Before Auschwitz

Routledge Studies in Twentieth-Century Literature

Before Auschwitz

Irène Némirovsky and the Cultural
Landscape of Inter-war France

Angela Kershaw

Routledge
Taylor & Francis Group
New York   London

First published 2010
by Routledge
270 Madison Ave, New York, NY 10016

Simultaneously published in the UK
by Routledge
2 Park Square, Milton Park, Abingdon, Oxon OX14 4RN

Routledge is an imprint of the Taylor & Francis Group, an informa business

© 2010 Taylor & Francis

Transferred to digital printing 2010

Typeset in Sabon by IBT Global.

Library of Congress Cataloging in Publication Data
Kershaw, Angela.
    Before Auschwitz: Irène Némirovsky and the cultural landscape of inter-war France / by Angela Kershaw.
        p. cm. — (Routledge studies in twentieth-century literature ; 10)
    Includes bibliographical references and index.
    1. Némirovsky, Irène, 1903–1942 — Criticism and interpretation.   2. Literature and society — France — History — 20th century.   I. Title.
    PQ2627.E4Z75 2010
    843'.912 — dc22
    2009014989

ISBN10: 0-415-95722-2 (hbk)
ISBN10: 0-415-89103-5 (pbk)
ISBN10: 0-203-86958-3 (ebk)
ISBN13: 978-0-415-95722-9 (hbk)
ISBN13: 978-0-415-89103-5 (pbk)
ISBN13: 978-0-203-86958-1 (ebk)

This project was funded in part by the Arts and Humanities Research Council.

Arts & Humanities
Research Council

Contents

Acknowledgments

The completion of this monograph was facilitated by support from the Arts and Humanities Research Council, which funded part of my sabbatical leave during 2007–08 under the Research Leave Scheme. I am also grateful to the School of Languages and Social Sciences at Aston University, where I was employed at the time, for the award of institutional sabbatical during this period. My thanks are due to colleagues and friends at Aston for their practical support in terms of providing teaching cover and for their interest in my project. I should also like to acknowledge my new colleagues in the Department of French Studies at the University of Birmingham, whose support in the final stages of the work has been very welcome indeed. The staff at the IMEC archive in Caen provided excellent support and assistance during my various trips to consult manuscript and other sources relating to Némirovsky held in their collection, and Denise Epstein is very generous in allowing such freedom of access to researchers wishing to consult her mother's papers. Various colleagues have been kind enough to give up their time to read parts of the manuscript: I should like to express my warmest thanks to Max Silverman, Nick Hewitt, and Martyn Cornick. Any errors or infelicities remain, of course, the responsibility of the author. Finally, I should like to thank my family: my parents, John and Irenee Kershaw, for their enthusiasm for all my projects, and John Snape, for his encouragement and support, which never wavers.

Introduction

The appearance of Irène Némirovsky's *Suite française* in 2004 was a major publishing success which introduced twenty-first century readers to the work of a writer who had first become a media sensation in 1929. With the novel's publication in English translation in 2006, the Némirovsky phenomenon became international. Much of the media interest in the novel in France and abroad was provoked by the almost unbelievable story of the manuscript's survival. Némirovsky wrote the book as a stateless Russian Jewish immigrant during the Second World War in Nazi-occupied France. In 1940 she left Paris, where she had been living since 1919, to take refuge in the village of Issy L'Evêque, which lay just inside the demarcation line, in the occupied zone. Arrested on 13 July 1942, Némirovsky was taken to the Pithiviers transit camp, from where she was deported to Auschwitz on 17 July. She died there on 17 August. Her husband, Michael Epstein, was deported in November 1942 and also perished. Their two daughters, Denise Epstein and Elisabeth Gille, survived the Holocaust and conserved, amongst their mother's papers, a large notebook which turned out to be a complete draft of the first two parts of a projected five-part novel based on the contemporary events of occupied France. Despite the impression given by some of the rather sensationalised media coverage, the manuscript's existence had been known long before 2004. Némirovsky's papers, including the manuscript, have been conserved in the IMEC archive (Institut Mémoires de l'Edition Contemporaine) since 1995, and her daughters were aware of the manuscript's existence in the 1970s. *Suite française* was not published sooner because Elisabeth Gille did not wish to publish an incomplete novel, and Denise Epstein did not wish the novel to be published at the same time as *Le Mirador* (1992), her sister's fictional biography of Némirovsky.[1] When *Suite française* finally appeared in 2004, it attracted the attention of critics as one of a very few works of fiction about the Occupation period written contemporaneously with the events described. The award of the 2004 Renaudot prize for *Suite française* caused further media discussion because this was the first time the prize had been awarded posthumously. The success of *Suite française* has led to the appearance of previously unpublished works of fiction by Némirovsky: 'Les Echelles du levant', which had first appeared in the journal *Gringoire* in 1939, appeared in book form under the title *Le Maître des âmes* in 2005; two short stories were published under the title *Ida* in 2006; *Chaleur du sang*, reconstructed from archival sources, appeared in 2007 and a further collection of stories, *Les Vierges et autres nouvelles* was published in 2009.[2] Most of Némirovsky's inter-war novels are now in print in French, and several have been translated into English by Sandra Smith.[3] Two biographies of Némirovsky have been published since 2004: Jonathan Weiss's *Irène Némirovsky* in 2005 and Olivier Philipponnat and Patrick Lienhardt's *La Vie d'Irène Némirovsky* in 2007.[4] In 2008, Denise Epstein published her own collection of reminiscences in the form of interviews with the French journalist Clémence Boulouque, entitled *Survivre et vivre*. Some academic work on Némirovsky is also beginning to appear, mostly in the form of articles.[5] In 2008, the University of Oxford's annual Zaharoff Lecture was delivered by Susan Suleiman, who discussed Némirovsky and Samuel Beckett as 'translingual' writers producing fiction in a language other than their mother tongue.[6] At the time of my writing this book, the Museum of Jewish Heritage in New York was hosting an exhibition on 'Irène Némirovsky: Woman of Letters'. In the United Kingdom, Némirovsky has received high profile media coverage in the broadsheets and on Radio 4, featuring on programmes such as *Front Row, Book at Bedtime,* and *Woman's Hour*. Némirovsky, whose fiction had been completely neglected in post-war France, is an astonishing case of a literary rediscovery.

My own discovery of Némirovsky goes back to the mid-1990s when I was researching French inter-war political fiction by women writers.[7] At that time I came across Némirovsky's 1933 novel *L'Affaire Courilof*, which tells the story of a Russian anarchist hired to kill a government minister. But none of Némirovsky's fiction was conceived with the intention of conveying an ideological message. Némirovsky has nonetheless attracted ideologically based criticism, both in our time and in her own, in relation to her portrayal of Jews and because of her association with right-wing anti-Semitic publications such as *Gringoire* and *Candide*. Some of this criticism has been intemperate, and much of it has failed to take account of the historical and literary conditions of production of Némirovsky's fiction. It is, paradoxically, quite straightforward to write neutrally about politically engaged literature because it is in the nature of the genre that the meaning of the text should be unambiguous. In the case of writing which is politically *disengaged*, it is more difficult for the literary critic or historian to maintain a neutral stance because the text remains open to a plethora of potentially contradictory interpretations. In this book, I attempt to maintain scholarly objectivity in relation to debates which necessarily arouse strong reactions amongst contemporary readers. This book does not pretend that reading Némirovsky after Auschwitz is easy. Its claim to objectivity is based on an approach which considers the entirety of Némirovsky's literary output and seeks to respect the chronological development of her representations, and to contextualise those representations in relation to the literary field in which they were produced. This book is however an *engagement*, because the material requires it to be so. It is an engagement in favour of a reading of cultural production which strives to avoid the 'apocalyptic history' to which Michael André Bernstein objects; it is a rejection of the failure to respect the particular situation of the writer at the moment of writing. This explains my choice of title: whilst much of the media discussion around Némirovsky has been generated through the perspective of readers with a knowledge of Auschwitz, this book seeks to place Némirovsky within the context in which she herself was writing—before Auschwitz.

How did Némirovsky's *œuvre* develop and achieve coherence between the mid-1920s and 1942? What was its place in the literary field of 1930s France? How was it defined by, and how did it help to define, that field? To address these questions, this book draws on the methodology developed by Pierre Bourdieu in *Les Règles de l'art* and elsewhere.[8] Bourdieu's sociology of literature seeks to understand 'literature' not just in terms of texts, but as a social field which is determined by relations and differences, and which is inhabited by agents who constantly struggle for dominance. Thus whilst the text itself and the author who produced it remain legitimate areas of study, they are viewed in relation to other agents in the literary field: commissioning editors, reviewers, readers, translators, and so on. Bourdieu rejects any division between an 'external' and an 'internal' reading of the literary text, seeking instead to demonstrate the ways in which the 'outside' and the 'inside' of the text constantly implicate each other. He rejects the structuralist conception of textuality which relegates or even excludes any attention to the author, the Cartesian view of the author as the sole source of meaning, and the vulgar Marxist notion that a text simply reflects its conditions of production. Bourdieu's attention to the author via the concept of habitus signifies his desire to maintain the notion of authorial agency whilst avoiding positing the author as the sole source of meaning. Bourdieu's theory is based on an understanding of the emergence of literature as an autonomous field of activity in the nineteenth century. Bourdieu understands the available positions which agents come to occupy within the field as disposed across two axes which oppose the absence or presence of cultural capital (exclusively artistic consecration or esteem) and the absence or presence of economic capital (financial reward). His theory has been criticised for positing a too rigid opposition between the *champ de grande production*—commercially motivated cultural production—and the *champ de production restreinte*—artistically motivated cultural production which seeks aesthetic and intellectual validation *as opposed to* financial reward. As James F. English argued, the 'map' of cultural fields Bourdieu offers is essentially a modernist one.[9] The opposition between 'high' culture and financial reward is much less clear-cut in the postmodern cultural environment of the late twentieth and early twenty-first century than it was in the nineteenth century, which is Bourdieu's starting point. English writes,

> There is no question of perfect autonomy or segregation of the various sorts of capital, such that one might occupy a zone or margin of

'pure' culture where money or politics or journalistic celebrity or social connections or ethnic or gender advantage mean nothing, or such that one might acquire economic capital that is free of all implication in the social, symbolic, or political economies. It is rather a matter of differing rates of exchange and principles of negotiation, both of these being among the most important stakes in the whole economy of practices.[10]

English analyses the cultural prize as one of the ways in which such negotiation, or *capital intraconversion*, is achieved in postmodern culture. My analysis of the success of *Suite française* in Chapter 6 draws on English's sympathetic rereading of Bourdieu, which seeks to extend the latter's theoretical framework in order to account for a twenty-first century cultural context which can no longer oppose 'literary' and 'commercial' success in absolute terms.[11] In the inter-war period, Bourdieu's modernist conception of an opposition between the literary and the commercial is much more obviously applicable, although here too, the positions Bourdieu describes should be viewed not as absolutes but as points along a continuum. With this caveat in mind, a structural opposition between the *champ de grande production* and the *champ de production restreinte* is a useful framework within which to understand Némirovsky's literary trajectory. The stark difference in nature and functioning between a journal such as the *Nouvelle Revue française*, whose function was to bestow artistic capital, and a publication such as *Les Nouvelles littéraires*, whose role depended entirely on the newly commercial nature of fiction in the inter-war period, suggests that the oppositions Bourdieu's theory posits did obtain during that period of France's cultural history. Gisèle Sapiro has adopted Bourdieu's framework most successfully for the inter-war period.[12]

Many commentators have pointed to the current 'social turn' in literary and cultural studies. In 2004, Jérôme Meizoz commented on the return of history and of the social in the study of literature since the end of the 1990s.[13] Wolfgang Iser, writing in 2006, suggested that in contemporary theory, 'art is always viewed in relation to its interaction with its context and with its recipient' and that 'the emphasis of modern theories is on relationships between the work of art, the dispositions of its recipients, and the realities of its context'.[14] Cultural theory is, in Terry Eagleton's words, not about asking 'Is this poem valuable?' but rather, 'What do we mean by calling a poem good or bad?':

> Instead of asking whether the clarinet concerto is slightly too cloying to be entirely persuasive, it inquires about the material conditions which you need to produce concertos in the first place, and how these help to shape the work itself.[15]

Eagleton goes on to say that 'None of these meta-questions need replace straightforward critical questions. You can ask both kinds of question together'. This book is an attempt to ask both these types of questions together, and indeed to affirm their interdependence. It seeks therefore to work in the 'middle zone' between close textual reading and the analysis of larger cultural trajectories which, as English remarks, is often neglected.[16] It is by offering both textual and contextual analysis that this book seeks to ascertain what kind of 'value' Némirovsky's fiction had for its contemporary readers, and what kind of 'value' it has for us today. It is not a eulogy, and it is not an attempt to 'rehabilitate' Némirovsky. There is no point in asking whether Némirovsky was 'as good as' Gide, or Sartre, or Elsa Triolet. What is important is to understand the nature of Némirovsky's literary project, to evaluate it on its own terms, and to interrogate the ways in which it was evaluated by contemporary critics. Significant space is therefore devoted to the study of reception. This book aims to provide not only an account of the works of a single author—though it does offer such an account—but also to shed light on the functioning of the inter-war literary field. As Bourdieu argues, an exclusive focus on the writer as the sole source of meaning occludes both the social space in which that writer moves, and the development of the aesthetic 'dispositions' which the author's position in the literary field implies.[17]

This book seeks to make the author's position in the field central to its analysis in order to understand the literary space in which the author was located, as well as to highlight that which the author contributed to that literary space. Paying close attention to reception is one way to achieve this goal. One of the reasons why Némirovsky interests me is that her *œuvre* functions as a lightning conductor on which many significant questions about inter-war French literary production converge: the popularity and commercial success of the novel as a genre; the 'crisis' of the novel and of representation more generally in the aftermath of the First World War; the politicisation of literary production; the relationship between 'particular' identities (such as Jewish identity) and 'French' cultural production; international cultural exchange and the presence of foreign writers and intellectuals in inter-war France; the representation and reconstruction of the French nation via imaginative literature; the re-imagining of gendered subjectivities in fiction. This book can only be a beginning, and much work remains to be done to deepen and broaden the suggestions I make here as to the nature of the relationships between Némirovsky's texts and those of other inter-war writers. It is of course impossible to explore comprehensively in a single work the very many potential textual connections between Némirovsky's fiction and that of her contemporaries. If this book stimulates other scholars to take up this challenge, it will have fulfilled an important function.

The starting point of my analysis is the reception of *David Golder* in 1929. Discussing the practice of cultural history, Alon Confino remarks that '[t]he study of reception is not an issue that simply adds to our knowledge. Rather, it is a necessary one to avoid an arbitrary choice and interpretation of evidence'.[18] It is through the study of reception that it is possible to reconstruct the questions posed by a given text in relation to the contemporary literary field. Having ascertained in Chapter 1 the nature of Némirovsky's literary reputation in 1929, Chapter 2 takes a step backwards in time to consider the development of Némirovsky's literary identity before the publication of *David Golder*. I thereby seek to apply Bourdieu's inversion of the traditional approach of the literary critic, which begins with the author, and to underline the role played by the literary field, expressed in critical discourses, in the definition of the 'meaning' of the work of art. In Chapter 3, I examine the Russian theme in Némirovsky's writing in terms of her engagements with the *mode russe*. In Chapter 4, I consider the Jewish theme in her writing, in the context of, but also in opposition to, the interwar *renaissance juive*. Chapter 5 addresses Némirovsky's ongoing attempt to construct herself as a French novelist, an aim which she pursued in the second half of the decade by portraying contemporary French society. Chapters 3, 4, and 5 analyse Némirovsky's perhaps somewhat opportunistic, but nonetheless creative, engagement with themes and motifs which were already well established in the French literary field. The concluding chapter focuses on *Suite française*, firstly locating it in relation to its original context of production, and, secondly, analysing its current reception, out of its own time. *Suite française*, along with the rest of Némirovsky's *œuvre*, must of course be read after Auschwitz. To do so is to embark upon a journey which is emotionally as well as intellectually demanding. Writing about Némirovsky is not just an academic exercise, because her personal tragedy was real. Némirovsky's own approach to writing fiction is also the most appropriate way to read it: critical detachment must be maintained, so as to facilitate a proper appreciation of the affective force of the story. In this respect, Denise Epstein's retelling of her mother's story has been exemplary. It is perhaps appropriate that the final words of this introduction should be Epstein's: 'Je n'éprouve aucune nostalgie, simplement un sentiment de frustration et d'un gâchis énorme' ('*I experience no nostalgia, simply a feeling of frustration and of enormous waste*').[19]

1 The Making of a Literary Reputation

Ce n'est pas seulement une création romanesque de grande valeur, c'est une vue pénétrante sur notre époque et les caractères particuliers qu'y revêt la lutte pour la vie. Toute une philosophie de l'amour, de l'ambition, de l'argent se dégage de ce roman qui, par sa puissance et par son sujet même, rappelle le Père GORIOT, et qui n'en est pas moins de la plus extrême nouvauté.

It is not only a literary creation of great value, it is also a penetrating portrait of our age and the particular character of our struggles for life. An entire philosophy of love, ambition, and money emerges from this novel which, in its power and even in its subject, calls to mind Balzac's Le Père Goriot, *and which is nonetheless extremely innovative.*

—Bernard Grasset, advertisement for *David Golder*,
Les Nouvelles littéraires, 7 December 1929

Roman bouleversant, intimiste, implacable, dévoilant avec une extraordinaire lucidité l'âme de chaque Français pendant l'Occupation [. . .] *Suite française* ressuscite d'une plume brillante et intuitive un pan à vif de notre mémoire.

An overwhelming, intimate and pitiless novel, an extraordinarily lucid revelation of the soul of every French person during the Occupation [. . .] Suite française *is the work of a brilliant and intuitive writer which makes a part of our memory live again.*

—Cover text, *Suite française*, Denoël, 2004

The literary reputation of Irène Némirovsky has been made twice, at an interval of more than seventy years and therefore in two very different historical, social, and literary environments. Némirovsky has acquired literary celebrity through two very different texts, *David Golder* and *Suite française*, the one published at the beginning of her career, when she was a virtually unknown Russian Jewish immigrant; and the other written at the end of her life, when she was a successful and celebrated French novelist. The quotations above suggest that the two texts have been presented to their readers in strikingly similar terms. In both cases, the publisher seeks to create a sense of community between novelist and readers by using the inclusive first person plural pronoun; here is a writer who can tell *us* about *our* memories, about *our* epoch. This is a writer who is in touch with French history and literary history, able to resuscitate characters from France's real and imagined past. That past is a traumatic place: Grasset's comparison of Golder with Balzac's Goriot, whose wealth is eroded by the extravagant frivolity of his daughters, is particularly resonant in the context of the *années folles* and the Wall Street Crash, as is the evocation of memories of the Occupation in the year of the sixtieth anniversary of the liberation of the Nazi concentration camps. And if Némirovsky is capable of making the past live again, and of interpreting the present, this is because of her extraordinary literary talent, thanks to which she can penetrate and unveil the truth of the subjects she approaches in her writing. From this brief comparison we begin to see the terms in which Némirovsky's publishers have constructed her phenomenal success: her Frenchness, her relevance to the contemporary world, and her literary skill. This chapter investigates the production and development of Némirovsky's success in the 1930s, and considers the repercussions of that success under the Occupation.

A SUCCESSFUL LITERARY CAREER

The present chapter is not concerned with questions of literary *quality*, but rather with questions of literary *success*. Bourdieu's conceptual framework provides a useful vocabulary for discussing literary success. A contextual approach to literary history and analysis relies on the notion that a work does not simply impose itself through its innate aesthetic qualities. This is a myth—a myth in which we may still need to believe, but a myth nonetheless. Literary success must be evaluated through analysis of the textual traces left by the creators of that success: those who caused the book to be produced and sold, and those who encouraged people to buy and read the text. Therefore it is by analysing the role of publishers and of critics in Némirovsky's literary trajectory that her success can best be appreciated. Bourdieu writes,

> Il suffit de poser la question interdite pour s'apercevoir que l'artiste qui fait l'œuvre est lui-même fait, au sein du champ de production, par tout l'ensemble de ceux qui contribuent à le 'découvrir' et à le consacrer en tant qu'artiste 'connu' et reconnu—critiques, préfaciers, marchands, etc. Ainsi, par exemple, le commerçant d'art (marchand de tableaux, éditeur, etc.) est inséparablement celui qui exploite le travail de l'artiste en faisant commerce de ses produits et celui qui, en le mettant sur le marché des biens symboliques, par l'exposition, la publication ou la mise en scène, assure au produit de la fabrication artistique

une *consécration* d'autant plus importante qu'il est lui-même plus con-
sacré. [emphasis in original][1]

> *It is enough to pose the forbidden question to perceive that the artist*
> *who makes the work is himself made, at the core of the field of produc-*
> *tion, by the whole ensemble of those who help to 'discover' him and*
> *to consecrate him as an artist who is 'known' and recognized—critics,*
> *writers of prefaces, dealers, etc. Thus, for example, the merchant in*
> *art (dealer in paintings, publisher, etc.) is inseparably both the one*
> *who exploits the work of the artist by making commerce of his prod-*
> *ucts and the one who, in putting it on the market of symbolic goods*
> *through exhibition, publication or staging, ensures that the product of*
> *artistic fabrication will receive a* consecration—*and the consecration*
> *will be greater the more consecrated the merchant himself is.*[2]

By analysing in some detail the debates which Némirovsky's novels provoked in the cultural press of the inter-war period, this chapter explores
the ways in which Némirovsky's literary success resulted from a series of
complex social relations in the inter-war literary field. As Linda Hutcheon
and Mario Valdés argue, the study of reception is an important aspect of
the 'storytelling project' that is literary history:

> The history of literature is in fact more accurately defined as the mul-
> tiple histories of its production and its reception. Literary historians
> over the centuries have always taken into account the complexities of
> literary production, but the new methodological paradigms developed
> by a variety of critical theories in the last few decades have made im-
> perative an awareness of the equally complicated and significant nature
> of literary reception.[3]

Such an approach is justified both by Némirovsky's own approach to
the task of being a writer, and by the aims of this book. Némirovsky was a
novelist who actively managed her relationships with her publishers and her
critics, and there is good reason to suppose that her choice of literary themes
was at least in part a response to the critical discussion her fiction was generating. Her case thus supports Bourdieu's view that 'on ne peut faire dans
la science des œuvres deux parts, l'une consacrée à la production, l'autre à
la réception' ('*all this means that one cannot divide a science of works into*
two parts: one devoted to production, the other to perception'): production and reception of the literary text are locked into an iterative relationship.[4] Whilst this book is focused on the work of a single author, it seeks to
view that author through a wide-angled lens, such that the entire literary
field of inter-war France comes into focus. It is through the analysis of the
reception of individual works that it is possible to reconstruct the proper-
ties of the field and thus eventually, understand the complex phenomenon

of the work of art.[5] The approach taken throughout this book to the study of Némirovsky's fictional output, and of French inter-war literature more generally, is firmly grounded in a belief in the importance of reception for an understanding of texts and their contexts. A literary review can both demonstrate the state of the contemporary literary field, and change it; the issues a reviewer raises in relation to a new text necessarily arise out of the current literary-critical status quo (there is no *tabula rasa*) but might also modify the literary-critical environment by raising a new question or by posing an existing question differently. The 'meaning' of a text and, not least, its ideological significance, is determined in relation to the literary field which produced it and is in significant measure a function of the ways in which that text is represented by its critics.[6] We return to the construction of literary value, celebrity, and success through the media in Chapter 6 in order to understand the phenomenon which has in part motivated the writing of this book—the success of *Suite française* in France in 2004 and in English translation in 2006. Here though, the rules of the game will have changed somewhat, since we shall observe the reception of a text in a literary and historical environment very different from that in which it was produced, or which produced it.

Before turning to a closer analysis of the construction of Némirovsky's celebrity and subsequent reputation as a novelist, it will be useful to have in mind an overview of the entirety of her output. Before the success of *David Golder* in 1929, Némirovsky had already published four short works in the subscription series *Les Œuvres libres*: 'Le Malentendu' (February 1926); 'L'Enfant génial' (April 1927); 'L'Ennemie' (July 1928); 'Le Bal' (February 1929).[7] *Les Œuvres libres*, launched by the publishing house Fayard in June 1921, was a monthly publication offering a selection of unabridged and previously unpublished stories by various authors in a single volume.[8] Two of the works Némirovsky published here were immediately reissued in book form in 1930 in the wake of the success of *David Golder*: 'Le Malentendu' by Fayard and 'Le Bal' by Grasset. These early texts treat the themes which were to occupy Némirovsky's literary imagination for the first half of the 1930s: Jews; the world of business and finance; Russian emigration; love. The order in which I present these themes is not coincidental: Némirovsky frequently pairs Jews with money and Russians with love. These early stories also depict the sometimes complex, sometimes frivolous relationships between love, money, and pleasure which developed as the *années folles* began to shade into the Depression. Between 1929 and 1935, Némirovsky drew on her personal history to produce a series of novels in which Jewish and Russian themes dominated. It is particularly in the early texts, notably *David Golder* (1929), *Le Bal* (1930), and *Le Pion sur l'échiquier* (1934) that we find stereotyped portrayals of Jewish characters, although the later novel *Les Chiens et les loups* (1940) is not exempt from this problem. *David Golder* and *Le Bal* recount very different stories of Jewish immigrants making a life in France: Golder is a successful and powerful financier, whilst *Le Bal*'s Alfred Kampf struggles to raise his social standing to match his newly acquired wealth. In *Le Pion sur l'échiquier*, Jewishness and money are again associated in the portrait of the businessman Beryl. That Némirovsky ceased to write about Jewish themes after 1933 is hardly surprising; she would however return to the theme of Jewish emigration in *Les Chiens et les loups* where she opposed the Eastern immigrant Jew to the assimilated European Jew in the context of the politics, economics, and society of inter-war France. This work offers a more nuanced account of Jewish identity than is to be found in the novels of the early 1930s. The theme of Russian emigration dominates *Les Mouches d'automne* (1931) and *Le Vin de solitude* (1935). The earlier text recounts the collective history of a land-owning family who flee the Russian Revolution and take refuge in Paris; the later novel focuses on an individual female protagonist, Hélène, who is Russian but adores France, and eventually fulfils her dream of making a life there. *L'Affaire Courilof* (1933) tells the story of a Russian anarchist hired to assassinate a government minister in the early years of the twentieth century. The scenario of this text anticipates those of Sartre's *Les Mains sales* and Camus's *Les Justes*. These six novels might be taken as a first phase of Némirovsky's writing project, with the mid-point of the decade as a turning point. In 1936 Némirovsky published *Jézabel*, a novel in which her ability to create narrative suspense and intrigue come to the fore. This novel is a psychological drama which explores mother-daughter relationships and the problems of ageing for women, themes which had already surfaced in her earlier texts. In the second half of the decade, Némirovsky turned her attention away from the problems of Russian emigration and the Jewish diaspora and toward those of inter-war France. *Le Pion sur l'échiquier* and *Le Vin de solitude* might be seen as transitional texts insofar as both anticipate what seems to have been a growing desire on Némirovsky's part to write in detail about France of the inter-war period. *Le Pion sur l'échiquer* (1934), *La Proie* (1938) and *Deux* (1939) analyse the effects of the First World War and the Depression on two generations of French men. *Le Pion sur l'échiquer* and *Deux* deal with the difficult re-integration of young war veterans into the changed economic and political environment of France in the 1920s and 1930s. *La Proie* considers the fate of their sons who, too young to have fought, experience a sort of *nouveau mal du siècle* and find themselves equally unable to make a satisfactory life in the uncertain inter-war years. The idea of a *nouveau mal du siècle* resulting from 'the catastrophic effects of the First World War on that generation of French writers who were never old enough to fight but who were brought up under a subsequently redundant militarist moral code' originated in an essay by Benjamin Crémieux published in the *Nouvelle Revue française* in 1923.[9] *Les Biens de ce monde*, serialised in the right-wing anti-Semitic journal *Gringoire* in 1941 and published in book form only posthumously (1947), and *Les Feux de l'automne*, not published in Némirovsky's lifetime, but also published posthumously as a book

(1957), offer an extended fresco of France from before the outbreak of the First World War to the armistice of 22 June 1940 and the beginning of the Occupation. These novels, which analyse the economic and emotional effects of two world wars on communities as well as individuals, might be seen as a prelude to *Suite française*, which takes up the story of the fall of France ('Tempête en juin') and the Occupation ('Dolce').

To summarise then, Némirovsky's fictional output falls into two main phases: up to 1935, she focused on Russian and Jewish themes; after 1935 she turned her attention to inter-war France, in particular, the effects of war on the French nation. These themes will occupy our attention in Chapters 3, 4, and 5, respectively. In addition to these novels, Némirovsky also published a large number of short stories in various journals and reviews. Four stories were published in 1934 in a collection entitled *Films parlés*.[10] Apart from a preface to a French translation of James Cain's *The Postman Always Rings Twice*, this was the only work Némirovsky published with Gallimard.

BERNARD GRASSET AND THE INTER-WAR LITERARY MARKETPLACE

On 11 January 1930, Frédéric Lefèvre devoted his famous 'Une heure avec . . .' column in *Les Nouvelles littéraires*, in which he interviewed the popular writers of the day, to Némirovsky. In the interview, Némirovsky recounted how Bernard Grasset came to publish *David Golder*. The manuscript had been rejected by Fayard for *Les Œuvres libres* on account of its length, so Némirovsky, unwilling to alter her work, sent it to Grasset with a *poste restante* address and bearing her married name, Epstein.[11] Némirovsky says in the interview that she wanted to keep her contact with Grasset a secret from her family and friends in case it was unsuccessful. Contemporary readers may have interpreted this as artistic modesty. Némirovsky's biographer Jonathan Weiss suggests that Némirovsky did not want Grasset to link *David Golder* to the author of the *Œuvres libres* stories (though two of these had in any case been published under a pseudonym).[12] It also seems plausible that Némirovsky wanted to keep her options open with *Les Œuvres libres*, since she could presumably have taken up their offer to publish a shortened version of the text if Grasset had not been interested, without Fayard ever knowing that she had approached a rival publisher. Némirvosky would go on to publish two further stories with *Les Œuvres libres*: 'Film parlé' (July 1931), which became the title story for the 1934 Gallimard collection, and 'La Comédie bourgeoise' (June 1932), also reprinted in that volume. How then did Némirovsky's choice of publisher position her in the literary field? *Les Œuvres libres* was situated at the commercial pole of literary production: it published popular, accessible literature, its volumes were cheap and it paid its authors well for their stories.[13] This did not, however, preclude the participation of aesthetically consecrated writers: Proust had published an extract from *Sodome et Gomorrhe* in *Les Œuvres libres* in 1921.[14] Némirovsky's move to Grasset was certainly not a move away from commercial publishing. Grasset firmly believed that book sales depended on making sure the author's name became well-known, and he expended a considerable amount of time and energy in making contacts with those he believed to be the 'opinion-makers'.[15] Némirovsky was fully aware of Grasset's commercial approach to publishing and was keen to benefit from it. She told an interviewer in 1930 that 'Grasset est un *as de la publicité*. Ce n'est pas moi qui le nierait et qui songerait jamais à m'en plaindre' [emphasis in original] (*Grasset is a* publishing ace. *I won't deny it and I would never think of complaining about it*).[16] Although Grasset was criticised for his commercial approach to literature, he made the careers of some of the most important writers of the inter-war period, including André Malraux, Philippe Soupault, Pierre Drieu la Rochelle and Blaise Cendrars.[17] Némirovsky's association with *Les Œuvres libres* and with Grasset, and the significant commercial success of her fiction, should not be taken as indications that she was a literary lightweight. Indeed, from 1935, she would contribute stories to the *Revue des deux mondes* which, whilst also a high-circulation publication, was close to the Académie française and represented a heavyweight, if conservative, literary voice.[18]

Bernard Grasset intervened extensively in the press on the publication of *David Golder* with the obvious intention of creating the novel as a literary sensation. This type of literary marketing was an important feature of the inter-war literary field, as the sale of books was a burgeoning area of economic activity. In his study of the French bestseller, Christopher Todd notes the increasingly sophisticated advertising techniques employed in the period, and the sharp rise in book production, which more than doubled between 1920 and 1928.[19] The publication of *David Golder* was announced in a large advertisement in *Les Nouvelles littéraires* on 7 December 1929 which, as we have seen, hailed the novel as a new *Père Goriot*. Lefèvre's 'Une heure avec Irène Némirovsky' interview on 11 January 1930 appeared on the front page of the paper, accompanied by a drawing of Némirovsky. On 18 January, Grasset published an article entitled 'Le succès foudroyant de *David Golder*' in *Le Matin* and *L'Œuvre*,[20] as well as another large advertisement in *Les Nouvelles littéraires* which included quotations from laudatory reviews in *L'Action française* and *Le Temps*, and from Lefèvre's interview of the previous week. On 25 January *Les Nouvelles littéraires* carried another, smaller, advertisement, and on 8 February a further large advertisement appeared in *Les Nouvelles littéraires* quoting yet more plaudits from high-profile critics in a range of well-known publications.[21] *Les Nouvelles littéraires*, founded in 1922 and owned by the publishing house Larousse, was the leading literary and cultural review of its time. It was exactly the right vehicle for Grasset's publicity campaign designed to launch his new literary discovery. *Les Nouvelles littéraires*, which had an extensive readership,[22] aimed to reflect the full range of contemporary cultural activity and was neither excessively conservative nor excessively experimental.

Anyone who was anyone in literary circles appeared in its pages.[23] Grasset's promotion of Némirovsky shows how clearly he understood the idea that literary value is not (only) a property of texts, but is conferred by the extra-textual discussion they generate. As Bourdieu puts it:

> Le producteur de la *valeur de l'œuvre d'art* n'est pas l'artiste mais le champ de production en tant qu'univers de croyance qui produit la valeur de l'œuvre d'art comme *fétiche* en produisant la croyance dans le pouvoir créateur de l'artiste. [emphasis in original][24]

> *The producer of the* value of the work of art *is not the artist but the field of production as a universe of belief which produces the value of the work of art as fetish by producing the belief in the creative power of the artist.* [emphasis in original][25]

Grasset's publicity campaign was a very successful attempt to create the sort of critical circularity which Bourdieu has disparagingly described as a game of mutually reflecting mirrors, whereby critics respond to the texts of other critics rather than to the novel in question;[26] by collecting together positive reviews, Grasset sought to create belief in the literary value of Némirovsky's novel by creating an impression of critical unanimity. Grasset's strategy suggests that Bourdieu's notion of a type of artistic legitimacy achieved via media visibility is not actually very new, but was operating most successfully in the inter-war period, thanks to the proliferation of literary, cultural, and political reviews and journals.[27] Following Bourdieu, Grasset's interventions in the literary field—specifically his prediction and underlining of her success—would be sufficient to place Némirovsky in the camp of the bourgeois (that is, 'commercial') novelist who occupies the *champ de grande production*:

> Pour les écrivains 'bourgeois' et leur public, le succès est, par soi, une garantie de valeur. C'est ce qui fait que, sur ce marché, le succès va au succès: on contribue à faire les *best-sellers* en publiant leurs tirages ; les critiques ne peuvent rien faire de mieux pour un livre ou une pièce que de lui 'prédire le succès'.[28]

> *For 'bourgeois' writers and their readers, success is intrinsically a guarantee of value. That is why, in this market, the successful get more successful. Publishers help to make* best-sellers *by printing further impressions; the best thing a critic can do for a book or play is to predict 'success' for it.*[29]

Various aspects of Némirovsky's literary trajectory suggest that this would be an appropriate interpretation—she published with 'commercial' publishers, managed her relationships with those publishers very carefully, and as a result her writing was financially remunerative.[30] However, there was space in the inter-war literary field for the widespread popularity and success of aesthetically interesting writers, thanks to the expansion of publishing, journalism, and education. The existence of a journal such as *Les Nouvelles littéraires* suggests that there was no absolute distinction between 'popular' and 'quality' writers—Christophe Charle says of *Les Nouvelles littéraires* that

> [l]eur éclectisme littéraire, leur apolitisme affiché, leur ouverture à tous les types d'activités culturelles et leurs interviews de personnalités par Frédéric Lefèvre entretiennent l'intérêt et profitent de l'élargissement du public cultivé au moment où les facultés de lettres sont en plein essor.

> *the journal's literary eclecticism, its overtly apolitical character, its openness to all types of cultural activities and Frédéric Lefèvre's interviews with famous personalities maintained readers' interest, taking advantage of the expansion of a cultivated reading public at the time when university literature departments were expanding).*[31]

Bourdieu's conceptualisation of the structuring of the literary field according to a fundamental opposition between 'heteronomy' (economic dominance) and 'autonomy' (aesthetic independence)[32] can lead to the positing of a stark and oversimplified opposition between 'commercial' and properly 'literary' consecration.[31] However, in the 1999 essay 'Une révolution conservatrice dans l'édition', Bourdieu convincingly stresses the *relationship* between economic and symbolic capital and the *continuum* between the two extremes of the commercial and the arcane:

> [. . .] du fait que le livre, objet à double face, économique et symbolique, est à la fois marchandise et signification, l'éditeur est aussi un *personnage double*, qui doit savoir concilier l'art et l'argent, l'amour de la littérature et la recherche du profit, dans des stratégies qui se situent quelque part entre les deux extrêmes, la soumission réaliste ou cynique aux considérations commerciales et l'indifférence héroïque ou insensée aux nécessités de l'économie. [emphasis in original][33]

> *A book's dual nature—as both a signifier and a commodity, a symbolic and an economic entity—requires an editor to have a dual character, one that can reconcile art and money, love of literature and the pursuit of profit, by devising strategies situated somewhere between the two extremes of cynical subservience and heroic indifference to the house's economic needs.* [emphasis in original][34]

Bourdieu's fundamental proposition that the cultural field operates according to an inverted economic logic, where financial disinterestedness is highly valued,[36] remains a useful one, as long as it is recognised that the positions he proposes are not absolutes: once the structure is applied, it becomes clear that most writers fall somewhere between the extremes. Bourdieu's project is to theorise the discursive production of literary value by examining the struggles which constantly take place between agents in the literary field for the right to determine what 'is' and 'is not' art. Bourdieu's theory should not lead us to say that a given author 'is' or 'is not' good, but rather that an author occupying a certain position in the literary field will not be deemed 'good' by authors or agents occupying an opposite position in that field. Bourdieu argues that the volume of sales is indicative of the position the writer occupies in the field, not of literary quality.[37]

THE CRITICAL RECEPTION

Némirovsky's relationship with Grasset lasted until 1933. Following the success of *David Golder*, she published *Le Bal*, *Les Mouches d'automne* and *L'Affaire Courilof* with Grasset before moving definitively to Albin Michel. A thematic analysis of the reception of these novels illustrates the nature and functioning of the literary field into which Grasset launched Némirovsky. My focus on these four novels is motivated by both methodological and practical considerations: these reviews form a coherent corpus, and consideration of them is facilitated by the survival of Grasset's dossiers of press cuttings relating to Némirovsky.[38] The existence of this resource makes it feasible to trace the major preoccupations of contemporary critics with considerable accuracy.

There is no doubt that the construction of *David Golder* as a 'masterpiece', a 'chef d'œuvre', was partly a result of Grasset's deliberate interventions in the press. But this strategy was only available to him because discussion of what constituted a masterpiece of French literature was already a significant feature of the inter-war literary field. Whilst many critics did immediately hail *David Golder* as a masterpiece,[39] others were more sceptical. In some cases this arose simply from a difference of opinion about the work, but in others the literary marketplace itself was called into question. Some argued that contemporary critics cannot judge what is or is not a masterpiece in their own time.[40] On the publication of *Le Bal*, Simone Ratel accused literary publishers of forcing the talents of their authors. She criticised the negative literary effects of the financial pressure to encourage authors to publish a second novel quickly on the back of a big success.[41] Claude Pierrey suggested to Némirovsky in an interview that critics were accusing her of a publicity stunt based on the sensationalised story of the anonymous manuscript. The fact that she had given birth to her first daughter between the writing of *David Golder* and the discovery of its author's identity only served to heighten readers' interest in this new literary star. 'On dit, Madame . . . Tout d'abord que vous êtes très riche, que la publicité, payée par vous, n'a fait qu'exploiter la légende adroite de la "poste restante", celle, plus touchante, des *relevailles*. . . . ' (*People are saying, Madame, firstly that you are very rich, and that the publicity campaign which you have financed has simply exploited the legend of the manuscript left with a* poste restante *address, and the rather more touching one of your convalescence after the birth of your child*).[42] In a similar vein, J. Ernest-Charles (who, it should be noted, tended not to review Némirovsky's work positively, and who had been objecting to the 'industrial' character of literary production since the turn of the century[43]) suggested that 'l'industrie moderne a inventé des procédés vigoureux pour imposer un chef d'œuvre aux foules' (*modern industry has invented robust strategies to impose a masterpiece on the mass of readers*).[44] Michel Raimond has identified two features of the post-First World War literary field out of which discussion of the commercialisation of the novel grew: the overproduction of novels, and the prestige of the novel in relation to other genres in the period, which was an economic and social phenomenon as much as a literary one.[45] It is in the context of a literary environment which was making a clear distinction between 'creative literature' and 'commercial literature'[46] that the critical wrangling over the label 'chef d'œuvre' in relation to *David Golder* should be understood.

The vigorous and heated nature of this discussion was more a function of the importance of a general debate in the French literary field in the 1920s about the value of the French novel than an indication that Némirovsky's novel was deemed by critics to be so significant as to make it imperative to determine its literary status. That is to say that the debate drew its significance primarily from the (extra-textual) contemporary literary-critical environment rather than from textual features: *David Golder* is not such a ground-breaking work that it could have provoked the sort of debate it did, had such debate not already been a feature of the literary field. It is important to bear in mind that *David Golder* was published at the end of a period which had seen extensive discussion of the definition, value, and future of the French novel. In his substantial study of the crisis of the novel in inter-war France, Michel Raimond identifies the 1920s as the years in which the critical debate reached its greatest intensity.[47] The debate around *David Golder* on the idea of a literary masterpiece was part of a general dissatisfaction on the part of critics and readers with many published novels, dissatisfaction which provoked a questioning of the criteria used to evaluate literary successes and failures, as well as a questioning of the value of the novel genre and of its definition.[48] During the course of the 1920s, critics had posed some fundamental questions: what is the novel? What is the novel worth? Is the novel a dying genre? And should writers seek to kill it off?[49] For Raimond, the crisis of the novel arose out of the combination of two potentially contradictory aesthetic needs: to define the novel, but also to free it from its conventions.[50]

Raimond sees the inter-war debate on the crisis of the novel in terms of a transition from a nineteenth-century conception of literature as storytelling, to a modern understanding of narrative underpinned by a recognition of the impossibility of adopting a position of total, global understanding of the world, but also motivated by the desire to seize and represent the immediacy of lived experience.[51] The discussion of realism in relation to Némirovsky's fiction was part of this transition. Raimond also notes that, despite the critical discussion of new narrative possibilities, the reading public still generally preferred a simple and moving story to a work which undertook subtle experiments with different modes of narration.[52] Némirovsky's accessible brand of realism was potentially attractive to readers and critics alike because it combined tradition and innovation: the comparison with Balzac suggests her fiction was received as reassuringly familiar, whilst suggestions that it could transform French realism show that it was also perceived as modern and original. Critics frequently remarked that Némirovsky's novels were truthful and well observed. Frédéric Lefèvre presented *David Golder* as being full of human experience, and noted that it was based on a sound knowledge of the business world; he also remarked on the deep, human truth of *Le Malentendu*. According to *Le Petit provençal* 'Mme Némirovsky a très bien observé ces types d'israélites gagneurs d'argent' (*Madame Némirovsky has very accurately observed these types of Israelites who make money*), and *Chantecler* praised her acute observations, though found *Le Bal* somewhat uneven.[53] *Les Mouches d'automne* was often presented in terms of sincerity and authenticity: the argument was of course a biographical one, insofar as it was suggested that Némirovsky's portraits of Russian and Jewish characters and milieux were 'real' precisely because of her origins. This aspect of the reception of Némirovsky's work illustrates the popularity of fictionalised works derived from authorial experience which was a feature of the contemporary literary field.[54]

Némirovsky's texts also gave rise to a more nuanced discussion of literary realism. *Comœdia* identified realism as the main aesthetic question on which the future of the novel depended, and went on to discuss the desirability or otherwise of presenting an unpleasant reality within a work of art without any obvious aesthetic mediation to render it more palatable.[55] This was the question naturalism had posed for novelists and critics in the 1880s—can fiction be a transcription of the real, or does the novel form imply a transformation of the real?[56] *David Golder* raised the question of naturalism for Raymond Millet in *Paris-Presse*:

> Elle apporte ainsi une transformation profonde à la formule du roman réaliste. Qu'on y prenne garde, cette conception peut déclencher un renouveau du naturalisme. Le naturalisme tel que semble le comprendre l'auteur de *David Golder* nous apparaît comme assaini et revigoré par la lointaine influence du roman classique français.[57]

> *She thus offers a profound transformation of the formula of the realist novel. Watch out, because this concept could provoke a resurgence of naturalism. Naturalism as the author of* David Golder *seems to understand it appears to be purified and revitalised by the distant influence of the French classical novel.*

Naturalism did not enjoy a high status among conservative defenders of good literary taste in the inter-war period, and the defence of classicism against naturalism and romanticism was a significant feature of the inter-war literary field.[58] Classicism was prized as the way forward for the regeneration of the French novel, as much by the *Nouvelle Revue française* as by the nationalist critics of *L'Action française* and *Gringoire*, whilst romanticism was rejected by both sides as decadent and disordered and thus as a corruption of French classical values such as balance and harmony. Naturalism was rejected by neo-classicists as vulgar materialism lacking any concern for composition or beauty. Inter-war exponents of naturalism, which was generally associated with popular, commercial literature, were to be found largely within the Goncourt academy, founded in 1902 to award the annual Goncourt prize.[59] In the quotation cited above, Millet comes down clearly on the side of classicism, arguing that whilst the more hard-hitting passages of *David Golder* might suggest naturalism, the novel is rescued by its classical structure. The same debate was in evidence in the pages of *Gringoire*, where de Pawlowski criticised *David Golder*'s narrow focus on a single character as reminiscent of the 'slice of life' doctrine of the naturalists which, for him, might adequately express sincerity, but cannot adequately express truth.[60] Marcel Augagneur, reviewing *Le Bal* in *Gringoire*, took up the same theme in an article significantly entitled 'Une tranche de vie', where he argues that Némirovsky successfully avoids falling into the trap of naturalism.[61]

The discussion of realism in relation to Némirovsky's early fiction had two important functions. On the one hand, *David Golder* provided an opportunity to discuss purely aesthetic concerns. On the other, the discussion of realism also opened up a space to deal with the historical, political, and ethical issues raised by Némiovsky's fiction. The criteria of observation, authenticity, and sincerity were frequently invoked by critics to explain and justify the appearance of stereotyped Jewish characters and situations in Némirovsky's texts, as well as to valorise the portrait of Russian émigrés in *Les Mouches d'automne*.

Némirovsky's life story was frequently cited by critics as a source of literary legitimacy. The reviews of *David Golder* reveal the construction of an author myth on the basis of which interest in the novel was generated. Gisèle Sapiro notes that the development of a culture of literary prizes in France in the early years of the century had encouraged the focusing of media and public attention on the person of the author:

Le prix contribue ainsi à la focalisation de l'attention du public sur le personnage de l'auteur, sur sa vie. Nouvelle manière de mettre en scène la littérature, dont les séries d'interviews d'écrivains réalisés à partir de 1924 par Frédéric Lefèvre pour *Les Nouvelles littéraires* sont l'expression.[62]

The literary prize thus contributes to the focusing of the readers' attention on the person of the author, on their life. This was a new way of staging literature, of which the series of interviews Frédéric Lefèvre conducted with authors for Les Nouvelles littéraires *from 1924 onwards is an example.*

This sort of framing of fiction in terms of the author's biography prefigures modern publishing strategies. Juliet Gardiner has demonstrated how such strategies are widely used by marketing experts in the twenty-first century literary marketplace. Clever marketing strategies certainly have been a dominant feature of the recent reception of *Suite française*. The mythologisation of Némirovsky's life story in 1929 had two key aspects: the story of her emigration and that of the arrival of a manuscript by a complete unknown at the Grasset offices. The 'mirroring effect' of journalistic literary criticism is very much in evidence here, as is the importance of Lefèvre's column: the information circulating appears to have been derived primarily from his 'Une heure avec Irène Némirovsky' interview in *Les Nouvelles littéraires*. Critics told and retold the story Némirovsky recounted there of how her family were forced to leave first St Petersburg and then Moscow in 1918, of their flight to Finland, Stockholm, and finally Paris. Némirovsky's origins were exoticised: Lefèvre described her as a 'beau type d'Israélite' (*one of those beautiful Israelites*) and remarked that 'en elle se mêlent, accord parfait et rare, l'intellectuelle slave, familière aux habitués de Sorbonne, et la femme du monde' (*she incarnates a perfect and rare combination of the Slav intellectual, familiar to those who frequent the Sorbonne, and the society lady*). Many critics related Némirovsky's fiction closely to her Jewish and Russian origins. With the publication of *Le Bal*, *L'Affaire Courilof,* and *Les Mouches d'automne*, more detailed discussion was generated about the relationship between Némirovsky's Russianness and Jewishness and her literary production, as we shall see in Chapters 3 and 4. Critics also persisted in repeating the tale of the mysterious manuscript received by Bernard Grasset, which made such an impression on him that he put an advertisement in the press to locate its author. In March 1930, as we have seen, Claude Pierrey referred to this tale as a legend, and, reviewing *L'Affaire Courilof* in June 1933, J. Ernest-Charles remarked that the story had been repeated *ad nauseam*.[63] This type of mythologisation leads the reader to believe that a literary work can impose itself simply through its innate aesthetic qualities. This is what Bourdieu calls 'the value of the work of art as fetish' and 'the belief in the creative power of the artist'. Contemporary readers were invited to believe in Némirovsky's creative power because her novel had impressed Grasset without the benefit of a famous name or literary intermediary to recommend it. Here we see Bourdieu's *illusio* in operation: the agents in the field—the critics—display their interest in the game which constitutes the very existence of the literary field, that is, their faith in the concept of literary value as a purely textual value.[64] Grasset's own position in the literary field as a successful publisher gave him the authority to consecrate *David Golder*.[65] It is worth noting briefly at this point—and we shall return to the question in Chapter 6—that the terms of the creation of the Némirovsky myth in 2004 were identical to those of 1929: the critical reception of *Suite française* also focused on the presentation of an extraordinary life and on the unexpected appearance and publication of an exceptional manuscript.

A further aspect of the person of the author which provoked discussion in reviews was Némirovsky's gender. The publication of Jean Larnac's *Histoire de la littérature féminine en France* in 1929 demonstrates the lively interest in the question of women and literature in the period. Larnac's historical survey led him to conclude that never before had there existed such a large number of female novelists in France.[66] However, the response of male writers to this 'invasion' of the literary field was often a hostile one.[67] Claude Pierrey, writing in *Chantecler*, implied that the context of reception of *David Golder* was largely unfavourable to women writers, saying that it appeared at a time when there was a veritable campaign against women writers on the part of those who sought to denigrate their contributions and to underestimate their value.[68] Paul Nizan remarked in 1937 that women's literature did not have a good reputation. This fact is very much in evidence in the reviews: when Némirovsky's gender is remarked upon, the reviewer generally points out that, given the poor quality of women's writing, Némirovsky's fiction is exceptional and her style is masculine. Critics said that there was no sign of a woman's touch in her novels,[69] that they were written in the way a man would write,[70] and that her talent was a male talent.[71] It is clear from the ubiquity of such remarks that the norm of literary quality is conceived of as masculine, and that literary success by women authors is a deviation from the norm. Characteristics of Némirovsky's writing considered not typically feminine include energy, sobriety, and density;[72] force;[73] narrative organisation;[74] style and construction;[75] and lack of sentimentality.[76] Larnac presented his study of women's literature as an attempt to demonstrate gender difference:

> J'aimerais enfin montrer la continuité de l'effort littéraire des femmes et révéler, dans leurs œuvres, ce qui est proprement féminin et en fait un ensemble fort différent de la littérature masculine.[77]

> *I should like to demonstrate the continuity between women's literary efforts and to show, in their works, what it is that is specifically feminine and makes their work significantly different from masculine literature.*

Although Larnac sets himself against critics who argue that women are incapable of producing literature of quality, and purports to affirm equality within difference, he nonetheless finds women writers incapable of innovation, objective observation, or formal rigour;[78] all are enslaved to their emotions, able only to write about themselves, and incapable of distancing themselves from their own experience in order to transform it into art;[79] they are incapable of concision and of the intellectual application required for the disciplines of history, philosophy, and literary criticism.[80] This sort of gendering of aesthetic and intellectual values shows why Némirovsky's work was labelled by critics as masculine in order to affirm its quality.

Female critics generally countered negative, essentialist evaluations of women's writing from their male colleagues by affirming women's ability to incarnate 'virile' values. They contested the notion that only men had access to the (male) literary norm, rather than celebrating that which was deemed specifically 'feminine' in literature. Arguments in favour of a gender-neutral approach to literature were not unusual in the inter-war period from the pens of female critics keen to promote the value of women's writing. Inter-war women who celebrated female difference from a radical perspective, for example, through an affirmation of lesbianism in life and in literature, were very much on the margins of cultural production.[81] Reviewing *Les Mouches d'automne*, Marcelle Gaston-Martin remarked on the particularly virile quality of the novel's conception, construction, and execution,[82] and argued that a 'virile' style should not be deplored in women, and that the work should simply be taken for what it is:

> Sans doute convient-il de louer un si peu féminin détachement de l'effet sentimental. Mais, par un illogisme bien humain, j'ai constaté que ce sont surtout ses lecteurs masculins—et non des plus frivoles ou naïfs— qui déplorent chez un écrivain aussi doué qu'elle, ce si curieux dédain du charme et de l'émotion. Ils vont jusqu'à sous-entendre l'inaptitude étrangement décevante dans une sensibilité de femme, à frôler ce domaine illimité.

> *It is probably appropriate to praise her detachment from any sentimental effect, which is not at all feminine. But, with an absence of logic which is typically human, I have noticed that it is particularly her male readers—and not the most frivolous or naïve ones—who deplore this very strange disdain for charm and emotion in a writer as talented as she is. They go as far as to imply an inability, strangely disappointing in the case of a female sensibility, to approach this limitless domain.*

Gaston-Martin here attacks male critics who criticise women writers for failing to be sufficiently 'feminine' whilst at the same time refusing any positive value to this 'femininity'. Perhaps she was referring to critics such as André Bellessort, a member of the Académie française, and its future Secretary under the Occupation. In an article entitled 'Un roman de femme', this defender of linguistic conservatism objected to Némirovsky's use of crude language, suggesting that this indicated a return to medieval times when women's language was characterised by the same crudity as men's, which he implied, was regression rather than progress.[83]

For most critics, it was Némirovsky's foreignness, rather than her gender, which identified her as an interesting and exotic literary curiosity. The fact that a Russian had chosen to write exclusively in French provoked discussion of the relationship between Occident and Orient in the context of the regeneration of French imaginative writing. Writing in the nationalist publication *L'Ordre*, Pierre Loewel located Némirovsky within a new literary trend:

> C'est bien un des phénomènes les plus réconfortants que d'assister à cet apport de voix du dehors, à cette importation constante de talents venus de l'extérieur pour servir l'art français. Mme de Noailles, la princesse Bibesco, Kessel hier, aujourd'hui Mme Némirovsky, latines et slaves prouvent avec quelle facilité et quelle maîtrise la culture française peut être appréhendée et rejettent bien loin, par leur exemple, la théorie de la formation traditionnelle indispensable à l'éclosion d'un talent national. Bien mieux: il semble que ces auteurs nouveaux apportent une vision fraîche, débarrassée de toutes les vieilles figurations, donnent aux mots une saveur nouvelle comme s'ils rajeunissaient, comme s'ils projetait sur le monde des images et un verbe qui n'aient pas encore servi.[84]

> *It is certainly a very comforting phenomenon, to witness the contributions of voices from elsewhere, the constant importation of talents from outside which serve French art. Yesterday, Mme de Noailles, princess Bibesco, and Kessel, today Madame Némirovsky, Latins and Slavs are proving how easily and with what success French culture can be understood, and, by their example, are demolishing the theory that a traditional training is required in order for a national talent to bloom. Even better: it seems that these new authors are bringing a fresh vision, divested of all the old forms, and are giving words a new flavour, a sort of rejuvenation, as if they were projecting onto the world images and a language which had never before been used.*

Loewel's comments are an affirmation of French universalism. Foreign elements can be incorporated and made French; alterity can be domesticated such that the foreign writer can master, and therefore contribute to, French culture and even become a *national* talent. This review testifies to a firm belief in the notion that French culture is the bearer of universal (Western) values, demonstrated here for Loewel by the ease with which French cultural forms can be mastered by outsiders. Loewel here rejects the idea, promulgated by *L'Action française*, that the highest achievements of the French (classical) mind were inaccessible to foreigners.[85] Nonetheless, it is French cultural values which are posed here as a source of aesthetic renewal, rather than any particular aptitude on the part of the foreign writers in question.

Loewel's suggestion that non-native speakers of French occupy a privileged position as regards the rejuvenation of the French language is also noteworthy: again he opposes the line taken by *L'Action française*, who strongly asserted that the French language should be protected from foreign influences.[86] An article in *Le Figaro*, significantly entitled 'Ecrivains francisés', pursued a similar line to Loewel, discussing the phenomenon of writers writing in French rather than in their native language, and likening Némirovsky to Doussia Ergaz (Russian), Amy Kher (Syrian Egyptian) and Daisy Fellowes (English).[87] The term *francisé* again suggests absorption and domestication of the cultural other rather than any notion of cultural exchange. J. Ernest-Charles's observation that the decision of various contemporary foreign women writers to write in French was very flattering for the French, expresses a similar opinion.[88]

The Jewish critic Benjamin Crémieux, a key member of the *Nouvelle Revue française* group, but writing here in *Les Annales*, also approached *David Golder* in terms of the ability of a foreign writer to engage with French linguistic and cultural models. He noted that Némirovsky was Russian Jewish novelist who wrote directly in French, and that:

> [l]a seduction la plus profonde de ce roman vient, sans doute, de voir une Barbare manier avec habileté et précaution des instruments de précision tels que la langue française ou la moule du roman psychologique français.[89]

> *The most seductive thing about this novel is probably seeing a Barbarian manipulating with skill and care such precise instruments as the French language or the model of the French psychological novel.*

One might read Crémieux's ironic juxtaposition of 'une Barbare' with 'des instruments de précision' as a direct reference to arguments about French cultural renewal advanced by right-wing nationalist critics who adhered to the literary and political doctrines of Charles Maurras. Maurras frequently used the term 'barbarie' to designate the rejection or disruption of his classical ideal.[90] The discussion of Némirovsky's fiction in terms of her foreignness is inscribed in the debate around the idea promulgated by the cultural and political right in the 1920s that France and French culture incarnated Western values which were universal and which derived from the French classical tradition, and which should be defended against the encroachment of the Orient in the form of bolshevism, Jews, mysticism, capitalism, socialism, and so on. A key text of this debate was Henri Massis's *Défense de l'Occident* (1927), in which he argued for the defence of the West against the advancement of the East, and attempted to contest some French intellectuals' fascination with the East as an answer to the spiritual, political, economic, and aesthetic failings of the contemporary West. André Malraux's *La Tentation de l'Occident* (1926) is one obvious example.[91] The crisis of the French novel in the 1920s manifested itself in conservative quarters as an assertion of the decadence of new French cultural forms which set themselves against the norms of French classicism. Raimond identifies a malaise in the French literary field in the early twentieth century provoked by comparisons with foreign—especially Russian and English—literature, and by the availability of a large number of foreign works in translation, which introduced readers to different literary techniques and thus facilitated shifts in literary tastes and in the criteria of literary evaluation operative in the literary field.[92] The widespread positive reception of Némirovsky's fiction testifies to her potential acceptability within the terms of the Occident/Orient binary: those for whom her Slav identity raised the possibility of Oriental decadence could view her texts as proof of the subjugation of Slav disorder by French classical forms.

Having identified the key thematic preoccupations of critics of Némirovsky's fiction—the nature and value of the French novel, realism, gender, national identity and culture—a clearer picture is emerging of the relationship between her novels and the contemporary literary field, a picture which suggests several reasons for her popularity. Némirovsky's fiction was both reassuringly familiar and promisingly modern. Its narrative structure and characterisation could be seen as products of the French realist and classical traditions, whilst also pointing towards future innovation. Némirovsky was the incarnation of the modern, professional woman writer, yet her representations of gender were not significantly transgressive and her own identity as a bourgeois wife and mother lent her credibility among traditionalists. The combination of her 'foreign' and 'Eastern' (Oriental) identity and her choice of the French language proved the accessibility and flexibility, and therefore the vigour, of French (universal, Occidental) cultural forms. Her novels thus corresponded to the criteria of literary value operative in a large swathe of the French literary field. There were however two notable exceptions to this broad acceptability: Némirovsky's fiction did not fulfil the ideological criteria operative among critics on the far left, and it did not fulfil the aesthetic criteria operative in the highly intellectualised sector of the literary field exemplified by the *Nouvelle Revue française*.

LOCATING NÉMIROVSKY IN THE LITERARY FIELD

A thematic reading of the reception of Némirovsky's early fiction suggests that in the literary review, a discourse of exceptionality cloaks the reality of critical familiarity. Whilst critics hailed Némirovsky's fiction as a success because of its originality, close examination of their arguments shows that it was deemed interesting more because it posed important questions which were *already* under debate in the literary field. Némirovsky's active awareness of the debates her work was provoking should not be underestimated: it is clear from the fact that, in interviews, she cited comments made by her reviewers that she read the literary press in some detail.[93] It is plausible therefore to imagine that her decision to pursue themes associated with Jewish and Russian identity in her early career was at least in part a response to the positive interest of the reviewers of *David Golder* in these aspects of her fiction and her personal history. If we consider the full range of Némirovsky's output between the wars, the iterative relationship between production and reception becomes even more apparent. According to Raimond, the 1920s debate on the crisis of the novel was superseded in the 1930s by a renewed faith in the power of narrative to depict the real, as exemplified by the great novel cycles of the period: he asks how one could possibly speak of a crisis of the novel when contemporary texts were aiming to tell the story of the real world over the course of a quarter of a century.[94] Sapiro also notes that, from the end of the 1920s, the *roman d'analyse* and the *roman de mœurs* gave way to novels which sought to explore contemporary history and to offer philosophical, historical, or psychological explanations of contemporary social reality.[95] Némirovsky's literary trajectory corresponds exactly to these broad trends of her literary environment. Her texts from the first half of the 1930s are *romans de mœurs* or *romans d'analyse,* which plausibly can be interpreted as a response to the debate on the crisis of the novel in the 1920s, whilst her literary production in the second half of the decade is an attempt to embrace twenty years of contemporary French history via an extended chronological narrative which is in some ways reminiscent of the *roman-cycle.* Némirovsky always wrote in accordance with the literary preoccupations of her time, and in this sense she was no innovator: she was a literary success because her textual production was closely attuned to its context of reception.

The reception of Némirovsky's fiction and the context of that reception demonstrate the applicability of Bourdieu's proposition that a relationship of structural homology exists between the production and consumption of culture:

> L'homologie qui s'établit aujourd'hui entre l'espace de production et l'espace de consommation est au principe d'une dialectique permanente qui fait que les goûts les plus différents trouvent les conditions de leur satisfaction dans les œuvres offertes qui en sont comme l'objectivation, tandis que les champs de production trouvent les conditions de leur constitution et de leur fonctionnement dans les goûts qui assurent— immédiatement ou à terme—un marché à leurs différents produits.[96]
>
> *The homology established today between the space of production and the space of consumption is the basis of a permanent dialectic which means that the most diverse tastes find that they can be satisfied by the works on offer, which appear as if they were their objectification, while the fields of production find the conditions of their functioning*

in the tastes which ensure—immediately or in due course—a market for their different products.[97]

Némirovsky's success resulted from a virtuous circle linking publisher, texts, critics, and their journals and reviews, and ultimately, readers. Her fiction found its 'right place' with Grasset,[98] and its 'right readers' in the critics and readers of the mainstream culturally literate but non-specialist literary press. As a result, her writing was highly remunerative, which allowed her to occupy a socially and economically advantaged position in Paris of the 1930s, a fact which she publicised by giving interviews from her comfortable home. In interviews in *Les Nouvelles littéraires* by Frédéric Lefèvre and Jeanine Delpech, the latter significantly entitled 'Chez Irène Némirovsky ou la Russie Boulevard des Invalides', the privileged bourgeois environment in which Némirovsky wrote is underlined. In Lefèvre's article, we learn that Némirovsky writes in a 'grand salon' stretched out on a divan; Delpech describes the covered balcony where a delightful view of Paris's gardens forms the backdrop for the author's imagination.[99] Claude Pierrey told readers of *Chantecler* that '[d]ans son salon d'un luxe raffiné, où les meubles et les objets de prix habilement disseminés n'en sont que mieux mis en valeur, l'auteur de *David Golder* s'avère, avant tout, femme du monde, infiniment gracieuse et accueillante' (*in her refined and luxurious sitting room, where the furniture and the precious objects are cleverly displayed to show off their value, the author of* David Golder *looks most of all like a society lady, perfectly gracious and welcoming*).[100]

A further indication of Némirovsky's position in the inter-war literary field is provided by the response of the *Nouvelle Revue française* (NRF) to her work. The *NRF* is widely acknowledged as the organ which had the most power to consecrate an author aesthetically in the inter-war period. It represented the fully 'autonomous' pole of the literary field where symbolic capital is bestowed by peers or specialists.[101] The literary values promulgated by the *NRF* were artistic independence (both economic and intellectual) and formal excellence. The *NRF* claimed to be the true locus of the new French classicism, in opposition to the right-wing nationalist critics who took their cue from Maurras and also claimed to represent the French classical tradition. The *NRF* rejected both conservative 'good taste' incarnated by the Académie française, and the 'vulgarity' of naturalism and populism. It celebrated literary innovation and originality and rejected all conformism and any attempt to achieve social ascension through literary activity.[102] The *NRF* did not consecrate Némirovsky. Decourdemanche (i.e. Jacques Decour) found the themes and narrative structure of *David Golder* conventional, and Denis Saurat dismissed *Les Mouches d'automne* in three sarcastic lines: 'Sentimental. Ce qu'il y a de plus faible en Tolstoï amené à la date de 1930; à la rigueur, suffirait à expliquer, et à justifier, la revolution russe' (*Sentimental. The weakest bits of Tolstoy brought up to date for 1930; it would almost be enough to explain, and to justify, the Russian revolution*).[103] The *NRF* did not review any of Némirovsky's subsequent novels. Its silence is eloquent—the *NRF* was clearly of the view that the aesthetic, social, and economic values which the Némirovsky phenomenon embodied were not in accordance with its own values.

Within the framework proposed by Bourdieu, Némirovsky should be located towards the socially and economically dominant pole of the inter-war French literary field, and within the *sous-champ de grande production*. Némirovsky's social dominance is indicated by her wealth, her bourgeois lifestyle, and by her educational status as a graduate of the Sorbonne. However, as a foreigner, a Jew, and a woman, she was unlikely to accede to the top of this axis. Némirovsky can be located around the midpoint of the axis which opposes symbolic capital (aesthetic recognition by peers and special-ists) to temporal capital (popular recognition by the general public). Her popular and media success indicates temporal capital, but the acknowledge-ment of specific symbolic (aesthetic) capital by critics—the affirmation of literary merit—means that she should not be located at the extreme point of this axis. The *type* of symbolic capital accorded to Némirovsky by her crit-ics is also crucial here: if Némirovsky does not belong at the other extreme of the horizontal axis (symbolic capital), this is because her texts were not received as examples of modernist literature characteristic of the *champ de production restreinte* and exemplified in the inter-war period by the *NRF* writers and critics. Némirovsky's place in the literary field corresponds to a well-established position, which Sapiro identifies, that is, a commercially successful writer, who was paid a monthly wage by a publishing house, and whose novels were serialised in advance of publication in large-circulation reviews for financial reasons.[104]

Némirovsky's literary success derived from an absence of conflict between the agents involved in the creation of her literary reputation: author, publishers, critics, and readers interacted harmoniously in the lit-erary field with the result that the field produced a certain type of value for her novels. Némirovsky succeeded in capitalising (aesthetically, finan-cially, and socially) on the literary sensation created on the publication of *David Golder* without becoming identified as a merely commercial writer. Her novels were widely read and reviewed throughout the 1930s because they were formally accessible, contemporary in theme, and yet reassur-ingly familiar.

LITERATURE AND POLITICS

One crucially important aspect of the French literary field of the 1930s, which we have not so far considered, is its politicisation.[105] In this decade, politically committed literature flourished because of the left/right polari-sation resulting from the international situation, and because of the active promotion of *littérature engagée* in various forms by the French left.[106]

Political engagement became a significant element of a writer's literary position between the wars, and the possibilities for the expression of politics through literature multiplied significantly thanks to a proliferation of literary-political journals, groups, and publishers.[107] Némirovsky was not a writer of political literature. In an interview in 1935 in *Candide* in which various writers were asked whether the threat of political unrest influenced their literary projects, Némirovsky expressed total disengagement:

> J'ai vécu une bonne moitié de ma vie sous la menace de troubles révolutionnaires (menaces souvent suivis d'effets). C'est vous dire que j'y suis habituée et que je n'y pense pas.
> Tous les lendemains sont incertains, d'ailleurs. Le travail a ceci de bon qu'il fait oublier.[108]

> *I have lived at least half my life under the threat of revolutionary disturbances, threats which have frequently become reality. That is to say that I am used to it and I don't think about it.*
> *In any case, you never know what tomorrow will bring. The good thing about work is that it makes you forget.*

Némirovsky's personal trajectory as an emigrée and therefore an enemy of the Bolshevik revolution placed her in direct opposition to the exponents of *littérature engagée* such as Nizan and Aragon, and to the conception of literature explored in journals such as *Commune*, *L'Humanité*, and *Vendredi*, and such publications generally ignored Némirovsky's fiction. One notable exception is *L'Affaire Courilof*, no doubt because of the political subject of the novel. The left-wing review *Monde* criticised Némirovsky for a lack of political understanding and accused her of demonstrating a very approximate knowledge of the revolutionary movement she depicts.[109] Jean-Baptiste Séverac remarked in an article published in *Le Populaire* and in *Midi-Socialiste* that he could not reconcile the portrait of Leon M . . .—for him 'une figure construite de toutes pièces et fort éloignée d'une réalité historique' (*cobbled together and a far cry from historical reality*)—with the real-life revolutionaries he had known before the war.[110] One might reasonably object to these ideologically motivated criticisms that they seek to apply inappropriate criteria to the text insofar as they read what is really a *roman d'analyse* or a psychological character study as if it were a *roman à thèse*. This is an example of the importing of evaluative criteria from a particular sector of the literary field into the discussion of a novel which belongs in quite a different part of that field, the result of which is, necessarily, rejection of the text by such critics.

The fact that Némirovsky's fiction does not belong in the highly politicised sector of the inter-war literary field does not, however, mean that this element of the literary landscape is irrelevant to an understanding of her work. On the contrary, Gisèle Sapiro has convincingly demonstrated in *La Guerre des écrivains* that it was precisely the politicisation of the French inter-war literary field which produced the tensions and political dilemmas of writers and intellectuals under the Occupation, tensions in which Némirovsky was inevitably to become embroiled, and which have significantly coloured the recent reception of *Suite française*. An important focus of the controversy over Némirovsky in our own time has been her literary contributions to certain right-wing anti-Semitic journals in the 1930s and into the 1940s. This has posed a serious ethical dilemma for modern readers—how can one evaluate the work of a Jewish author who was herself a victim of the Shoah, but who had been closely involved with individuals and publications ultimately held responsible for the promotion of the anti-Semitic policies of the Vichy regime? This question has proved particularly problematic for English and American readers. Evidence of this is to be found in the pages of the *Guardian* of February 2007, in a series of articles published after the appearance of *David Golder* in English. Carmen Callil raised the question of the publication of Némirovsky's short stories in the 'notoriously anti-Semitic French journals' *Gringoire* and *Candide*. On 22 February, the *Guardian* ran a lengthy article by Stuart Jeffries entitled 'Truth, Lies and anti-Semitism' which gave an overview of the 'transatlantic row' which had erupted over the issue of Némirovsky's potential anti-Semitism in relation to her collaboration with far right reviews, her personal associations, and the presence of anti-Semitic stereotypes in her novels. Having surveyed the various arguments, Jeffries concluded his article with Callil's somewhat agnostic question, 'Who are we to judge?' In the French press, the approach has been rather different. The *Guardian* debate was covered in *Libération* in utterly dismissive terms in a short article entitled 'Haine de soi' which discussed the 'accusation' that Némirovsky was a 'self-hating Jew': 'Seuls, en effet, le politiquement correct et l'aseptisation du discours (et de la fiction) aujourd'hui, en particulier aux Etats-Unis, permettent d'avancer une hypothèse aussi absurde' (*In fact, only modern political correctness and the sanitisation of discourse, particularly in the USA, could produce such an absurd hypothesis*). The term 'self-hating Jew' is presented in inverted commas in English within the French text (and without reference to its academic context—Sander Gilman's 1986 study, *Jewish Self-Hatred*), as if to reject the notion that such an idea could have any place in the French intellectual landscape. This sort of response risks precluding any real engagement in France with the question of Némirovsky's potentially problematic position in the literary field of the late 1930s and early 1940s. French critics did make reference to her association with *Gringoire* and *Candide* when *Suite française* was originally published, but tended to minimise its significance, for example by pointing out that in any case, this sort of 'collaboration' was not sufficient to save her from deportation.[111] The publication of the first biography of Némirovsky in French by the American Jonathan Weiss produced more detailed discussion of Némirovsky's Jewish identity, but even so, the idea that Némirovsky's association with *Gringoire* and *Candide* might be taken as evidence of anti-Semitism was rejected.[112] Treatment of the issue in biographical studies has varied. Jonathan Weiss's *Irène Némirovsky* certainly is willing to explore its ambiguities and to advance the idea that it is 'inquiétant' (*worrying*). [113] Weiss concludes that Némirovsky's right-wing associations and her decision not to flee France left her in 'une situation sans issue' (*a situation with no way out*),[114] and that under the Occupation, her real identity became incompatible with the cultural identity she had created for herself throughout her career.[115] By contrast, the more recent and much longer biography by Olivier Philipponnat and Patrick Lienhardt works very hard to exculpate Némirovsky both as regards general accusations of anti-Semitism and specifically over her involvement with *Gringoire*. The authors advance some interesting and persuasive arguments: that her involvement with *Gringoire* was primarily financially motivated,[116] that she wrote for a very wide range of journals regardless of their political bias, and that in any case anti-Semitism was ubiquitous in the French press of the time;[117] that her association with *Gringoire* began before the hardening of this publication's political line in the mid-1930s, and that many other writers also published here (though it should also be noted that some, including its literary editor Joseph Kessel, also a foreign Jew, broke publicly with the journal precisely because of its anti-Semitism);[118] that the obvious anti-Semitism of *Gringoire*'s principal political polemicist Henri Béraud should not be taken to imply either that the entire journal was anti-Semitic, or that literary contributors such as Némirovsky were;[119] that the context of publication of her stories deformed their intended message.[120] They also explain that paradoxically, *Gringoire* was prepared to continue to publish Némirovsky even after the passing of restrictive laws against Jewish writers and journalists under Vichy, and therefore that this journal offered Némirovsky a source of income at a time when literally no other options were available.[121]

The sensitivity of this issue is amply demonstrated by certain alterations made both to Weiss's biography and to Myriam Anissimov's biographical introduction to *Suite française* for their English translations. In the case of Weiss, the original French version of the biography had suggested that *Les Biens de ce monde* and *Les Feux d'automne* expressed a certain outmoded celebration of the permanence of rural France which the Vichy regime was promoting. In the English (American) version, Weiss qualifies the argument, adding the sentence 'Yet these novels do not really reveal Irène's attitude at the time'. In the French version, Weiss had suggested that some unpublished works suggested doubts on the part of Némirovsky about Vichy, but that this did not indicate a complete break with the regime, whilst in the English version, these doubts have become out-and-out criticism:

> Si on examine de près les textes qui n'ont pas été publiés de son vivant et les projets de romans, on y voit se formuler quelques doutes sur la nature de la politique menée par le gouvernement de Vichy, *doutes qui*

ne vont jamais jusqu'à provoquer une rupture, mais qui indiquent une indépendance d'esprit que les autres écrits—ceux déstinés à la publication pendant l'Occupation (même s'ils n'ont été publiés qu'après)— n'affichent pas. [emphasis added]

> *If we look closely at the other texts unpublished in her lifetime and at other literary projects, we see evidence of doubts about the Vichy government and its ideology*, as well as a sometimes harshly critical attitude toward those who cooperated with the regime. [emphasis added][122]

In the (considerably edited) English version of Myriam Anissimov's preface to original French edition of *Suite française*, a reference to Némirovsky's associations with the far right is omitted: 'Irène Némirovsky devint aussitôt célèbre, adulée par des écrivains aussi étrangers l'un à l'autre que Joseph Kessel, qui était juif, et Robert Brasillach, monarchiste d'extrême droite et antisémite'[123] becomes '*David Golder* was an overnight success, unanimously acclaimed by the critics and admired by other writers'.[124] The sentence 'Quelle relation de haine à soi-même découvre-t-on sous sa plume!' is part of the (generally quite extensive) cuts. In pointing out these changes, I do not wish to imply any criticism of the authors or of their translators or editors: it is a well-known fact that translated works are frequently adapted in view of the expectations of their new audience in the target culture. Certainly, neither author would wish to define Némirovsky as anti-Semitic. The changes to their texts should be seen as an attempt to avoid provoking misinterpretations of their work which, as we shall see in Chapter 6, might well have emerged in the context of a sometimes hostile reception of Némirovsky in Britain and America.

In my view, Némirovsky's association with *Gringoire* and other right-wing journals can best be understood using the approach proposed by Gisèle Sapiro in *La Guerre des écrivains*. This approach has the major advantage of shifting the focus from admonishment to explanation, from the ethical to the literary. It is also important to examine in detail the discourse actually produced in the journals in question, and to distinguish carefully between journals with whom Némirovsky actively chose to be associated by agreeing to publish her fiction in their pages, and journals whose reviewers took notice of her work but with whom she was not otherwise linked.

Sapiro's key thesis is that the position-taking of intellectuals under the Occupation was determined by their literary trajectory in the inter-war period and their consequent position in the literary field, and that previously apolitical aesthetic stances became politicised because of the situation of political crisis and because of practical constraints imposed by the Nazis in the occupied zone in the domain of cultural production.[125] For Sapiro, straightforward political oppositions and commitments are not sufficient to explain the structure of the literary field and the positions of writers within it under the Occupation. The fall of France posed a stark choice for intellectuals—to accept or to refuse the Occupation.[126] This theoretical choice had however to be translated into practice, which for writers generally meant, to publish or not to publish in legal publications. As a result, a range of positions between the two extremes of acceptance and refusal became possible.[127] Sapiro insists that the question of whether and, if so, where to publish, was posed differently for a given writer according to his or her position in the literary field, and that this decision was determined by literary factors and was not a free ideological choice.[128] Sapiro's research reveals a correspondence between the literary opposition 'temporal capital/ symbolic capital' and the political opposition 'collaboration/resistance':

> Le champ littéraire se structure ainsi, dans un premier temps, autour de l'opposition entre un pôle temporellement dominant, formé par des écrivains institutionnalisés qui cumulent toutes espèces de capitaux (économique, scolaire, social) et jouissent d'une notoriété de type mondain, et un pôle temporellement dominé, principalement constitué par des jeunes prétendants en ascension sociale, démunis de ressources économiques mais dotés d'un important capital culturel à la fois hérité et acquis, qui s'orientent vers la reconnaisance des pairs et les profits symboliques. La superposition partielle entre cette opposition structurale et la principale opposition politique illustre la relation entre attitudes politiques et positions occupées dans le champ littéraire: tandis que les représentants du premier pôle se ralient majoritairement aux nouveaux pouvoirs, le régime de Vichy et/ou la Collaboration, la plupart des représentants du second s'engagent dans la clandestinité.[129]

> *The literary field is structured, firstly, around the opposition between a temporally dominant pole, constituted of institutionalised writers who have all the different types of capital (economic, educational, social) and enjoy a worldly reputation, and a temporally dominated pole, primarily made up of young pretenders seeking social advancement, without economic resources but benefiting from a significant amount of cultural capital which they have both inherited and acquired, who seek the recognition of their peers and symbolic profit. The partial coincidence between this structural opposition and the main political opposition illustrates the relationship between political attitudes and positions occupied in the field: whilst representatives of the first pole mostly rallied to the new powers, the Vichy regime and/or Collaboration, most of the representatives of the second pole became involved in clandestine resistance.*

Némirovsky's position as closer to the first, temporally dominant pole, makes it more likely that she would adopt a position of professional accommodation with the Vichy regime, and this for *literary* rather than *ideological* reasons. In order to refuse the Vichy regime *through her professional activities*, she would have had to gain access to the types of literary groups with which she had never been previously associated, that is, those associated with the NRF, with the Gallimard publishing house, with the Communist party or with small-circulation, avant-garde reviews, since these were the sorts of literary milieux out of which intellectual resistance to Vichy was to be born. As the responses cited above of the NRF to *Les Mouches d'automne* and of *Monde* to *L'Affaire Courilof* suggest, this would have been highly unlikely: the structure of the literary field does not allow an author simply to change her literary allegiances at will. I would suggest then, following Sapiro, that on the one hand, Némirovsky's position in the literary field in the 1930s precluded her participation in the intellectual opposition to Vichy, and, on the other, that the political overdetermination under the Occupation of previously *apolitical* literary choices lent a political significance to Némirovky's involvement with *Gringoire* which it did not have in the 1930s.

Of all the reviews with which Némirovsky was associated, there is no doubt that her closest relationship was with *Gringoire*. *Gringoire* was the best-selling literary and political weekly in 1930s France. Founded in 1928, its far right political tendencies developed after the departure of Joseph Kessel and the arrival of Henri Béraud in 1934.[130] Its polemical tone attracted a large audience of middle-class French readers discontent with the contemporary political regime. Its popularity has been attributed to its eclecticism—though clearly a right-wing publication, it gave a platform to a range of (sometimes contradictory) opinions.[131] Under the Occupation, *Gringoire* removed its centre of operations to the unoccupied south (as did *Candide*); these two journals, which had dominated the right-wing cultural press throughout the 1930s, thus relinquished much of their readership to Alphonse de Chateaubriant's *La Gerbe*, which was controlled and financed by the Nazis and preached active collaboration.[132] Nonetheless, *Gringoire* enjoyed the highest circulation of all the publications based in the unoccupied zone.[133] Pro-Vichy, *Gringoire* wholeheartedly embraced Pétain's National Revolution from mid-1940.[134]

Between January 1930 and February 1942, *Gringoire* regularly reviewed Némirovsky's novels, often at some length, published nineteen of her short stories and serialised three of her novels (*La Proie* in 1936, *Deux* in 1938, and *Les Biens de ce monde* in 1941). Her first story appeared in *Gringoire* in December 1933, that is, before Béraud's arrival heralded a hardening of the journal's political content. Béraud would be tried in December 1944 for 'intelligence with the enemy' on the basis of his contributions to *Gringoire*; he was sentenced to death, but his sentence was commuted to 20 years of hard labour.[135] The paradox of Némirovsky's association with *Gringoire* is that despite the journal's political evolution after 1934, in *literary* terms it was an obvious choice as an outlet for her fiction, insofar as its position in the literary field corresponded very closely to hers: it was the leading conservative, popular publication, it had a large general readership and it paid its authors extremely well. It is certainly not difficult to see why Némirovsky would choose to further her career through such a journal which, as we shall see, received her novels with great enthusiasm. As Philipponnat and Lienhardt demonstrate, financial concerns accompanied literary ones: it was around 1933 that Némirovsky began to publish a significant number of stories in a range of reviews, in order to supplement her income, after the death of her father.[136] Némirovsky's choice of *Gringoire* was not ideologically motivated, except in the vaguest sense that the anti-bolshevism of a Russian émigrée might dispose her towards a right-wing publication.[137] Némirovsky's contributions to *Candide* might be seen as more problematic. She published two stories in *Candide*, which appeared in November 1938 and August 1940, and *Les Chiens et les Loups* was published here in serialised form between October 1939 and January 1940. She had also given interviews to the journal in June 1931, February 1935 and September 1935.[138] However, Némirovsky did not contribute to either *L'Action française* or *Je suis partout*, journals which were more militant—and in the case of the latter, overtly fascist—than either *Candide* or *Gringoire*, both of which were as much cultural as political in focus.

Comparing the reception of Némirovsky's fiction in *Gringoire* and *L'Action française*, it is immediately obvious that the latter produced a more militantly racist, anti-Semitic discourse in response to her characters and to her Jewish identity. The Maurassian *L'Action française*, nationalist, monarchist, anti-Semitic, and anti-German, was ideologically more specific and politically more militant than *Gringoire*.[139] *L'Action française* reviewed *David Golder* on 9 January 1930, *Les Mouches d'automne* on 7 January 1932, *L'Affaire Courilof* on 25 May 1933, and *Le Pion sur l'échiquier* on 31 May 1934.[140] The first two were received positively and the second two negatively. This shift may have had as much to do with the development of the literary policy of *L'Action française* as with Némirovsky's literary production. Paul Renard notes that from 18 February 1932 (that is, shortly after the publication of the second of these reviews), the title of the literary section of the paper changed from 'La Vie littéraire' to 'La Vie littéraire française' in order to underline its newly vigorous defence of French literature and the French literary tradition, and its attempt to safeguard the material and moral interests of French writers.[141] Perhaps in this context, the positive reception of a Russian Jewish novelist was no longer desirable. Even the positive reviews contained negative references to Jewishness. In his review of *David Golder*, Robert Le Diable took the opportunity to repeat the contemporary *idée reçue* that in the business world 'les Israélites sont nombreux et puissants' (*Israelites are numerous and powerful*). His conclusion is telling:

> L'impression finale, je l'ai dit, est très favorable au vieux juif [. . .] Il ne faudrait pas pour cela s'apitoyer sur tous les financiers juifs. Qu'au fond

de leur âme, ces potentats soient tristes, et dégoûtés de leur puissance, c'est leur affaire. Mais leurs jeux, les jeux de la 'fortune anonyme et vagabonde', ce sont-là jeux de princes, dont nous autres, les chrétiens, nous faisons les frais.

The final impression, as I have said, is very favourable to the old Jew [. . .] But that is no reason to feel any sympathy for all Jewish financiers. The fact that deep within their souls, these potentates are sad, and disgusted with their power, that is their business. But their games, their games with anonymous and unstable fortunes, those are games played by princes for which we Christians are paying the price.

Comparing *Les Mouches d'automne* to Antonine Coulet-Tessier's *Chambre à louer*, Robert Brasillach focused on Némirovsky's foreign identity and took the opportunity to assert the ubiquity of Jewish assimilation:

Mme Irène Némirovski [sic] est, si je ne me trompe, d'origine à la fois russe et israélite, émigrée en France après la Révolution de 1917. Elle a choisi pour s'exprimer le français, comme le firent au XVIIIe siècle le prince de Ligne et l'abbé Galiani. Mme Coulet-Tessier est, si nous ne nous abusons, Française. Nous regrettons d'avoir à lui indiquer Mme Irène Némirovski comme modèle.
   Des deux, c'est l'étrangère en effet qui sait le mieux les secrets de notre race. La sienne, il est vrai, est prompte à l'assimilation, et on l'a bien vu lors du précédent roman de Mme Némirovski, *David Golder*.[142]

If I am not mistaken, Madame Irène Némirovski [sic] has both Russian and Jewish origins, and emigrated to France after the 1917 revolution. She has chosen to express herself in French, as did the Prince of Ligne and the abbot Galiani in the eighteenth century. Madame Coulet-Tessier is, if I am not wrong, French. We regret that we have to suggest Madame Irène Némirovski to her as a model.
   Of the two, it is in fact the foreigner who best knows the secrets of our race. Hers, it is true, is quick to assimilate, as we saw very well in Madame Némirovski's previous novel, David Golder.

This sort of xenophobic, militant, and deliberately provocative discourse within literary reviews was, according to Renard, a deliberate attempt to convert readers to political anti-Semitism.[143] It was not generally a feature of the reviews in *Gringoire*. Only the first and the last reviews *Gringoire* published (of *David Golder* and of *Les Chiens et les loups*[144]) evoked the Jewish theme because of the subject matter of the novels in question. The reviewers repeated the troubling vocabulary of *David Golder*—'âme de vieux Juif' (*the soul of an old Jew*); 'vieux Juif sordide' (*sordid old Jew*); 'petit Juif dégoûtant' (*disgusting little Jew*). De Pawlowski used *David*

Golder as an excuse to philosophise about the Jewish soul taking pleasure in its current misery as a promise of future happiness, and wondered
whether this perpetual searching was in fact the condition of all men. In the
(much shorter) review of *Les Chiens et les loups*, the reader learns that 'Les
torments de l'âme juive, l'insatisfaction perpetuelle qui la stérilise, ce goût
morbide de l'argent sont traités par Mme Irène Némirovsky de main de
maître' (*The torments of the Jewish soul, the perpetual lack of satisfaction
which paralyses it, that morbid taste for money, are masterfully treated by
Madame Irène Némirovsky*). Thus, whilst *L'Action française* focused on
the highly inflammatory questions of economics and Jewish assimiltaion,
Gringoire focused on the Jewish 'soul' and 'character'.

The first two articles *Gringoire* devoted to Némirovsky—both lengthy—
worked hard to identify a specific position for Némirovsky within the literary field and in relation to the view of literature the journal sought to
promote. As we have already seen, de Pawlowski and Augagneur set *David
Golder* and *Le Bal* in the context of the opposition of classicism to naturalism and romanticism. This *aesthetic* debate was by no means politically
neutral. A nationalist (Maurassian) discourse associated French cultural
identity with classical forms, and condemned romanticism as the source of
the corruption of French values which had produced the weakness and decadence of the France of the Third Republic.[145] After the defeat in 1940, such
intellectual corruption was cited by those who had been proclaiming the
'decadence' of French intellectual production between the wars as a reason
for the fall of France.[146] De Pawlowski used a metaphor of a bouquet and a
seed to describe the opposition between classical construction and romantic freedom, and associated both Némirovsky's narrative approach and 'the
Jewish character' with the latter. However, his review was equivocal as
regards the values associated with the terms 'romanticism' and 'classicism'
in the contemporary literary field. Augagneur rejected naturalism as an
extension of romanticism, and populism as an extension of naturalism, and
praised *Le Bal* for avoiding the populist–naturalist approach, despite the
fact that its subject matter might be seen to be appropriate to such a narrative treatment. Henceforward, all the reviews in *Gringoire* of Némirovsky's
work were laudatory: she was held up as a model of good writing against
modernist writers. Marcel Prévost said that '[l]'écrivain qui, par un art si
dédaigneux de tout procédé facile, impose aux lecteurs des créations imagi-
natives, celui-là mérite le renom de romancier. Cela nous change de tous les
fantômes inconsistants qui hantent certaines productions chères à nos modernes précieuses' (*the writer who, through an art which disdains all facile
writing strategies, provides readers with imaginative creations, that writer
deserves the title of novelist. It makes a change from all the insubstantial
ghosts which haunt some of the literary efforts dear to our precious modernists*).[147] In a similar vein, Jean-Pierre Maxence compared Némirovsky's
style favourably with that of an aspiring avant-garde writer of philosophical
fiction and recent recruit to the *NRF* circle, one Jean-Paul Sartre[148]: 'Tous

deux [i.e. Sartre and G.-A. Odic, whose *L'Ombre à la Barraquer* is discussed in the same review alongside Sartre's *La Nausée* and Némirovsky's
La Proie] ont en commun un grave défaut: un style contourné, artificieux,
pesant, pâteux même. M. Jean-Paul Sartre alourdit son texte d'un vocabu-
laire philosophique qui le rend assez insupportable' *(they both share the
same serious fault: a convoluted, artificial, heavy, style, which might even
be called turgid. Jean-Paul Sartre weighs his text down with a philosophical vocabulary which makes it pretty unbearable.)*[149] *Gringoire* was keen
to oppose Némirovsky's fiction to that of modernist writers, presenting it
as stylistically and narratively robust whilst insisting that it was not simply
commercial and popular literature. Marcel Prévost repeatedly affirmed that
Némirovsky had resisted the temptation to exploit her success by bringing
out a series of hastily written novels in quick succession.[150] Writing in 1939,
Maxence made exactly the same point—that Némirovsky did not give in to
the temptation simply to capitalise on the success of *David Golder*.[151] Prévost and Maxence thus rejected the charge of pure commercialism made in
relation to Némirovsky in publications such as the exclusively cultural journal *Comœdia*, where Simone Ratel talked of the forcing of literary talent.[152]
Gringoire celebrated Némirovsky as a good example of the type of writing
the journal sought to promote: writing which avoided the opposite extremes
of naturalism and modernism. *Gringoire*'s reviews of Némirovsky's work
represent an attempt to prise accessible, realist literature with a clear composition, a strong narrative thread and convincing characterisation away
from accusations that its only virtues were saleability and a lack of intellectual challenge. The *NRF* was not sufficiently persuaded either by *David
Golder* or *Les Mouches d'automne* to attempt to wrest Némirovsky from
Gringoire's clutches and claim her as its own.

All of the questions raised by Némirovsky's relationship with *Gringoire*
are highly ambiguous. How far did the responsibility of intellectuals extend?
What was the status of purely literary involvement in a collaborationist
organ? Should writers attempt to maintain France's cultural voice during
the Occupation or fall silent? Némirovsky's involvement with the far right
press must ultimately be evaluated in the light of the fact that if there is one
thing upon which historians of the Occupation period agree, it is that any
straightforward binary opposition between collaboration and resistance is
woefully inadequate. Furthermore, Némirovsky's case relates only to the
period 1940–1942, that is, before Stalingrad and before the German occupation of the whole of France, a period during which France was 'reasonably united' in the belief that Pétain's Vichy regime was 'the best means of
assuring a decent and honourable return to normalcy'.[153] During this period,
the attitude of intellectuals to collaboration with particular journals was
generally fluid and uncertain, and for many, a deliberate choice against such
activity—a choice which would be coded ethically after the Liberation in
terms of the collaboration/resistance binary—was taken later.[154] Although
the organisation of clandestine and contraband intellectual resistance had

begun in the summer of 1941, it did not come to full fruition until the beginning of 1943; the first edition of the clandestine publication *Les Lettres françaises* appeared in September 1942, after Némirovsky's death.[155] Furthermore, as Sapiro's analysis suggests, the writers involved in literary resistance occupied a position in the literary field which was diametrically opposed to Némirovsky's. Generally composed of Gallimard and *NRF* writers, the Conseil national des écrivains (CNE), the hub of intellectual resistance, included hardly any well-known writers, other than its three central figures Jean Paulhan, Louis Aragon, and Paul Eluard, and very few novelists, apart from Mauriac, Malraux, and Martin du Gard. Those associated with the CNE were generally located at the pole of *production restreinte*, and did not include writers involved with publishers such as Albin Michel or reviews such as the *Revue des deux mondes*, where Némirovsky published.[156]

It is certainly true that, under the Occupation, some writers defended the idea that to publish anything at all in a legal source was an act of betrayal. But this was a controversial view. The slogan 'littérature légale veut dire: littérature de trahison' (*legal literature is treasonous literature*) adopted by Georges Politzer in the review *La Pensée libre*, was contested by Louis Aragon, the leading exponent of contraband literature, and a position of radical refusal was very rare—most writers, including those who would be at the forefront of post-war French literature (such as Sartre, de Beauvoir, and Camus) did publish.[157] Even the Communist-dominated CNE, which played a central role in calling for the *épuration* of intellectuals at the Liberation, did not insist on this extreme position of radical refusal, but deemed a purely literary contribution to the legal press to be an innocent activity.[158] Robert Pickering, who has studied the specific case of works published legally under the Occupation, which express neither collaboration nor resistance, stresses the idea of absurdity as a way of approaching such writing. Pickering underlines the inherently transgressive nature of absurdity as a literary theme (as in a text such as Camus' *L'Etranger*, published in 1942), but also proposes absurdity as a way of describing the very fact of publishing under such circumstances:

> To publish legally in this context equates not to an act of betrayal or of unscrupulous opportunism, but to the expression of a deep despair, of experience adrift and uncontrollable; more, it could be seen as an attempt, conscious or unwitting, to neutralise or negate such absurdity, by its very formulation, in a way which appears to stand beyond the prescriptions of a specific set of beliefs or directives.[159]

This is a fitting evaluation of the context of publication of Némirovsky's Occupation writing: its very existence seems absurd, and yet Némirovsky's determination to continue to write and to publish could equally be interpreted as a negation of that very absurdity through an affirmation of her writing identity.

The foregoing discussion has demonstrated that the literary position Némirovsky occupied in the late 1930s and under the Occupation, in relation to *Gringoire*, is explicable in *literary* terms and was not an *ideological* choice. Close consideration of the construction of Némirovsky's success and literary reputation through analysis of the reception of her work reveals a striking coherence between all the actors and elements which contributed to the construction of Némirovsky as a popular French novelist over the course of the 1930s. From the perspective of cultural history, Jonathan Weiss is right to assert that the endpoint of this trajectory in the Occupation years was an *impasse*; from a biographical perspective, Philipponnat and Lienhardt are right to underline the very real constraints—such as financial considerations—which in practice left Némirovsky little room for manoeuvre. Sapiro's analysis of the literary logic underlying apparently ideological positions in *La Guerre des écrivains* suggests that the *impasse* in which Némirovsky found herself is explicable in terms of her literary position in the inter-war period. It is the role of the biographer, not the literary critic, to propose ethical judgements: this chapter has sought rather to elucidate the ways in which complex relationships between literature and politics are rooted in reception as much as in production, and always threaten to exceed authorial control.

2   Before *David Golder*

It is a function of the way in which literary success is created that most readers do not read a contemporary author's fictional output in the order in which it was written. Readers generally begin with the work which made the author's name, and only then, if their interest has been captured, do they go back and attempt to retrace the imaginative and intellectual journey which led to the author's later reputation. This tendency is present in its most exaggerated form in the recent success of *Suite française*: since it is Némirosky's very last novel which has made her reputation in the twenty-first century, most readers have approached her fiction in reverse chronological order. For this reason, they have found aspects of her 1940s writing difficult to understand; Némirovsky's literary and political predicaments under the Occupation are only fully comprehensible in the context of an appreciation of the development of her literary career through the 1930s. Similarly, most of the first readers of *David Golder* were unaware that it was the culmination of a literary journey which had begun well before the explosion of critical interest in Némirovsky in January 1930. Némirovsky had already published 'Le Malentendu', 'L'Enfant génial', 'L'Ennemie' and 'Le Bal' in *Les Œuvres libres*. *Le Bal*, which contemporary readers took to be Némirovsky's second novel, was in fact written before *David Golder* was finished, and *Le Malentendu* was already four years old when it appeared in book form in 1930. Even *Les Mouches d'automne*, Némirovsky's third published novel, was partly based on a story written in the early 1920s.[1] Thus *L'Affaire Courilof* (published in 1933) was the first text Némirovsky originated entirely after the success of *David Golder*. An understanding of these early works is important for an appreciation of Némirovsky's subsequent literary career, as it is here that we find evidence of the sort of position-taking which would contribute to her location in the literary field of 1930s France. We already have established that the novels Némirovsky published in the first half of the 1930s were a response to the literary debates of the 1920s: her stories published between 1926 and 1929 provide an aperture through which we might observe the development of her perspective on the literary environment surrounding her. My focus in this chapter then will be on the part of Némirovsky's fictional production which predates *David Golder*.

An examination of Némirovsky's literary pre-history necessitates a methodological shift: whilst the analysis will remain contextual, there is no reception to speak of for these texts. To understand their genesis, it will be necessary to reconstruct other aspects of Némirovsky's literary environment. Nonetheless, we should read them in the context of the more general critical discussion of the contemporary novel, since Némirovsky was aware of the literary debates of her time and wrote in response to them. It will also be important to trace the relationships between her formal literary education at the Sorbonne and her creative writing. Némirovsky's reflections on her own reading and writing will provide a means of assessing how she sought to position herself in relation to other writers of her own generation and of the past. In Bourdieu's terminology, it will be a question of tracing the relationship between a habitus and a field:

> Ainsi, la hiérarchie réelle des facteurs explicatifs commande d'inverser la démarche qu'adoptent à l'ordinaire les analystes: il faut se demander non point comment tel écrivain est venu à être ce qu'il a été—au risque de tomber dans l'illusion rétrospective d'une cohérence reconstruite–, mais comment, étant donné son origine sociale et les propriétés socialement constituées qu'il lui devait, il a pu occuper ou, en certains cas, produire les positions déjà faites ou à faire qu'offrait un état déterminé du champ littéraire (etc.) et donner ainsi une expression plus ou moins complète et cohérente des prises de position qui étaient inscrites à l'état potentiel de ces positions.[2]

> *Thus the real hierarchy of explanatory factors requires a reversal of the approach ordinarily adopted by analysts. On no account do we ask how such and such a writer came to be what he was—at the risk of falling into the retrospective illusion of a reconstructed coherence. Rather we must ask how, given his social origin and the socially constructed properties he derived from it, that writer has managed to occupy or, in certain cases, produce the positions which the determined state of the literary (etc.) field offered (already there or still to be made), and thus how a writer managed to give a more or less complete and coherent expression to the position-takings inscribed in a potential state within these positions.*[3]

It is worth underlining that the relationship between habitus and field is always one of dispositions, of potentialities realised or unrealised, and never a deterministic one. In this chapter, we will not lose sight of the iterative relationship between literary production and literary reception, but in contrast to Chapter 1, more space will be devoted to production. I aim to go some way toward addressing the objection that the sociology of literature neglects textual analysis. Jérôme Meizoz noted in 2001 that the neglect of textuality was one of the main criticisms levelled at the sociology of literature, and one of its main challenges for the future.[4] There is no theoretical contradiction between the sociology of literature and attention to textual detail—Bourdieu constantly underlines the interdependence of the production and consumption of literature. However, for pragmatic reasons, the development of the theory has often precluded detailed textual analysis. It is to be hoped that since the theory is now well established and well-known, more work will be produced which truly combines the textual and the contextual. My discussion of the critical response to Némirovsky's fiction in Chapter 1 has demonstrated the ways in which reception aligned her texts with certain available positions within the literary field. In this chapter I explore the ways in which Némirovsky's intellectual and creative trajectories—specifically, her education and her awareness of certain contemporary literary debates—disposed her towards certain positions. For clarity, I treat in two separate chapters the reception of *David Golder* and the subsequently published novels, and the production of the stories published in *Les Œuvres libres*, but they are of course two sides of the same question: how did Némirovsky come to occupy particular positions offered by the literary field of 1930s France? The order in which I approached these issues is derived from the type of critical 'inversion' proposed by Bourdieu. The traditional point of departure for literary analysis is the author. To begin with the critical reception of an author's work is to stress the importance of the field in defining the status of a writer. It also minimises the risk of falling back into the sort of biographical (psychological or sociological) determinism which produces the illusion of coherence, and it avoids the perpetuation of the myth of the author as the sole source of meaning.

In this chapter, I contextualise Némirovsky's early fiction in relation to three types of evidence: her educational trajectory, her unpublished notes about her writing, and her published interviews. Némirovsky's interest in literature was academic as well as creative. She was a student in the Faculty of Letters at the Sorbonne between the autumn of 1920 and the summer of 1925.[5] She spent the first two years of her French university education studying Russian literature and language and in July 1922 obtained the *certificat d'études supérieures de littérature étrangère (russe)* and the *certificat d'études pratiques (Russe)*, gaining the highest mark in her group in both papers.[6] As Philipponnat and Lienhardt point out, it was thus in France and not in Russia that Némirovsky became familiar with the great works of Russian literature.[7] During the academic session 1922–1923, Némirovsky returned to the Sorbonne, this time to study comparative literature, gaining the *certificat d'études supérieures de littératures modernes comparées* in July 1924.[8] The Sorbonne in the early 1920s is extremely significant in the history of comparative literature as a discipline. Fernand Baldensperger, 'the patriarch of French comparatism' in the twentieth century,[9] established the Sorbonne's Institut de littérature comparée in collaboration with Paul Hazard and Paul van Tieghem, following Baldensperger's appointement in 1910 from the University of Lyon. The Institute became the leading centre for comparative research in the inter-war period.[10] In 1921, Baldensperger, Hazard, and van Tieghem launched the *Revue de littérature comparée*, a journal which survives to this day and remains a central point of reference for the discipline. The academic session 1922–1923 was particularly significant, since this was the year Baldensperger returned to Paris after a secondment to Strasbourg.[11] In the academic sessions 1922–1923 and 1923–1924, three courses specifically devoted to comparative literature were offered at the Sorbonne, whilst in 1921–1922 there had only been one.[12] Thus Némirovsky was a student of a new and burgeoning academic discipline (the university chair of comparative literature established at the Sorbonne in 1910 was only the second in France[13]), and she was working within the orbit of leading French academics, whose work was crucial to the definition and development of comparative literature in Europe and in America. However, there is some evidence to suggest that Némirovsky's studies in comparative literature were not a complete success. Her marks were considerably lower than in her previous examinations.[14] She did not, unlike some of her classmates, sign up for this programme the following year, but instead returned to her study of Russian, and obtained the *certificat d'études supérieures de philologie russe* in March 1925, with a *mention très bien*.[15]

Némirovsky was in the habit of writing extensive notes and reflections on her writing, and we are fortunate that much of this material has survived and is now conserved in the IMEC archives. For the most part, these documents date from the latter part of Némirovsky's writing career: the earliest set of complete notes for a novel appears to be that relating to her 1934 novel *Le Pion sur l'échiquier*, although the archives do also contain much interesting material dating from the earlier part of her career. These texts give a fascinating insight into both Némirovsky's writing methods and her literary interests. As well as plans and drafts of novels and stories, and extensive reflections on her work in progress, Némirovsky also noted down details of the books she was reading and copied out quotations from the work of critics she found illuminating.

In addition to these private reflections, Némirovsky was also keen to discuss her approach to writing in interviews. Given her literary education, we can assume that when Némirovsky evoked particular writers or certain contemporary literary debates, she was doing so *en connaissance de cause*. However, evidence from published interviews should be treated with some caution since, as we saw in Chapter 1, Némirovsky knew how to use the press to her advantage—she used interviews in order to construct a certain image of herself as a writer. It is justifiable to take seriously the comments Némirovsky made about her writing in the press because they reveal her knowledge of, and ability to manipulate, the rules of the contemporary literary field. However, Némirovsky was well aware of the benefits of publicity. There is no doubt that her press interviews were a means of seeking readers' assent and thereby generating a larger audience for her novels.

Certain preoccupations recur in Némirovsky's accounts of her approach to writing. Firstly, she is often asked which authors she reads and appreciates. Secondly, she raises the question of which aspects of her writing might be termed 'French' and which 'Russian'. Thirdly, she describes her own writing method. She says that she writes biographies of her characters and produces extensive reflections on her work in progress before beginning the writing of the novel itself, a claim which is amply borne out by the surviving manuscripts. And fourthly, she tells interviewers that her texts are generated from three sources—memories, personal reflections, and documentary evidence. Whilst there are significant developments as regards the ways in which Némirovsky presents her approach to fiction over time—the published interviews span almost the whole of her career, from 1930 to 1940—these four questions remained of interest to her.

LITERARY ALLUSIONS

'Le Malentendu', first published in February 1926, tells the story of Yves Harteloup, a young war veteran, who falls in love with Denise, the wife of his former army comrade Jessaint, whilst on holiday in Hendaye. The second part of the novella recounts the progression of the affair once the characters return to Paris, and its eventual disintegration. In the contemporary terminology, it is a *roman d'analyse*, a realist novel which analyses the interior life and motivations of its characters.[16] French novelists of the inter-war period were interested in novels of marriage and love because they presented fruitful thematic and formal possibilities: they raised moral issues, and invited narrative experiments with point of view.[17] In her study of *La Femme et le couple dans le roman, 1919–1939*, Fernande Gonthier links the interest in marriage as a literary topic in inter-war France to the development of attitudes to marriage in the social field. This was a transitional period during which the notion of marriage as a means of securing social and financial advantage and ensuring the future prosperity of the bourgeois family was being replaced by a concept of marriage based on a free choice and the personal inclinations of individuals.[18] Gonthier suggests that the novelty of this theme in the literature of the period was its focus on the couple as an entity in its own right. Previous literary interrogations of relationships tended rather to depict the couple in terms of the two individuals constituting it. Némirovsky's choice of title certainly focuses the reader's attention on the relationship rather than on the protagonists. Her first published story drew on a literary mode which was both well established and popular. Its main focus is the instability of the couple in the social environment of the *années folles*, and the difficulties of the male subject who comes back from the war and cannot reintegrate into French society. These are questions to which Némirovsky would return in much more detail in her novels of the later 1930s: Yves Harteloup is a sort of prototype for the male protagonists of *Le Pion sur l'échiquier, La Proie,* and *Deux.* Yves describes his psychological malaise in terms of a nineteenth-century literary model:

> Et pourtant, ce n'était pas un jeu, pensa-t-il . . . vraiment, une espèce de dégoût, de lassitude amère demeurait au fond de son cœur, depuis quelques années, depuis la guerre ? . . . avec persistance . . . 'comme un mesquin mal du siècle, sans phrases romantiques', se dit-il encore.[19]

> *And yet, it wasn't a game, he thought . . . really, there had been a sort of disgust, a bitter weariness deep within his heart, for a few years now, since the end of the war? . . . persistently . . . 'Like a petty little* mal du siècle, *without any romantic declarations', he said to himself.*

The *mal du siècle* was also a feature of the contemporary literary field, as we have noted: it was in 1923–1925 that the *NRF* published the articles which defined the concept of the *nouveau mal du siècle.* The appearance of these essays was directly contemporaneous with the setting and the writing of 'Le Malentendu'.[20] The motif of the *mal du siècle* recurs explicitly in *Le Pion sur l'échiquier,* as we shall see in Chapter 5: the problem of postwar malaise was to become a major literary preoccupation for Némirovsky when she turned her attention to the depiction of contemporary French society in her later work. Yves's malaise in 'Le Malentendu' is not in fact that of the *nouveau mal du siècle* generation—the sons of the war veterans—but of their fathers: Yves fought the war, and his disorientation is a direct result of this experience. Whilst the younger generation have to face a society in which the militarist values of their childhood are redundant, Yves's problem is one of economics. In the third chapter of the novella where the narrator recounts Yves's life story, we learn that, as an adolescent, he was prepared for a privileged life of financial security and leisure which has become impossible in the post-war economic situation.[21] Already in 'Le Malentendu', Némirovsky was beginning to interrogate the consequences of the economic crises of the 1920s.

'Le Malentendu' seems to have developed out of a combination of autobiographical material and Némirovsky's reading experiences. The various geographical references reveal that Némirovsky was writing about places with which she was very familiar. We know for example that Némirovsky holidayed in Hendaye in the early 1920s. Certain passages are clearly and convincingly painted from life:[22] Yves's and Denise's night-time encounter on the beach;[23] the description of the carnival at Fontarabie (the Spanish port of Hondarrabia).[24] The accounts in the second part of the text of the Parisian nightclubs of the *années folles* and the excursions to Montmartre and to the Bois de Boulogne[25]—locations which recur in Némirovsky's fiction—document Némirovsky's own social life in the period.[26] Her experience of emigration also finds its way into the text in the form of Yves's eventual departure for Finland, and Yves's father's affair with a Russian artist.[27] The literary references in 'Le Malentendu' give an insight into the type of writing with which Némirovsky was familiar. These references would also have created certain associations for the contemporary reader, thus contributing to the positioning of the text in the literary field.

Némirovsky makes reference to four authors in 'Le Malentendu': Pierre Loti (1850–1923), Paul Bourget (1852–1935), Alphonse Daudet (1840–1897), and Charles Baudelaire (1821–1867). At the beginning of 'Le Malentendu', we learn that the Harteloup family villa is next door to Loti's. There is a further reference to Loti's house, with its overgrown garden and its fading shutters, which Yves and Denise pass as they take a walk.[28] Perhaps this evocation of Loti was intended as a gesture toward the well-informed contemporary reader, who might have known that Loti had died at Hendaye in 1923. Loti, like Yves, was a veteran of the First World War. In her notes for *Les Biens de ce monde* (1941), which describes Pierre Hardelot's experience of the First World War, Némirovsky transcribed a passage from Loti's 1916 'Il pleut sur l'enfer de la Somme'.[29] Loti is not then the only link between these two texts: the similarity of the protagonist's names is striking. However the account of Pierre's idealised marriage to Agnès in the later novel is quite the opposite of Denise's unfaithful marriage and unsuccessful affair. The reference to Alphonse Daudet in 'Le Malentendu' is not made explicit, and may or may not have been recognised by contemporary readers. Waiting for Yves, Denise recalls four lines of a poem: 'Aimer sans être aimé, / Etre au lit sans dormir, / Et attendre sans voir venir / Sont trois choses qui font mourir, dit-on à peu près' (*To love without being loved, / To be in bed without sleeping, / And to wait without seeing anyone coming, / Are three things which kill, they say, or something like that*). Alphonse Daudet quotes this Provençal proverb in the final volume of his three-part saga *Tartarin de Tarascon* (1890).[30] Némirovsky does not indicate the source of the quoted text, which is presented as common knowledge ('dit-on'). A reference to Baudelaire is used by one of the protagonists to characterise Denise's attitude to love. According to Jean-Paul, her cousin, she is, like Baudelaire, the last of the romantics, in that she has not lost her faith in words.[31] But unlike Baudelaire, she is not the first of the modernists. Her romantic faith in words is out of place in the cynical post-war world in which belief in love has been destroyed.[32] Jean-Paul misquotes Baudelaire's 'Sonnet d'Automne' from *Les Fleurs du mal* in order to explain to Denise that modern women accept a man's preference for brief flirtation instead of offering and requiring eternal fidelity: 'Les autres femmes ont mis depuis longtemps en pratique le vers de Baudelaire avec une variante: 'Sois charmante, tais-toi et f. . le camp ' (*For a long time now, other women have put into practice a variant on Baudelaire's lines: Be beautiful, shut up and f . . . off*).[33] The function of the quotation is then to indicate the decadence of the sexual morality of the *années folles*. It is in relation to sex that the reference to Paul Bourget occurs. In conversation with her mother about contemporary sexual relationships, Denise remarks that the era of Paul Bourget has passed; unlike Bourget's protagonists, men are now required to give up their leisure and work: 'Il est passé le temps des héros de Bourget, qui collectionnaient les femmes et les cravates et ne faisaient rien. Ne rien faire! Ils mourraient de faim, les héros de Bourget! . . . ' (*The time of Bourget's heroes has passed, men who collected women and ties and didn't do anything else. Doing nothing! Bourget's heroes would die of hunger!*)[34] This is by no means an isolated reference to Bourget in Némirovsky's *œuvre*. In the short stories 'Destinées' and 'Le Sortilège', both published in *Gringoire* in 1940, Bourget is cited as an expert on the subject of adultery.[35] We also know that Némirovsky was familiar with Bourget's literary criticism, since she transcribed passages from his 1922 *Nouvelles pages de critique et de doctrine* in her notes.[36] Indeed, some contemporary critics likened Némirovsky's novels to Bourget's. Reviewing *Jézabel* in *Marianne* in 1936, Ramon Fernandez remarked that the Montparnasse night clubs depicted in the novel seemed to represent an updated version of the *fin de siècle* cosmopolitan society Bourget portrayed.[37] There is some justification for making such a connection. Given Némirovsky's choice of theme, as well as her use of an often intrusive omniscient narrator who explains the characters' motivations,[38] one might be tempted to read 'Le Malentendu' as a Bourgetian novel updated for the *années folles*. In a sense, 'Le Malentendu' closely resembles what Diana Holmes calls 'the archetypal Bourget narrative':

> an established heterosexual union [. . .] is put under threat by the intervention of a third party, a man who is more seductive, appealing and dangerous than the husband or established lover. Most of the narrative is concerned with the nature of the adulterous relationship that develops and with the possibility and extent of its fulfilment. The dénouement on the whole is catastrophic: desire is irresistible but its indulgence leads to disaster.[39]

However, Némirovsky does not simply reproduce the model. In 'Le Malentendu' the dénouement is indeed a disaster for Denise—Yves rejects their relationship and leaves for Finland—but this is not the same sort of narrative punishment Holmes finds characteristic of Bourget's novels.[40] Denise is punished not for her adultery, but for her idealised view of love and her inability to recognise happiness in her flawed relationship with Yves.

Can any conclusions be drawn from these literary allusions? There is no doubt that they are slight. At one level, they simply suggest a young, inexperienced writer attempting to demonstrate her familiarity with well-established literary models. In his study of literary influence, Claudio Guillén distinguishes between 'allusion' and 'intertext', noting that 'it is clearly one thing to make a simple allusion or reminiscence, necessarily implying a memory from the past, or the externality of what is alluded to, and to include in the poetic fabric of the work itself—adding to its verbal surface, one might say, words of forms or foreign thematic structures'.[41]

For Guillén, an allusion is a simple citation, whose effect is 'horizontal', whilst a properly intertextual feature 'interven[es] decisively in the vertical semantic structure' of the work in question. The literary references in 'Le Malentendu' are straightforward allusions. This tendency to make passing reference to other works of literature continued to be a feature of Némirovsky's writing. Though not particularly sophisticated from a narrative point of view, such allusions nevertheless represent a sharing of cultural knowledge between author and reader. They therefore establish a degree of intellectual complicity which is surely not insignificant in the case of a foreign writer producing literature in a language which was not her mother tongue, to be consumed in a cultural environment which was not her own. It is legitimate therefore to ask what kind of French literary tradition these allusions suggest, and whether there is any relationship between the type of writing evoked and the later development of Némirovsky's own literary practice. It is perhaps significant that Loti and Bourget (along with Maurice Barrès) were amongst the first French novelists to be elected to the Académie française.[42] Should we read in the pairing of Loti and Bourget a kind of homage to the recognised literary masters of the *fin de siècle* (Loti, Bourget, Maurice Barrès, Anatole France) against whose orthodoxy the *NRF* had set itself when it was launched in 1909?[43] Is Némirovsky already nailing her colours to the traditionalist mast, in opposition to the avant-garde? This reading is plausible in the context of her later association with the conservative *Revue des deux mondes*. Comparison with the authors Némirovsky cited when asked about her reading in interviews is also instructive here. In each of the two interviews she gave in 1930 to Frédéric Lefèvre (January) and Claude Pierrey (March), she was asked which authors she admired. Only Proust, André Maurois, and the Tharaud brothers are mentioned in both interviews. Like the allusions in 'Le Malentendu', this suggests a dominant identification with the conservative, traditionalist sectors of the literary field. Maurois and the Tharauds (all three future Academicians) were by no means progressive writers. The reference to Proust in this context is probably merely suggestive of Némirovsky's desire to appear interested in contemporary French literature. Otherwise, it is the range and diversity of the authors Némirovsky cites which are striking. In her reply to Lefèvre, we find representatives of *fin de siècle* decadence (Huysmans, Oscar Wilde); of naturalism (Maupassant); of the Westernising, progressive strand of Russian literature (Turgenev); of French modernism (Valéry Larbaud); of the contemporary novel of bourgeois marriage (Jacques Chardonne). In Némirovsky's reply to Pierrey, the Russian context is evoked by the rather more traditionalist Tolstoy and Dostoevsky, whilst her favourite French authors are Racine (classicism), Chateaubriand (romanticism) and Prosper Mérimée (pioneer of the French short story in the 1830s). This eclectic range of references suggests a young writer whose position in the literary field is not yet fixed. Later, Némirovsky's definition of her own literary position via references to other authors became more specific. In an interview in 1933 with Lefèvre, she explicitly distanced herself from Huysmans and Proust and professed to enjoy the novels of George Sand which, she said, were generally viewed as 'old fashioned'. She expressed her admiration for the specifically French classical values of clarity, moderation, and reason exemplified by Mauriac's novels, which she found superior to the English novel. She said that she valued Tolstoy's general human appeal over the more explicitly Russian Dostoevksy. She distanced herself from the cultural left by remarking that she knew nothing about the 'new' (i.e. Soviet) Russian literature.[44] There is a perceptible shift away from Russian models and towards a more traditionalist and specifically French literary conservatism. Regarding the descriptions she gives of her habit of writing extensive reflections on her novel in progress, there is similarly a progression from an assertion of her Russian heritage, to an embracing of French neoclassicism, and then an affirmation of literary nationalism: in 1930, she had likened her writing method to that of Turgenev,[45] whilst in 1933 she referred to this as Gide's method,[46] and in 1935, as Barrès's method.[47] By 1938, Némirovsky's preference for the traditional seemed even clearer: she told Jeanine Delpech that she was currently rereading Balzac and Sainte-Beuve, and that she very much admired Kleber Haedens, who was one of the prominent young literary figures of *L'Action française*.

The textual and paratextual references to a certain strand of traditionalist, conservative French writing I have identified at the beginning of Némirovsky's career is indicative of Némirovsky's later literary trajectory, though cannot be said to determine it. It is important not to exaggerate the significance of literary allusions, though they do function as both 'sources' and 'influences'. The identification of such 'sources' can never provide a complete explanation of a given text, and the analysis of literary influences should not lead to a search for some point of textual origin. Concrete relations do exist between works of literature, and they can be traced, but the search for influences must not be fetishised. It is perhaps helpful to keep in mind the image of a web of interrelations, and to reject the idea of a chain of causality leading back to some point of origin.[48] I would not wish to suggest that the examples discussed above are the only sources of Némirovsky's early fiction, nor that they define the nature or meaning of those texts, nor even that Némirovsky's inclusion of them was fully conscious. I am simply proposing that these examples are significant in relation to Némirovsky's subsequent position in the literary field, and that they can plausibly be traced back to the reality of Némirovsky's reading experience and cultural knowledge.

A FICTION OF CREATIVITY

Némirovsky's second published story, 'L'Enfant génial' (1927), is a fascinating fable about the nature of creative genius. According to Némirovsky, this text was written in 1923, before 'Le Malentendu'.[49] This short text of less than fifty pages tells the story of Ismaël Baruch, a Jewish boy from a poor family who scrapes a living running errands around the port of his Russian hometown on the shores of the Black Sea. His natural poetic and musical talent is discovered by Romain Nord, a failed poet who has come to the sailor's tavern to drown in alcohol the sorrows of his own artistic and amorous failures. Nord takes the boy poet to an opulent palace of decadence where he discovers the delights of gypsy women and champagne. Ismaël is fascinated by the 'Princesse', Nord's mistress, who undertakes to educate him. He falls ill. But, as he recovers from his fever, grows up, and is introduced to the work of other writers, he begins to despise his own poetry, and his talent is destroyed. Rejected by the 'Princesse' and apprenticed to a tailor, Ismaël hangs himself. Curiously, this rather disturbing story was reissued in 1992 as a children's book, prefaced by Elisabeth Gille, who presented it as a tale in which a child's spontaneous genius is lost through the transitional traumas of adolescence.[50] This is a plausible reading, as is Philipponnat and Lienhardt's interpretation of the story in terms of Ismaël's failure to recognise the artistic value of traditional Jewish music, which is his heritage and which courses through his veins.[51] But this is a multi-layered text which repays more detailed scrutiny. It bears the signs of a young writer engaged in literary experimentation, insofar as it is not completely coherent. Nonetheless, 'L'Enfant génial' prefigures certain literary preoccupations and affinities which turn out to be characteristic of Némirovsky's later writing.

The character of Ismaël is derived from the literary type of the *déraciné*, the individual uprooted from his original milieu and placed in a new environment. Ismaël is removed from a situation of poverty into one of wealth. Under the influence of Nord and the 'Princesse', his previously spontaneous and unreflective creativity is placed in an academic context. The story of the gifted adolescent from a modest background whose education is his downfall had been expressed in fiction by Bourget in *Le Disciple* (1889), and was taken up by Maurice Barrès in *Les Déracinés* (1897). Némirovsky was familiar with Barrès as well as with Bourget, and cited him in interviews and in her notes.[52] In both of these novels, the education of a boy from a modest background leads not to achievement and self-realisation, but to moral demise: the boy's attempt to attain the intellectual and creative horizons which have been revealed to him results in confusion and moral disorder, symbolised in the texts by murder and suicide. Bourget's novel is an attack on certain strands of modern and contemporary philosophy, and Barrès's is a right-wing denunciation of the French Republican education system. Although 'L'Enfant génial' is too slight and immature a work to constitute a deliberate engagement with the philosophical and political subtexts of Bourget and Barrès, the narrative framework is similar, and, as we shall see, a certain thematic strand of the story is potentially reminiscent of ideas about education characteristic of the French intellectual right of which Bourget and Barrès were key representatives.

The central problematic of 'L'Enfant génial' is the reason for the disintegration of Ismaël's talent. At the outset, Ismaël's poems are a divine gift,[53]
the outpourings of untutored creativity:

> —Qui t'a enseigné à traduire ainsi ce que tu penses et ce que tu sens?
> —Personne . . . Toutes ces choses que je dis chantent en moi . . . [54]

> *'Who taught you to translate what you think and feel like that ?' 'No-
> one . . . All these things which I say sing within me'.*

Romain Nord realises the danger inherent in educating Ismaël:

> Il est heureux, ainsi . . . Il est heureux, parce qu'il ne connaît pas son
> génie . . . Du jour où il le connaîtra, il sera malheureux. . . . [55]

> *He is happy the way he is . . . He is happy, because he is not aware of
> his genius . . . The day he discovers it, he will be unhappy. . . .*

Nord's prediction is correct. Once Ismaël begins to learn, he can no longer
bear either his own poetry or the port which used to be his home:

> Quant aux livres, ils le rendaient jaloux et malheureux; inconsciem-
> ment, il se prenait à imiter les vers des autres; alors une espèce de rage
> haineuse le bouleversait; ses anciennes chansons lui paraisait risibles,
> pitoyables, et les nouvelles, il ne savait pourquoi, étaient pires encores.
> [. . .]
> Mais, dès qu'il arriva au bout du rempart, il recula devant l'odeur
> oubliée de vase et de poisson pourri; de même le quartier juif lui parut
> petit, misérable, plein de vacarme et de puanteur.[56]

> *As for books, they made him jealous and unhappy; without realising,
> he started to imitate other people's poems; and then a sort of rage over-
> came him, full of hatred; his old songs seemed laughable and pitiful to
> him, and his new ones were even worse, and he didn't know why.*
> *[. . .]*
> *But as soon as he arrived at the limits of the city walls, he recoiled
> before the smell of mud and rotten fish which he had forgotten; simi-
> larly, the Jewish quarter seemed small and miserable to him, noisy and
> stinking.*

From then on, he walks the path which is to lead to his suicide. His
malaise first expresses itself as physical illness. When he is sent to the
countryside to complete his convalescence, he stops writing and becomes
fascinated with the natural world; the 'enfant génial' of the title becomes
just another 'beau gars' as he abandons the cerebral entirely in favour of

the physical.[57] His talent entirely destroyed, he is rejected by his beloved 'Princesse', who was only interested in his poems, and by his family, who was only interested in the money those poems provided. It is Nord, who he meets for the last time in the tavern lamenting his own losses, who suggests that death is the only solution; the next morning, Ismaël is found hanged.[58] There seems to be an attempt in the text to set up an opposition between natural creativity and the academic study of literature. The narrator explains that Ismaël is dismayed when he discovers the existence of works of literary analysis:

> Alors, il se mit à lire des ouvrages de critique, de doctrine, s'imaginant dans son innocence que la poésie s'apprend, comme les mathématiques, à force d'application et de bonne volonté. Ce fut le désastre. Au nom de lois qu'il ne déchiffrait pas plus que du chinois, il vit que les uns condamnaient ce que les autres approuvaient; il s'égara dans la forêt inextricable des jugements littéraires; il perdit complètement la tête; mon Dieu! il fallait donc répondre à tant d'objections quand on écrivait, satisfaire à tant d'exigences multiples et contradictoires! Puis, pour son malheur, il lut les livres savants où on analyse l'action d'écrire, tous les rouages complexes du mécanisme de la création; et, alors, il fut pareil à un homme qui, au moment où il va accomplir un geste insignifiant, rechercherait tous les infiniment petits dont se compose sa volonté d'agir, et il demeurait hébété, désemparé en face de sa feuille de papier obstinément blanche.[59]

> *So he started to read works of criticism and doctrine, imagining, in his innocence, that you could learn how to write poetry, like you can learn maths, by applying yourself willingly. It was a disaster. He saw that, in the name of laws which were no more understandable to him than Chinese, one person condemned what the others praised; he got totally lost in the tangled forest of literary judgements; he lost his head completely; my God! So when you write, you have to deal with so many objections, satisfy so many different and contradictory expectations! Then, unfortunately, he read learned books which analysed the act of writing and all the complex parts of the creative mechanism; and then he was like a man who, when he is just about to carry out an insignificant task, starts to seek out every infinitesimal element of his desire to act, and he was stupefied, thrown into confusion before his obstinately blank piece of paper.*

It is difficult not to hear in this passage an expression of the frustrations of a recent graduate of the Sorbonne with her own literary aspirations. Could the reference to 'ouvrages de critique, de doctrine' be a direct reference to Bourget's 1922 *Nouvelles pages de critique et de doctrine*? We can only speculate as to the extent to which this passage accurately represents

Némirovsky's opinions about her own academic and creative experiences. It certainly prefigures a comment Némirovsky made in an interview in 1940, where she asserted that '[s]i un écrivain s'interroge trop sur son œuvre, il est inquiet, incertain, et le métier d'écrire devient pour lui un tourment au lieu d'être une joie. Du moins, il en serait ainsi pour moi.' (*if a writer questions herself too much about her work, she becomes worried and uncertain, and the task of writing becomes a torment instead of a joy. At least, that's how it would be for me*).[60] Némirovsky appears to have held ambivalent views about literary theory. For in 1940, she was writing also about Chekhov's narrative technique in *La Vie de Tchekhov* and reflecting on E. M. Forster's *Aspects of the Novel* and Percy Lubbock's *The Craft of Fiction*, as she wrote *Suite française*.[61] And yet, in *La Vie de Tchekov*, she wrote that most rules in art are purely arbitrary.[62] Whilst she may have found literary theory frustrating, she certainly did not shun it completely.

If Némirovsky really was attempting to oppose academic study to creative ability in the context of her own education at the Sorbonne, she was doing so in a very specific context. The reform of the French higher education system in the early years of the twentieth century had provoked outcry from some on the intellectual right who argued that *la nouvelle Sorbonne* prized pedantic scholarly methods over inspiration, and sacrificed French talent, genius, and creativity in the name of democracy.[63] 'L'Enfant génial' seems to reproduce the oppositions which structured the debate on the *nouvelle Sorbonne*, and it appears to promote some of the arguments of the intellectual right: talent is presented as specifically artistic and creative, as opposed to scientific (Ismaël understands nothing about numbers); Ismaël's intuitive invention is an innate gift and is directly opposed to acquired knowledge taught through books. Perhaps Romain Nord and his 'Princesse' are examples of the type of 'mauvais maître'[64] which Bourget and Barrès had fictionalised in the characters of Adrien Sixte and Paul Bouteiller: a mentor whose influence is ultimately dangerous. But we must be careful in pursuing such a line of argument: whilst there are echoes of contemporary intellectual and artistic debates within the text, they are by no means woven into a coherent 'message'. My intention in reading 'L'Enfant génial' in the context of Bourget, Barrès, and the debate on the *nouvelle Sorbonne* is not to ascribe to the text a sophisticated political or philosophical thesis which it clearly cannot support. It is rather to suggest that resonances of the contemporary literary environment can be heard in Némirovsky's early work, and that the types of literary contexts in relation to which her writing might be situated are those of the conservative sector of the French literary field. Whether or not the coincidence of ideas and literary structures I have identified was deliberate—it is in fact much more likely that it was not—it is meaningful insofar as it suggests a writer whose affinities are with traditional literary forms, and not with the politically and aesthetically experimental modes of literary expression which were also developing in the immediate post-war years.

Némirovsky's story does not reproduce a Barrèsian ideology. The implication of 'L'Enfant génial' is not that Ismaël would ultimately have been better off if he had never transcended his origins, but rather that the *type* of education he received could not benefit him:

> Hélas! c'était tout simplement qu'il entrait dans la difficile période de l'adolescence, que son corps, brusquement devenu celui d'un homme, dérobait à l'intelligence sa sève, que la nature, bienfaisante, en voulant le faire vivre, interrompait, dans sa sagesse, la source divine de son génie. Mais personne ne le lui disait; personne ne lui faisait espérer retrouver plus tard le don délicieux et fatal, plus tard, quand il serait un homme . . . personne n'était là pour lui chuchoter: 'Attends, espère' . . . Ils étaient tous penchés sur lui, autour de lui, accrochés à lui, comme des humains qui veulent ouvrir de force de leurs doigts sacrilèges une fleur.[65]

> *Alas! it was simply that he was entering the difficult period of adolescence, that his body, suddenly become that of a man, was masking the core of his intelligence, that, in her wisdom, benevolent nature, wanting to make him live, was interrupting the divine source of his genius. But no-one told him this, no-one made him hope that later, he would rediscover the delicious and fatal gift, later, when he was a man . . . no-one was there to whisper to him: 'Wait, hope . . . '. They all crowded over him, around him, latched on to him, like humans who want to force open the petals of a flower with their sacrilegious fingers.*

Ismaël's talent could have been nurtured to its maturity had he been exposed to the right sort of education. The text does not however tell us what sort of education that might be. Whilst Bourget and Barrès set out to ascribe responsibility for their heroes' fates, Némirovsky leaves the question of why Ismaël lost his talent for the reader to answer. 'Pourquoi s'étaient-elles tues, les chansons qui naissaient autrefois spontanément sur ses lèvres?' (*Why did they fall silent, the songs which used to spring spontaneously from his lips?*)[66] Because of his illness? Because of his recovery? Because he needed his old environment of the bars, the women, the booze, in order to create? Or simply because he experienced adolescence and exchanged his child's body for that of a man? Characteristically, Némirovsky does not tell us. This story, like the novels which were to follow it, is radically *disengaged* in its refusal to ascribe responsibility. The reader cannot ultimately be certain as to its meaning. Is the title ironic or serious? Is the story a defence of popular, spontaneous art, as Philipponnat and Lienhardt suggest? Was Ismaël really a genius, or is his own mature assessment of the mediocrity of his work correct? Such a refusal of narratorial judgement runs throughout Némirovsky's work. It is what distinguishes her literary production from that of the *fin de siècle* literary production of Bourget and Barrès, but it was often out of step with the literary landscape of the 1930s in which responsibility was a key literary value. It has also posed difficulties for readers of *Suite française* who expected to find in that novel an easily digestible political interpretation of the Occupation.

Whilst 'L'Enfant génial' displays some features which link it to the literary environment of the 1920s, on another level, it is derived from a much older literary model—that of the folk tale or fairy story. This aspect of the text sounds another note of caution as regards too close a comparison with Barrès or Bourget, for we are not dealing here with a realist novel. The inter-war period saw a growth in interest in the genre of the folk tale. Arnold van Gennep's multi-volume companion to French folklore has its roots in research undertaken in the 1920s.[67] It was during the 1930s that researchers began to achieve an extensive classification of folkloric motifs.[68] Comparative literature had also interested itself in folklore as a means of identifying the roots of the 'national' character of literature. This was an approach which Baldensperger rejected, on the basis that he believed the establishing of an unbroken chain of literary development back to some folkloric origin to be methodologically impossible. Ismaël's story rather resembles the folkloric motif of the child sold or promised to a rich or influential person.[69] This motif appears, for example, in certain tales retold by the brothers Grimm, such as Rapunzel and Rumpelstiltskin. One might also posit certain similarities between 'L'Enfant génial' and some of Hans Christian Andersen's tales. Ismaël's experiences at the palace of the 'Princesse' are reminiscent of Kay's abduction by the Snow Queen. The problem of Ismaël's artistic genius recalls Andersen's 'The Nightingale'. In this story, a common, humble bird delights the Emperor with his singing, just as Ismaël delights Nord with his music. The Emperor then receives a gift of an artificial bird, which according to the music master, has one important advantage over the real bird:

> with the real bird, we can never tell what is going to be sung, but with this bird everything is settled. It can be opened and explained, so that people may understand how the waltzes are formed, and why one note follows upon another.[70]

Like the 'Princesse', the music master values an analytical approach to art. The description of Ismaël's talent in 'L'Enfant génial' is strikingly reminiscent of the music master's description of the difference between the mechanical bird and the real one:

> Jamais le petit ne réfléchissait d'avance à ce qu'il allait dire: les paroles s'éveillent en lui comme des oiseaux mystérieux auxquels il n'y avait qu'à donner l'essor, et la musique qui leur convenait les accompagnait aussi naturellement.[71]

The young boy never thought about what he was going to say in advance: the words awoke within him like mysterious birds to which he only had to give flight, and the music which suited them accompanied them so naturally.

When the artificial bird is installed in the palace, the real bird flies away, rather like Ismaël's talent. But eventually, the mechanical bird breaks down—artificial, explicable music turns out to be no substitute for the spontaneous singing of the real bird. Andersen's stories of creative genius tend to have happy endings. Andersen saw genius as a gift from God—which is how Ismaël's talent is initially described—which gets its reward regardless of the lowly status of the protagonist.[72] In 'The Nightingale' the real bird eventually returns to sing once more for the Emperor. Némirovsky is less optimistic, and so Ismaël is not so lucky.

Reading Némirovsky's early stories in relation to the folktale or fairy tale genre is instructive insofar as it demonstrates the extent to which her writing derives from an appealing desire simply to tell a good story. In interviews, Némirovsky often said that her own literary development had begun with an interest in fairy tales, and it is possible that she was familiar with the stories of Hans Christian Andersen. She told Frédéric Lefèvre and Michele Deyroyer that she had written fairly stories in Finland as an adolescent.[73] She explained to Marie-Jean Viel that, as a child, she would tell herself stories, and eventually began to write them down.[74] So whilst certain features of 'L'Enfant génial' link the tale to Némirovsky's contemporary environment, it is also related to much more generic models. Reading 'L'Enfant génial' as a folktale does not however clarify its meaning. Whilst the folktale generally has a straightforward and comprehensible meaning or moral, interpreting the message of 'L'Enfant génial' is far from straightforward.

EXPERIMENTS IN FORM

In an interview in 1940 for *Les Nouvelles littéraires*, part of a series entitled 'Les Conrad français' (after the Polish writer Joseph Conrad who wrote fiction in English) on foreign writers who wrote in French, Némirovsky described her bi-cultural literary identity as a combination between French form and Slav content:

Eh bien! je m'éfforce de couler dans une forme française, c'est-à-dire claire et ordonnée et aussi simple que possible, un fond qui est naturellement encore un peu slave (ou oriental, si vous préférez).[75]

Well! I try to pour something that is of course fundamentally still a little Slav (or oriental, if you prefer) into a French mould, that is to say, clear and ordered and as simple as possible.

She remarked in the same interview that 'je désire, j'espère, je crois être un écrivain plus français que russe' (*I desire and hope to be, and believe I am, more of a French writer than a Russian one*). French form, for Némirovsky, meant the classical ideals of moderation, clarity, reason, harmony, and self control.[76] She tended to represent the Russian influence in her writing as thematic rather than formal: describing the interaction between the French and Russian elements in her work in interviews, she generally presented her Russian heritage as a question of identity and not of specific literary influence. Apart from citing Turgenev as a source of her writing method (who she later displaced in favour of Gide, then Barrès, as we have seen), and an acknowledgement of her admiration for Tolstoy and Dostoevsky, the interviews offer little evidence as to specific Russian intertexts. In her personal notes on the other hand, there is clear evidence that Némirovsky's approach to writing was significantly influenced by Chekhov. Before embarking upon her biographical study *La Vie de Tchekhov*, she had imagined writing a work of literary criticism about Chekhov's writing technique.[77] In her notes for the short story 'Fraternité', she qualified a writer's objectivity and detachment from the characters as Chekhovian: 'Il faudrait que cela soit purement objectif, l'impression que moi, je sais . . . que moi, auteur, je suis un peu au-dessus des personnages. V. Tchek [= voir Tchekhov]' (*It should be purely objective, the impression that I know . . . that I, the author, am a little above the characters. See Chekhov*).[78] She does not, however, qualify Chekhov's style as specifically Russian. When she refers specifically to Russianness in her notes, there is a strong sense, as in the interviews, that it is a question of experience and identity rather than of literary form. For example, reflecting on a possible story about Russian émigrés in Paris, she imagines them living in 'un de ces petits appartements parisiens dans les vieux quartiers, qui donnent une impression étrange de mystère, *mais pour moi seulement. Un Français ne comprendrait pas . . .* ' [emphasis added] (*one of those little Parisian apartments in the old quarters which give a strange impression of mystery, but only to me. A French person would not understand . . .*).[79] One might plausibly trace Némirovsky's idea of combining a visceral Slav identity with French narrative forms back to her training in comparative literature at the Sorbonne. But it is important not to exaggerate this influence, for when Némirovsky came to write her literary biography of Chekhov, she did not seriously embrace the methodology of comparative literature which she would have encountered during her studies under Hazard and Baldensperger. *La Vie de Tchekhov*, written at Issy l'Evêque in 1940, reads more like a novel than a work of objective, scientific literary history of the sort Hazard and Baldensperger would have condoned. Their interest was in actual and provable literary interactions and influences; they sought to analyse international contacts between national literatures in cases where there was evidence, for example, that a given author had read the work of a foreign author and incorporated precise aspects of that work in his or her own literary production.[80] When Némirovsky discusses the relationship between Chekhov and other writers (Maupassant, Mérimée and Katherine Mansfield, for example),[81] she presents only similarities of style, without advancing any proof of specific influence.

How exactly should the French 'mould' into which Némirovsky began to pour her Slav experience be defined? The presentation of the stories in *Les Œuvres libres* offers a point of departure for an analysis of Némirovsky's genre choices. 'Le Malentendu' and 'L'Ennemie' were both classified as *romans*, whilst 'L'Enfant génial' and 'Le Bal' were designated as *nouvelles*. According to Michel Raimond, one of the salient features of the debate around the crisis of the novel in the 1920s was an attempt to define the novel as a genre in relation to the *conte*, the *nouvelle* and the *récit*.[82] Raimond concludes that the distinction between *récit* and *roman* was somewhat academic and ultimately unsatisfying.[83] The differentiations between *roman*, *conte*, and *nouvelle* were more constructive, and can be productively employed to distinguish between different types of writing in relation to Némirovsky's early stories.

Raimond identifies Paul Bourget as a key source for the debate in the 1920s on the distinction between *nouvelle* and *roman*.[84] Bourget suggested in *Nouvelles pages de critique et de doctrine* that whilst the *nouvelle* was focused on one episode, and was a highly concentrated form, the *roman* followed a series of episodes which privileged development over concentration.[85] We have already seen that Némirovsky knew Bourget's work; there is clear evidence that she was familiar with his distinction between *roman* and *nouvelle*, since in her notes, she transcribed a passage on Mérimée from the essay in which Bourget made this distinction.[86] In *La Vie de Tchekhov*, Némirovsky appears to reject Bourget's notion that a *nouvelle* must be focused on a single episode:

Maupassant, Mérimée, d'autres encore, dans leurs nouvelles mettent en lumière un épisode, un événement unique. La multiplicité des personnages et des scènes est réservée au roman. Cela semble logique; en fait, cela est arbitraire comme la plupart des règles artistiques. Lorsque, dans une nouvelle ou un roman, on met en relief un héros ou un fait, on appauvrit l'histoire; la complexité, la beauté, la profondeur de la réalité dépendent de ces liens nombreux qui vont d'un homme à un autre, d'une existence à une autre existence, d'une joie à une douleur.[87]

Maupassant, Mérimée and many others in their stories bring a single episode or a single event into the limelight. Multiplicity of characters and scenes is kept for the novel. This seems logical, but in fact, is purely arbitrary, like most rules in art. Whenever, in a short story or novel, one hero or event is thrown into relief, the narrative itself is impoverished: the complexity, beauty and depth of reality depend on the innumerable ties that exist between one man and another, one life and another, and between joy and suffering.[88]

Némirovsky here recommends exactly the technique she was using in *Suite française*, which she was writing at the time. Whilst this writing strategy is indeed very successful in the longer novel, Némirovsky's best short stories are those in which she achieves concision and economy precisely by focusing on a single episode or character. Némirovsky's own definition in *La Vie de Tchekhov* of the difference between the *nouvelle* and the *roman* is in fact not too far away from Bourget in spirit:

> Par un roman, on pénètre dans un milieu déterminé; on s'en imprègne; on le chérit ou on le haït. Mais une nouvelle est une porte entr'ouverte un instant sur une maison inconnue et refermée aussitôt.[89]

> *A novel allows one to enter into a particular setting, to become impregnated with it, to love it or to hate it. But a short story is a door flung open for an instant on an unknown house, and swiftly closed again.*[90]

For Némirovsky, simplicity and concision were the cardinal virtues of the short story writer, as we can see from the two passages by Bourget on Mérimée which she transcribed in her notes:

> La nouvelle: cette brusque et brève evocation, presque hallucinatoire, est son but.
> [. . .]
> L'apparition de José Navarro (dans Carmen) vous étonne d'autant moins que le narrateur ne commet pas la faute de vous annoncer un personnage remarquable. A peine vous le décrit-il: 'C'était un jeune gaillard de taille moyenne, mais d'apparence robuste, au regard sombre et fier'. Quelques traits plus appuyés, et vous sentiriez l'écrivain désireux d'un effet à produire. Vous vous défendriez. La bonhommie simple est ici la ruse savante de l'artiste. . . . [91]

> *The nouvelle: that brusque and brief evocation, almost hallucinatory, is its aim.*
> *[. . .]*
> *The appearance of José Navarro (in Carmen) surprises you because the narrator does not make the mistake of announcing a remarkable person to you. He hardly describes him to you: 'He was a strapping young man of medium height, but he looked strong, and his eyes were dark and proud'. If he were described in more detail, you would be able to tell that the author wanted to produce an effect. You would resist. Here, simple geniality is the artist's clever ruse.*

In her notes accompanying the draft of *Le Vin de solitude*, Némirovsky reminded herself to reread Mérimée before starting work.[92] These manuscript sources show that Némirovsky formulated her literary techniques by engaging with the classics of the short story genre and with the discussions about genre which were a feature of the literary field in which she was operating.

The genre designations which *Les Œuvres libres* applied to Némirovsky's stories are logical in relation to Bourget's definitions. The difficulty with 'Le Malentendu' and 'L'Ennemie'—both described as *romans*—is that in each case, whilst there is indeed enough episodic and psychological material for a full-length novel, these texts are short, with the result that they are overloaded with content. In 'L'Ennemie' in particular, the narrative development lacks any clear focus: the variety of episodes and characters is ultimately unsatisfying, and there are too many narrative climaxes for such a short text (Michette's tragic death; the adulterous relationship between Francine, Michette's mother, and Charles; Gabri's desire for vengeance against her mother; the rape of Gabri by Génia Nikitof; Gabri's suicide). As a result, the text seems melodramatic, and extensive narrative explanation must be substituted for the cumulative exposition of characters' motivations through their interactions with other characters and with events. 'L'Ennemie' appears to be inspired by a naturalist or populist aesthetic, and as such anticipates certain aspects of *David Golder* and *Le Bal* on which contemporary critics commented, as we saw in Chapter 1. The depiction of the popular quarters of Paris just after the war, and the story of the death of the child Michette Bragance in a shocking domestic accident because she is neglected by her sexually promiscuous mother, are reminiscent of the preoccupations of the naturalist school, but Némirovsky's novelistic technique in 'L'Ennemie' has more in common with Bourget's psychologism than with Zola's experimental novel. In 'Le Malentendu', the exposition of character is more successful, and there is evidence here of experiments with point of view and the interior monologue, technical aspects of the novel which were debated at length in literary journals in the period, and which Némirovsky would come to exploit more successfully in her later fiction.[93] Although Némirovsky's work is not generally characterised by significant narrative self-reflexivity—her texts are certainly not the sorts of *romans du roman* of which Gide's *Les Faux-monnayeurs* is an obvious example[94]— the reader is invited to reflect on the nature of the narrative when, within a passage of free indirect narration, Denise remarks that 'Elle ne voulait pas de la facile poésie d'un roman d'été' (*she didn't want the easy poetry of a summer romance*):[95] is this just a tale of a holiday romance, we wonder, or is it something more? 'Le Bal' is the first story in which Némirovsky achieved the sort of narrative concision she later discussed in *La Vie de Tchekhov*. This story is indeed her first true *nouvelle*—here, Némirovsky reveals the complex relations between individuals and situations whilst also achieving the simplicity of composition she praised in Chekhov. The narrative framework is slim: M and Mme Kampf, newly wealthy Jewish émigrés in Paris, are to hold a ball in order to consolidate their rising social status. As the title suggests, the ball is the single episode around which the narrative gravitates. Like 'L'Enfant génial', this story is an account of a traumatic adolescence. Humiliated by her mother's refusal to allow her to attend the ball, and by her governess's flirtations, Antoinette sabotages the ball by throwing the invitations into the Seine. This *nouvelle* is a triumph of dramatic irony: in the final two chapters, the reader witnesses Mme Kampf's frantic preparations for the ball to which no guests have in fact been invited. The horror of Mme Kampf's disappointment is matched only by that of Antoinette's pitiless silence.

Although 'L'Enfant genial' is also designated as a *nouvelle* in *Les Œuvres libres*, various textual indicators strongly suggest that it has more in common with the *conte*. This term was available in the contemporary literary field to describe short fiction which takes liberties with the reader's credulity:

> Le conteur reléguait la vie au second plan, il la survolait, il l'évoquait, il jouissait, en tout cas, par rapport à la réalité fictive qu'il suscitait, d'une marge appréciable de liberté, qui lui permettait de déployer ses caprices. Le conteur, plus libre que le romancier de suivre sa fantaisie, triomphait dans le fantastique, le surréel, le fabuleux.[96]

> *For the writer of the* conte, *real life takes second place: he might glide over it, evoke it, but in any case he enjoys a considerable margin of freedom in relation to fictive reality, which allows him to give free reign to his caprices. The writer of the* conte, *freer than the novelist to follow his fantasies, is particularly successful in the modes of the fantastic, the surreal or the fabulous.*

Modern critics have underlined the fluidity of the boundaries between the *nouvelle* and the *conte*.[97] In the inter-war period, the term *conte* was generally associated with children's literature and would not therefore have been a good choice for an aspiring writer who wanted her fiction to be taken seriously.[98] However, it is very appropriate to the folkloric aspect of 'L'Enfant génial'. The characteristics of the *conte* on which critics agree are that it is about storytelling (from the verb 'conter'), that is, it is derived from an oral genre and does not confine itself to strict realism.[99] The opening sentence of 'L'Enfant génial' resists the temporal and geographical specificity typical of Némirovsky's other stories, suggesting to the reader right from the outset that the fictional world they are about to enter has more in common with the folktale than with the realist novel: 'Ismaël Baruch était né, un jour de mars où il neigeait très fort, dans une grande ville marine et marchande du sud de la Russie, au bord de la mer Noire' (*Ismaël Baruch was born, one very snowy day in March, in a large commercial port in the south of Russia, on the shores of the Black Sea*).[100] The temporal vagueness of 'one very snowy day in March' and the geographical vagueness and exoticism of 'a large port in the south of Russia' are highly characteristic of the folk tale. The text's final sentence also signifies the folktale genre via an easily recognisable linguistic formulation: 'C'est ainsi que vécut et mourut Ismaël Baruch, l'enfant génial' (*And that is how Ismaël Baruch, the genius child, lived and died*).[101] The final line of the early unpublished story 'La Niania' uses the same linguistic marker: 'Ainsi mourut la Niania sans avoir revu danser la neige dans les plaines de son pays' (*And that is how Niania died, without ever having seen the snow dance again in the plains of her homeland*).[102] Here it is the 'ainsi vécut' which is significant, recalling the classic 'and that is the story of . . . ' formulation which traditionally concludes a fairy story. 'La Niania' is derived from the motif of the old-fashioned Russian nanny, ubiquitous in nineteenth-century Russian novels.[103] Némirovsky told Frédéric Lefèvre that she destroyed her early fairy stories because they were not original. But originality is not prized in the folktale: its purpose is to hand on stories that are already known.[104] Generally speaking, Némirovsky did not pursue her early interest in the *conte* in her later writing; her mature work is very much in the mode of realism. There is however a small cluster of short stories in which strict realism is abandoned in favour of an evocation of the fantastic. 'Magie' (*L'Intransigeant*, 1938) and 'Le Sortilège' (*Gringoire*, 1940) are uncanny tales in which the evocation of Russian superstitions about magic and love provides a framework within which Némirovsky can construct stories based on the supernatural. Némirovsky's notes for 'Le Sortilège' reveal her interest in the fantastic as a literary mode: she noted that 'J'ai toujours voulu faire un conte fantastique' (*I have always wanted to write a story in the fantastic mode*).[105] 'Les Revenants' (*Gringoire*, 1941) appears initially to be in the mode of realism, but it turns out to be a ghost story in which the narrator's dead cousin Marc appears to her children as a little boy in a room in their flat where the old furniture from his former home is being stored.

The four stories which Némirovsky published before *David Golder* bear witness to a young writer trying out different forms and themes, some of which she would refine and reuse in her later work. The short novels 'Le Malentendu' and 'L'Ennemie' are flawed insofar as they lack the narrative concision Némirovsky would later achieve, and they are dogged by over-intrusive narratorial explanations of the character's motivations. In her later work, Némirovsky would return to the themes she had evoked in these stories—post-war male malaise and the fragility of the couple in *Le Pion sur l'échiquer*, *La Proie* and *Deux*; the disastrous mother–daughter relationship in *Le Vin de solitude* and *Jézabel*. In these later novels, she found ways to articulate her ideas in a much more convincing narrative format. 'Le Bal' also prefigures the theme of the negative mother-daughter relationship. It is this text which perhaps best illustrates Némirovsky's skill as a writer able to construct a compelling narrative in few words. Here she amply overcame the structural problems of 'Le Malentendu' and 'L'Ennemie'. In terms of genre, 'L'Enfant génial' is the least representative of her later work, although its caricatural portrait of Jewish characters sets the tone for later depictions of Jewish identity, as we shall see in Chapter 3. Némirovsky repudiated this text in the 1930 interview with Frédéric Lefèvre, saying that she had recently reread it and now thought it very bad, and stressing that she was very young when she wrote it. And yet, this text is perhaps the most interesting and the most revelatory of the four early works as regards Némirovsky's writing practice, insofar as it is the only sustained discussion of the nature of artistic creation Némirovsky ever published.[106]

NÉMIROVSKY AND THE *NOUVELLE*

In 1935, reviewing the collection *Films parlés* in *Gringoire*, Jean-Pierre Maxence suggested that the composition of Némirovsky's stories was reminiscent of Maupassant and the tone characteristic of Chekhov.[107] He also argued that, from the moment *David Golder* appeared, it was clear that Némirovsky was a born *nouvelliste*. Evidence from published interviews and unpublished notes demonstrates that the classic nineteenth-century writers of the short story genre—Maupassant, Mérimée, and Chekhov— were crucial to Némirovsky's literary development. Némirovsky began her writing career as an author of short stories, and this highly specific approach to fiction remained crucially important to her development as a writer. Némirovsky often defined herself as a writer of *nouvelles* when she talked about her fiction. Interviewed by Janine Boussounouse in *Les Nouvelles littéraires* in 1935, she remarked: 'Dès que j'ai commencé à écrire, j'ai toujours voulu faire des romans . . . ou des nouvelles plus ou moins longues' (*As soon as I started writing I wanted to write novels, or rather, long or short* nouvelles). Némirovsky seemed to prefer the term *nouvelle* to *roman*. She also described 'Le Malentendu' as 'ma première nouvelle' (*my first* nouvelle) in an interview with Marie-Jeanne Viel.[108] Némirovsky deserves a place within the French literary tradition of the short story inaugurated by Mérimée in the 1830s and popularised by Maupassant in the 1860s. Within this tradition, Némirovsky's voice is a distinctive one. Even in the longer texts, the reader is constantly aware that the hand of the short story writer is guiding the hand of the novelist. Nowhere is this more obvious than in the 'Tempête en juin' section of *Suite française*, where each of the intersecting narrative threads could plausibly function as a short story in its own right. To illustrate: prototypes of the characters of Gabriel Corte, a writer, and Charles Langlet, an art collector, provide the material for two independent stories: 'Le Spectateur', published in *Gringoire* in December 1939, and 'M. Rose', published in *Candide* in August 1940.[109] Such migration of characters and situations between Némirovsky's short stories and her novels is frequent.

Némirovsky's continuing association with *Les Œuvres libres* indicates her ongoing interest in the narrative possibilities offered by the short story.

The two further stories she published here—'Film parlé' in July 1931 and 'La Comédie bourgeoise' in June 1932—were designated by the term 'scénario inédit'. These stories explored the potential influence of the film scenario on the *nouvelle*. Némirovsky once again succeeded in linking her fictional output closely to questions of interest in the contemporary literary field: the effect of cinema on the novel was a significant focus of the debate on the crisis of the novel. The technique of montage pointed the way towards narrative discontinuity and juxtaposition, whilst the interior monologue was deemed cinematographic by contemporary commentators.[110] The relationship between film and fiction was taken up in the review of *Films parlés* which appeared in the *Revue des deux mondes* in March 1935, though the conclusion reached here was that cinema was superfluous as a stimulus to literary creation.[111] Some critics went as far as to decry the negative effects of cinema on literature: *Le Figaro* objected to Némirovsky's use of characters and situations drawn from popular cinema, and concluded that '[i]l est inquiétant de se demander ce que le mauvais cinéma peut fournir de bon à la littérature' (*it is worrying to ask oneself what good poor cinema can do for literature*).[112]

These stories were collected in the 1934 volume *Films parlés*, accompanied by two additional stories, as part of the 'Renaissance de la nouvelle' collection edited by Paul Morand and published by Gallimard. This collection, which ran to more than thirty titles between 1934 and 1939, was a response to the perception that in the inter-war period, the short story as a genre had had its day, and was no longer of interest either to publishers or to readers.[113] Morand, himself a successful writer of short stories, was not of this view: in his preface to the first volume in the collection he remarked that it was not in fact a question of renaissance, since the genre had never really died out.[114] Némirovsky's stories show that, contrary to the opinions of some critics, the short story in the period could be more than just a commercially motivated subspecies of the novel. Although she certainly did write short stories for financial reasons—in notes dated 1936 she remarks that she will soon have two children to feed and therefore needs another novel and another story[115]—her best stories are much more than frivolous commercial productions. And although there is plenty of cross-fertilisation between her novels and her short stories, the latter are not merely some sort of 'bottom drawer' in which to store ideas unsuitable or insufficiently interesting to be developed into novels.[116] In René Godenne's terminology, Némirovsky was a '*nouvelliste* by vocation' and not merely an 'occasional *nouvelliste*'.[117]

The publication of *Films parlés* is also significant as regards the progress of Némirovsky's literary trajectory, insofar as it was part of a repositioning of Némirovsky in the literary field. Although this book was published by Gallimard, the publishing house most closely associated with the *Nouvelle Revue française*, its appearance did not result in Némirovsky being associated with the sector of the literary field represented by these two literary institutions. However, it is significant that *Films parlés* was the first of Némirovsky's works to be reviewed in the *Revue des deux mondes*. This journal was well-known as a vehicle for short stories—Mérimée had published here in the 1830s. As we saw in Chapter 1, it closely reflected the aesthetic values of the Académie française (Mérimée became an Academician in 1844), and was the incarnation of established literary conservatism in the inter-war period.[118] Martyn Cornick opposes the *Revue des deux mondes*, 'produced by Academicians for a conservative audience which expected it to publish "conservative" texts', to the *NRF*; the former 'would never seriously have contemplated publishing texts which might have threatened established, even institutionalised, norms of literary or intellectual acceptability', unlike the *NRF*.[119] As Philliponnat and Lienhardt point out, it was both a literary and a national honour to be published here, a honour which, as a stateless foreigner, Némirovsky had a clear interest in accepting.[120] A single Gallimard imprimatur was not enough to make Némirovsky into an *NRF* writer, but it does indicate a change in her perceived status. A certain logic links Némirovsky's association with the *Revue des deux mondes* and the intertextual references to the Academicians Loti and Bourget in her earliest works. The journal continued to review Némirovsky's novels positively,[121] and in 1936 welcomed her as a contributor of fiction,[122] accepting four short stories: 'Jour d'été' (April 1935); 'Liens du sang' (March–April 1936); 'La Confidence' (October 1938), and 'Aïno' (January 1940).[123] It was also in 1934 that Némirovsky broke with Bernard Grasset's publishing house and signed a contract with Albin Michel. This did not indicate a move away from the *champ de grande production*.[124] But whilst Albin Michel had begun as a publisher of popular novels at the turn of the century, the publishing house cemented its reputation in the field of the contemporary novel after the First World War when a number of its authors won prestigious literary prizes.[125] As Philipponat and Lienhardt point out, Némirovsky was exactly the sort of writer Albin Michel tended to publish: commercially successful, well-respected, but not predictable.[126]

Through her association with Albin Michel and the *Revue des deux mondes*, Némirovsky was able to continue to capitalise on the reputation she had established with Grasset as a successful, popular, and widely read novelist, whilst also claiming for herself a significant degree of aesthetic— and conservative—literary consecration. Sapiro's research has demonstrated that writers who occupied such a position in the literary field were likely to find themselves associated through their literary activities with cultural institutions appropriated by the Vichy regime—the *Revue des deux mondes* was to become a Vichy organ under the Occupation.[127] Nonetheless, the position Némirovsky had come to occupy by the mid-1930s was very much that of the majority. In his study of the literary criticism of *L'Action française*, Paul Renard concludes that the type of cultural conservatism it espoused was very much the dominant view in the 1930s, even during periods when the political climate was leftist (for example, during the

Popular Front).[128] In her earliest published work, Némirovsky cited authors consecrated by the Académie française and occupying a conservative position in the literary field; she affirmed the value of French neo-classicism; she expressed views on the teaching of literature which echoed arguments being proposed on the political right; and she subordinated Russian themes in her texts within the boundaries of acceptable French formal conventions. However, through her experiments with populism and with the folktale, she also affirmed the value of literary subjects rejected by conservatives— the Parisian and Russian Jewish popular classes. It would be all too easy to trace a direct line backwards through Némirovsky's *œuvre* to early references to Bourget and Barrès, and to cite this as evidence of an inevitable literary conservatism. Such retrospective affirmations of coherence are, as Bourdieu warns, deceptive. There is no doubt that the seeds of the later Némirovsky are contained in her early stories, that the story of her development as a novelist is one of consistency rather than rupture, and that this development can be plausibly reconstructed. Literary influences are real, but their effects are not predetermined. Némirovsky's literary life before *David Golder* was remarkable for the diversity of its composite parts and for its well-informed engagement with its aesthetic environment, but the literary career to which it gave rise was by no means a foregone conclusion.

3   A Russian Soul

The Martinican anti-colonial theorist Frantz Fanon observed in 1952 that '[w]hat is often called the black soul is a white man's artefact'.[1] The 'Russian soul' in the literary field of 1930s France was a Frenchman's artefact, as was the 'Jewish soul' which will occupy our attention in Chapter 4. The present chapter investigates the ways in which the historically and culturally specific concept—or stereotype—of the 'Russian soul' influenced both the production and the reception of Némirovsky's 'Russian' novels. Némirovsky had been writing about Russia since the very earliest moments of her literary production. As we have seen, the unpublished 'La Niania' would provide the basis for a longer fictional evocation of Russian emigration; 'L'Enfant génial' was set in Odessa, and 'Le Malentendu' and 'L'Ennemie' both included Russian references. After the success of *David Golder*, and the republication of *Le Bal* as a book, Némirovsky turned to her experience of Russia for material for her next two novels, *Les Mouches d'automne* (1931) and *L'Affaire Courilof* (1933). The depiction of the revolution in Finland in 'Les Fumées du vin', first published in *Le Figaro* in June 1934 and included in the collection *Films parlés* in the same year, anticipates the Finnish episode in *Le Vin de solitude* (1935), Némirovsky's second emigration novel. Némirovsky's two most detailed studies of Jewish identity—*David Golder* (1929) and *Les Chiens et les loups* (1940)—are also stories about Russian émigrés. However, these novels are more closely related to the 'mode juive' than to the 'mode russe' and I therefore discuss them in Chapter 4. The subject of the present chapter is the interplay between Némirovsky's fictionalisation of her personal experience of Russia and her awareness of, and ability to manipulate, the stereotype of the 'Russian soul', which was a significant feature of the French literary environment within which her texts operated.

MODELS OF CULTURAL EXCHANGE

Bourdieu's sociology of literature provides a means of approaching a writer's literary choices which avoids both simplistic biographical readings and the mythologisation of literary 'inspiration'. It is not sufficient to say that Némirovsky wrote about Russia because she was Russian, or because she was inspired by Russia, though both of these statements are undoubtedly true. For Bourdieu, the literary field is a 'space of possibilities' and the literary text is the result of 'choices' made by the agent (author) in favour of certain possibilities and against others. Such 'choices' are not completely free, but are conditioned by the agent's habitus and by their position both in the literary field and in the field of power. The field is structured by the key opposition orthodoxy/heresy, and change occurs when certain agents find themselves in a position where they are able to adopt 'heretical' choices, that is, when they have a high level of cultural capital and of autonomy.[2]

The choice of Russia as a theme in the literary field of 1930s France could be either orthodox or heretical. The space of possibilities related to this theme was determined by a series of factors historically anterior to the 1930s, including discussions of Russian literature (especially Dostoevsky) in the pages of French literary reviews, in particular the *Nouvelle Revue française*, in the 1920s; the Russian revolutions of 1917 and 1905; and the longstanding history of French and Russian cultural exchange going back to the eighteenth century. Némirovsky's perception of the ways in which it was possible for her to write about Russia in the 1930s was conditioned by her position in the literary field. The analysis presented in Chapters 1 and 2 suggests that her choices will be orthodox, and as we shall see, evidence from the novels supports this argument. However it is also interesting to explore the extent to which Némirovsky was aware of the orthodoxy of her choices, and she thus was able to produce a sometimes ironic discourse on such orthodoxy whilst at the same time conforming to it.

As a Russian writing in French about Russia, Némirovsky was necessarily involved in a process of cultural exchange.[3] The binary model of cultural exchange with which Némirovsky was familiar thanks to her studies in comparative literature at the Sorbonne must have influenced her understanding of her own bi-cultural identity. As we saw in Chapter 2, Némirovsky saw herself as a writer pouring Slav content into a French mould. Comparative literature as Baldensperger, Hazard, and van Tieghem understood it focused on a pair of national literatures and aimed to understand the relationships between them.[4] This approach was an attempt to go beyond the type of comparatism pioneered by Joseph Texte at the turn of the century. Texte concluded that comparative literature only became possible once national literatures had emerged and understood themselves to be coherent entities. Thus what Claudio Guillén describes as 'a fruitful historical paradox' could occur: 'the rise of nationalism will lay the foundation for a new internationalism'.[5] Comparative literature in the interwar period defined a national literature according to the language in which it was written, but rejected the determinist conception of the relationship between the nation and its culture which had frequently led to assertions of superiority and inferiority. The Sorbonne group rejected Texte's biological analogy according to which each national literature was viewed as a specific genre which grew and developed in a definable manner in a particular sociogeographical location.[6] The group thus promulgated the opposite view to that espoused by nationalist critics in inter-war France such as those associated with *L'Action française*, for whom French 'génie' certainly was a question of race and national soil, was inaccessible to foreigners, and constituted proof of French superiority.[7] Instead the Sorbonne comparatists aimed to demonstrate the ubiquity of international influences in any national literature and thus, to affirm the reality of cultural interaction. They did not however contest or problematise the existence of 'national' literatures. There was a humanitarian and ethical aspect to inter-war French comparative literature, which was explicitly rooted in the post-First World War political context. Both Baldensperger and van Tieghem called for comparative literature to engage in the project of ensuring that nations begin better to understand, and therefore to respect, each others' differences as well as to appreciate what connects them to each other. Comparative literature, argued Baldensperger, could provide a dislocated humanity with a solid basis for the affirmation of common values.[8]

The importance of the binary type of comparatism for the production and reception of Némirovsky's Russian novels should not be underestimated, since it was the dominant contemporary theoretical model. However, for modern readers, this model has of course been superseded. Traditional studies of authorial 'influence' have been overtaken by the broader and more flexible notion of intertextuality. The conflation of the nation with a particular linguistic space has been exploded by postcolonial theory: it is now generally accepted that not all literature written in the French language can be described unproblematically as 'French literature'. Theorists of culture have shown us that it is in the nature of culture to have 'leaky boundaries', that, as Terry Eagleton puts it, '[o]ur cultural identity leaks beyond itself just by virtue of what it is, not as an agreeable bonus or a disagreeable haemorrhage'.[9] As Homi Bhabha remarks, '[t]he very concepts of homogenous national cultures, the consensual or contiguous transmission of historical traditions, or 'organic' ethnic communities—*as the grounds of cultural comparativism*—are in a profound process of redefinition' [emphasis in original].[10] Modern cultural theory is rejecting essentialised categories of identity in favour of the liminal space, the interstices, the hybrid, Bhabha's 'third space' in which we find that which is 'neither the one [. . .] nor the other [. . .] but something else besides'.[11] However, the positive value ascribed to hybrid cultural forms is a modern perspective. Writing in 1886, in the preface to his much-read study *Le Roman russe*, Eugène Melchior de Vogüé argued, as Baldensperger and van Tieghem would, that understanding another culture could promote a rapprochement between two nations such as France and Russia.[12] But for Vogüé, as for later critics, the point of cultural interaction was certainly not the creation of a cultural hybrid: indeed, he expressed his fear that the result of cultural exchange might be cultural uniformity and the loss of French cultural prestige.[13] The ideal result of cultural exchange would be, for Vogüé, the *absorption* of Russian influences:

Comme tout ce qui existe, la littérature est un organisme qui vit de nutrition; elle doit s'assimiler sans cesse des éléments étrangers *pour les transformer en sa propre substance.*[14] [emphasis added]

Like everything which exists, literature is an organism which needs nutrition to live; it has constantly to assimilate foreign elements in order to transform them into its own substance.

The endpoint of cultural exchange according to this view is not the creation of mixed forms, but the reinforcement and improvement of a specifically and recognisably French literature. As Blaise Wilfert convincingly demonstrates in his study of foreign literary influences on modern French literature, the result of international 'importations' into the French literary field of the early twentieth century was a strong affirmation of the national character of literary production.

The present chapter does not aim to uncover the *nature* of Némirovsky's cultural identity,[15] but rather to assess the relationship between the Russian theme in her writing and the contemporary literary field which both produced and received it. For this reason, and to avoid an anachronistic interpretation, it is crucial to understand the relevance of a historically and culturally specific binary model of international cultural relations, whilst also appreciating that from a twenty-first century perspective, such a model is no longer adequate as an explanation of the reality of cultural identity and exchange.

COSMOPOLIS

The presence of foreigners in Paris in the inter-war period, and the reaction of the French to émigré communities in their capital, has been extensively documented by Ralph Schor.[16] As an émigré novelist, Némirovsky was part of a much wider sociological and literary phenomenon. According to Schor, the proportion of foreigners in the Paris region rose from 5.3% of the total population in 1921 to 9.2% in 1931.[17] The phenomenon of immigration was so marked that Paris became known as a new Babel, a Cosmopolis.[18] The Russian émigré community was the fourth largest immigrant group in 1931,[19] though the participation and visibility of Russian émigrés in the cultural life of the French capital was such that people tended to overestimate the numbers involved.[20] Inter-war Parisians were fascinated by the Russia of the émigrés, and were keen to consume Russian books, films, and entertainments of all kinds. This fascination with things Russian was primarily a feature of the 1920s, and the fashion relied on superficial and stereotyped representations of Russia and Russian culture. Discussions of the phenomenon of Russian emigration were of course politically encoded: whilst conservatives portrayed the émigrés as victims of the Bolshevik revolution and as a good example of heroic resistance to the dangerous spread of communism, the French left vilified them as reactionaries.[21]

French pride in French culture and civilisation is a very well-known feature of the European cultural landscape. The presence of so many foreigners in Paris led French commentators, particularly on the political right, to express their fears for the integrity of French culture in the face of so much potential and actual foreign cultural contact. Schor concludes that public opinion in relation to the presence of foreigners was divided between two contradictory but related feelings: pride and anxiety.[22] In Chapter 1, I noted this dichotomy in the reception of Némirovsky's early fiction, insofar as her novels flattered a conservative French readership interested in the exotic but keen to affirm its faith in the superiority of French cultural forms and to resist the supposed encroachment of the Orient. The same dichotomy was also in evidence in the domain of education, where the massive influx of foreign university students after the First World War was seen as proof of the prestige of French culture and of the excellence of the French education system. However, the aim of welcoming such students was to extend France's intellectual influence abroad, not to provoke competition from foreigners within the culture and economy of the Hexagon.[23] Némirovsky was a beneficiary of the 1896–1897 legislation which founded the reformed French university and enabled the creation of special courses for particular groups of foreign students.[24] Presumably the existence of such courses fulfilled the aim of demonstrating the superiority of the French system whilst avoiding the production of large numbers of foreign graduates who would otherwise be able to obtain the same qualifications as French students. As we saw in Chapter 2, Némirovsky spent her first two years at the Sorbonne studying Russian language and literature and her fourth year studying Russian philology. She appears to have studied almost exclusively with other Russians. The names of her fellow students, indicated in the examination records of the Sorbonne, suggest their Russian origin,[25] and Némirovsky wrote to her friend Madeleine that '[n]ous sommes une bande sympathique, jeunes gens et jeunes filles, tous Russes' (*we are a great group of young men and women, all Russians*).[26] Némirovsky's letters to Madeleine indicate that her social life brought her into contact to a significant extent with other Russians, fellow students, and members of the 'Cercle russe'. The courses advertised by the Russian section of the Sorbonne's Institut d'études slaves suggest that Némirovsky would have been taught through the medium of Russian by Russian lecturers. A bilingual poster for the 1924–1925 academic session advertised a series of lectures in Russian by a range of visiting Russian professors, and practical language classes were given in the 1929–1930 session by one Mlle Kantchalovski.[27] So although Némirovsky was studying within a prestigious French institutional environment, her experience of the Sorbonne must have constituted a powerful reinforcement of her Russian cultural identity.

From a literary perspective, the presence—or perceived presence—of so many foreigners in Paris who, in the case of the Russian émigré community, were culturally extremely active, underlined the urgency of the question of the 'national' character of cultural production. We saw in Chapter 1 that this was part of a wider intellectual debate focused on the Occident/Orient binary. Right-wing intellectuals such as Henri Massis viewed the Orient as a disruptive force threatening Western culture, citing the decadence of contemporary French culture as one of the factors facilitating the perceived advance of the East. Others believed the Orient might offer potential solutions to the obvious post-war economic and political problems afflicting the West. In such a context, how could, or should, the 'génie français' be defined, protected, or developed? According to Gisèle Sapiro, the 'génie français' was the key term in the inter-war debate around the reconstruction and reaffirmation of a national culture, as opposing literary-political groups attempted to appropriate the term as their own, and to use it to disqualify the arguments proposed by their adversaries.[28] In this context, French classicism was strongly associated with the 'génie français'. Paul Bourget's contribution to the debate on the crisis of the novel in his 'Note sur le roman français en 1921' was an attempt to define what constituted the excellence of the French novel. It is a classic statement of the conservative position on this question. He first identifies composition—structural precision and clear organisation—as characteristic of all French classical writers and as strikingly absent in the works of Goethe, Walter Scott, Dickens, George Eliot, Tolstoy, and Dostoevsky. Composition is, for Bourget, a national virtue which must never be sacrificed.[29] He goes on to identify psychological analysis as a quality proper to the French novel, and one that, in his opinion, should be conserved.[30] He contrasts Dostoevsky, and all foreign writers, who he calls neurotic visionaries, to the French exponents of psychological analysis, which he defines as the lucid dissection of states of mind.[31] Bourget argues that the main difference between the French and the Russian novel is that the French novel presupposes a more advanced stage of society. He says that Turgenev, who he sees as the most Westernised Russian writer, was aware of this, which is why he came to France to study Mérimée.[32] Némirovsky's claims in interviews that she was influenced by Turgenev and Mérimée were clearly an attempt to define herself as a French novelist within the terms of the contemporary debate. Critics who responded positively to her fiction by praising the composition of her texts and her sparse and analytical psychological studies were implicitly defining Némirovsky as a representative of the 'génie français'. Bourget did not of course acknowledge in his discussion of French national literature that cultural exchange might work in two directions: he did not refer to the fact that Mérimée spoke Russian, was heavily influenced by Pushkin, and sought to introduce French readers to Russian literature through his many translations.

The publication of a number of works of literary history and criticism indicate the extent of the interest in Russian literature in the inter-war French literary field. Eugène Melchior de Vogüé's *Le Roman russe* is generally seen as emblematic of the vogue for Russian culture in France at the *fin de siècle* and in the early part of the twentieth century. The discussion of the nature of Russian literature provided an opportunity to discuss the nature of French literature. Vogüé's stated aim in *Le Roman russe* was to identify the nature of the 'génie russe' in contradistinction to the 'génie français'. Gide's *Dostoevsky*, another landmark, appeared in 1922 at the high point of Gide's personal fascination with Dostoevsky. In the preface to the English edition of this work (1925), Arnold Bennett remarked that '[i]f anyone wants to appreciate the progress made by Western Europe in the appreciation of Russian psychology, let him compare the late Count Melchior de Vogüé's *Le roman russe* with the present work'.[33] Gide certainly had not abandoned the idea of a national 'génie', but argued strongly against what he called 'intellectual protectionism' and in favour of a conception of the 'génie français' which would be open to foreign cultures.[34] The official recognition of the Soviet state by the French government in 1924 provided a new impetus for French intellectuals to interest themselves in Russian—or Soviet—culture. The Gallimard publishing house sought to make Russian literature accessible to French readers through two series entitled 'Les Classiques russes' and 'Les Jeunes Russes', established in 1925 and 1926 respectively.[35] In 1929, Vladimir Pozner published his *Panorama de la littérature russe* which, according to Henri Peyre's study of the influence of Dostoevsky on French writers of the inter-war period, was the most influential contemporary account of twentieth century Russian literature.[36] Also in 1929, Vsevolod Fokht set up the 'studio franco-russe'. Fokht was part of the community of Russian writers and intellectuals in Paris who were politically opposed to the new Soviet regime and rejected the cultural policies it was promulgating, and who sought therefore to maintain 'authentic' Russian cultural production in exile. The aim of the 'studio franco-russe' was to convey to the host culture the difference between Russian literary production in exile and the new Soviet literature coming out of Soviet Russia. The studio, a public forum for intellectual debate, was an important point of contact between the community of Russian writers in exile in Paris and French intellectuals.[37]

The community of Russian émigré writers in Paris was composed of an older generation, well-known in Russia before their departure, who sought to conserve the traditions of Russian culture in exile, and a younger generation who made their names abroad and who wanted to renew Russian literature through contact with European modernism.[38] Both generations wrote exclusively in Russian. The discourse of the émigré writers reproduced exactly the terms of the French/Russian opposition we saw in Bourget, but valued them differently: Russian texts strove for spiritual depth instead of Latin clarity of composition; Russian psychological analysis was profound and sincere whilst the French version was superficial.[39] As Soviet literature became better established in Soviet Russia, the younger émigré generation established a triangular structure of identification and rejection, defining itself against Soviet culture and against the conservatism of the older émigré generation. In this context, 'Russian' became a complex signifier: Soviet culture was designated as 'un-Russian', whilst aspects of French modernism which émigrés sought to emulate could be labelled 'Russian'.[40] Némirovsky took no part in the 'studio franco-russe',[41] perhaps because her attitude to exile was diametrically opposed to that of the émigré writers. According to Leonid Livak's study of the émigré writers:

> They modelled their situation as a state of cultural crisis, alienation, solitude, and anxiety resulting from the social turmoil that marked their lives. This interpretation of their cultural situation motivated their 'modernist' refusal of 'traditional' literature.[42]

Némirovsky tended to reject an interpretation of exile in terms of crisis, alienation, and anxiety and instead normalised her experience of emigration. She told Jeanine Delpech that although the circumstances of her life had never been peaceful, and although she had always lived with anxiety and danger, 'malgré tout, j'ai mené une vie de jeune fille normale, je travaillais, je lisais, comme maintenant . . .' (*despite everything, I have led the life of a normal young woman, working, reading, just as I do now*). Her writing was focused toward the goal of cultural assimilation, and she adopted traditional, rather than experimental models of cultural expression which were easily recognisable within the French literary field. Her choice of language defined her literary identity insofar as the Russian-language writers dismissed exiles who chose to write in French.[43] Although one might trace some thematic connections between the work of the Russian-language exile writers and Némirovsky's novels—Martina Stemberger suggests that Némirovsky's evocation of the chaos and apparent unreality of the world, and her investigation of the impossibility of real communication with others are also typical of the émigré writers[44]—Némirovsky's literary project was quite different from theirs. Her education at the Sorbonne would have familiarised her with the Russian classics of the nineteenth century rather than with contemporary debates over Russian cultural identity. Although she did read contemporary Russian literature—she told Frédéric Lefèvre in 1933 that she had recently read Zotchenko's short stories and Valentin Katev's *Les Mangeurs de grenouille*[45]—her manuscript notes strongly suggest that she was more influenced by the classics: Chekhov, Tolstoy, Dostoevsky, Pushkin, and Turgenev. Perhaps her assertion in the same interview that she knew nothing about the new Russian literature was a tactful attempt to avoid becoming embroiled in somewhat abstruse debates over the opposition between Russian exile literature and Soviet literature. Livak notes that internecine arguments of this nature were not particularly interesting to French readers. Becoming identified with this type of debate would not have enhanced Némirovsky's reputation amongst the majority of her audience.[46]

The debates on émigré literature around the 'studio franco-russe' and on French–Russian cultural exchange in the pages of the *NRF* were a feature of the *champ de production restreinte*. The domain of popular, commercial literature, where Némirovsky found an audience, was dominated by the 'mode russe' which, as Schor makes clear, indicated neither an interest in Russians as individuals, nor a desire for fruitful cultural exchange, but rather the perpetuation of a fixed stereotype. The 'mode russe' made frequent appearances in fiction, film, and theatre where Russian heroes were seemingly ubiquitous.[47] A significant number of novels taking Russian emigration as their theme had been published in French by both French and Russian novelists the 1920s, and had found an extensive readership. The best known is perhaps Joseph Kessel's *Nuits de princes* (1927); one might also mention Jean Vignaud's *Niky* (1922), Francis Carco's *Verotchka l'étrangère ou le gout du malheur* (1923), Etienne Burnet's *Loin des icônes, roman des émigrés russes* (1923) and Max du Veuzit's *John, chauffeur russe* (1931).[48] The foreignised, enticing, and somewhat melodramatic titles of these novels suggest that they were intended to have a popular appeal. They were published not by the *NRF*/Gallimard, but by the more mainstream, commercial publishing houses (Plon, Albin Michel, Flammarion, and Tallandier, respectively). Schor identifies a series of recognisable themes which made up the 'mode russe'.[49] The Russian émigré of popular literature was an impoverished aristocrat, obliged to sell the family jewellery, to work as a valet or a taxi driver, or to trade in second-hand bric-a-brac. The traditional Russian remained attached to the orthodox faith and its exotic rituals. Russian heroes were formidable lovers, given to strong passions and, ultimately, violence. The stereotype of the 'mode russe' depended on a belief in the existence of an essential national character or temperament linked to the native soil and impervious to other considerations (such as class).[50] The Russian character, strongly marked by the trauma of exile, was deemed to be melancholy and nostalgic, constantly plagued by the hardships of the new life in France and by longing for the old life in Russia. The 'Russian soul' was perceived as mysterious and impenetrable, especially to the rational French mind. 'Russianness' was understood in terms of excess, apathy, fatalism, superstition, and the simultaneous existence of contradictory states of mind. The Russian was perceived as a troubled and troubling amalgam of Occident and Orient, of Europe and Asia. The myth of the 'Russian soul' could be ethnographic, political, and literary; it had its roots in the work of the nineteenth-century historian Jules Michelet as well as in the French reception of Dostoevsky which found in this classic of Russian literature the incarnation of the Russian character.[51] Vogüé must bear some responsibility for the perpetuation of the myth of the Russian soul, for his preface to *Le Roman russe* presents the Russian classics in very much these terms, affirming that the study of Pushkin, Gogol, Turgenev, Dostoevsky, and Tolstoy reveals the mysterious nature of the Russian soul as well as the excessive and formless character of Russian literature.

Not everyone of course was persuaded by the myth. Vladimir Pozner, a member of the 'studio franco-russe' and a future activist in the French communist party, ridiculed the 'mode russe' in an article in *Les Nouvelles littéraires* on 26 June 1926.[52] Livak remarks that the widespread adoption of the stereotype in popular fiction shocked the émigrés.[53] But there is no doubt that, for most Parisians, the 'mode russe' was a much more familiar motif than the more intellectualised debates around the 'Paris note' aesthetics of the Russian writers in exile. The 'mode russe' was an example of the type of exoticism which presents a radical and stereotyped image of Otherness, with the result that the 'home' culture perceives no connection between Self and Other and is therefore not troubled by cultural difference. The 'mode russe' served to reinforce a series of oppositions which confirmed existing French views of Frenchness, such as emotion/intellect; chaos/order; irrational/rational; excess/restraint. Such representations confirmed existing, stable concepts of identity, leaving notions such as the 'génie français' intact and undisturbed.

LA RUSSIE, BOULEVARD DES INVALIDES?

Given this intellectual and literary context, it is unsurprising that many commentators were keen to emphasise Némirovsky's dual cultural identity. Jeanine Delpech entitled her *Nouvelles littéraires* interview 'Chez Irène Némirovsky, ou la Russie boulevard des Invalides', suggesting that Némirovsky's apartment was like an outpost of Russia in the very heart of Paris. George Higgins (an Englishman) included Némirovsky in his 'Les Conrad français' series. As we saw in Chapter 2, in this interview, Némirovsky presented a series of propositions about her cultural identity, all of which have their roots in the sort of cultural dualism we have been discussing, and which ultimately serve to stress her identity first and foremost as a French writer. Némirovsky set her answer to the survey in the context of the conventional associations of the words 'French' (balance, self control, harmony) and 'Slav' (disorder, fatalism, mysticism, pessimism). She affirmed that her writing was French in its form, even if it contained Slav content, and said that she desired, hoped, and believed that she was a French writer rather than a Russian one. She reinforced the idea that her literature was only a little bit Slav by pointing out that she had only ever written school essays in Russian (which may not actually be true), that she had learned to speak French before she ever spoke Russian, and that she had spent half her childhood and all her adolescence and adult life in France. Her Russian identity is 'ce qui demeure en moi de ma race et de mon pays' (*what remains in me of my race and my country*), which suggests a passive residue of another nationality rather than an active cultivation of a bi-cultural or exilic identity.[54] Thus, when she concluded that she could not ultimately separate her knowledge of French and her experience of France from her Russian origin, she was asserting an assimilated identity rather than a foreign or exilic one: 'Tout cela est tellement amalgamé à ce qui demeure en moi de ma race et de mon pays, qu'avec la meilleure volonté du monde, il m'est impossible de distinguer où finit l'un, où commence l'autre' (*All that is so inseparable from what remains in me of my race and my country that, with the best will in the world, it is impossible for me to distinguish where one ends and the other begins*). This interview indicates a clear awareness on Némirovsky's part of the terms in which national cultural identity was being discussed in France at the time. Her strong affirmation of her identity as a French writer is of course completely unsurprising in 1940, and the interview is very much a product of the contemporary political environment—it was published in April 1940, during the Phoney War, shortly before the fall of France in May. However, the way in which Némirovsky presents the relationship between her French and Russian identities has its roots in a much earlier period—it is very much in tune with Vogüé's model of cultural exchange as the *absorption* of the foreign. She may have overstated her case, for Higgins suggests that the issue is more complex than his interviewee implies:

> Pour la célèbre romancière de *David Golder* [. . .] est français la mesure, la clarté, la logique, en somme toutes les qualités que devait posséder le discours latin fort à la mode dans nos lycées il y a encore cinquante ans. Il y aurait beaucoup à dire à ce sujet. Par exemple, qu'il y a une intuition, une sensibilité françaises; que Victor Hugo n'est ni clair, ni logique, ni mesuré et qu'il est néanmoins un des plus grands poètes de notre langue . . . Mais plutôt que de nous engager dans un débat hérissé d'embûches, donnons la réponse de Mme Irène Némirovsky.

> *For the famous author of* David Golder, *moderation, clarity and logic are French, that is, all the qualities supposedly to be found in Latin discourse that was so fashionable in our schools fifty years ago. There is a great deal to be said about this. For example, that there is a French intuition, a French sensibility; that Victor Hugo is neither clear, nor logical, nor moderate and that he is nonetheless one of the greatest poets of our language . . . But rather than becoming involved in debates which are fraught with difficulties, here is Madame Irène Némirovsky's answer.*

Higgins uses the example of Hugo to suggest that Némirovsky's definition of 'Frenchness' is too essentialised; he seeks to problematise the categories on which Némirovsky's explanation of her cultural identity in terms of national origin depends.

This sort of essentialised notion of cultural identity also emerges from Némirovsky's forays into the genre of literary biography. In 1931, she wrote a review of André Maurois' recent biography of Turgenev. This review, in Russian, was published in the émigré journal *Chisla*, disproving Némirovsky's later statement that all her mature work was in French, and suggesting that she did have at least some contact with the émigré writers in Paris, whatever their differences in aesthetic approach.[55] In Némirovsky's unpublished notes, there is a page in French headed 'Critique du Tourguéniev de Maurois' which relates to this review. She begins,

> Fait avec scruple, mais forcément superficiel de la difficulté d'un Français qui veut décrire l'âme profonde d'un Russe, surtout les paysages, et cela par quoi un pays ou un être ne ressemblent pas à un autre pays.[56]

> *Meticulously written, but necessarily superficial because of the difficulty of a French writer trying to describe the profound soul of a Russian, and especially the landscapes, and that which makes a country different from another country.*

Némirovsky argues that, as a Frenchman, Maurois is incapable of fully understanding Turgenev. Her own biographical writing tends to reinforce rather than to contest stereotypes of national identity. In the 1946 preface to *La Vie de Tchekhov*, Jean-Jacques Bernard presented Némirovsky as a cultural mediator who had removed a screen separating French readers from the Russian writer.[57] However, Martina Stemberger is right to point out that this text actually provides a highly stylised image of Russia:

> Die gezielte Exotisierung des "Russischen" für ein französisches Publikum ist hier unübersehbar; den Blick, die Rezeption eines durchschnittlichen französischen Leserpublikums vorwegzunehmen, das Interesse am *Fremden*, an einem hyper-stilisierten Russland zu befriedigen, ist offensichtlich eine der Intentionen des Textes.[58]

> *The selective exoticising of the 'Russian' for a French public is undeniable here; the attempt to anticipate the reception by an ordinary French reading public, to satisfy their interest in the foreign, and in a hyper-stylised Russia is obviously one of the text's intentions.*

If, thanks to Némirovsky, the screen has been removed between France and Russia, this is because she succeeds in presenting Chekhov in terms of a conventional and exoticised image of Russia with which her French audience were already familiar. The biography relies to a significant extent on the opposition Asia/Europe or Orient/Occident, not only in terms of its account of the Russian character and landscape but also as regards its presentation of national literatures. According to Némirovsky, Russian literature and French literature address fundamentally different questions: whilst a European reader would expect a novel to answer the question, what are we? a Russian reader would seek an answer to the question, what should we be?[59] Russian literature is doctrinaire whilst French literature is existential. The Russian character is frequently presented via brief formulations which the reader is intended to recognise and accept: Chekhov's father is a Russian patriarch who behaves like an Oriental despot;[60] the inhabitants of Chekhov's native village display an unconcerned Slav resignation;[61] the Russian male is dreamy and passive.[62] Némirovsky's imaginative description of Chekhov's response to the first signs of his illness combines the Occident/Orient opposition with a conventional portrait of the Russian character which is very much in tune with the 'mode russe':

> Il avait appelé à son secours non pas sa résignation, son orgueil ou sa science, non pas une vertu d'Occident, mais cette paresse slave qui consiste à s'asseoir en face de la vérité, à regarder longtemps, fixement, sans faire un geste pour la fuir, à la regarder si bien qu'elle finit par perdre toute forme, par se fondre en une sorte de brume, par se dissoudre et disparaître.[63]

> *He did not seek an escape through submissiveness, nor through his pride or his knowledge or any Western virtue, but through that Slav laziness which consists in stationing oneself before the truth and regarding it fixedly for a long time, without any attempt to flee, merely gazing so long that its contours become blurred, until it merges into a kind of mist, dissolves, and disappears.*[64]

The rather comedic account of Chekhov's father's chaotic and dusty shop—which sells purgative herbal teas as well as religious relics!—and its impoverished clients, who are as likely to want a drink and some company as they are to purchase anything, is deliberately exotic, entertaining, and picturesque.[65] The evocation of the abduction and sale of Russian women to Turkish harems and the practice of drowning illegitimate children suggest a Russia that is barbaric and uncivilised.[66] As we noted in Chapter 2, Némirovsky's biography of Chekhov is not a serious academic work of comparative literature but an accessible, imaginative, and often fictionalised portrait of Chekhov's character and of his native Russia. Némirovsky recreates Chekhov for her readers using very similar techniques of characterisation to those she adopted in her fictional writing; the book was clearly destined for French readers familiar with the discourse of the 'mode russe'.

The ways in which Némirovsky addressed questions around national cultural identity in interviews and through comparative literary biography is problematic insofar as she maintained a rather deterministic notion of the relationship between national origin and cultural production whilst at the same time strongly asserting that she herself was a French novelist. Némirovsky perhaps did herself a disservice in published sources such as these, since as we saw in Chapter 2, her experiments in literary technique were much more sophisticated than some of the comments she made in interviews imply. At a formal level, her writing draws on the work of a wide range of novelists—French and Russian certainly, but also English, American, and German. The range of international literary influences to which Némirovsky's unpublished notes bear witness disproves any notion that France–Russia is the only relevant node of cultural contact: she also had a detailed knowledge of, and interest in, contemporary English language fiction, which was popular in France at the time,[67] including Evelyn Waugh, James Hilton, James Cain, Kate O'Brian, T.S. Stribling, Pearl S. Buck,[68] Sinclair Lewis,[69] and John Galsworthy.[70] However, at the level of theme and content, Némirovsky was not particularly interested in using her fiction to discuss the complexities of international cultural interactions or to dramatise the psychological itineraries of the exile. She saw her Russian origin as a rich seam that could be exploited in order to capture the interest of French readers with a taste for novels about exotic locations and foreign identities. It is in this sense that Némirovsky's literary choices in relation to the description of Russian identity in her novels can be termed 'orthodox' rather than 'heretical'. The 'mode russe' of the 1920s provided a literary context in relation to which Némirovsky could make use of her memories of Russia and her knowledge of Russian culture as the subject matter of her writing. Némirovsky's writing about Russia, in the early part of her career at least, should then be understood as a response to a literary vogue that had been established in the 1920s. As we shall see in Chapter 4, this was also the case as regards her representation of Jewishness in *David Golder*.

Némirovsky's first two emigration novels bristle with easily legible motifs of the 'mode russe'. In *Les Mouches d'automne*, the exotic subject matter of the text is established immediately through naming: Yourotchka (the diminutive of Youri), Nicholas Alexandrovitch, Alexandre Kirilovitch, Nianiouchka (the pet name for the main protagonist, Tatiana Ivanovna, the family's nanny), Platocha, and Piotre all appear in the first few pages. The theme of nostalgia is established on the second page of the novel when Tatiana recalls her fifty-one years of service in the Karine household and the generations of Karine children she has brought up. For Tatiana, the war the young generation is going to fight is a repetition of the wars their fathers and grandfathers fought: her attitude is one of typically Russian fatalism and resignation. Tatiana Ivanovna is a literary type: the faithful Russian nanny who has been with the family for longer than anyone can remember and whose identity is entirely defined by nostalgia. The depiction of the Russian character in this novel continually reproduces the stereotype of the melancholy 'Russian soul'. Tatiana often says that everything is in the hands of God; Youri, faced with his impending death, wearily remarks that whatever is to happen, is to happen, and his mother, reflecting on their past wealth and current poverty, says there is nothing to be done but to accept God's will.[71] Némirovsky evokes recognisable Russian customs and proverbs, such as the idea that smashing the glasses after a toast brings good luck, and the belief that a cockroach in the house announces future prosperity.[72] Némirovsky's émigrés sew the family jewellery into their clothing;[73] poverty-stricken Russian aristocrats are reduced to doing manual labour[74] or to selling second-hand Russian bric-a-brac to curious Parisians.[75] The Karine's lifestyle in Paris corresponds to the popular image of the destitute émigré: they live in a tiny, dark flat and sleep during the day and eat their meals at night.[76] The responses of the three generations to exile life is also entirely typical: whilst the elderly Tatiana is completely unable to cope with life in Paris, the parents of the Karine family succeed in assimilating partially, whilst the children are able to embrace the European capital with enthusiasm.

In *Le Vin de solitude*, cultural exoticism is again established in the opening pages, this time via a description of the landscape: 'le vent ramenait vers la ville l'odeur des plaines ukrainiennes, une faible et âcre senteur de fumée et la fraîcheur de l'eau sur des joncs qui poussaient sur les rives. Le vent soufflait d'Asie; il avait pénétré entre les monts Oural et la mer Caspienne' (*the wind brought the perfume of the Ukrainian plains to the town, a faint and bitter smell of smoke and the coolness of the water on the rushes which grew on the riverbank. The wind blew from Asia, it had penetrated between the Ural Mountains and the Caspian Sea*).[77] Némirovsky would use the same motif of the East wind in *La Vie de Tchekhov* to evoke the steppe on the outskirts of the author's native village: 'Ces vastes étendues de terre, sans une montagne, sans une forêt, étaient traversées par les vents violents venus de l'Est, de l'Asie' ('*a vast plain, without a single mountain or forest, swept by furious winds from from the East, out of Asia*').[78] In *Le Vin de solitude*, the melancholy Slav character is again underlined: Hélène's *angoisse* is the inheritance of her race and she takes a melancholy pleasure in her solitude.[79] However, Hélène is a transitional character because, although she is Russian, she loves France and wants to be French. Her childhood identification with Napoleon dramatises the ambivalence of both her national and her gender identity.[80] Nonetheless, the novel reproduces clearly delineated stereotypes of 'Frenchness' and 'Russianness'. French order confronts Russian disorder: Mademoiselle Rose, Hélène's French governess, is calm and quiet, moderate and reasonable, but Hélène's character is wild and strange, her family home is described as incoherent, and her country is without moderation.[81] Hélène's dual identity is a juxtaposition of elements and is not therefore an example of hybridity: 'Il lui semblait parfois que dans son corps deux âmes habitaient, sans se mêler, se juxtaposaient sans se confondre' (*sometimes she thought that two souls inhabited her body, without mingling, they were juxtaposed, without combining*).[82] When they arrive in Paris, the Karol family illustrate a different stereotype compared with the Karine family of *Les Mouches d'automne*. Boris Karol is not a member of the landed aristocracy but rather a *nouveau riche* financial speculator, and so unlike the Karines, he and his family become the type of émigrés who can enjoy the decadent Parisian lifestyle of the *années folles*. It is against this background that the combative and sexually competitive relationship between Hélène and her mother Bella is played out. The two women's love affairs with Max Safronov draw on the stereotype of excessive, violent, and vengeful Russian passion. In this novel, it is interpersonal relationships which are the source of emotional conflict. There is no sense in which Hélène's exilic identity produces intrapersonal conflict. Similarly, in *Les Mouches d'automne*, it is Tatiana's relationship with her external environment which causes her crisis—she is an elderly Russian woman who simply cannot comprehend life in Paris. The exiled characters in Némirovsky's Russian novels do not experience identity conflict as a result of their dual national allegiances. Hélène represents the extreme of successful assimilation whilst Tatiana represents the extreme refusal of assimilation. It is not until *Les Chiens et les loups* that we find representations of the sorts of conflictual identities more usually associated with exile writing.

The discourses of the 'mode russe' also provided content for a good number of Némirovsky's short stories. In 'L'Ennemie', Génia Nikitof is another violent Russian lover. 'Et je l'aime encore . . . ' tells the story of Olga, a Russian émigrée in Paris separated from her lover by the 1917 revolution. Her apartment is rather similar to the Karines':

> Il n'y avait pas de feu, pas de fleurs; des vêtements étaient jetés en désordre sur le lit. Ces cendres de cigarettes sur le tapis, ces hideux bibelots loués avec le mobilier et l'appartement et dont on n'avait jamais pensé à se débarrasser, ce décor de bohème mélancholique, ces logements d'émigrés, comme je les connaissais![83]

> *There was no fire, no flowers; clothes were strewn in a disordered heap on the bed. Cigarette ash on the carpet, horrible ornaments rented along with the furniture and the apartment which no one had ever thought to get rid of, that bohemian, melancholy décor, how well I knew those places where the émigrés lived.*

The phrase 'ces logements d'émigrés' is obviously intended to be recognised by readers. 'Magie' and 'Le Sortilège' use the motif of Russian superstition to construct stories revolving around the supernatural: 'Magie' is a ghost story in which young Russians in exile in Finland take part in a séance, whilst in 'Sortilège', set in Russia, Klavdia Alexandrovna can read the cards and knows all sorts of other techniques for predicting the future.[84] 'La Confidence' is about a French literature tutor, a single lady who, in her youth, had been a French governess in Russia where she had a passionate affair with a Russian man. This story opposes the French classicism Blanche Lajunie teaches to her student to her memories of Russia and the Slav soul.[85] In 'Déstinées' the narrator's Russian friend is the very incarnation of the French perception of the 'âme russe': 'Mon amie est une Russe très belle et qui a eu quelques aventures, mais à mesure que les années passent, ce qui domine en elle, c'est ce qu'on appelle en France le mysticisme slave. Tout simplement de la piété, mais non disciplinée, quelque chose d'un peu désordonnée et sauvage' (*my friend is a very beautiful Russian who has had a few love affairs, but as the years go by, the thing that dominates her character is what in France we call Slav mysticism. Simply piety, but without discipline, something a little disordered and wild).[86]

L'Affaire Courilof is a different case. It is not an emigration narrative: the story takes place entirely in Russia. Intercultural dislocation and the identity of the 'foreigner' are not therefore thematised in this text. The novel begins by focusing the reader's expectations in terms of genre and narrative suspense, rather than of subject matter. The frame narrative evokes the reader's curiosity by posing a series of enigmas (Who is Léon M.? Why does he refuse to reveal his real name to his interlocutor? What was his role in the Courilof affair?). The 'found' manuscript is the testimony of an anarchist revolutionary whose mission is to infiltrate the household of the politician Courilof by posing as a doctor in order ultimately to assassinate him. *L'Affaire Courilof* is not however a political novel. Critics who objected to its lack of political precision did so with some justification: it evokes an atmosphere of Russia at the turn of the century, and studies the characters of two men through their strange relationship. It does not attempt to offer a detailed analysis of Russian politics, relying instead on a conventional view of Russian history and politics as being shot through with corruption and violence. The 'Russian soul' also underpins the characterisation in this novel: as many critics noted, Courilof and Léon M. are further examples of the melancholy and fatalistic introspection deemed typical of the Russian character.

The motifs of the 'mode russe' recur in the later novel *Les Chiens et les loups* (1940). Certain familiar signifiers of a traditional Russian identity appear in this text, such as the Russian proverb about the cockroach.[87] Tante Rhaissa's newfound profession as a seamstress in Paris is a typical trajectory for an impoverished émigrée, and the flat the family occupy in the Ternes district of Paris is another typically poor émigré residence. However, as we have already noted, Némirovsky is more concerned in this novel with images of Jewishness than she is with images of Russianness. In 1940 the 'mode russe' was a thing of the past, whilst the fate of foreign Jews in Paris was yet to be determined. Némirovsky's evocations of Russia in this novel are secondary to her investigation of a specifically Jewish experience of emigration. The protagonists have left their native country not as dissident Russians opposed to the Bolshevik revolution, as in *Les Mouches d'automne* and *Le Vin de solitude*, but as Jews forced to flee a pogrom.

Already outsiders in Russia, they do not assert a Russian identity in exile. Their Russian nationality has been called into question by their experience of persecution, and it is therefore their Jewish identity which primarily determines their experience of emigration.

Némirovsky's engagement with the 'mode russe' in the first half of the 1930s was, in a sense, opportunistic. We saw in Chapter 1 that Némirovksy's life story, and in particular her experience of emigration, was a significant aspect of the construction of an 'author myth' which generated interest amongst readers and contributed to the creation of Némirovsky's literary success. It was logical then for Némirovsky to continue to exploit her experience of Russia in her writing in order to attract a readership already predisposed towards this subject thanks to the vogue for emigration novels in the 1920s. Némirovsky was exceptionally well placed to 'package' Russia and sell it to her French readers in terms they would recognise and accept. However, Némirovsky's depictions of Russia should not be viewed as mere cynical commercialism. Bourdieu rejects a simplistic opposition between 'cynicism' and 'innocence' on the part of writers as they establish their positions in the literary field.[88] For Bourdieu, the existence of a homology between the literary field, that is the producer of cultural goods, and the field of power, that is the consumers of cultural goods, means that supply and demand respond to each other without the need for conscious (cynical) intervention on the part of the producer (except in the case of cultural products whose value is solely commercial):

> Lorsqu'une œuvre 'trouve', comme on dit, son public, qui la comprend et l'apprécie, c'est presque toujours l'effet d'une *coïncidence*, d'une rencontre entre des séries causales partiellement indépendantes et presque jamais—et, en tout cas jamais complètement—le produit d'une recherche consciente de l'adjustement aux attentes de la clientèle, ou aux contraintes de la commande ou de la demande. [emphasis in original][89]

> *When a work 'finds', as the saying goes, an audience which understands and appreciates it, this is almost always the effect of a coincidence, of a meeting between causal series which are partially independent and is almost never—and, in any case, never completely—the result of a conscious search for adjustment to the expectations of customers, or to the constraints of command or demand.*[90]

The Russian theme in Némirovsky's writing in this period was a result of a series of partially independent chains of causality of which she was not necessarily fully conscious, but whose coming together are comprehensible sociologically. Némirovsky's personal trajectory and the nature of the literary field of France in the 1920s and early 1930s provided the conditions of possibility for such a 'coincidence' which allowed Némirovsky to occupy what turned out to be an advantageous position in the literary field.

THE 'MODE RUSSE' IN THE DISCOURSE OF CRITICS

The reception of Némirovsky's 'Russian' novels bears witness to the ubiquity and familiarity of the 'mode russe' in the contemporary literary field. Reviewing *Les Mouches d'automne* in *Les Nouvelles littéraires*, Maurice Bazy suggested that the French were rather too familiar with the émigré question:

> On sait assez que rien ne ressemble plus à une histoire d'émigrés russes qu'une autre histoire d'émigrés russes. On sait aussi que trois chauffeurs de taxi sur quatre sont d'anciens altesses et que les ex-colonels des Preoobrajensky en sont réduits, par un retour de choses que ce n'est pas l'endroit ici de juger, à vous apporter votre vestiare.[91]

> *We all know that nothing resembles a story about Russian émigrés more than another story about Russian émigrés. We all know that three out of four taxi drivers are former counts and that, thanks to a strange reversal of circumstances which this is not the place to judge, the former Preobrajensky colonels have been reduced to bringing you your coat.*

Critics of *L'Affaire Courilof* generally viewed it either as an illustration of the Russian soul or as a revolution novel which some found historically plausible and others did not. A typical commentary described the text as 'ce livre qui est une étude profonde de l'âme russe et reflète son nihilisme désolé, irremediable et sincère' (*this book which is a deep study of the Russian soul and reflects its desolate nihilism*);[92] another remarked on its psychological portrait of a specifically Russian type.[93] For Henry Bidou, Léon M. was a Slav of the soft type. For Ramon Fernandez, *L'Affaire Courilof* illustrated Némirovsky's essentially Russian literary skill:

> Il est des gens qui savent conter, comme d'autres savent danser, naturellement. C'est le cas de beaucoup de Russes, et Mme Némirovsky est du nombre [. . .] De plus, elle sait créer, à la russe, les atmosphères.[94]

> *Some people know how to tell stories, as others know how to dance, naturally. This is the case with many Russians, and Némirovsky is among them [. . .] Also, she knows how to create an atmosphere in a very Russian way.*

In a similar vein, Bidou remarked that 'Madame Némirovsky jouera du violon sur vos nerfs, à la russe, pendant deux cent pages' (*Madame Némirovsky will play on your nerves like a bow on the strings of a violin, for hours, in a very Russian way*). Critics similarly read *Les Mouches d'automne* as an illustration of Némirovsky's own typical Russianness: 'L'auteur de *David Golder* possède au plus haut degré le don d'émouvoir le lecteur par une nostalgie poétique comme seules les âmes slaves en sont imprégnés' (*The author of* David Golder *posseses at the very highest level the skill of moving the reader through a poetic nostalgia, in which only Slav souls are steeped*).[95] Some critics tried to disentangle 'French' and 'Russian' elements of Némirovsky's work. *Echo de Paris* found the concision of *Les Mouches d'automne* to be more effective in conveying the experience of the émigrés than the more lengthy narratives typical of Russian literature: 'Ce petit livre nous en dit plus sur le désarroi des émigrés et sur l'âme russe que de longs romans et de gros volumes' (*This little book tells us more about the distress of the émigrés and about the Russian soul than long novels and weighty tomes could*).[96] *Excelsior* held the opposite view, maintaining that the text's concision detracted from its 'Russianness': 'On souhaiterait un récit moins uni, moins sagement composé, mais plus riche en coups de sonde, en révélations mystérieuses. En s'exprimant dans notre langue, on dirait que Mme Némirovsky a perdu beaucoup des qualités de sa race' (*We would have liked a less unified narrative, less dilligently composed, but more probing, with more mysterious revelations. By writing in our language, it seems that Madame Némirovsky has lost many of the qualities of her race*).[97] For Robert Brasillach, in *L'Action française*, Némirovsky's conformity to French literary models neutralised the potentially abrasive and destructive character of her depiction of the Russian soul:

Il y a dans ce conte une vertu d'émotion, et en même temps une discrétion qui sont aujourd'hui chose rare. Mme Némirovksy a fait passer l'immense mélancholie russe sous une forme française, et lui a presque ôté sa force dissolvante.[98]

This story is pleasingly emotional, and at the same time discrete, which is a rare thing today. Madme Némirovksy has conveyed the immense Russian melancholy through a French form, and has thereby almost removed its abrasive character.

It was a condition of her acceptability within the pages of the right-wing *L'Action française* that Némirovsky's literary production should be received as an illustration of French literary norms and as a negation of potentially dissolute and dangerous foreign disorder. Reviewers of Némirovsky's novels often used her dual cultural identity as a justification for attributing fixed national characteristics to literature, even when discussing later texts not specifically focused on Russia. A commentator on *La Proie* found Jean-Luc to be a Russian hero whose character was not at all characteristic of the French novel, and believed him to be a Russian hero treated in the French manner.[99] Critics tended to take for granted the meanings of terms such as *the French novel* or *the Russian soul* rather than attempting to negotiate the literary significance of the type of cultural hybridity Némirovsky represented, and therefore their discourse reinforced the conventional terms of the French/Russian opposition. Critics who sought to portray Némirovsky as a bridge between two cultures nonetheless reinforced the customary oppositions:

> On se console (de ne jamais comprendre tout à fait les Russes, disait Georges Imann) en songeant qu'ils se comprennent encore moins eux-mêmes. Avec Mme Némirovsky, on a l'impression que les histoires slaves ne sont plus inintelligibles pour les têtes françaises, éprises de construction et de logique.[100]

> *One consoles oneself (that one can never completely understand the Russians, according to Georges Imann) by thinking that they understand themselves even less. With Madame Némirovsky, one has the impression that Slav stories are no longer unintelligible to the French mind, which is so much in favour of construction and logic.*

By exploiting and sustaining the stereotypes of the 'mode russe', Némirovsky created a virtuous circle which generated literary success: because she made use of motifs already familiar within the literary field, her texts fulfilled the expectations of critics and readers.

However, the fact that the majority of critics did not simply reject Némirovsky's work as stereotyped and therefore uninteresting suggests that her Russian novels are something more than a simplistic recreation of the terms of the 'mode russe'. Indeed, Maurice Bazy, amongst others, praised Némirovsky's ability to avoid the familiar clichés of the emigration narrative. To some extent, as we have seen, such praise is unmerited, since her novels do very recognisably reproduce the terms of the 'mode russe'. How then can we account for it? Two factors should be taken into account: firstly, the structure of the texts in question, and secondly, the presence of slight variations in narrative perspective which begin to undermine the discourse of the 'mode russe'. One of the disconcerting features of Némirovsky's writing is that she frequently combines stereotyped content with a narrative structure which, whilst not particularly innovative, is nonetheless highly competent and convincing. Némirovsky's broad and multilingual reading experience manifests itself in a technical ability to create tightly constructed narratives which nonetheless use some fairly conventional thematic material. Contemporary critics picked up on the formal interest of Némirovsky's novels, as we saw in Chapter 1 when we surveyed the critical engagement with literary realism provoked by her early fiction. Several critics commented favourably on the concision of *Les Mouches d'automne*, though they did not agree as to whether this enhanced or detracted from its 'Russianness'. Reviewers praised the construction of *L'Affaire Courilof* by comparing it to a *roman policier*.[101] *Le Vin de solitude* is constructed according to the structure of the *Bildungsroman*: the story of emigration is also the story of Hélène's emotional and intellectual maturing and her discovery of a feasible social role. In her notes, Némirovsky described the text as a an apprentice-ship novel after the model of Goethe's *Wilhelm Meister*,[102] demonstrating once again that France/Russia is not the only significant opposition in her literary trajectory. Her concern with the formal construction of this text is demonstrated by an extended analogy in her manuscript notes whereby the framework of *Le Vin de solitude* is mapped, chapter by chapter, onto the movements of a symphony by César Franck.[103] In addition to the successful construction of these texts, there is also evidence of a variation in narrative perspective which is slight, but effective. In both *Les Mouches d'automne* and *Le Vin de solitude*, there are moments where Némirovsky's character-istic irony is directed not the émigrés themselves, but at the way in which they are perceived through French eyes:

> Ils descendirent dans le port de Marseilles le 28 mai 1920 [. . .] Ils étaient vêtus de haillons, ils avaient des figures étranges et effrayantes, misérables, dures.[104]

> *They stepped out on the port in Marseille on 28 May 1920 [. . .] They were dressed in rags, their faces were strange and frightening, miser-able, harsh.*[105]

> La cendre parsemait les tapis; le domestique méprisant et silencieux ver-sait le café sur un coin du bureau et disparaissait avec un aigre sourire qui jugeait sévèrement 'ces étrangers loufoques'.[106]

> *Ash was scattered on the carpet, the scornful and silent butler poured out the coffee on a corner of the bureau and disappeared with a sour smile which was a harsh judgment on 'these crazy foreigners'.*

In these examples, the adjectives convey not the narrator's opinion, but that of a French observer: it is for the French inhabitants of Marseille that the émigrés are strange and frightening; it is for the French servant that they are crazy. Némirovsky's texts thus adopt both the stereotyped perspective of the French gaze on the Russian émigrés, by depicting them in the conventional terms of the 'mode russe', and at the same time, disrupt that perspective by revealing the French audience to themselves. Némirovsky-as-narrator occupies both the position of the indigenous French and that of the immi-grant. The reader therefore absorbs the Russian as the Frenchman's arte-fact, but is also prompted to see the immigrant being seen by the pejorative French gaze. It is as if Némirovksy, having first drawn the reader into the familiar stereotype, then throws down a challenge: have you ever thought of Russian émigrés as strange and frightening, as crazy? Némirovsky uses a similar narrative strategy in *Les Chiens et les loups* when she describes Harry's mother and her sisters who organise social gatherings *à la russe* and who have not lost their Russian accents. To their French friends, they seem exotic and quaint: 'On disait même "charme slave", mais sans aucune malice' (*People even talked about 'Slav charm', but without any malice*).[107] She satirises the 'mode russe' via the response of Harry's French friends to Ada and her paintings: 'Vous ne trouvez pas qu'elle a quelque chose de dostoevskien?' (*Don't you think she's a little bit Dostoevskian?*)[108] In the mouths of these featherbrained French socialites, 'dostoevskien' is vague shorthand for 'Russian' rather than a serious commentary on Ada's work. But nowhere is Némirovsky's dual discourse on the 'mode russe' as evident as in the short story 'Espoirs', published in *Gringoire* in 1938.[109] The story relies on a delightful irony: Sophie, a hat maker, and Vassili, her husband, struggling Russian émigrés in Paris, are happy to discover a distant French relative who they hope might prove to be a source of income. They are at first pleased at his enthusiasm for the rediscovery of a long-lost family connection, but then are tragically disappointed when they discover that he too is destitute, and that his positive attitude is motivated by the hope that his newfound Russian cousins will support *him* financially! On the one hand, the story is pure 'mode russe'. But on the other, it is a biting satire on the gullibility of the Parisian *bourgeoises* who, as Sophie has realised, want some Russian exoticism along with their purchases:

> Pour leurs cent-soixante-quinze francs, il ne leur suffit pas d'avoir un chapeau; il leur faut par-dessus le marché un aperçu de l'âme russe. Je leur en donne pour leur argent.[110]

> *For their one hundred and seventy five francs, they don't just want a hat; they also want a glimpse of the Russian soul into the bargain. I give them their money's worth.*

Sophie maintains just the right level of dirt and disorder in her shop, in order to conform to her clients' expectations without shocking them too much. She exaggerates her Slav accent, deliberately makes mistakes in French, and invents terrible stories of the hardships of her life so that 'quand elles recevront à dîner Mme Duraton et le député Chose, elles pourront parler de la mentalité étrangère, de l'âme slave et de la mystique de l'Orient' (*when they have Madame Duraton for dinner with that politician, Mr Whatshisname, they'll be able to talk about the foreign mentality, the Slav soul and the Oriental mystique*).[111] It is tempting to conclude that Némirovsky made and presented her Russian novels in the same spirit as Sophie makes her Russian hats.

The success of Némirovsky's Russian novels is due to her ability to engage creatively with the space of possibilities with which the literary field presented her. It is certainly true that her use of the 'mode russe' is of a different order—that is, occupies a different position in the literary field— than, say, Gide's playful literary interactions with Dostoevsky which produced a novel such as *Les Caves du Vatican*. Nonetheless, Némirovsky is, in Bourdieu's vocabulary, a *conscious* writer, not a *naïve* one, that is, her literary identity is not a passive product of the forces at work in the field, but rather, is a result of her ability to manipulate those forces.[112] If Némirovsky resembles Sophie of 'Espoirs', it is because she understood only too clearly that her skill as a craftswoman was potentially insufficient in itself. Both Sophie and Némirovsky understand that, to sell their product, they must manipulate the discourses surrounding their craft.

GENDER AND GENRE: WOMEN OF THE PAST, WOMEN OF THE PRESENT

Némirovsky's emigration narratives are more than just stories of emigration. In her notes relating to 'Espoirs', Némirovsky wrote that the story was not about exile but about *déclassement*, about the human being whose life is suddenly reduced to the basic and brutal realities of material existence.[113] Némirovsky's narratives do not simply resemble all the other emigration stories with which Maurice Bazy was familiar because she treats this narrative situation as a point of departure which opens out onto other questions, rather than as an end in itself. It is for this reason that the question of form is crucial in these texts. *Les Mouches d'automne* is an emigration story, but it is also an experiment with the *nouvelle*. *Le Vin de solitude* uses an emigration narrative to construct a *Bildungsroman*. *L'Affaire Courilof* deliberately avoids the genre of the *roman à these* and borrows instead from the *roman policier*.

In each of Némirovsky's emigration novels, there is a close relationship between the choice of genre and the narrative focus on a central female protagonist. *Les Mouches d'automne* had first appeared with Editions Kra under the title *Les Mouches d'automne ou la femme d'autrefois*. It was part of a series entitled 'Femmes', which sought to illustrate the different 'types' of the 'modern woman'. Other writers published in the series included Paul Morand, Jean Giraudoux, Joseph Kessel, and Colette.[114] It is perhaps thanks to the title of this series that the novel achieved the narrative focus on which its technical success depends: it is through the close concentration of the narrative on Tatiana, 'la femme d'autrefois' (*the woman of the past*), and on the latter's perception of time, that Némirovsky achieves the narrative concision characteristic of the French *nouvelle* or the Chekhovian short story. Like 'La Niania' on which it is based, the story of Tatiana Ivanovna is as much that of a woman out of her right time as it is of a woman out of her right place. In 'La Niania', the Russian nanny is defined entirely by her great age. She is subsumed into the ancestral home and landscape:

> La Niania était très vieille, si vieille qu'elle ne changeait plus depuis des années. Elle paraissait immuable, comme le château, comme le parc centenaire, comme l'étang silencieux ou se balançait de grands nénuphars, tous roses au soleil couchant.[115]

> *Niania was very old, so old that she hadn't altered for years. She*
> *seemed immutable, like the house, like the hundred year old park, like*
> *the silent pond where the huge water lilies floated, pink in the sunset.*

Her body functions as the guardian of the family's memories: 'On la chéris-
sait justement, à cause des souvenirs inscrits dans les rides de sa figure,
comme les pages d'un livre' (*She was cherished because of the memories
inscribed in the wrinkles in her face, like the pages of a book*).[116] As Tatiana
Ivanovna, Niania has a more personal identity which allows Némirovsky to
explore both her role as the (often disregarded or unappreciated) lynchpin
of the family, and her ultimately fatal disorientation when faced with the
modern European city. The confusion which, in the final pages of the novel,
leads to her drowning in the Seine[117] is temporal as well as geographical: she
believes she is crossing the frozen river to reach the family estate of Karinovka, but it is for the Karinovka of the years before the revolution that
she longs. Tatiana is one of a series of older women in Némirovsky's *œuvre*.
The reader understands that their sense of uselessness in a world that has
moved on is doubled by a certain pride in their extensive life experience,
which their children and grandchildren disregard. Yet the irritation felt by
the younger generations is also very real and very comprehensible in these
texts.[118] One of the most significant contributions Némirovsky made to
women's writing may well be her unusual ability to describe female identity
at each stage of its evolution through time: she depicts children, adolescents,
young lovers, brides, mothers, and grandmothers with her characteristic
combination of cruel irony and touching sympathy.

Two modern critics have taken Némirovsky seriously as an example of
twentieth-century women's writing. In *The Forgotten Generation*, Jennifer Milligan reads Némirovsky primarily in terms of her dissection of the
myth of romantic love and her account of traumatic and sexually charged
mother–daughter relationships.[119] The latter theme is a major focus of Martina Stemberger's *Irène Némirovsky: Phantasmagorien der Fremdheit*, a
psychoanalytically focused study of identity in Némirovsky's fiction which
analyses the 'bad mother' as an example of destructive femininity.[120] Stemberger has also analysed the function of prostitution in Némirovsky's fiction, comparing her treatment of this theme with the works of Colette.[121]
The mother–daughter relationship is central to *Le Vin de solitude*. In her
own description of the novel, Némirovsky presented it not as an exile novel
(this was also the case with 'Espoirs', as we have seen), but as a study of
problematic family relationships:

> Ce livre-là n'a pas été écrit pour ceux qui, au sein d'une famille unie et
> heureuse, se forgent une solitude imaginaire, ni pour ceux dont les pre-
> mières années ont été entourées de soin et de tendresse. Mon ambition
> est de toucher quelques-uns des autres, ceux qui ont connu le desespoir
> à l'âge qu'on appelle heureux, mais qui ont eu le courage (ou le bon-
> heur) de continuer à vivre et à aimer la vie.[122]

> *This book was not written for those who create an imaginary solitude for themselves within a loving and united family, nor for those whose early years were surrounded by care and tenderness. My ambition is to reach some of the others, those who knew despair at the age that is called happy, but who have had the courage or the good fortune to continue to live and to love life.*

Whilst the psychoanalytic aspects of these relationships are indeed fascinating and complex, as Stemberger shows, the form Némirovsky adopts in order to convey these themes is also crucial. The story of Hélène's struggle to continue to live and to love life constitutes a powerful example of a female *Bildung*. Research on women writers' use of the *Bildungsroman* genre has tended to focus on the ways in which female authors have transformed its conventional structure in order to express a specifically female trajectory.[123] However, women writers of non-experimental, realist fiction in the inter-war period often maintained and adapted the existing structures of the genre in order to tell a story of female development.[124] Némirovsky's writing is not *écriture feminine*.[125] *Le Vin de solitude* is an example of a female-authored apprenticeship narrative which adopts the features and motifs of the male-authored generic model. The conventional male apprenticeship is achieved through travel and through sex. In Hélène's case, journeys to Finland and to Paris facilitate her *Bildung*; although travel is forced upon her by the political situation, her ultimate emigration to France corresponds to her own strong desire to live in this country. The female subject of the early twentieth century was not as free as her male counterpart, either socially or economically, to choose to travel, but nonetheless, travel functions as a key component of her apprenticeship. Hélène's sexual relationships with Fred Reuss in Finland and with Max Safronov are crucial milestones along her journey to maturity. However, it is through Hélène's rejection of these relationships that *Bildung* is achieved: although sex is crucial to male and female apprenticeship narratives alike, it is by refusing oppressive sexual relationships that the female subject progresses. The end point of the female *Bildung* is often a positive embracing of solitude, as the title of Némirovsky's novel suggests. Whilst the goal of male apprenticeship is the integration of the subject into society and the assumption of a social role[126] that of female apprenticeship must be creative, since it is by no means certain that a pre-existing model of autonomous, independent female subjectivity will present itself. The end point of the female apprenticeship narrative is 'terminal' in the sense in which Margaret Attwood has used this word, that is, 'not "the end of the line, where you get off" but "where you get on to go somewhere else"'.[127] At the end of *Le Vin de solitude*, Hélène has severed her ties with the family home, has liberated herself from destructive relationships with both Max and her mother, and is ready to 'go somewhere else', that is, to define her own, independent existence:

Je n'ai pas peur de la vie, songea-t-elle. Ce ne sont que les années d'apprentissage. Elles ont été exceptionnellement dures, mais elles ont trempé mon courage et mon orgeuil. Cela, c'est à moi, ma richesse inaliénable. Je suis seule, mais ma solitude est âpre et enivrante.[128]

I am not afraid of life, she thought. These have just been the years of apprenticeship. They have been exceptionally hard, but they have strengthened my courage and my pride. That is a treasure which no one can take away from me. I am alone, and my solitude is bitter and intoxicating.

As Stemberger suggests, there is a marked tendency throughout Némirovsky's *œuvre* to represent the triumph of young women who manage to achieve freedom (Hélène in *Le Vin de solitude*, Ada in *Les Chiens et les loups*) as opposed to the downfall of young male characters who often succumb to failure and despair (Christophe Bohun in *Le Pion sur l'échiquier*, Jean-Luc Daguerne in *La Proie*).[129] Némirovsky's *dénouements* open up the possibility for a gendered reading of her texts which is emancipatory.

The conclusions to Némirovsky's two emigration narratives offer a striking contrast which illustrates the diversity of her portrayal of female trajectories. Two Russian women respond in opposite ways to Paris, the modern European city *par excellence*. Tatiana Ivanovna, a woman of the past, is defined by another time and another place and cannot achieve the reshaping of her identity which is necessary for a positive experience of exile. Hélène, a woman of the present, or perhaps of the future, redefines her identity such that the blue sky she sees emerging from the clouds between the pillars of the Arc de Triomphe in the novel's closing lines is the path to freedom.

MAKING AND BREAKING THE RULES OF THE 'MODE RUSSE'

By setting Némirovsky's emigration narratives in the context of other contemporary novels on the same theme, we can begin to reconstruct the reading experience of her contemporary readers and to understand more clearly the ways in which her novels both adopt and diverge from the discourse of the 'mode russe'. Francis Carco's *Verotchka l'étrangère ou le gout du malheur* (1923) and Joseph Kessel's *Nuits de princes* (1927) had contributed to the definition of the 'mode russe' and were frequently cited by Némirovsky's critics as points of comparison. Carco and Kessel occupied a similar position in the literary field to Némirovsky, insofar as both were considered to be aesthetically respectable writers who produced popular fiction; they were published by mainstream, commercial publishers (Carco's novel was published by Albin Michel, and Kessel's by Les Editions de France) and their novels sold in large numbers. Carco (1886–1958) was a French writer of Corsican origin who published a large number of novels based on exotic locations and themes. His interest in the émigré question derives from his more general interest in depicting the foreign in his writing. Joseph Kessel (1898–1979) was, like Némirovsky, a Jewish émigré from Russia. Like Carco, he began his writing career in journalism, and became a prolific writer of fiction. He served in the First World War and is often cited alongside Malraux as one of the first exponents of the inter-war novel of action. *Nuits de princes* was not his first book about Russia: his first published work, *La Steppe rouge* (1923), is a collection of pithy and often brutal stories about the Bolshevik revolution.

Verotchka l'étrangère and *Nuits de princes* are both based around the lives and loves of a group of Russian immigrants in Paris. Both novels trade on stereotypes of Russian character and behaviour. The plot of these novels is strikingly similar: both depict Russians falling victim to their own extravagant and excessive behaviour. Their addiction to drugs, alcohol, sex, and luxury leads them to a physical, emotional, and economic crisis point which may or may not be resolved. Carco's Serge recovers from his cocaine addiction with the help of the eponymous Verotchka, only to be tempted back to his old lifestyle by Maroussia, who refuses to dry out and who, in the novel's closing lines, lies collapsed in a Russian night club in Paris after an overdose. Kessel's Hélène manages to leave her dissolute lifestyle behind—she gives up her profession as a nightclub dancer and glorified prostitute, recovers from her alcoholism and departs with Chouraloff for a new life in Africa. Both stories depend for their décor on depictions of Russian émigré nightlife in Paris, and for their plot on excessive Russian sexual passion and jealousy. In each case, the interest of the narrative is derived from complicated sexual intrigues between the various characters. The dominant Russian male is a stock character of these novels: Carco's Gourdourov and Kessel's Fédor Achkeliani are socially and sexually powerful men who use fear to control the lives of other members of the group. Némirovsky's Max Safranov (*Le Vin de solitude*) and Génia Nikitof ('L'Ennemie') are also examples of this character type. The Russian woman is these novels is beautiful, passionate, sexually uninhibited, and well able to manipulate men sexually and economically: Verotchka, Maroussia, and Hélène all correspond to this type, from which Némirovsky's Hélène (*Le Vin de solitude*) is also derived.

Verotchka l'étrangère and *Nuits de princes* rely on an opposition between the Russian lifestyle as disordered and unstructured and the French lifestyle as disciplined and controlled. This is frequently exemplified by Russian entertainment: Carco describes Russian dancing as 'toute en sauts et en tourbillons d'un caractère désordonné' (*full of disordered jumps and twists*), and Kessel evokes 'le souffle barbare, désespéré et parfois sublime que la Russie sans limites et sans formes a déposé dans ses chants' (*the barbarous whispering, desperate, and sometimes sublime, which limitless and formless Russia has deposited in her songs*).[130] However, this opposition is deliberately compromised by the fact that it is precisely *in Paris*—Paris, city of pleasure[131]—that Russian émigrés are able to pursue their dissipated lifestyle. The reader is thus invited to reflect on the fact that the Paris of the *années folles* is itself sufficiently decadent as to support this type of ('foreign') existence. The cultural and sexual exoticism of these novels is titillating in itself, but part of their thrill derives from the way they dramatise the scandal of the existence of such debauchery *in Paris*. Their aim is not seriously to investigate the psychological, cultural, or economic effects of emigration, but to perpetuate an exoticised and eroticised image of Russians in Paris. To this end, Carco and Kessel both provide their French readers with a predominantly external view of Russians. Carco's novel is focalised throughout via a French first person narrator. Kessel focalises the first chapter of his narrative through the perspective of Mlle Mesureux, the French proprietress of the *pension* where the émigrés live. In both texts, Russians and their habits are depicted *en bloc* and from the perspective of the French characters with whom they interact. Unlike Carco, Kessel does also offer internal presentation of Russian characters as the novel progresses, however, given the focus of the plot on the twists and turns of excessive and violent passionate relationships, there is little room for subtle psychological analysis. Neither do these texts aim to present a realistic or nuanced picture of Russian politics. Their political perspective is resolutely and simplistically anti-Bolshevik: the émigrés, and indeed Russia itself, are presented as victims of an incomprehensible and violent uprising which is in the process of destroying the country.

The characters, situations, and locations which Némirovsky brings to life in her Russian novels are very clearly derived from the 'rules' of the genre established by novels such as Carco's and Kessel's. The political perspective is the same, the same character types recur, and, in *Le Vin de solitude*, the plot revolves around violent and passionate sexual intrigue (especially in Part IV, which recounts the Karols' new life in Paris). However, Némirovsky's portraits of émigrés are primarily internal: she makes the departure from Russia into a crucial and substantial part of the plot (both Carco's and Kessel's novels begin when the characters are already established in Paris) and focalises the narrative mostly through the Russian émigrés themselves. When she shifts the focalisation to dramatise a French perspective on the émigrés, it is to make that perspective the focus of her irony, as we have seen. She therefore achieves some critical distance in relation to the 'mode russe' which is not a feature of Carco's novel and which is underplayed—though occasionally present—in Kessel's. Kessel's novel, written after Carco's, demonstrates a degree of critical awareness of the functioning of the 'mode russe' in contemporary Parisian culture. French clients are attracted to Russian bars because there, they can taste the distress of an entire nation and glimpse the soul of the suffering Russians.[132] Also, the character of Stéphane Morski, a writer, is an interesting insertion of the 'Paris note' aesthetics of the exile writers into a text which is a clear example of the 'mode russe'. Kessel, who had published a substantial essay on 'La nouvelle littérature russe' in *La Revue de Paris* in 1925, was fully aware of the literary complexities created by the revolution and the phenomenon of exile. The stories collected in *La Steppe rouge* (1923) present a very different discourse on Russianness. However, there is more variety of theme and a greater degree of narrative sophistication in Némirovsky's emigration novels than is to be found in either *Nuits de princes* or *Vérotchka l'étrangère*. As we have seen, *Les Mouches d'automne* is an atmospheric investigation of the related themes of place and time; it is a concise and effective study of the relationship between memory and identity which shows how the relationship between nostalgia and the construction of the self varies according to age or generation. *Le Vin de solitude*, a much longer text, supports a diverse range of themes relating both to personal identity and to the contemporary socio-political environment. It investigates childhood, ageing, mother–daughter relationships, and sexual awakening; it dismantles the myth of the 'happy bourgeois family' and constructs a convincing female *Bildung*. It dramatises the social divisions which characterise both Russian and French society, considers the idea of emigration in the opposite direction, via its portrait of Mademoiselle Rose, Hélène's French governess, and portrays the world of business and financial speculation in Russia, France, and beyond. This novel is a depiction of 'le royaume du trompe-l'œil' (*the kingdom of illusions*).[133] One of its central preoccupations—and indeed one of the key themes of Némirovsky's *œuvre* as a whole—is the human need to live through illusions: 'Car l'homme, pour vivre, a besoin d'un minimum d'air respirable, d'une certaine dose d'oxygène et d'illusion' (*For man, in order to live, needs a minimum amount of air he can breathe, a certain dose of oxygen and illusion*).[134] Némirovsky's emigration narratives are more than just melodramatic, exoticised page turners—though they are this too. They also include passages of some narrative sophistication. The scene in which Boris Karol announces to his wife that he has lost his job is a careful and effective interweaving of different narrative perspectives. Hélène witnesses the scene through her child's perspective such that the reader hears Hélène hearing the quarrel, rather than having direct access to the scene. Hélène uses her game of soldiers to mask the quarrel, so that she is both in the apartment and also, in her imagination, on the battlefield at Wagram. She is so involved in her game that she barely recognises the reflection of the child she sees in the mirror. Different elements of the scene collide: the words spoken by Mademoiselle Rose (to Hélène) and by Boris and Bella (to each other) are juxtaposed with the imaginary dialogues of Hélène's game and her thoughts about parents' behaviour, such that the narration of the scene resembles a mosaic or a kaleidoscope.[135] In *Les Mouches d'automne*, Némirovsky makes extensive use of Flaubertian *style indirect libre* to convey the opinions and feelings of her characters. Flaubert appears to be a significant point of reference in *Les Mouches d'automne*. One reviewer compared Tatiana to Flaubert's Félicité of *Un Cœur simple*.[136] Némirovsky invited the comparison by describing the woman on whom the portrait of Tatiana was based as 'une femme au cœur simple' (*a woman with a simple heart*)[137] and by calling the Karines' daughter Loulou, the name of Félicité's parrot. There are various passing references to works of French and classical literature in *Le Vin de solitude*. Hélène's grandfather teaches her to recite Hugo and reads Chateaubriand to her.[138] Bella is both Medusa and Medea.[139] One of the guests at Mme Manassé's house looks like the oracle at Delphi.[140] As we noted in Chapter 2, this sort of literary allusion is common in Némirovsky's fiction. Her engagement with the 'mode russe' is a more developed version of this playful type of intertextuality. It suggests that Némirovsky's fiction can be approached as a well-informed literary game.

Némirovsky's presentation of Russia in her emigration narratives and elsewhere in her *œuvre* is the result of a carefully controlled affirmation of cultural difference. Because her ultimate goal was assimilation, Némirovsky's writing left the notion of French cultural superiority largely intact and did not challenge the myth of French cultural prestige. She negotiated the contemporary interest in Russian culture and identity in the French literary field with some skill, producing texts which were recognisable to readers in terms of the literary discourses established in the 1920s, but which were not entirely bound by those discourses. Some reviewers responded positively to Némirovsky's ability to domesticate Russia's potentially disruptive foreignness. Jeanine Delpech concluded that her work showed '[u]n tempérament, une appréhension du monde et des êtres bien slaves' (*a temperament and an understanding of the world and of people which are very Slav*) as well as 'une clarté et un sens de la composition bien français' (*a clarity and a sense of composition which are very French*). According to Delpech, 'ce mariage d'inclination permet à cette Russe de nous donner des œuvres qui nous passionnent sans trop nous déconcerter' (*this marriage of inclination allows this Russian to give us works which delight us without disturbing us too much*). There is no doubt some irony in Delpech's 'sans trop nous déconcerter', but it is directed as much at French readers as it is at Némirovsky. Némirovsky's works were sufficiently exotic to be interesting, but not so unfamiliar as to be inaccessible. Her domestication of Russian cultural difference occasionally attracted a hostile response. When J. Ernest-Charles discussed Némirovsky's portrait of Russians in *L'Affaire Courilof*, he described Léon M . . . dismissively as 'un révolutionnaire atténué pour salons d'Occident' (*a revolutionary watered down for Western sitting rooms*).[141] However Némirovsky's portraits of Russia and of Russians are judged, her fiction must be seen as an active engagement with, and not a simple reproduction of, the 'mode russe'.

4   A Jewish Soul

J'avais raison de refuser l'essentialisme. Je savais déjà à quels abus
entraînent des notions tels que l'âme slave, le caractère juif, la mentalité primitive, l'éternel féminin. Mais l'universalisme auquel je me ral-
liais m'emportait loin de la réalité. Ce qui me manquait, c'était l'idée
de 'situation' qui seule permet de définir concrètement des ensembles
humains sans les asservir à une fatalité intemporelle.[1]

*I was right to reject essentialism; I knew already what abuses could
follow in the train of abstract concepts such as the 'Slav soul', the
'Jewish character', 'primitive mentality', or das ewige Weib. But the
universalist notions to which I turned bore me equally far from reality. What I lacked was the idea of 'situation', which alone allows one
to make some concrete definition of human groups without enslav-
ing them to a timeless and deterministic pattern.*[2]

So wrote Simone de Beauvoir in *La Force de l'âge* (1960), the second volume of her autobiography. This quotation encapsulates some of the challenges posed by the question of Jewishness in Némirovsky's work. Whilst
various methodologies might be employed to approach this aspect of her
œuvre, the avoidance of essentialism is, as de Beauvoir claims, absolutely
crucial. Here, describing an intellectual dilemma she was facing in 1934,
de Beauvoir gives an account of her own search for an anti-essentialist
methodology which would also avoid the abstraction of French universalism. Her answer was, of course, the existentialist notion of 'situation',
which Jean-Paul Sartre would employ in order to approach the 'Jewish
question' in his *Réflexions sur la question juive*, in the aftermath of the
Second World War.[3] De Beauvoir's remarks demonstrate Némirovky's
interpretive vulnerability. She was, and is, constantly at risk of being
subsumed into precisely the essentialised categories de Beauvoir cites as
examples: the Slav soul; the Jewish character; the eternal feminine. There
is no doubt that some aspects of Némirovsky's fiction invite such reductive
readings, as we saw in Chapter 3. However, as the various manifestations
of the 'Russian soul' in her work demonstrate, she was able to manipulate
such discourses of identity without falling into a naïve reproduction of
essentialised categories. This is important because, as de Beauvoir says,
essentialism leads to abuses which are very real.

THE UNIVERSAL AND THE PARTICULAR

As Arlette Elkaïm-Sartre points out in her preface to *Réflexions sur la question juive*, Sartre could not, and did not attempt to ascribe specific 'content' to Jewish authenticity.[4] Némirovsky embarked upon a more problematic venture: to give substance to fictional Jewish characters in the mode of popular, accessible, and entertaining literature directed at a French audience whose frame of reference in relation to Jewishness inevitably included the sorts of anti-Semitic stereotypes cemented in the public consciousness by texts like Drumont's *La France juive* (1886). We are faced with a different dilemma: how can we, in the twenty-first century, after Auschwitz, read the results of her efforts? It is important to bear in mind that, unlike some other French-Jewish writers of the period, Némirovsky's prime motivation for writing was not to investigate Jewish identity, but rather, as should by now be clear, to select and fictionalise aspects of her own experience which would resonate with contemporary readers in order to construct herself as a successful and respected French writer of literary fiction. To approach the sensitive and politically charged question of Jewishness in Némirovsky's fiction, a methodology which respects this motivation is required. Némirovsky must not be reproached for failing to accomplish something she never set out to achieve.

There is no doubt that Némirovsky's representation of Jewishness presents something of a methodological challenge. We saw in Chapter 1 that after the publication of *Suite française*, and once certain biographical details as regards Némirovsky's close association with right-wing intellectuals and journals began to be discussed, accusations and counteraccusations of anti-Semitism emerged. We saw that, whilst modern readers have found it difficult to reconcile Némirovsky's choice to publish in organs such as *Gringoire* and *Candide* with her own Jewish identity and with her persecution by the Vichy regime, these choices are explicable in terms of the dynamics of the literary field in which Némirovsky and her texts were operating. In this chapter, we shall again be concerned with these issues, but at a more closely textual level. Why did a Jewish writer choose to portray Jewish characters in terms of the sorts of stereotypes which were highly characteristic of contemporary right-wing anti-Semitic discourses? Why are Némirovsky's Jewish characters predominantly negative and unattractive? How close does she come to producing a racial account of 'Jewishness' which could be interpreted as dangerous essentialism? How can we approach and evaluate the work of a writer who apparently reproduced precisely the sort of fictional discourse which according to some theorists—notably Michaël Prazan—legitimised an ideological and political anti-Semitism and thus led directly to the Nazi genocide? These questions appear at first to be unanswerable, to place us before a set of paradoxes which seem to suggest, as Neil Levi and Michael Rothberg put it, that the Holocaust is 'a series of events [. . .] that seems to defy all attempts at comprehension'.[5] But as the vast, diverse, and productive range of research in the field of Holocaust studies shows, ways of understanding can and must be found: we cannot simply affirm that Némirovsky has been rendered incomprehensible by the Shoah.

In 1934, de Beauvoir was struggling with the relationship between universalism and particular human identities. In 1946, Sartre argued that the apparently pro-Jewish democrat ultimately sought to destroy the Jew *qua* Jew in order to preserve him as 'le sujet abstrait et universel des droits de l'homme et du citoyen' (*'the abstract and universal subject of the rights of man and the rights of the citizen'*).[6] Issues of ethics and justice posed by the Holocaust have been addressed in terms of the value of universalism:

> Are the death camps the culmination of this tradition, a sort of fulfilment of the Enlightenment dream of universal reason in which the desire for universality demands the elimination of all that is not identical with this universal model, as Horkheimer and Adorno claim? Or do the camps rather, as Jürgen Habermas and others have argued, signify precisely the *failure* to properly understand and implement the Enlightenment project? [emphasis in original][7]

The problem of the relationship between the universal and the particular is at the heart of the dilemma posed for modern readers by Némirovsky's representations of Jewishness. The dominant line of argument now views the Nazi death camps, after Horkheimer and Adorno, as 'the rage of homogeneity at difference'[8] and thus seeks, from an ethical perspective, to value difference positively. Némirovsky had not resolved—or rather, did not see any pressing need to resolve—the tension between French universalism and Jewish (or indeed Russian, or female) particularity in her work: she believed that a French-Russian-Jewish novelist was a possible identity. As Jonathan Weiss concludes, she died without having resolved the ambiguity of her triple allegiance.[9] Neither did she see any need to represent difference positively. As modern readers however, we tend to want to resolve this tension and to find positive representations of difference. When we do not find them, it is all too easy to slip into a discourse of blame. Why did Némirovsky risk using stereotypes when she must have been aware of the nefarious political uses to which they were increasingly being put? Why did she risk a definition of Jewish identity in terms of heredity and the body, which could be interpreted in racial terms? Here we must be careful to avoid what Michael André Bernstein terms *backshadowing*, which results from a tendency to see the Holocaust as both unimaginable and inevitable:

> Backshadowing is a kind of retroactive foreshadowing in which the shared knowledge of the outcome of a series of events by narrator and listener is used to judge the participants in those events *as though they too should have known what was to come*. Thus, our knowledge of the Shoah is used to condemn the 'blindness' and 'self-deception' of Austro-German Jewry for their unwillingness to save themselves from a doom that supposedly was clear to see. [emphasis in original][10]

In the case of France, historians have clearly demonstrated firstly, that the French population, Jewish and non-Jewish, was unaware of the precise significance of the deportations, and secondly, that Jews in France had no means of imagining that the nation within which they were integrated could expel them on the basis of their Jewishness:

> The accounts written before the return of the survivors by those not deported show the latter to be unaware of the exact process and scale of extermination [. . .] Darville and Wichené, themselves imprisoned at Drancy, and so interested in the Jewish tragedy as to write one of the very first works on the subject, were unaware, even after Paris had already been liberated, of the fate of those who had not yet returned and who for the most part never would return. What then can be expected from the majority of French society?
>
> [. . .]
>
> For the Jews of France, whether French for generations or immigrants, it was difficult and perhaps impossible to acknowledge that the French model of emancipation and integration, born of the Revolution and barely compromised by the Dreyfus affair, could have been rendered null and void by the Vichy government. They did not understand that they could be expelled de facto from the French nation, that their French citizenship meant nothing to the occupying forces, that they had become merely Jews to annihilate.[11]

Bernstein's argument tempers any suggestion that might be made following the sort of approach proposed by Michaël Prazan about *écriture génocidaire*, that Némirovsky *should not* have produced anti-Semitic stereotypes in her fiction because such writing paved the way for the Holocaust. It also sounds a note of caution in relation to the type of reading which might see Némirovsky's representations of Jewish otherness as an example of what Bryan Cheyette has termed *semitic* discourse, that is, textual representations, either positive or negative, which construct Jews ambivalently in terms of a fundamental difference and which for Cheyette, are therefore implicated in the Holocaust.[12] If we see the Holocaust as 'the rage of homogeneity at difference' then indeed, we can posit a causal relationship between 'semitic' discourse and genocide. However, this is obviously not a reason to berate Jewish writers of the early twentieth century for investigating what might constitute Jewish identity in their own time, even if they sometimes did so in terms which post-Holocaust readers find problematic. This is not to deny the possibility that anti-Semites may indeed have found support for their arguments in Némirovsky's writing. But this is a problem of reception and not of production: as Sartre says, it is of course anti-Semitism, not Jewishness that is at issue:

> Or, nous l'avons montré, il ne saurait être question d'agir sur le Juif. Le problème juif est né de l'antisémitisme; donc c'est l'antisémitisme qu'il faut supprimer pour le résoudre.[13]

As we have shown, it cannot be a matter of acting on the Jew. The Jewish problem is born of anti-Semitism; thus it is anti-Semitism that we must suppress in order to resolve the problem.[14]

We cannot but read with hindsight because we know how events unfolded; we can however, as Bernstein recommends, show 'respect for people living at a time *before* that unfolding was complete who could not, and should not, be expected to have any knowledge of the future'.[15]

In this context, Boudieu's sociology of literature has two major advantages. Firstly, it avoids the historical determinism against which Bernstein warns, allowing the reader to understand both how things were and how things might have been. Bourdieu's notion of habitus points to the analysis of 'les systèmes de dispositions qui, étant le produit d'une trajectoire sociale et d'une position à l'intérieur du champ littéraire (etc.), trouvent dans cette position une occasion plus ou moins favorable de s'actualiser' ('*the systems of dispositions which, being being the product of a social trajectory and of a position within the literary (etc.) field, find in this position a more or less favourable opportunity to be realized*'):[16] the sociology of literature proposes relationships between *dispositions* and *possibilities* as the focus of analysis. Secondly, as we saw in Chapter 3, Bourdieu conceives of the literary field in terms of a range of possibilities which result from previous struggles for legitimacy in that field: the sociology of literature provides a way of discerning which literary choices were and were not possible for an author at a given moment occupying a certain position in the field. As we saw in Chapter 1 in relation to Némirovsky's decision to publish in *Gringoire* and *Candide*, this approach shifts the debate from the moral to the literary plane, and facilitates a more balanced assessment of choices made in a literary-political context very different from that in which the textual results of those choices are received in our own time. It also points to a consideration of the interplay of discourses rather than to a description of identity. Consonant with the approach taken to the Russian theme in Némirovsky's writing in Chapter 3, the present chapter does not seek to discover the nature of Némirovsky's Jewish identity, but rather to analyse the functioning of discourses around Jewishness in her work in relation to the contemporary literary field.

THE 'MODE JUIVE'

Although there is comparatively little biographical evidence, outside of her novels, as regards what Némirovsky actually thought about her Jewish identity and Jewish culture, various factors allow us to identify her Jewish identity sociologically, in relation to the Parisian Jewish communities of the 1930s. Both Némirovsky and her husband Michael Epstein were Russian émigrés from Jewish families who had arrived in Paris after the Russian revolution, Némirovsky in 1919 and Epstein in 1920. They thus were part of the third wave of emigration: Paris had already experienced Jewish Russian immigration in the 1880s and 1890s, and again after 1905.[17] However, Némirovsky's family sought to integrate themselves from the outset within the native community of French Jews and did not identify themselves with the immigrant community of Eastern European, Yiddish-speaking Jews. Already fluent speakers of French, they were members of the professional, affluent, cultured bourgeoisie. They lived in the sixteenth arrondissement (first at 115, rue de la Pompe and later at 18, avenue du Président Wilson), an area to which affluent French Jews had migrated before the First World War.[18] Both Michael Epstein and Némirovsky's father worked in banking at a time when 75% of Jewish bankers in Paris were native French Jews.[19] Neither Némirovsky nor Epstein was a practising Jew in a religious sense. Although their marriage in 1926 was celebrated in a synagogue, this was more out of respect for Michael's family's wishes than out of any sense of religious observance on the part of the couple.[20] It is however perhaps significant that the marriage was celebrated in a non-consistorial synagogue, for most French Jews who sought to maintain a sense of their Jewish identity were involved with the Paris Consistoire, the quasi-official organ of the French Jewry, whilst immigrant Jews would be more likely to practise their religion in synagogues and organisations not affiliated to the Consistoire.[21] David Weinberg's research on Jews in Paris in the 1930s reveals the difference—and indeed hostility—between the immigrant Jewish community and the native Parisian Jewish community. They lived in different areas of the city and were divided economically, linguistically, and spiritually: the immigrant community was largely working class or artisan, maintained the use of Yiddish and was more religiously observant. French Jews, who believed in the compatibility of French post-Revolution ideals of equality with Jewish belief and identity, generally viewed the immigrant community as backward looking and old fashioned, whilst immigrant Jews were appalled by the assimilation of the native French Jewish population.[22] The complex nature of Némirovsky's Jewish identity derives from her ambivalent position in relation to the sharply dichotomised Jewish communities in Paris. Politically, socially, economically, and intellectually, Némirovsky was closely aligned with the native French secular Jewish community, and had little in common with the immigrant community. However, she was, and remained, a stateless immigrant, and as such, could not hope to achieve total identification with the French Jewish community. Némirovsky's complex national, cultural, and ethnic identifications support Nadia Malinovich's argument that whilst tensions clearly existed between 'native' and 'immigrant' Jews, a certain group of middle-class, French-speaking immigrants transgressed this opposition.[23] Némirovsky's Russian identity further complicated her Jewish identity, since it was generally recognised that anti-Semitism was a feature of the Russian exile community.[24] Joseph Kessel represents precisely this in his depiction of Fédor Achkeliani's anti-Semitism in *Nuits de princes*, and Némirovsky makes passing reference to it in *Le Vin de solitude* where the narrator remarks that as emigrants in Finland, Jews and Russians, the two irreconcilable races, are forced by circumstances to cohabit and cooperate.[25] It is this complexity which, largely unresolved, is inscribed in Némirovsky's fiction.

In published interviews, the only obvious reference to an interest in Jewish culture on Némirovsky's part is her high praise for the work of the Tharaud brothers.[26] This may seem strange to modern readers for whom the works of Jean and Jérôme Tharaud appear at best ambivalent and at worst obviously racist. However, their works were very widely read in the 1920s and 1930s and were not necessarily received in this way. The Tharaud brothers were the authors of a large number of commercially successful works on the lives and customs of Eastern European Jews. These were works of fiction, history, and journalism, based on the authors' travels, which presented Judaism and Jewishness to their French audience through exotic and picturesque narratives. Whilst modern critics draw attention to an underlying seam of racist anti-Semitism, their texts were received positively by their Jewish and non-Jewish contemporaries as sympathetic, philosemitic works, at least in the 1920s.[27] Némirovsky's enthusiasm for the work of the Tharaud brothers is perfectly understandable in its historical context: she might plausibly have appreciated their widely acknowledged talent as creators of convincing and engaging narratives, as well as recognising that their popularity indicated a receptivity on the part of French readers to the Jewish and Oriental themes which were also a feature of her own writing. It is also important to note that it is only in the interviews she gave in early 1930, in the wake of the success of *David Golder*, that Némirovsky referred positively to the Tharaud brothers; she did not evoke them in the more obviously problematic political context of the mid to late 1930s. It was the publication of *Quand Israël n'est plus roi* by the Tharaud brothers in 1933, which expressed support for Nazism, which made their ambivalent attitude to Jews clear. Némirovsky's personal notes do not indicate any familiarity with or interest in other contemporary French Jewish writers. The only exception is André Maurois, but her interest was not in his Jewishness but in his study of Turgenev, as we saw in Chapter 3. The comparison here with Némirovsky's deep knowledge of Russian literature is striking: she was steeped in Russian culture through her education and through her reading, and actively sought inspiration from Russian models in order to develop her own literary practice.

Nonetheless, it is certainly not the case that Némirovsky wanted to deny or to hide her Jewish identity. Her most extensive public discussions of the question are to be found in two interviews she gave to *L'Univers israélite*, a monthly conservative religious and literary journal, one of the central press organs of French Jews in the inter-war period, and widely seen as a barometer of mainstream Jewish opinion.[28] Interviewed by Nina Gourfinkel in 1930, Némirovsky proclaimed: 'Et on me taxe d'antisémitisme? Voyons, c'est absurde! Puisque je suis juive moi-même et le dis à qui veut l'entendre!' (*People are calling me anti-Semitic? Come on, that's absurd! Since I am Jewish myself and I tell anyone who cares to listen).*[29] In 1935, she expressed herself even more clearly on the topic. Janine Auscher reported their conversation:

> Il me semble, reprend-elle soudain grave, que je n'ai jamais songé à dissimuler mes origines, bien au contraire. Chaque fois que j'en ai eu l'occasion, poursuit-elle en s'animant, j'ai clamé que j'étais [sic] juive, je l'ai même proclamé! Je suis beacoup trop fière de l'être pour avoir jamais songé à le renier.[30]

> *'It seems to me', she goes on, suddenly more serious, 'that I have never tried to conceal my origins, quite the opposite. Whenever I have had the opportunity,' she continues more animatedly, 'I have affirmed that I am Jewish, I have even proclaimed it! I am much too proud to be Jewish to have ever thought of denying it'.*

Philipponnat and Lienhardt acknowledge that Némirovksy made such statements rarely, but with vehemence, and suggest that she was averse both to the denial and to the assertion of her Jewish identity: she was very resistant to the idea that she should have to justify herself. She readily acknowledged her Jewish and Russian identities, but wanted to see herself first and foremost as a French novelist. However, by 1935, the external political situation was beginning to require these sorts of justifications.[31]

The 1920s were the decade of a Jewish vogue in the French literary field, as both Jewish and non-Jewish writers turned to an investigation of Jewish identity in their work.[32] The writers involved in this intellectual and artistic current used the terms *mode juive*, *renaissance juive*, or *réveil juif* to describe and to stimulate this phenomenon. In the context of a new conceptualisation of French national identity in the years before and after the First World War which sought to integrate rather than to erase particularisms within the concept of the nation, the relationships between 'Frenchness' and other potential personal identities was a significant focus of intellectual attention. The idea of a 'mode juive' differs considerably from the 'mode russe' discussed in Chapter 3. The 'mode russe' was a fashion and a stereotype, and provided a stark contrast to the more serious literary activities of the Russian émigré writers. The 'mode juive' encompassed a wide range of cultural and political activities associated with the Jewish renaissance of the early twentieth century. Leading French Jewish intellectuals such as Edmond Fleg, André Spire, Armand Lunel, and Albert Cohen elaborated their ideas about a new Jewish consciousness through their activities in the domains of journalism and publishing as well as through their novels and poetry.[33] Fleg published his *Anthologie juive* in 1923, a novel entitled *L'Enfant prophète* in 1926, and a defence of Judaism, *Pourquoi je suis juif*, in 1928. In 1919, Spire, who would become one of the leading figures of French Zionism, brought out a new edition of his *Poèmes juifs*, which had first appeared in 1908, and in 1928 published a two-volume work entitled *Quelques juifs et demi-juifs*. Cohen's *Solal* (1930) is perhaps one of the best-known inter-war works by a French Jewish writer, not least because of his later success, the vast and complex novel *Belle du seigneur* (1968). Cohen founded the short-lived *Revue juive* in 1925 with Gallimard, and collaborated with Josué Jehouda's better-established *Revue juive de Genève*. He published his second novel, *Mangeclous*, in 1938. Lunel was a Provençal writer; his modern folkloric tale *Nicolo Peccavi ou l'affaire Dreyfus à Carpentras* won the first Renaudot prize in 1926. Other important figures of the Jewish renaissance include the communist writer Jean-Richard Bloch, whose . . . *Et Cie*, a novel about a nineteenth-century French Jewish family which first appeared in 1917, was published by the *NRF* in its definitive version in 1925, and Bernard Lecache, whose novel *Jacob* was published with Gallimard in 1926. Lecache is better known for founding the Ligue internationale contre l'antisémitisme (LICA) in 1928. Other Jewish women writers also gained some prominence in the period. Elissa Rhaïss published several novels about Algerian Jews in the 1920s and early 1930s,[34] and Myriam Harry produced a significant number of novels and works of reportage, from the turn of the century and throughout the inter-war period and beyond, including the 'Siona' series (1914–1927).[35] Sarah Lévy's *O mon goye!* (1929), about a marriage between a Catholic nobleman a Jewish woman from a family of rich financiers, and *Ma chère France!* (1930) were best-sellers which posed similar problems to *David Golder* as regards the presence of potentially anti-Semitic stereotypes.[36] Non-Jewish writers also interested themselves in the 'Jewish question', notably Jacques de Lacretelle in his *Silbermann* (1922), which was received as philosemitic work, and its sequel, *Le Retour de Silbermann* (1929).[37]

Whilst these works are relevant to the reception of Némirovsky's novels, as we shall see, the textual production associated with the 'mode juive' was being carried out in a different section of the literary field to that which Némirovsky occupied. Just as the textual production resulting from the interest in Russian culture in the literary field can be located along the axis *champ de grande production / champ de production restreinte*, so literary evocations of Jewishness occurred both in the domain of popular culture and in the more intellectualised sector of the literary field. This becomes clear if one considers the publishing houses involved in disseminating the key texts of the 'mode juive'. The novels of Edmond Fleg, Albert Cohen, Armand Lunel, Jean-Richard Bloch, and Jacques de Lacretelle were all published by the *NRF*/Gallimard. The collection Fleg directed, entitled 'Judaïsme', was published by Rieder, a leftist and internationally focused publishing house which, like Gallimard, was keen to promote new, modern writing and hosted significant collections of fiction designated as 'romans juifs'.[38] Catherine Fhima notes the close relationship between the *NRF*/Gallimard and the Jewish literary renaissance, and points out that the movement had its roots in the literary avant-garde of the pre-war years.[39]

The esoteric genre of poetry and the intellectualised genre of the essay are strongly represented in the work of these writers. Furthermore, the French Jewish intellectuals were characterised by strong political and religious engagements: Spire's Zionism and Fleg's spiritual devotion to Judaism were far removed from Némirovsky's experience. The 'mode juive' was a feature of the *champ de production restreinte* rather than of the *champ de grande production*. From the perspective of the structure of the literary field and her own position within it, Némirovsky's enthusiasm for the work of the Tharaud brothers and her apparent lack of engagement with the 'renaissance juive' are therefore logical. The Tharaud brothers were published by Plon, a traditionalist publishing house founded in the nineteenth century and impervious to modern, avant-garde literary production;[40] like Némirovsky, they were closely associated with the conservative *Revue des deux mondes*, which serialised several of their works. Némirovsky's positive comments about the Tharaud brothers are consistent with their similar positions within the literary field. Several critics picked up on the connection immediately: Franc-Nohain's remark in *Echo de Paris* in January 1930 that one couldn't help calling the Tharaud brothers to mind is typical.[41] By contrast, there is no evidence to suggest that Némirovsky perceived any community of interest between her literary project and that of Spire, Lunel, Fleg, or Cohen, and critics did not make such a connection.

Nonetheless, Armand Lunel, writing in the 1970s, identified Némirovsky, along with Fleg, Cohen, Bloch, and himself, as one of the most representative novelists of the 'mode juive', citing her 'unforgettable' *David Golder*.[42] However, post-war critics have had some difficulty in locating Némirovsky in relation to the 'mode juive'. Chanan Lehrmann mentions her briefly in his 1961 survey of the Jewish theme in French literature, but only in a footnote which occurs in a chapter primarily devoted to non-Jewish writers. He does not discuss her work in his chapter on French language Jewish literature, where he deals with Spire, Fleg, and Cohen.[43] In his 1960 survey *Ecrivains juifs de langue française*, Raph Feigelson notes only that '[s]ur le theme du riche juif solitaire, *David Golder*, Irène Nimerowski [sic], avec un ton d'amertume et d'orgueil, rapporte certains aspects de la frustration juive' (*on the theme of the rich and lonely Jew, Irène Nimerowski's [sic] David Golder gives an account of certain aspects of Jewish frustration, in a bitter and proud tone*).[44] Nadia Malinovich locates *David Golder* within a cluster of novels by Jewish writers which criticise Jewish materialism and social *arrivisme*.[45] Elsewhere, retrospective assessments of Némirovsky which treat her specifically as a Jewish writer have been less neutral. In his *Histoire de l'antisémitisme* (1977), Léon Poliakov accuses her (alongside Gide and Lacretelle) of a virulent but surreptitious anti-Semitism. Nonetheless, he acknowledges her talent and says that her portrait of Judeo-Russian financial milieux is not without accuracy.[46] Poliakov argues that these writers contributed to the cultivation and promulgation of timeless, essentialised myths of Jewish difference. In an article on Némirovsky and Sarah Lévy,

Alan Astro avoids both Feigelson's neutrality and Poliakov's condemnatory tone by refusing to conflate textual representations with an assertion of authorial or narratorial opinion. He remarks carefully that 'the novel is as full of symptoms of feminist misogyny as it is of Jewish anti-Semitism' and notes that there are 'many anti-Semitic moments' in Némirovsky's novel, but also shows that anti-Semitism is the focus of irony in the text. And whilst Astro suggests that a naïve form of Jewish self-hatred is represented in the text, he does not go as far as to say that this is a characteristic that should be ascribed to the author.[47] Norman David Thau by contrast affirms—albeit in a footnote—that Némirovsky could certainly be seen as a case of Jewish self-hatred.[48] Myriam Anissimov is similarly categorical in her preface to the original French edition of *Suite française*, as we saw in Chapter 1: she interprets the cruel and pejorative portraits of Jewish characters in Némirovsky's *œuvre*, and the use of certain physical stereotypes common in anti-Semitic discourse of the period, in terms of Jewish self-hatred.[49] Jonathan Weiss makes specific reference to Sander Gilman's *Jewish Self-hatred* (1986) in the conclusion to his biography, but not necessarily in order to suggest that Némirovsky was anti-Semitic.[50] Rather, Weiss is seeking to suggest the complexity of her relationships to Jewishness:

> Dès lors, nous sommes en présence d'un exemple de la théorie de l' 'antijudaïsme juif' avancé par Sander Gilman dans son étude du domaine littéraire allemand. Rappelons que, pour Gilman, l'antijudaïsme juif est le résultat de l'intériorisation chez un écrivain juif de son image négative dans la société et sa projection sur une œuvre littéraire. Il en résulte, chez Irène Némirovsky, une appropriation d'une certaine image stéréotypée du juif dans la société française; en intériorisant ces stéréotypes qui la révulsent, elle invente une autre image du juif imaginaire, du juif 'pur', dont les caractéristiques sont nécessairement aux antipodes du stéréotype.
>
> L'antijudaïsme d'Irène Némirovsky nous semble donc moins un effort pour renier ses origines qu'un désir de les réinventer.[51]

> *This brings us to the theory of 'Jewish self-hatred'[52] suggested by Sander Gilman in his study of the German literary world. Gilman suggests that Jewish anti-Semitism results from the internalization in the Jewish writer of the negative image of the Jew in society and its projection onto the literary work. The result in Némirovsky's novels and stories is the appropriation of a certain stereotypical image of the Jew in French society. While internalizing the stereotypes that repel her, Irène also creates another image of the imaginary Jew, one who is 'pure' and whose characteristics are consequently exactly opposite to the stereotype.*
>
> *The anti-Semitism of Irène Némirovsky seems thus less an effort to deny her origins than a desire to reinvent them.[53]*

What Weiss identifies here is an interiorisation and a re-projection of certain representations existing within the culture in which Némirovsky produced her texts; he does not say that Némirovsky was in agreement with such representations; on the contrary, he says that she was revolted by them. Olivier Philipponnat and Patrick Lienhardt by contrast reject the label 'self-hatred'—without any specific reference to Gilman or to Weiss— whilst making an argument that is in fact similar to Weiss's: Némirovsky's fiction 'présente l'image que lui renvoie une France couverte de miroirs déformants' (*presents the image which a France covered with deforming mirrors reflected back to her*).[54] Philipponnat and Lienhardt prefer the idea of a 'hatred of reflections of the self' to the term 'self-hatred'.[55] Their biography (which makes no reference to Weiss's work) practises extensive contextual recuperation in order to refute any suggestion of anti-Semitism. The authors locate the roots of Némirovsky's stereotypes in her literary antecedents, citing in particular Gogol and the Tharaud brothers, and in the contemporary literary discourses she sought to emulate;[56] they affirm that the images in question never convey anti-Semitic arguments, and that any ideological anti-Semitism in relation to Némirovsky's fiction was a function of reception rather than production.[57]

Martina Stemberger's extensive study of Némirovsky's representations of Jewishness is quite different in its approach. Stemberger remarks that she would like to be able to avoid deploying the concept of Jewish self-hatred, but nonetheless seems to find it unavoidable. She notes that the behaviour of most of Némirovsky's Jewish characters appears to illustrate precisely this psychological configuration, if somewhat schematically and superficially, particularly regarding the depiction of the negative reaction of Western, assimilated Jews to Eastern, Yiddish-speaking immigrant Jews, which occurs frequently in Némirovsky's novels.[58] Stemberger's work is a detailed textual analysis of the motifs in Némirovsky's published fiction which construct the closely related themes of Jewishness, foreignness, and femaleness. In the first—and longest—section, Stemberger proposes to analyse the existence and function of concrete stereotypes and the narrative strategies via which Némirovsky's texts construct an uncanny (in the Freudian sense) Jewish identity.[59] Stemberger frames her analysis in terms of an inseparable link between anti-Semitism and matriphobia, suggesting that negative Jewish stereotypes generally function in Némirovsky's texts not to convey hatred for Jews in general, but rather to convey a different and specific hatred: most often, hatred for the bad mother.[60] She also makes the important point that, whilst the stereotypes Némirovsky employs are very recognisable features of the contemporary discursive environment, there are other anti-Semitic discursive practices which Némirovsky avoids, such as Manichean depictions of the 'bad Jew' versus the 'good non-Jew', or stereotypes based on religious anti-Semitism.[61] Stemberger then traces every imaginable motif associated with Jewishness across the range of Némirovsky's published texts. She argues that Némirovsky's representations of certain physical characteristics labelled as 'Jewish' construct the body as the site of the inevitable return of a suppressed Jewish identity.[62] Following Norman David Thau's main argument in *Romans de l'impossible identité. Etre juif en Europe occidentale (1918–1940)*, Stemberger asserts that in Némirovsky's fiction, the mixed identity of the foreign, immigrant Jew in Europe is an impossible identity, a non-identity. She concludes, as does Thau, that 'Jewishness' in Némirovsky's work is ultimately presented as uncanny, unimaginable, and impossible to define: it is an intangible combination of physicality, memory, and psychology, impossible either fully to assume or fully to reject.[63] Thau reads Némirovsky principally alongside Albert Cohen and Armand Lunel, and with some reference to Edmond Fleg and Bernard Lecache. His conclusion—that Némirovsky rejects her Jewish origins[64]—demonstrates the danger inherent in a methodology which conflates Némirovsky with the 'mode juive'. Writers such as Cohen, Lunel, Fleg, and Lecache committed their life's work to the exploration of Jewish identity through fictional and non-fictional texts and in the public sphere; Némirovsky did not. And so it is unsurprising that, in comparison, Némirovsky's work looks like a rejection of Jewishness. As I noted above, it is very important to avoid reproaching Némirovsky for not achieving something which was never her goal: Jewishness was certainly a crucial part of Némirovsky's literary identity, but it was by no means its only, nor even its central focus. The approach taken by Stemberger and Thau, whilst admirable and impressive in its detailed attention to textual features, risks occluding the contextual environment which conditioned Némirovsky's textual production to a significant extent. It also potentially exaggerates the significance of Némirovsky's own psychological relationship to Jewishness which, though clearly important, interesting, and complex, cannot ultimately be distilled in any straightforward way from her fictional works.

FROM CONTRADICTION TO COMPLEXITY

As we read Némirovsky's 'Jewish' texts in the twenty-first century, it is crucial to appreciate both the distance travelled, in terms of Némirovsky's writing practice, between her texts of the late 1920s and those of the late 1930s, and the contextual features—both literary and political—of her cultural environment, which had a significant effect on her approach to representing Jewishness in fiction. Both of these aspects are masked by the detailed textual and thematic approach of Stemberger and Thau. It is certainly true, as their works amply and convincingly demonstrate that certain significant motifs recur throughout Némirovsky's fiction in relation to her depiction of Jewish identity, but the thematic identification of these motifs does not always reveal particularly clearly the ways in which their meanings change significantly over time. It might indeed be the case that the recurrence of certain motifs in an author's work is indicative of a particular psychological relationship to an aspect of that author's identity. But in Némirovsky's case, it might also be a function of the fact that, particularly if one takes her short stories into account, she wrote a large number of works in a relatively short space of time, and thus drew repeatedly from a certain cultural repertoire of familiar images in order to construct her narratives. These two interpretations are not contradictory: the choice of images from a cultural repertoire is obviously also a function of individual psychology. But in approaching Némirovsky's representations of Jewishness chronologically, I want to emphasise the ways in which the questions raised by each text are significantly different.

Némirovksy's first detailed portrait of a Jewish character is in the mode of folklore. We saw in Chapter 2 how Némirovsky adopted and adapted the genre of the *conte* to tell the story of Ismaël Baruch in 'L'Enfant génial' (1927). The depiction of the Jewish ghetto in the port of Odessa in this story is exoticised and picturesque, and draws on images which are difficult for the modern reader to receive (and some of which were excised from the 1992 edition). We learn that 'les enfants naissaient dans le quartier juif comme pullule la vermine' (*children were born in the Jewish quarter like swarming vermin*) and that the Baruch family 'prospéraient comme les rats qui couraient sur la plage, autour des vieux bateaux' (*prospered like the rats which ran across the beach around the old boats*).[65] The physical descriptions of Ismaël's parents come straight from the type of discourse employed by the Tharaud brothers: his father 'portait encore le caftan usé, les babouches et les courtes mèches bouclées, appelées "peiss", de chaque côté du front' (*still wore the worn-out caftan, the slippers and the short curls, called 'peiss', on each side of his forehead*) and his mother wears 'une perruque noire, laineuse et frisée, qui lui donnait la vague apparence d'une négresse lavée par les neiges et les pluies du Nord' (*a black, woolly, curly wig, which made her look vaguely like a Negro woman washed by the Northern snow and rain*).[66] The description of the Jewish traders is in the same vein: they are 'vêtus de leurs houppelandes graisseuses, bavards, obséquiuex, qui sautillaient comme de vieux oiseaux, des échassiers déplumés, et qui comprenaient tout, connaissaient tout, vendaient de tout et achetaient davantage' (*dressed in their long greasy coats, talkative and obsequious, they hopped along like old birds, featherless waders. They understood everything, knew everything, sold everything and bought even more*).[67] Némirovsky is constructing the Eastern European Jew in terms already familiar to her readers when she likens Jews to vermin and evokes the Oriental caftan and coiffures and the sycophantic, omnipresent, and omniscient Jewish merchant. This is the extreme point of the stereotype of the Eastern European Jew, and it is obviously caricatural. It might plausibly be read as an attempt to engage the interest of readers already familiar with such representations thanks to Jean and Jérôme Tharaud. As we saw in Chapter 2, 'L'Enfant génial' might also be situated more generally in relation to the burgeoning interest

in folklore between the wars, which manifested itself in literary regional-
ism and in the academic study of folklore, and which had its counterpart
within the 'mode juive' in the form of an interest in Jewish folk tales.[68]
The positive reception of the work of the Tharaud brothers relied largely
on a reading of their exoticism as folkloric. The type of representations
of Eastern European Jews which the Tharaud brothers had popularised
provided both a possible source of inspiration and a potential readership
for a text such as 'L'Enfant génial'.

In the climate of optimism which surrounded the expression of Jewish
identity and Jewish difference in the 1920s, which was both a cause and
an effect of the Jewish renaissance and which was based on a perceived
decline in anti-Semitism in France after the First World War, Némirovsky,
in common with other French Jewish writers, did not necessarily need to
fear any negative repercussions in relation to ethnically based and caricatural depictions of Oriental Jews. In the 1920s, French Jews felt newly confident as regards their place in French society,[69] and therefore able to express
Jewish difference without calling their allegiance to France into question.[70]
After all, in 1917, the right-wing nationalist Maurice Barrès famously had
included Jews amongst the various 'spiritual families' whose particulari-
ties were henceforth to contribute to the greatness of the French nation.[71]
Insofar as 'L'Enfant génial' can be said to evoke the Barrèsian *déraciné*, an
issue we explored in Chapter 2, it could also be said to be in dialogue with
Les Familles spirituelles de la France (1917). If Ismaël calls into question
the inevitability of the downfall of the *déraciné*, Irène constructs her own
literary identity as a French-Jewish writer and a writer of Jewish stories on
the basis of the promise of an assimilation able to accommodate difference,
which the Maurice Barrès of 1917 seemed to be offering. In a climate not
only of tolerance but of active interest in all the varieties of Jewish culture
and traditions, why should Némirovsky have been concerned if her readers
conflated Irène with Ismaël?

Two years after the publication of 'L'Enfant génial', Némirovsky hit the
headlines with another Jewish story, *David Golder*. Its eponymous hero—
or anti-hero—shares with the characters of 'L'Enfant génial' his Russian
and Jewish origins and a textual existence as an easily recognisable stereotype. But David derives his identity from a different set of discourses: he is
not (only) the traditional, timeless, and foreign Oriental Jew; he is the modern Jewish financier pursuing his shady business interests in contemporary
France. He incarnates many of the conventional negative associations made
between Jews and money, and appears to provide an example of their applicability to the economic realities of 1920s France. Whereas Ismaël seemed
to inhabit the ahistorical and geographically distant realm of the fairy tale,
David moves in real time and real space. For this reason, the questions
posed by *David Golder* are more obviously contemporary, political, and
ethical, which goes a long way towards explaining its immediate success in
1929, and the difficulties it poses for modern readers.

In *David Golder*, Némirovsky draws on the usual physical attributes stereotypically associated with Jews: Mme Marcus has a 'maigre visage au grand nez dur, en forme de bec' (*'thin face with its large, beak-like nose'*) and Fischl is 'un petit juif gras, roux et rose, l'air comique, ignoble, un peu sinistre, avec ses yeux brillants d'intelligence' (*'Fat little Jew . . . he had a comical, vile and slightly sinister air as he stood in the doorway with his red hair, ruddy complexion, and bright, knowing eyes'*).[72] Athough he now appears to be a civilised Western businessman, David Golder cannot deny that he used to be just a 'petit juif, qui vendait des chiffons et de la feraille, à New York, avec [son] sac sur le dos' (*'the little Jew who sold rags and scrap metal in New York, from a sack on [his] back'*), one of the 'schouroum-bouroum', the 'marchands du Levant, qui essaiment dans le monde entier avec leurs ballots de tapis et de vieilles fourrures' (*'traders from the Levantine who travelled all over the world with their bales of rugs and second-hand fur coats'*), as his wife Gloria reminds him.[73] But now he lives the life of the wealthy cosmopolitan jet set of the *années folles*, frequenting the bars and casinos of Biarritz as well as the Jewish cafés of the rue des Rosiers. His life is dominated entirely by the need to make money; his wife and daughter are grotesques motivated solely by the enjoyment of wealth, leisure, and sex. The whole family is caught within a narrative web of motifs associated with gold: their name is obviously symbolic; David's daughter Joy has golden hair and a golden voice, and his wife, Gloria, whose name contains the word *or*, has gold teeth.[74] David's social and professional identity, constructed on the basis of a complete absence of moral or humane sentiments, seems to confirm the worst excesses of right-wing anti-Semitic prejudice. His ultimate fate—to die alone and destitute on a boat in between France and Russia, muttering words of Yiddish, might be read as a fable of the inevitable failure of assimilation. The overwhelmingly negative portrait of all the characters in this story seems to confirm the text as a repository of a range of stereotypes via which, according to Elaine Marks, Jews have been represented in French literature:

> Accused of being communists, revolutionaries, capitalists, bankers, accused of being rootless and conspiratorial, physically grotesque and uncontrollably libidinous, contaminating the health and the order of France and of Europe, Jews are persistently denounced as foreigners and parasites who disrupt, subvert, menace and threaten.[75]

The evaluation of Némirovsky's use of stereotypes is made problematic by the fact that it does not conform to our expectations as experienced readers, and therefore does not respond well to the usual explanations. Stereotyped formulations occur not only in dialogue but also in narratorial discourse. In Némirovsky's novels, stereotypes coexist with a close internal presentation of character such that the reader's sympathy is engaged in relation to a character who is also a negative stereotype, which renders the fictional discourse paradoxical and ultimately unstable, as Stemberger points out.[76] The use of negative stereotypes does not support any clear textual 'message', and contradicts contextual sources, such as interviews, which would seem to disprove completely the idea of any anti-Semitic intention on Némirovsky's part (and here, comparison with obviously politically anti-Semitic writers such as Drieu la Rochelle or Céline is instructive). Given the instability of Némirovsky's representations, we can usefully move away from the straightforward identification of stereotyped images as 'acceptable' or 'unacceptable', as Homi Bhabha recommends in relation to colonial discourse:

> To recognize the stereotype as an ambivalent mode of knowledge and power demands a theoretical and political response that challenges deterministic or functionalist modes of conceiving of the relationship between discourse and politics. The analytic of ambivalence questions dogmatic and moralistic positions on the meaning of oppression and discrimination. My reading of colonialist discourse suggests that the point of intervention should shift from the ready recognition of images as positive or negative, to an understanding of the *process of subjectification* made possible (and plausible) through stereotypical discourse. [emphasis in original][77]

It is too simplistic to suggest either that Némirovsky's use of negative stereotypes of Jewishness shows that she was a self-hating Jew, or that her texts must be condemned as anti-Semitic because the stereotypes they contain facilitate political oppression and ultimately genocide. This is to perpetuate the unsophisticated opposition between political correctness, which banishes any text which appears to reinforce stereotypes, and an idealised view of the Western canon as 'ameliorating' and never racist, which Bryan Cheyette and Laura Marcus seek to reject:

> This rather crude debate, we believe, merely reproduces the complacent self-image of a civilising western modernity which considers racists or antisemites to be pathological fanatics who are, in turn, banished to the margins of society. This commonplace view of modernity is challenged in this volume.[78]

Cheyette and Marcus seek instead to bring out the complexities of racism and anti-Semitism in Western culture. Susan Suleiman argues in a similar vein when she remarks that '[Némirovsky's] portrayal of Golder himself is complex, and to call it an antisemitic stereotype is simplistic and wrongheaded. One needs to show some interpretive respect before making such accusations'.[79] As Bhabha has demonstrated, the stereotype is a complex '*mode of representation of otherness*'[80] which dramatises both horror and desire for the perpetrator of colonial discourse and for the colonised subject:

The stereotype, then, as the primary point of subjectification in colonial discourse, for both colonizer and colonized, is the scene of a similar fantasy and defence—the desire for an originality which is again threatened by the differences of race, colour and culture.[81]

For Bhabha, the use of the stereotype does not dramatise hatred of the self, but rather the primal desire for unitary subjectivity which is always thwarted by the reality of split subjectivity. Theorists who have examined the function of the stereotype in relation to ethnic, and specifically, Jewish, humour have made a similar point as regards the absence of a deterministic relationship between the subject who produces the stereotyped, hostile discourse and the meaning of that discourse:

> Jokes are *ambiguous* comic utterances without a single clear meaning, and their relation to aggression or fear is variable and problematic. Jokes are playful aggression and play with aggression are [sic] not necessarily a mask for real but temporarily hidden or unrecognised hostility. [emphasis in original][82]

Bhabha does not exclude the possibility that the joke might be a strategy of cultural resistance.[83] Bhabha's focus on the ambivalence of the stereotype points to the ways in which such discourses open up a space of anxiety which reveals the weakness of the colonizer, and as such leads not only to oppression but also to potential resistance:

> Stereotyping is not the setting up of a false image which becomes the scapegoat of discriminatory practices. It is a much more ambivalent text of projection and introjection, metaphoric and metonymic strategies, displacement, over-determination, guilt and aggressivity; the masking and splitting of 'official' and phantasmic knowledges to construct the positionalities and oppositionalities of racist discourse.[84]

David Golder does not simply erect a false image of Jews which can then be accepted (by anti-Semites) or rejected (by those who oppose anti-Semitism). It draws on discourses available in the literary field to tell a story which, according to the reading strategies employed—as the mixed reception the text encountered amply demonstrates—construct a range of different and potentially contradictory subject positions and intersubjective oppositions in relation to Jewish identity and immigration in 1920s France.

There is no definitive answer to the question of whether *David Golder* 'is' or 'is not' anti-Semitic. It is an ambivalent work of fiction which uses negative stereotypes of Jewishness but which does not propose anti-Semitic arguments and is (unlike the work of Drieu or Céline) politically disengaged. The main focus of this *roman d'analyse* is David's complex and contradictory psychological motivations: was he really responsible for Marcus's death? Why does he accede to Joy's request that he should resume his business activities in order to provide her with an income, even though he now knows she is not his biological daughter? Comparison with a novel such as Paul Morand's *France la doulce* (1934)—which Némirovsky read[85]— serves to underline the ambivalence of Némirovsky's writing. *France la doulce* is a transparent *roman à thèse* in which the title of the film whose production the novel recounts, and which gives the novel its title, is an easily legible metaphor for France itself. The text's unambiguous message is that France's economy is being weakened by the financial activities of foreign and Jewish immigrants. The culmination of the business projects pursued in the novel by the German Jew Max Kron is a huge cinema on the Champs Elysées. The 'Ciné-Triomphe' is an enormous, fragile, and tasteless edifice, made entirely of insubstantial, synthetic materials unable to withstand any external pressure: it is a metaphor for a France whose economy has been constructed by foreigners on insecure foundations and which is ready to collapse.[86] To modern readers unfamiliar with the frequently crass and unsophisticated xenophobia of the inter-war *roman à thèse*, Némirovsky's fiction might appear ideologically unacceptable. In the context of the contemporary literary field, the absence of any xenophobic or anti-Semitic thesis in her work becomes obvious. *David Golder* is not a precursor of *France la doulce*.[87] Némirovsky's study of the effect of France on a certain group of wealthy immigrants is a far cry from Morand's indiscriminate condemnation of the effect of all foreigners on France.

As Nadia Malinovich shows, *David Golder* was certainly not the only novel of the period by a Jewish author to rely on essentialised ethnic portrayals of Jewishness or to offer a negative portrait of Jews.[88] The reasons Malinovich cites for the existence of such representations are firstly the widespread acceptability of racial definitions of ethnic difference in the France of the 1920s, secondly the belief on the part of Jewish writers that portraits of Jews should be 'realistic' as opposed to idealised—and this is precisely the argument Némirovsky used when she told Nina Gourfinkel in *L'Univers israélite* that 'c'est ainsi que je les ai vus' (*that is how I saw them*)[89]—and thirdly that in the new context of confidence and perceived security in the France of the 1920s, Jewish writers did not feel it necessary to censor negative representations. Crucially then, and as we established in Chapter 1, we must see *David Golder* as a response to the literary and cultural debates of the 1920s and not as an anticipation of the crises of the 1930s. We must, in Bernstein's terminology, avoid backshadowing. In formal terms, as we have seen, *David Golder* is a literary response to the *crise du roman* of the 1920s. In thematic terms, it is a cultural response to the tide of interest and optimism in relation to Jewish writing created by writers such as Fleg, Spire, and Cohen. To view the text in this way is to adopt Bernstein's 'prosaics of the quotidian', that is, to recognise its importance as an event or moment 'not for [its] place in an already determined larger pattern, but as significant in [its] own right'.[90] Némirovsky herself addressed the question of the retrospective assessment of *David Golder* in the light of subsequent events:

> Il est tout à fait certain que s'il y avait eu Hitler, j'eusse grandement adouci *David Golder*, et je ne l'aurais pas écrit dans le même sens, ajoute la jeune femme pensivement. Et pourtant, conclut-elle en souriant, j'aurais eu tort, c'eût été une faiblesse indigne d'un véritable écrivain ! . . . [91]

> '*It is quite certain that had Hitler been around at the time, I would have toned down* David Golder *considerably, and I would not have written it in the same way', the young woman adds thoughtfully. 'And yet', she continues, 'I would have been wrong to do so; it would have been a weakness unworthy of a real writer!*'

In this interview, Némirovsky at first appears to concede that retrospective evaluations are valid. But her affirmation that a writer must express herself at whatever cost is also a rejection of the notion that subsequent events be allowed to determine definitively the meaning of extant works of literature.

Stereotypes of Jewishness continued to appear in Némirovsky's work after *David Golder*. *Le Bal*, composed during the writing of *David Golder*, tells the story of Alfred Kampf, 'un sec petit juif aux yeux de feu' ('*a dry little Jew with fiery eyes*'),[92] and the Kampf family's failure to assimilate into the Parisian haute bourgeoisie. In the texts of the mid-1930s, stereotyped representations persist, but are no longer the main focus of the narrative. In *Le Pion sur l'échiquier* (1934), Christophe Bohun's professional antagonist Beryl, who used to be called Biruleff, is the only Jewish character in the novel; he is introduced to the reader through a negative physical description[93] and is characterised in terms of his business and financial acumen. Stemberger identifies his unruly red hair as a stereotype of Jewish physical appearance borrowed from Russian literature.[94] The focus of this novel is not Jewish identity, but Christophe's inability to find a meaningful existence within the commercial environment that is his father's legacy to him. The fact that Christophe's father is a Greek immigrant might suggest a superficial similarity of theme with *France la doulce*, but again, unlike Morand's novel, this text lacks any political thesis and focuses not on the fate of France but on the social and psychological disintegration of an individual. For this reason perhaps, and also because of Christophe's quasi-accidental suicide at the end of the book, the publisher's presentation on the back cover likens *Le Pion sur l'échiquier* to Drieu la Rochelle's *Le Feu follet* (1931). But again, any likeness is superficial. *Le Feu follet* is an emotionally and physically brutal story of drug addiction and despair which constructs the claustrophobic inner world of the addict Alain with little substantial reference to his socio-political environment. When his friend Dubourg attempts to relate Alain's crisis to his bourgeois identity and to his époque, his arguments are dismissed as unconvincing.[95] By contrast, whilst *Le Pion sur l'échiquier* also depicts Christophe's inner world in some detail, the point of the text is to locate Christophe's despair at the centre of a nexus of relations with other people, with the business environment he rejects and with the social, cultural, and economic realities of post-war France. In *Le Vin de solitude* (1935), the Jewish theme takes second place to the Russian theme; Hélène's father is Jewish but her mother is not, and Hélène is not portrayed as Jewish. The conventional associations between financial speculation, love of money, and Jewishness do however occur in this text: Karol is another Jewish *arriviste*, another speculator with international business interests. Chapter 2 of the second part of the novel is a set-piece scene in which we see Karol negotiating deals with the Jew Slivker and the Russian politician Chestov in order to profit from the war.

The texts of the mid- and late-1930s must be read in the context of a growing and newly political awareness of anti-Semitism on the part of Jews in France. Whilst anti-Semitism had not been a central issue for French Jews in the 1920s, significant changes on the national and international level because of the rise of Nazism in Germany obviously had a serious impact. Although 1933 did not mark the complete cessation of the Jewish renaissance in France, as it necessarily did in Germany, the changing European political context led to the fragmentation of Jewish organisations and, in literature, to an appreciable degree of caution as regards the production of obviously 'Semitic' discourses.[96] David Weinberg analyses the attitude of native French and well-established immigrant Jews to the 'Jewish question' between 1933 and 1937, that is, between Hitler's accession to power and the fall of Leon Blum's Popular Front government. He concludes that 'they placed uncertain faith in the humanitarianism of the French government while cautioning fellow Jews not to arouse anti-Semitism among their fellow Frenchmen'.[97] In this context, the persistence of potentially anti-Semitic stereotypes in *Le Pion sur l'échiquier* and *Le Vin de solitude* requires some explanation. For Stemberger, Beryl and Boris Karol are the most negative and dangerous stereotypes in Némirovsky's *œuvre*.[98] These representations must, I think, be understood in terms of the type of audience Némirovsky was targeting in the mid-1930s. We saw in Chapter 1 that her association with right-wing and conservative literary institutions was a function of her position within the contemporary literary field. The sort of 'popular' anti-Semitism[99] with which such representations might be conflated is typical of this milieu. Even if we read this feature of her literary identity politically, Némirovsky's position was typical of a certain section of the Jewish community:

> Imbued with a faith in the politics of compromise, they were helpless to react to the polarization of French society on the Left and Right. When eventually forced to choose, their fear of the association of Judaism with Bolshevism led them into the arms of the right-wing forces whose

calls for national unity were mistaken by natives as an appeal to the French democratic tradition.[100]

It is not surprising that Némirovsky should identify with this section of French-Jewish public opinion—she certainly had no sympathy with the revolutionaries who had driven her family from Russia.

In the late 1930s, Jewish characters and themes disappeared from Némirovsky's fiction—they do not feature in *Jezabel* (1936), *La Proie* (1938) or *Deux* (1939). At the end of the decade, Némirovsky returned to the theme of Jewishness, but now moved away from stereotyped characters based on Jewish social and professional identities and instead began to interrogate the notion of an inescapable and timeless Jewish essence or 'soul', a spiritual and physical Jewishness which an individual must ultimately acknowledge and assume. This is the central theme of the short story 'Fraternité' (1937) and of the novel *Les Chiens et les loups* (1940). 'Fraternité', published in *Gringoire*, recounts the chance meeting between an assimilated French Jew and an impoverished, Yiddish-speaking Eastern immigrant Jew who discover they share the same name and therefore the same identity. The assimilated French Jew, Christian Rabinovitch, realises that he is the irreconcilable contradiction his name encapsulates. But although he is forced to acknowledge that he shares with the stranger what the narrator calls 'le vieil héritage', he re-affirms his identity as a rich French bourgeois at the end of the story by asserting his similarity with his archetypally French friend Robert de Sestres, whose château he is visiting.[101] The manuscript proves that Némirovsky was acutely aware of the political context in which she was writing. As she was planning the story, she wrote: 'Je vais certainement me faire engueuler encore en parlant des Juifs en ce moment, mais bah!' (*I shall certainly get myself yelled at again by talking about Jews at the moment, but so what!*)[102] At the end of the manuscript, there is a note in Némirovsky's hand which reads: 'Refusé par René Doumic comme antisémite! 31 octobre 1936. Paru das *Gringoire*, 5 février 1937' (*Refused by René Doumic as anti-Semitic! 31 October 1936. Published in* Gringoire, *5 February 1937*). Doumic was the director of the *Revue des deux mondes*; he presumably interpreted the story as a dangerous assertion of a fundamental Jewish difference lurking beneath the veneer of assimilation. The manuscript source is richly suggestive as regards Némirovsky's attitude to the ways in which Jewishness could be written about in fiction in a very particular socio-political context. She maintains exactly the position she had expressed to Janine Auscher in 1935 in relation to *David Golder*, that a writer should not censor her work because of external political circumstances. The exclamation mark suggests however that Némirovsky was surprised that 'Fraternité' should be deemed anti-Semitic. But the fact that she then offered the story to *Gringoire* shows that she was willing to publish a text already labelled as anti-Semitic in a journal whose political colour must have been clear to her in 1937.[103] By March 1938,

Némirovsky had apparently altered her attitude: attempting to decide on the names of the characters in the short story 'Espoirs', also destined for *Gringoire*, she noted: 'Malheureusement ce ne peut être un Lévy ou un Rabinovitch' (*unfortunately it can't be a Lévy or a Rabinovitch*).[104]

Nonetheless, in 1939 Némirovsky published her most detailed and sustained fictional interrogation of Jewish identity. *Les Chiens et les loups* was serialised in *Candide* from October 1939 and was published as a book by Albin Michel in 1940. The author's preface which accompanied the 1940 edition shows that, as with 'Fraternité', Némirovsky was only too aware of the potential problems of reception her text might encounter. In this preface, she explicitly defines the novel as a story about Jews, but makes clear that it is about Eastern, not French, Jews, and should not therefore be taken as representative, since 'la variété d'une race humaine est infinie' (*the variety of a human race is infinite*). She counters the potential objection from Jewish readers that, in the current climate, she ought not to be writing about Jews at all, and certainly not in a negative way, by using the same argument she had advanced in 1935 in relation to *David Golder*: 'il n'est pas de sujet "tabou" en littérature. Pourquoi un peuple refuserait-il d'être vu tel qu'il est, avec ses qualités et ses défauts?' (*no subject is taboo in literature. Why should a people refuse to be seen as they are, with their qualities and their faults?*).[105] Such arguments might have been effective in 1929, and even in 1935, but by 1939 the situation was significantly different. *Les Chiens et les loups* is problematic because of the absence of any obvious literary context in relation to which it could be received. Malinovich's bibliography of novels in French on Jewish themes between 1900 and 1940 testifies to the scarcity of such texts at the end of the decade—only Cohen's *Mageclous* (1938) and Lunel's *Jérusalem à Carpentras* (1938), a collection of short stories, countered the decline in the 'renaissance juive'. With *Les Chiens et les loups*, Némirovsky, uncharacteristically, was writing against the dominant trend of the contemporary literary field. The manuscript of 'Fraternité' and the preface to *Les Chiens et les loups* bear witness to Némirovsky's clear understanding that her own individual desire to write about Jewishness was in contradiction with her literary and socio-historical environment. Yet a biographical interpretation of Némirovsky's desire to write about Jewishness in the late 1930s is far from straightforward, since the writing of *Les Chiens et les loups* was exactly contemporaneous with her conversion to Catholicism.[106]

Like 'Fraternité', *Les Chiens et les loups* opposes the assimilated, Westernised branch of a family, the Sinners, to their poor Oriental, Yiddish-speaking relations, whilst demonstrating that they are linked by an ineffable and hereditary 'Jewishness'. The novel opposes two couples, Ben and Ada, poor Jews from a Ukrainian ghetto, and the wealthy and cultured Harry, Ben's cousin, who marries the stereotypically French Laurence once all the characters are reunited as émigrés in Paris. Harry is a dual figure, representing the assimilated, Western Jew in relation to Ben and Ada, but nonetheless rejected by Laurence's traditionalist bourgeois family because of his foreign and Jewish identity. A love triangle exists between Ada, Ben and Harry, which is also the textual vehicle for Ada's identity crisis. Ada resembles Hélène of *Le Vin de solitude* insofar as she is a broadly positive heroine who achieves a successful resolution of her identity at the end of the text: although an exile once more, expelled from France, she discovers solidarity and a sense of self through motherhood. *Les Chiens et les loups*—as is clear from the title—relies to a significant extent on the narrative principle of doubling or pairing, which as Stemberger shows is a recurrent textual strategy in Némirovsky's fiction: Ben is opposed to Harry, and Ada to Laurence.[107] However, the central theme of this text is the ways in which other identities cut across apparently well-established binaries. This is as significant and interesting a feature of the novel as its affirmation of a hereditary and inescapable 'Jewishness', and these two aspects of the text must be read in conjunction with each other. The text's opening pages describe the highly segregated environment of the Ukrainian town where 'les Juifs infréquentables' (*unsavoury Jews*) live in the ghetto, whilst 'de riches Israélites' (*rich Israelites*) enjoy the luxurious surroundings of the wealthy suburbs, and the Jewish, Russian, and Polish bourgeoisie occupy an indeterminate middle space. However, whilst ethnic or religious identity is the overt reason for segregation, the point of this opening section of narrative is to demonstrate that it is money which actually divides people, not race, for 'les défenses n'existaient que pour les pauvres' (*the barriers only existed for the poor*): in practice, wealthy Jews live in the affluent suburbs along with the Russian *haute bourgeoisie*, even though the law forbids it.[108] This opening passage establishes a framework for the novel as a whole, which constantly demonstrates the ways in which access to money and therefore to a Western, affluent, cultured existence transforms binary structures of identity into triple structures. Ben, Ada, and Harry form a trio whereby Ben and Harry are separated by wealth and culture but linked by 'Jewishness'; Ada is the fulcrum—as is indicated by her palindromic name, as Stemberger suggests[109]—insofar as she shares Ben's poverty but Harry's culture. Harry realises that he is both like and unlike Ben:

> Il savait qu'il ressemblait à Ben et, cependant (c'était son malheur), il ne lui ressemblait que par quelques traits, et par d'autres il était aussi différent de lui que de Laurence elle-même.[110]

> *He knew that he resembled Ben, and yet—and this was his misfortune—he only resembled him in certain ways, and in others he was as different from him as he was from Laurence herself.*

A few pages later, another trio is established along similar lines, this time between Harry's mother, Harry's French wife Laurence, and Ada. Laurence implies that she is separated from her mother-in-law by 'les coutumes de votre pays et de votre race' (*the customs of your country and of your race*), yet for Mme Sinner, Ada is just 'une simple fille de la ville basse' (*a simple girl form the lower town*).[111] In the final scene between Ben and Ada (Chapter 28), the protagonists' conversation constantly posits the instability of oppositions such as Jew/non-Jew and Eastern/Western Jew. Economic identity confuses relations of sameness and of difference. *Les Chiens et les loups* explores the *multiple* complexities of a *dual* identity. Némirovsky's presentation of Jewish identity in this text differs from her presentation of Russian identity in *Les Mouches d'automne* and *Le Vin de solitude* insofar as the latter texts do not explore the complexity of multiple ethnic allegiances to the same extent: as we saw in Chapter 3, in these novels, the identity of the exile is not one of internal psychological conflict. By 1940 however, a Jewish-Russian-French identity has unsurprisingly become a conflictual identity in Némirovsky's fiction. The exploration of dualism in *Les Chiens et les loups* is typical of the approach adopted by other French Jewish writers of the period. The writers of the Jewish renaissance did not simply affirm particularism, but explored their dual identity in terms of complexity rather than opposition.[112] There is conflict in *Les Chiens et les loups*, but there is also the possibility of resolution. To understand duality in terms of complexity and not of opposition in Némirovsky's later work avoids the negative conclusion reached by Thau and reiterated by Stemberger that the representation of dual identity is an assertion of non-identity.[113] Ada's trajectory and the final positive resolution of her identity crisis do not support a reading of the text as an assertion of non-identity. Her experience as an artist in exile demonstrates not that cultural identity is fixed and that a dual cultural identity is therefore impossible, but rather that any cultural identity is relative and therefore fundamentally unstable. In Paris, Ada sells Russian and Jewish art to curious Parisians in search of exoticism, but in exile in an unspecified country in Eastern Europe, she sells Parisian fashions to local women eager for a taste of French sophistication.[114] Again the structure is a triangular one: in Paris, Ada seemed Oriental, but in the East she seems Western because she has lived for so long in France. The message of this text—if it can be said to have one—is that the term *étranger* (foreigner or stranger) is always relative and partial. From this point of view, *Les Chiens et les loups* might be read as a subtle contestation of racial anti-Semitism. Contrary to the assertions of Thau and Stemberger,[115] this novel does depict external (that is, non-Jewish) anti-Semitism in relation to which the characters are obliged to construct and reconstruct their identities. In the opening section, we see Ben and Ada as children forced to flee a pogrom; in Paris, Laurence's father opposes his daughter's marriage to a foreign Jew, and Laurence herself feels a specific aversion to Jews which the narrative does not encourage the reader to share.[116] The novel also opens up the question of anti-Semitism and culture when it makes reference to the archetypal Jew in literature: Ada's grandfather is writing a book entitled 'Caractère et Réhabilitation de Shylock'.[117]

Némirovsky's decision to interrogate Jewish identity in *Les Chiens et les loups* was a personal choice which went against the grain of the French literary field of the late 1930s and 1940s. It seems this was not an experience Némirovsky wanted to repeat—in June 1940 she wrote in her notebook that if her literary inspiration was failing her, this was partly because of the critical reception of *Les Chiens et les loups*.[118] Her subsequent novels (*Les Biens de ce monde*, serialised in *Gringoire* between April and June 1941, *Les Feux de l'automne* and *Suite française*, both unpublished in her lifetime) contain no Jewish characters.

Over the course of the decade in which Némirovsky was writing, her representation of Jewishness progressed from contradiction to complexity. 'L'Enfant génial' both proposes an ethnically based Jewish authenticity and calls this into question by refusing to conclude as to whether Ismaël really was a genius; *David Golder* evokes the reader's sympathy for a character who is also presented stereotypically as a money-obsessed Jew. *Le Pion sur l'échiquier* and *Le Vin de solitude* run the risk of presenting stereotypes without contradiction. 'Fraternité' announces the problems of identity which would be explored fully in *Les Chiens et les loups*. The latter novel has failed to satisfy modern readers as regards its definition of Jewishness. For example, Thau argues that

> la découverte d'une alterité juive, d'une permanence identitaire, ne peut être vécue que négativement. Trop assimilée, ayant voulu surtout s'assimiler complètement, Némirovsky ne donne, ne peut donner aucun contenu positif à cette judéité dont *David Golder* et *Les Chiens et les loups* disent (et déplorent) la permanence. Elle ne peut ressentir et présenter celle-ci que comme irrationnelle, inexplicable, voire donc d'origine raciale.[119]

> *the discovery of Jewish difference, of an unchanging identity, can only be experienced negatively. Too assimilated, and above all desiring total assimilation, Némirovsky does not and cannot ascribe any positive content to the Jewishness whose permanence* David Golder *and* Les Chiens et les loups *depict and deplore. She can only feel and present it as irrational, inexplicable, and therefore as being of racial origin.*

Stemberger makes much the same argument, but in more textual detail; however her judgements are less categorically negative, and she avoids the condemnatory tone of Thau's biographical reading.[120] It is important to bear in mind that the characterisation of a secular Jewish identity remained problematic for the intellectuals of the 'mode juive': according to Malinovich, '[w]hilst the idea of an ethno-cultural Jewish identity generated a good deal of excitement in the 1920s, a means of perpetuating a non-religious Jewishness in real practical terms was never really articulated'.[121] One might conclude in the terms Elaine Marks uses to describe Proust's

A la recherche du temps perdu, which, she says, 'both recapitulates and scrambles the signs by which we usually read *la France* and *le Juif*'.[122] It is only by reading Némirovsky's novels in their historical and cultural context and by paying attention to the chronological progression of her treatment of Jewish identity that it is possible to understand why Némirovsky reiterated stereotypes of Jewishness at the beginning of her career, and why the 'scrambled signs' of a text such as *Les Chiens et les loups* are so difficult to untangle and to evaluate.

UN ROMAN JUIF?

In their preface to the 2005 reprint of *Le Maître des âmes* (first published in *Gringoire* in 1939 under the title 'Les Echelles du Levant'), Philipponnat and Lienhardt make the point that the critical reception of Némirovsky's novels has been significant in defining their 'meaning', arguing that it was *David Golder*'s anti-Semitic readers which made it problematic.[123] This preface itself illustrates how paratextual material has defined and continues to define Némirovsky as a novelist. The preface discusses the question of anti-Semitism and literature at some length, and reads the novel's anti-hero, the Faustian Dario Asfar, in this context. This approach is clearly justifiable insofar as the vocabulary Némirovsky uses repeatedly to describe Asfar— *levantin*, *métèque*—was also used in contemporary discourse to signify Jewishness. However, Asfar is not Jewish. Asfar's origins are obscure: all we know is that, like his wife Clara, he was born in the Crimea; his father was Greek and his grandparents came from Greece, Italy, or Asia Minor.[124] This is a novel about immigration and xenophobia but not explicitly about Jews and anti-Semitism.[125] This probably did not prevent contemporary readers from constructing anti-Semitic readings around Dario, given the prevalence of the contemporary (pejorative) vocabulary of Jewishness in the text, and Némirovsky must have been aware of this. Even Némirovsky's husband Michael Epstein thought that Dario Asfar probably was Jewish: when he was looking for examples of literary anti-Semitism in his wife's fiction in order to mount a case to rescue her from deportation in 1942, he recalled this text along with *David Golder*.[126] However, once again, the point of this story is to show the ways in which economic status cuts across racial or ethnic identity. According to Dario, there are only two categories of people—*les repus* (the well-fed) and *les affamés* (the starving), and it is this opposition which structures the narrative.[127] At the end of the story, Dario asserts that his son Daniel will only understand his father if he ever experiences the grinding and terrifying poverty his father has known. Daniel's conclusion that they are barely of the same race is an acknowledgement that the opposition affluence/poverty defines each man's identity over and above their blood ties. Dario on the other had has come to realise that he is of the same 'race' as his own father. But it is not a question of their common ethnic roots but rather of economic identity: Dario has succumbed to the poverty his own father experienced, despite his pretensions to a professional identity. The question of Daniel's ultimate fate remains open. A xenophobic reading of this ending is of course possible—all 'foreigners' ultimately share the same 'race' and are all therefore destined to share the same miserable fate. But this simplistic reading masks the complexity of Némirovsky's interrogation of 'race': her point is that 'race' is defined differently according to whether you are an *affamée* or a *repus*. The text's preface risks provoking a reading of *Le Maître des âmes* as an essentialised portrait of Jewish identity and potentially occludes the deconstruction of essentialised racial portraits contained within Némirovsky's account of the intersections of racial and economic identity.

Unfortunately, as Philipponnat and Lienhardt point out, some contemporary critics took the opportunity to read Némirovsky's fiction precisely as an essentialised account of Jewish racial difference in order to lend weight to their own ideological agendas. As we saw in Chapter 1, critics writing in *Gringoire* and *L'Action française* published obviously and unambiguously anti-Semitic responses to *David Golder*. Various journals used the opportunity to stereotype the author via exotic designations: for example, for *D'Artagnan*, Némirovsky was a 'piquante israélite' (*exciting Israelite*).[128] Other critics on the political right used their reviews to validate the stereotypes they found in the novel. Robert de Saint-Jean's characterisation of David in the right-wing *Revue hebdomadaire* as 'l'un des financiers israélites qui gouvernent le marché' (*one of the Israelite financiers who govern the market*) is an affirmation his readers were obviously intended to recognise and accept.[129] In the conservative *Journal des Débats*, the academician André Bellesort bemoaned the fact that literary representations of this type had not succeeded in modifying the reality they purported to represent: 'cet homme et ces hommes nous sont connus de longue date, nous les avons rencontrés si souvent! Trop souvent à notre gré, puisque le roman ou le théâtre, qui, depuis cent ans, se plaisent à nous en inspirer l'horreur, n'ont causé aucun dommage à leur pouvoir ni même à leur préstige' (*that man, and these men, have been known to us for a long time, we have met them so many times! Too often in our view, since neither the novel nor the theatre which for over a hundred years has delighted in portraying them in horrifying terms, has caused any damage at all to their power or to their prestige*).[130] Reviewing *Le Pion sur l'échiquier* in the far right publication *Le Jour*, François Porché likened James Bohun to David Golder, asserting that they are both financial rogues, that they share the same 'extraction', coming from the Levant or from the Balkans, and that their caricatural presentation only heightens their value as a representation of reality:

> Parce qu'elle correspond à un type qui est devenu classique dans la caricature, on pourrait croire que cette variété d'hommes est une invention d'humouriste. Mais quand la caricature s'empare d'un

personnage pour en faire un poncif, c'est que le personnage existe depuis longtemps à une foule d'exemplaires. Seulement, la vérité est toujours pire que la caricature. La caricature semble grossir, alors qu'elle se borne à simplifier. La peinture vraie écarte le trait sommaire et reinstitue la vie dans son détail affreux. Là fut le talent de Mme Némirovsky lorsqu'elle entreprit d'étudier ces voraces à grandes gueules qui nagent dans nos eaux.[131]

Because it corresponds to a type which now frequently occurs in caricatures, one might think that this type of man was invented by humourists. But when caricature seizes hold of a character and makes a cliché out of him that means that that character has existed for many years and in many different ways. Except that the truth is always worse than the caricature. The caricature seems to exaggerate, but all it actually does it simplify. The realistic portrait avoids the common element and depicts life in all its appalling detail. That is where Madame Némirovsky's talent is obvious when she undertakes to study the hungry monsters with their huge mouths which are swimming in our waters.

The question of the possibility of anti-Semitic reactions to *David Golder* was raised explicitly. Jean Blaise suggested in *La Dépêche* that if Némirovsky were not Jewish, her work would be considered anti-Semitic, and that some people think this in any case.[132] The fact that Némirovsky was Jewish did not endear the book to Ida See, who expressed her reaction in *Le Réveil juif* : 'Nous savons que ce tableau des Juifs "rois de l'or ou du pétrole" agrée aux nombreux antisémites, et nous n'avons pas assez le sens de l'adulation pour joindre nos pauvres flatteries à celles de tant de hauts personnages, pour féliciter une Israélite (?) [sic] d'avoir si bien décrit des Juifs et des Juives odieux . . . !' (*We realise that this portrait of Jews who are 'kings of oil or gold' is pleasing to many anti-Semites, and we are not so intent on heaping praise on her that we should seek to join our little words of flattery to those of many well-placed commentators to congratulate a Jewess (I assume?) for having described odious Jews and Jewesses so well!*)[133] Nina Gourfinkel was concerned that a book such as *David Golder* could place a weapon in the hands of anti-Semites which they could use against Jews. But she concluded her interview with Némirovsky by affirming that the author was neither anti-Semitic nor in fact Jewish in any meaningful way.[134] For Gourfinkel, the real subject of *David Golder* was the fashionable cosmopolitan jet set composed of people of all nations: she refused to see the novel as a representation of Jewish identity.

Gourfinkel was one of a handful of critics who used the publication of *David Golder* as an opportunity to write longer and more considered articles about the concept of 'le roman juif' than was possible in a brief review. In a substantial article entitled 'De Silbermann à David Golder' published in the *Nouvelle Revue juive* in March 1930, very shortly after the appearance of her interview with Némirovsky in *L'Univers israélite*, Gourfinkel concluded that the non-Jewish Jacques de Lacretelle came closer to having produced a convincing study of Jewish experience than Némirovsky. Gourfinkel again asserts in this article that David is a cosmopolitan, not a Jew; she argues that he has neither a positive sense of his Jewish heritage nor any desire deliberately to reject his Jewish origin. His tragedy is not specifically Jewish, like Shylock or Silbermann, but universal.[135] Two conservative critics used their discussions of *David Golder* to argue that the expression of a 'Jewish soul' in fiction was possible. The novelist and critic Robert Bourget-Pailleron thought that Némirovsky's writing style was an illustration of her own Jewish 'nature':

> [C]e qui étonne un peu dans le livre de Mme Némirovsky, c'est un certain romantisme des propos, une couleur de drame que prennent les personnages et qui est parfois un peu trop violente. Peut-être, après tout, convient-elle bien à la peinture des milieux israélites. Cette fébrilité incessante, ce passage de la jovialité au tragique, ce désir insatiable de jouir et de brûler sa vie sont dans la bonne tradition de la race.[136]

> *What is rather surprising in Madame Némirovsky's book is a certain romanticism in the language, a rather dramatic attitude which the characters adopt and which is sometimes a little too violent. Perhaps, after all, this is appropriate to the depiction of Israelite circles. This perpetual movement, the shifts from humour to tragedy, the insatiable desire to enjoy life until you are burnt out are very much in the tradition of the race.*

However, for Bourget-Pailleron, *David Golder* was not and probably not intended to be, a true Jewish novel because it did not contain the type of portrait of the non-assimilated Jew found in the novels of the Tharaud brothers. This comment demonstrates the extent to which the Tharaud brothers were taken in some sectors of the literary field as the model for Jewish literature. Whilst frequent reference was made in the reception of *David Golder* to the Tharaud brothers, the intellectuals of the 'mode juif' were hardly ever mentioned. Bourget-Pailleron was the only critic to compare Némirovsky with any of the major figures of the Jewish renaissance, and it is not a substantial reference. He compared *David Golder* briefly to Lecache's *Jacob*, finding it superior from a literary point of view. Jean de Pierrefeu also cited the Tharaud brothers as the writers who had defined 'le roman juif'. For Pierrefeu, 'le roman juif' is an offshoot of travel writing, a depiction of particularism stimulated by the modern writer's desire to travel and to write about other (exotic) human identities.[137] He concludes that *David Golder* should be described as a Jewish novel because it really succeeds in demonstrating what he calls the Jewish temperament. Pierrefeu expresses a highly essentialised concept of Jewish identity:

> David Goldberg [sic], sous sa modernité aiguë, parmi son entourage vingtieme siècle, semble, tel le juif errant, incarner sa race dans la succession des siècles, comme s'il avait vécu de toute éternité [. . .] Mlle Irène Némirovsky a reussi avec des elements ultra modernes une synthèse du génie juif qui n'est pas loin d'être un chef d'œuvre.

> *David Goldberg [sic], in his acute modernity, with his twentieth-century entourage, seems to be the incarnation of his race throughout the centuries, like the wandering Jew, as if he had lived through all eternity [. . .] using the most modern components, Mademoiselle Némirovsky has succeeded in creating a synthesis of the Jewish spirit which is not far from being a masterpiece.*

By contrast, critics on the left refused such an essentialisation of Jewish identity as a foundation for their appreciation of the novel. The Jewish critic Benjamin Crémieux found *David Golder* to be a successful expression of a specific aspect of Jewish identity, arguing that the text dramatises an individual caught between the traditions of the past and the assimilation of the future:

> [C]'est une expression de l'âme juive, non pas de l'âme juive dans sa totalité (ce qui est bien impossible), mais de l'âme juive saisie au moment ou le soutien de la religion et de la tradition familiale vient lui manquer et avant que la civilisation occidentale l'ait affinée, moderée.[138]

> *It is an expression of the Jewish soul, but not of the Jewish soul in its totality, which would be impossible, but of the Jewish soul seized at the point at which it is no longer supported by religion and family tradition, and before Western civilisation has refined and moderated it.*

Emile Bouvier, writing in the leftist *La Lumière*, argued that it was pointless to categorise 'le roman juif' according to the spurious notion that the 'Jewish soul' might be seized in its totality.[139] For Bouvier, 'le "type juif" est un mythe, que les écrivains chrétiens cultivent avec une obstination puérile (quand elle n'est pas malveillante) et les écrivains israélites avec une noble, mais aveugle, passion' (*the Jewish 'type' is a myth, which Christian writers cultivate with childish obstinacy (when it is not maliciously intended) and which Israelite writers cultivate with a noble but blind passion*). However, this does not preclude the investigation of Jewish identity in literature; like

Crémieux, Bouvier argues for a historically specific interrogation of certain types of Jewish experience:

> En somme, si 'l'esprit juif' est une chimère qu'il serait oiseux de pour-suivre, l'histoire juive, la condition juive, la famille juive et, si l'on veut, la complexité de certains caractères juifs, constituent de substantielles réalités, dont le roman moderne a raison d'aborder l'étude loyale.

> *All in all, if the 'Jewish spirit' is a phantom which it would be vain to pursue, Jewish history, the Jewish condition, the Jewish family, and if you will, the complexity of certain Jewish characters do constitute substantial realities, which the modern novel should certainly attempt faithfully to study.*

For Bouvier, *David Golder* is a good example of this type of writing.

The reception of *Les Chiens et les loups* was, given its publication date, unsurprisingly sparse.[140] *Gringoire* reviewed the novel briefly, present-ing it as another illustration of the 'Jewish soul' by the author of *David Golder*. The features of the 'Jewish soul' Pierre Loewel thought the text illustrated were (predictably) unflattering: he identifies a tormented nature, a paralysing sense of eternal dissatisfaction and a morbid love of money. Amid the clamour of politics in 1939–1940, Némirovsky's small voice insisting that racial identity is relative to other identities could not make itself heard. Unfortunately, as we saw in Chapter 1, the type of conserva-tive readership she had cultivated through the decade was now embracing political positions she could not have anticipated when she was writing *David Golder*, with the result that a partial, partisan, and ideologically undesirable interpretation of her work became all the more likely. Had she been able to interest less aesthetically conservative critics, or those on the political left, in her work, the response might have been quite different. It is for this reason that texts such as Cohen's *Mangeclous* (1938) or Lunel's *Jéruslaem à Carpentras* (1938), both published by *NRF*/Gallimard, were not subject to the same lack of an ideologically sympathetic literary context. In the very different literary and political climate of 1929–1930, the recep-tion of *David Golder* was of course much more extensive and much more varied politically. The discussions of 'le roman juif' which *David Golder* provoked reveal the malleability of this text in the hands of its critics: for some it was an expression of the timeless 'Jewish soul', and for others it was a refutation of this very concept. It is due to the difference in the character and functioning of the French literary field in 1929 and 1939, and to the cementing of Némirovsky's position within it over the course of the decade, that a text such as *David Golder*, which appears to rely on unambiguously negative stereotypes, could produce such an ambivalent response amongst critics, whilst an ambiguous and complex text such as *Les Chiens et les loups* produced a limited and unitary reading.

FROM SILBERMANN TO HARRY SINNER

The differences between the dynamics of the literary field which surrounded *David Golder* and *Les Chiens et les loups* can be illustrated by comparing Némirovsky's novels with the contemporary works which helped to establish the literary context in relation to which they were received. Nina Gourfinkel rightly had identified one of the most significant points of reference for *David Golder* when she compared it to Lacretelle's *Silbermann*. There is an entirely coincidental contextual connection between these two novels. The secondary school which provides the setting for *Silbermann* is a fictionalised version of the Lycée Janson-de-Sailly, where Lacretelle himself had been educated. This school is situated in the sixteenth arrondissement of Paris, on the rue de la Pompe, directly opposite number 115, where Némirovsky lived with her family when they first arrived in Paris in 1919. We know that Némirovsky had read Lacretelle, and liked his work, because she refers to him as a great novelist in the interview with Gourfinkel, although she also questions the authenticity of his portrayal of Jews.[141] Némirovsky must have recognised intimately the milieu Lacretelle portrays, since the events of the novel take place quite literally on her front doorstep. The way in which Silbermann conceives of the relationship between his French education at Janson and his Jewish identity is very close to the statements Némirovsky made about the relationship between her French and Russian identities, which we discussed in Chapter 3. Like many Jews persuaded by French post-Revolution republican rhetoric, Silbermann believes in the possibility of combining a French and a Jewish identity into an ideal synthesis: 'être Juif et Français, je ne crois pas qu'il y ait une condition plus favourable pour accomplir de grandes choses [. . .] Seulement, le génie de ma race, je veux le façonner selon le caractère de ce pays-ci; je veux unir mes resources aux vôtres. Si j'écris, je ne veux pas que l'on puisse me reprocher la moindre marque étrangère' (*to be a Jew and to be French: I don't think that there could be a more favourable situation in which to accomplish great things [. . .] But I want to mould the spirit of my race according to the character of this country, I want to unite my resources with yours. If I write, I don't want anyone to be able to accuse me of the least sign of foreignness*).[142] At the beginning of her career, and no doubt in part because of her educational experience at the Sorbonne, Némirovsky was more concerned with synthesising a French-Russian identity in her literature. Nonetheless, Silbermann's view of the compatibility of the French intellectual tradition with 'foreign' importations is close to Némirovsky's own position on the question of cultural exchange. It is also plausible—though impossible to prove—to suggest a more direct connection between *David Golder* and *Silbermann*. The similarity of the titles is underscored by a further textual echo relating to the names of the central characters. Facing the reality of racial persecution, David Silbermann decides to abandon his dreams of academic success and go to America to make money. He imagines his name on the sign hanging outside his future business: 'David Silbermann, cela fait mieux sur la plaque d'un marchand de diamants que sur la couverture d'un livre!' (*David Silbermann! That would look better outside a diamond merchant's than on the cover of a book!*).[143] And yet the names of both David Silbermann and David Golder do of course appear on the cover of a book. The eponymous David Golder also muses on the name of his business. After Marcus's death, he scribbles out his name on his company's headed paper, leaving simply 'David Golder', which will now replace the portmanteau 'Golmar' which combined 'Golder' and 'Marcus'. He imagines the company's neon signs which bear this name: 'Six lettres d'or, lumineuses, éclatantes, qui tournaient, elles aussi, comme des soleils, cette nuit, dans quatre grandes villes du monde' (*'Six shimmering gold letters that tonight would be turning like suns in four of the world's greatest cities'*).[144] Could this evocation of a Jewish name for a Jewish company be a reference by Némirovsky to Lacretelle's by then famous novel? Whether or not the reference was deliberate, it demonstrates that the two texts are fishing in the same waters for their imagery. In a cultural environment where the name of Rothschild was ubiquitous, these passages evoke once more the stereotype of the essential connection between Jews and money (which Silbermann has internalised at this point in the narrative, when he rejects writing and embraces commerce) and the idea that Jewish businesses are everywhere and easily recognisable by their names. Similarly, the reference in *Le Retour de Silbermann* to a rich Jewish banker from Russia who moves in Parisian high society[145] might almost be a reference back to David Golder, had the publication of Lacretelle's sequel not predated that of *David Golder* by a few months.[146] *Le Retour de Silbermann* evokes the literary type of which David Golder is also an example, demonstrating again the common frame of reference governing the two novels. There is also considerable stylistic similarity between Lacretelle's and Némirovsky's fiction. Discussing the critical reception of *Silbermann*, Douglas Alden notes that '[h]is works have a modern appeal because of their themes, but they also provide a classical refuge from the more eccentric forms of contemporary literature'.[147] As we saw in Chapter 1, this was absolutely the case as regards the reception of *David Golder*. Richard Griffiths' interpretation of *Silbermann* as a primarily psychological novel without a clear 'message' also applies to *David Golder*,[148] though *Silbermann* is a psychological study of the (Protestant) first person narrator, not of Silbermann, whilst *David Golder* is a psychological study of Golder, and Némirovsky does not thematise 'external' anti-Semitism in detail, as Lacretelle does. The novels are linked by the fundamental ambiguity of their attitude to Jewishness: Silbermann's 'great statement of the Jewish case'[149] corresponds in this respect to Némirovsky's evocation of the reader's sympathy for the character and fate of Golder, but these potentially philosemitic aspects of the texts are rendered unstable by the simultaneous presence of racialised conceptions of ethnicity and the use of negative stereotypes. The 'problem' of *Silbermann* is also the 'problem' of *David Golder*: as Griffiths argues, it is difficult, if not impossible, to receive these works positively after the Holocaust, but, nonetheless, we must avoid a retrospective reading which imposes a post-war world view onto pre-war texts.[150]

Whilst the work of Lacretelle provided a positive context for the reception of *David Golder*, *Les Chiens et les loups* suffered from an absence of any obvious literary context, as we have already noted. This can be illustrated through an appreciation of the lack of any meaningful literary or contextual connections between Némirovsky's fiction and the work of Albert Cohen. In 1930, works as diverse as *Solal* and *Silbermann* could coexist in the literary field. By 1938, when Cohen's *Mangeclous* appeared, Lacretelle was no longer writing about Jews, and Némirovsky's treatment of Jewish identity had little in common either stylistically or thematically with Cohen's. Némirovsky's tendency towards concision and narrative restraint is diametrically opposed to Cohen's epic excess. Cohen's novels are often described as 'rocambolesque': extravagant and full of extraordinary adventures. Némirovsky's novels rely on realism, both psychological and social, whilst Cohen's discourse constantly exceeds realism. At the conclusion of *Solal*, the eponymous hero dies, only to be born again to pursue his adventures in *Mangeclous* and *Belle du seigneur*. It is of course much more difficult to make direct links between the contemporary socio-political environment and the literary text in relation to obviously non-realist texts such as Cohen's than it is in relation to a text such as *Les Chiens et les loups*. Cohen's fiction was thus less open to ideological manipulation by critics than was Némirovsky's.[151] Cohen is well known for his creation of Rabelaisian characters such as the Valeureux, Solal's five absurd cousins: Cohen's warm and humorous sympathy for his characters is very different from Némirovsky's ironic and merciless dissection of hers, which Nina Gourfinkel likened to the action of a scalpel.[152] Cohen and Némirovsky held radically different views about the relationship between their French and foreign Jewish identities. David Coward suggests that, whilst Cohen bridged two value systems, he used his Western identity to underline his Jewish heritage.[153] His Zionism derived from his desire to bring the civilising values of the Law of Moses to the West.[154] Némirovsky also bridged two cultures, yet her identity was very European from the outset; in Némirovsky's case, cultural hybridity did not result in the coexistence of two value systems, for she had no sense of Jewish spiritual values, and in any case subordinated her foreign-Jewish identity to her French identity, as we have seen. There is no sense in which *Les Chiens et les loups* could be read as an assertion of Jewish values, even though it is a discussion of the problems posed by assimilation. Harry Sinner has more in common with David Silbermann than he has with Solal; as a literary type emanating from the pen of a Jewish novelist in the French literary field of the late 1930s, he was dangerously anomalous.

The problem of the ethical evaluation of Némirovsky's representations of Jewishness is ultimately a question of whether the images and situations which occur and recur in her novels are received as generally valid or as specific descriptions of particular individuals and situations. The diversity of responses to *David Golder* demonstrates that the answer to this question does not lie in the text itself. The 'problem' of Némirovsky's descriptions of Jewish identity is a problem of reception. The reception of her fiction could not possibly be the same in 1939 as it had been at the start of her career: in 1929 the author of *David Golder* was an unknown writer whose position in the literary field was yet to be determined, who could yet be 'claimed' by a variety of groups or positions within the field. By 1939 her position in the literary field was established, and it was not a position likely to facilitate a positive or tolerant response to *Les Chiens et les loups*. In assessing Némirovsky's representation of Jewishness, it is crucial to avoid ahistorical or anachronistic readings. We must avoid backshadowing. We must instead embrace what Bernstein terms *sideshadowing*: 'a gesturing to the side, to a present dense with multiple, and mutually exclusive, possibilities for the future':[155]

> For a prosaics of sideshadowing, the question of how to live one's ethnic, racial, or sexual heritage is a subset of the more general issue of finding a proper relationship to temporality and communal identity. Against current ideologies that compete about which one of these aspects, most commonly either the ethnic or the sexual, should be seen as somehow foundational for the entirety of one's being, prosaics regards each one as an equally valid ground base upon which one learns to play out the infinitely complex variations that constitute our freedom.[156]

It is not necessary—nor is it possible—to attempt to integrate all of Némirovsky's literary choices into a single narrative which makes sense retrospectively. Nor is it desirable to approach her writing in such a way as to force a choice between different aspects of her identity, or indeed to impose a coherent integration of this diversity. Bourdieu's approach has the advantage of allowing this sort of sideshadowing in *literary* history: the acknowledgement that each literary event is the one potentiality amongst many that was actually realised, and the recognition that each literary event occurs *in its own time*, without the benefit of hindsight.

5 Crisis and Conflict
Constructions of National Identity

In the preceding chapters, I discussed the fictional manifestations of Némirovsky's multiple cultural and ethnic allegiances. I noted the wide range of international literary influences on her writing. And I underlined the lively interest in the 'exotic' aspects of her life and work displayed by readers in the early 1930s. But I also argued that the ultimate goal of Némirovsky's writing project was cultural assimilation: she attempted to subordinate the 'foreign' aspects of her literary identity to an overriding 'Frenchness' by adopting formal conventions which the contemporary literary field deemed to be specifically French. In the novels dating from the early 1930s, Némirovsky successfully 'contained' Jewish and Russian themes within recognisably French literary models, and presented 'foreign' identities in ways which were both alluring and palatable to French readers. She thus achieved her stated intention to be more of a French writer than a Russian one. Némirovsky continued to pursue this goal in the second half of the decade, but she adopted different literary strategies in order to achieve it. With the exception of *Les Chiens et les loups*, which is in some respects anomalous, Russian and Jewish themes disappeared from Némirovsky's novels after 1935, to be replaced by a depiction of the contemporary French socio-economic environment from the perspective of French protagonists. Having convinced her readers of her ability to portray the 'foreign' in French terms, she started out on what might be seen as a perilous enterprise for an immigrant: to present the French to themselves. That Némirovsky was able to undertake such a venture is indicative of the success of her quest to be accepted as a French writer in the early part of the decade. The ways in which she approached this venture are indicative of her understanding of the contemporary literary field. This chapter considers how Némirovsky's fictionalisations of the crises and conflicts of the 1930s and early 1940s reinforced the construction of her own identity as a French novelist.

We saw in Chapter 2 that 1934 was a significant turning point in Némirovsky's literary trajectory. In 1934, *Films parlés* appeared with Gallimard and was reviewed in the *Revue des deux mondes*, which inaugurated a period of collaboration between Némirovsky and this respected, conservative review. The year 1934 also marked the end of Némirovsky's relationship with Grasset and the beginning of her publishing contract with Albin Michel, which was to last until her death and even beyond. *Le Pion sur l'échiquier*, the first book Némirovsky published with Albin Michel, was also the first of her novels to be serialised in a review (it appeared in *L'Intransigeant* from October 1933) before appearing in book form in the early summer of 1934. Némirovsky and Albin Michel continued to use this highly remunerative publishing strategy: *Le Vin de solitude* appeared in *La Revue de Paris* from March 1935; *Jézabel* was serialised in *Marianne* from October 1935; *La Proie* appeared in *Gringoire* from October 1936; *Deux* appeared in *Gringoire* from April 1938 and *Les Biens de ce monde*, which did not appear as a book until 1947, was published in *Gringoire* from April 1941. Némirovsky's biographers link the notable increase in the volume of material Némirovsky published in wide-circulation reviews of various political colours after 1933 to her personal financial circumstances: the death of her father left her in need of additional sources of income in order to support the lifestyle to which she was accustomed.[1] Reviewing *Le Pion sur l'échiquier* in *Gringoire*, Marcel Prévost noted that Némirovsky had changed her way of writing in this novel.[2] It is the first of Némirovsky's mature works to turn its gaze away from the experiences of the immigrant. However, as I have already noted, it is a transitional text: Christophe Bohun, though he was born in France and fought for France in the First World War, is the son of a Greek immigrant; his professional antagonist Beryl—formerly Biruleff—is Jewish and is portrayed in highly pejorative stereotypical terms. In *Le Pion sur l'échiquier*, Némirovsky retuned to a narrative situation she had first used in 1926 in *Le Malentendu*: the young war veteran attempting to create a psychologically and economically viable existence in post-war France. Thus, in relation to Némirovsky's previous fictional output, *Le Pion sur l'échiquier* represents a repositioning in the literary field which was both a consolidation and a reorientation.

For Bourdieu, understanding the work of given a writer amounts to reconstructing the artistic position-taking in relation to which that writer constructed her or his artistic project. The adoption of a given position is also necessarily the refusal of other positions, as Bourdieu demonstrates in *Les Règles de l'art* via the example of Flaubert:

> Lorsque Flaubert entreprend d'écrire *Madame Bovary* ou *L'Education sentimentale*, il se situe activement, par des choix impliquant autant de refus, dans l'espace des possibles qui s'offrent à lui. Comprendre ces choix, c'est comprendre la signification différentielle qui les caractérise au sein de l'univers des choix compossibles et la relation intelligible qui unit ce sens différentiel à la différence entre l'auteur de ces choix et les auteurs de choix différents des siens.[3]

> *When Flaubert embarks upon writing* Madame Bovary *and* Sentimental Education, *he actively situates himself, by choices (implying the same number of refusals) in the space of the possibles offered him. To*

understand these choices is to understand the differential signification that characterizes them within the universe of compossible choices and the intelligible relationship that joins this differential meaning to the difference between the author of these choices and the authors of choices different from his.[4]

We saw for example in Chapter 3 that, in depicting Russianness, Némirovsky occupied a position opposed to that chosen by the Russian-language exile writers of the 'Paris note', and which had been established in the literary field of the 1920s in novels by writers such as Carco and Kessel. In Chapter 4, we saw that Némirovsky occupied a position opposed to the spiritually and politically engaged writings of the Jewish renaissance, and which had been made possible by novels such as Lacretelle's *Silbermann* and *Le Retour de Silbermann*. Of course, such a schematic description is a simplification, and we also saw the various ways in which such oppositions are complicated in Némirovsky's fiction. It is nonetheless via this sort of differential understanding of the literary text that plausible readings can be offered and the misreading produced by a decontextualised reading can be avoided. Although 1934 marks a change in the thematic focus of Némirovsky's novels, she continued to produce the type of books she had always written and which were intended to ensure that she was widely read and therefore financially successful: accessible novels which, like the short stories which she also produced in large numbers, relied on the author's ability to create narrative suspense. Her fiction of this period is highly typical of a large swathe of French novelistic production originating in the immediate pre-First World War period, and represented in the works of writers such as Roger Martin du Gard, Georges Duhamel, Jules Romains, André Maurois, Romain Rolland, and Jacques de Lacretelle. Broadly speaking, such writing is traditional in form and focuses on the relationships and conflicts between the individual and contemporary French society. These novels reached a wide audience of middle-class readers in the 1920s and 1930s. The commercial aspect of Némirovksy's writing is not atypical, and must be understood in the context of the newly emerging market for literary fiction in the period. Discussing the vitality of the novel as a genre in the post-war period in his *Histoire de la littérature française* of 1936, Albert Thibaudet remarked that, with a public clamouring for novels, literature had never before been required to such an extent to defer to the public's wishes and to the requirements of the market.[5] As Bourdieu argues, the fact that the logic of supply and demand governs the literary field does not mean that fiction which corresponds to the dominant tastes of the majority of readers should be dismissed as a cynical exercise in commercialism. In her novels of the second half of the 1930s, through her thematic and formal choices, Némirovsky adopted a position which was already well established in the French literary field. As was the case at every stage of her development as a novelist, she did not create her position in the literary field through startling innovation, but rather by manipulating discourses already available in the cultural context in which she was operating. Her engagement with the French novel of contemporary social analysis in the second half of the decade was a turning away from the very obvious markers of cultural difference which she had previously foreground in her fiction. She continued to define herself in opposition to certain dominant trends in the literary field of 1930s France which were more typically to be found in the *champ de production restreinte*: the formally experimental novel primarily motivated by the search for aesthetic innovation, and the politically committed and explicitly militant novel. It is important to recognise what kind of novelist Némirovsky was, but also, what she was not. As we saw in the case of her writing about Jewishness, we should not criticise Némirovsky for not achieving something that was never her aim: she did not see her fictional project in terms of striking formal innovation, nor as an opportunity to convey complex political or philosophical theses.

Taking Némirovsky's *œuvre* as a whole, the reader is struck by the recurrence of themes and motifs. Philipponnat and Lienhardt even go as far as to speak of the entirety of Némirovsky's literary output as one long uninterrupted novel, and in a sense, this is justifiable.[6] However, in recognising such consistency, it is important not to overlook the clustering of certain themes and motifs. Némirovsky's fictional production after 1934 is strikingly coherent and significantly different in focus from her earlier work. Her account of the experiences of two generations of French men in the wake of the First World War in *Le Pion sur l'échiquier* (1934), *La Proie* (1938), and *Deux* (1939) is sufficiently coherent across the three texts to suggest that these works should be seen as a sort of trilogy. Similarly, *Les Biens de ce monde* (1941), *Les Feux de l'automne*, and *Suite française* (the latter two texts were written during the early 1940s but remained unpublished during Némirovsky's lifetime) are linked by a common aim and theme: the construction of a chronologically complete account of French society from the turn of the century to Némirovsky's very last moments of writing in 1942. There is a deliberate transition between these two 'trilogies': *Deux* and *Les Biens de ce monde* are both partly set in the fictional Northern French village of Saint-Elme. But there is also a shift in emphasis: in the first 'trilogy', the narrative focus is on the experiences of individuals, whilst in the second, the focus is on the effect of history on communities. *Les Biens de ce monde*, *Les Feux de l'automne*, and *Suite française* were written over a much shorter period of time than *Le Pion sur l'échiquier*, *La Proie*, and *Deux*; in the case of the first 'trilogy', the sequence of publication was interrupted by *Le Vin de solitude* (1935) and *Jézabel* (1936). The status of *La Proie* as a 'sequel' to *Le Pion sur l'échiquier*, despite the interval of four years and the appearance of two other novels between their publication, is suggested by the various references to pawns and chess boards in *La Proie*. As a student, Jean-Luc's rooms are above a club and, as he sleeps, he can hear the sound of chessmen moving on the board.[7] Jean-Luc likens the political intrigues in which he becomes involved to a game in which the pawns are real men; as he loses control, the pawns start to play their own game; ultimately, all his pawns turn against him.[8]

Némirovsky's novels of the latter part of the 1930s and the early 1940s display various points of similarity with the great French novel cycles of the inter-war period. At a formal level, it is obviously important not to push the analogy too far, since her texts were clearly not produced within as deliberate and consistent a framework as a cycle such as Jules Romains' twenty-seven-volume *Les Hommes de bonne volonté* (1932–1946), and their scope is more limited. However, there is a definite coincidence between these types of works and Némirovsky's later fiction. The briefest of considerations of any work of literary history of the period shows this to be the case.[9] Roger Martin du Gard presented the failure of a man's quest for freedom in *Jean Barois* (1913) and the revolt of the bourgeois son against his family in *Les Thibault* (1922–1940). Georges Duhamel's five-volume *Vie et aventures de Salavin* (1920–1932) traced the hopeless undertakings of a failed man, thus creating the archetypal *raté*, and *La Chronique des Pasquier* (1933–1945) recorded the hazards of social ascendancy and material success—and failure. Like *Les Pasquier*, but on a larger scale, Romains's monumental *Les Hommes de bonne volonté* sought to portray contemporary French society faced with the challenges of modernity. Such novels portray French life over a period of time, they tend to create representative characters, and they focus on two, three, or even four generations of the same family, all of which are features of Némirovsky's fiction of this period. As Germaine Brée notes, such 'traditionally structured' novels flourished in the 1930s:

> [. . .] whether based on the story of individual lives or on society as a whole, they revolve thematically around the relations individuals have with each other and how they react to their social code. To oversimplify a little, we can say that, in this type of novel, what the characters do reveals their psychology and that interactions between them triggers [sic] events which in turn reveal the moral values of their milieu.[10]

In this context, one might also cite novelists such as André Maurois and Jacques Chardonne, also widely read in their time, though much less so in our own. The style and themes of their fiction are close to Némirovsky's. The story of the son who takes over the family business under difficult economic circumstances and gradually merges his identity with that of the firm had been told by Maurois in *Bernard Quesnay* (1926), to which *Le Temps* likened *David Golder*.[11] Maurois and Chardonne were well-known exponents of the novel of bourgeois marriage. Chardonne's *Les Varais* (1929) and Jacques de Lacretelle's four-volume *Les Hauts-Ponts* (1932–1936) are centred on the fate of the family house and land. Némirovsky's later fiction is generated almost exclusively out of these related themes of the French bourgeois family and its business and property interests. Todd notes that 'novels with family-centred plots reigned supreme for most of the 1930s', thanks to the influence of Mauriac.[12] Némirovsky's texts are examples of a strong trend in the inter-war French novel. Brée notes the dominance of 'novels that, while cautiously modifying their narrative style, still remained faithful to the aesthetic of *subject* and *mimesis*' [emphasis in original].[13] Némirovsky's novels are highly characteristic of this mode of writing, as Marcel Prévost implied with pleasure when he compared the solidity of Némirovsky's characterisation to the insubstantial protagonists created by more aesthetically experimental modernist writers.[14]

Thus, in the second half of the 1930s, Némirovsky wrote about France by drawing on a repertoire of themes which constituted a very recognisable feature of the contemporary national literary landscape. That is to say that she began to write about France in the ways in which French novelists had been writing about France for some years. This is not to say that there is nothing distinctive about her writing. It is to underline the fact that her *œuvre* was, and increasingly so, an exercise in cultural assimilation. There is no doubt that Némirovsky was familiar with this tradition of contemporary French writing, for she cites its representative authors in her notes and in interviews. She refers to Maurois's *Le Cercle de la famille* in relation to *Le Vin de solitude*, and to Duhamel's *Pasquier* in relation to 'En raison des circonstances', an unpublished story on which *Les Feux de l'automne* was based.[15] As we have already seen, Némirovsky used interviews published in the literary and cultural press to reinforce her literary identity as a French novelist, and there is consistency between the writers she cited in such sources and the thematic preoccupations of her work. In the interviews she gave to Frédéric Lefèvre and Claude Pierrey in 1930, she cited Maurois and Chardonne amongst her favourite French authors, and in the interview with Lefèvre in 1933, she praised *Les Thibault* as a successful example of the French novel cycle.[16] However, in this interview she also expressed some scepticism about the genre, remarking that 'je l'aime beaucoup quand il jaillit de la source. C'est-à-dire quand l'histoire écrite en deux tomes ne pouvait pas être écrite en un seul' (*I really like it when it is completely justified by the work, that is, when a story written in two volumes could not have been written in just one*), but pointing out that 'dans d'autres cas, cela s'appelle tout bonnement du remplissage' (*in other cases it really is a question of padding*). She also praised Mauriac, who, she felt, incarnated French clarity and moderation. Given that, for Némirovsky, the 'Frenchness' of French fiction resided in its concision and precision, it is not surprising that her engagement with the portraits of contemporary France typical of the *roman-cycle* was ultimately more thematic than formal.

MONEY AND MELANCHOLIA

Two themes dominate *Le Pion sur l'échiquier*, *La Proie*, and *Deux*: suicide and money. In these novels, a self-destructive malaise afflicts two generations of French men: the young war veterans (Christophe Bohun in *Le Pion sur l'échiquier* and Antoine Carmontel in *Deux*) and their sons (Philippe Bohun in *Le Pion sur l'échiquier* and Jean-Luc Daguerre in *La Proie*). These novels investigate the social roots of psychological malaise. As the *Revue des deux mondes* remarked of the protagonists of *Le Pion sur l'échiquier*, all are victims of '[l]a malediction d'une époque sans pitié' (*the curse of a pitiless era*).[17] Money had of course been the main thematic preoccupation of *David Golder*, where the brutal account of the machinations of the cosmopolitan circles of high finance had brought Némirovsky tremendous success as well as—or thanks to—a certain degree of controversy. In *Le Pion sur l'échiquier*, *La Proie*, and *Deux*, money is a crucial ingredient of the malaise of the French male subject. Némirovsky's manuscript notes tell us that she conceived *Le Pion sur l'échiquer*—set in 1934—explicitly as a novel of the generation following that of David Golder,[18] and it is very much a development of the thematic preoccupations of her first success. Success was clearly in Némirovsky's mind as she planned the text: musing on different possibilities for the family groupings in her embryonic novel, she wrote: 'Décidement, je crois que cela vendrait mieux, la seconde solution' (*I really think that the second solution would sell better*).[19] Némirovsky's biographers are right to point out the financial motivation behind her writing at this moment in her life.

Némirovsky conceived *Le Pion sur l'échiquer* as a portrait of 'l'homme, écrasé par la fatalité, le pion que les forces économiques et sociales tiraillent dans tous les sens' (*a man crushed by fate, a pawn which economic forces pull in all directions*).[20] Whilst the story of Christophe's failure to re-integrate into the social, emotional, and economic realities of post-war France is closely related to French literary models, the direct source of inspiration for the text was Sinclair Lewis's *Babbitt*, the American literary success of 1922, whose eponymous hero was to become an international cultural phenomenon. In the notes Némirovsky wrote whilst drafting her novel, she remarked:

> Il faudrait le baser sur *Babbitt*, prendre une année de la vie de X, une année d'homme moderne, avec les sordides embêtements qui le caractèrisent (trop sordides, peut-être, mais si vrai). Montrer comment l'argent (et là, pas l'amour de l'argent, mais la simple nécessité de vivre, le gagne-pain quotidien) peut empoisonner la vie d'un homme.[21]

> *It should be based on Babbitt. Take a year in the life of X, one year of a modern man, with the sordid annoyances which characterise him (maybe too sordid, but very real). Show how money (and I don't mean the love of money, but the simple necessity of living, earning enough to eat) can poison a man's life.*

Babbitt was published in French translation in 1930, with a preface by Paul Morand who Némirovsky knew well.[22] *Babbitt* is a satirical denunciation of the commercial environment of small-town America in the 1920s, a society whose values are exclusively financial and which has produced a standardised culture and standardised human beings. The property dealer Babbitt, like Christophe, gradually loses his faith in the values which govern his life and the society in which he operates, but, despite his rather pathetic attempts, he cannot escape and create new values. Rebecca West described him in a review of the novel in 1922 as 'a strayed soul disconsolate through frustrated desires for honour and beauty'.[23] Although Bohun's frustrated desires are perhaps less noble, Lewis's satirical account of American modernity is a plausible model for Némirovsky's ironic presentation of French modernity. However, *Babbitt* was, in Mark Schorer's words, a demonstration that 'conformity is the great price that our predominantly commercial culture exacts of American life'.[24] It was not therefore directly applicable to the French cultural context, with its strong tradition of social protest and rejection of cultural conformity. Némirovsky rejected this culturally specific aspect of Babbitt's identity when she noted that 'je ne peux pas faire ce brave type, genre Babbitt. Mes héros sont toujours conscients' (*I can't do those well-behaved types, like Babbitt. My heroes are always self-aware*).[25] Her characters do not follow Babbitt's trajectory. Whilst Babbitt ultimately turns away from his moment of rebellion and reintegrates into his original family and professional situation, Némirovsky's characters are both unable and unwilling to resolve their personal and financial dilemmas through conformity. They are not *brave types*, and their self-awareness manifests itself precisely in a refusal of conformity. The impossibility of a compliant resolution is also a function of changed socio-economic circumstances. Whilst *Babbitt* is about the boom years of the American economy before the crash, *Le Pion sur l'échiquier, La Proie,* and *Deux* are all very much post-Wall Street: in the economic climate of 1930s France, a return to stability is not a choice open to Némirovsky's protagonists. There are no overt references to Babbitt in *Le Pion sur l'échiquier*, but the American depression finds its way into the text through the jazz number which Christophe hums, and which comes to symbolise his malaise:

> No more money in the bank
> No cute baby we can spank
> Oh, what to do? Oh, what to do?
> Put out the lights and go to bed.[26]

Rudy Vallée, an American radio star and the original 'crooner', recorded this song, entitled 'Let's put out the lights', in 1932.[27] The presence of the song in the text is more a marker of modernity than of Americanisation; Christophe also hears strains of Maurice Chevalier's 1925 'Valentine' coming from a neighbour's gramophone.[28] This story of a young and beautiful former lover who has become old and unattractive is as appropriate to Christophe's middle-aged sexual malaise as the Rudy Vallée song is to his economic anxieties. What these examples suggest is that the interest of Némirovsky's texts lies in her ability to weave together suggestive snippets of discourses on the malaise of modernity. As we saw in Chapter 2, intertextual allusions in Némirovsky's fiction tend not to be very developed, but they are frequent, and although they act only on the surface of the text, they form a network of contextual allusions which is not without coherence. Their variety suggests that, whilst the thematic centre of Némirovsky's novels is very obviously derived from a recognisable current of contemporary French fiction, her texts are not limited to this model.

Melancholy was, as Nicholas Hewitt has demonstrated, an important and multifaceted theme in French literature of the inter-war years:

> [. . .] as a sickness which contains within itself its own cure, [melancholy] continues through the nineteenth century, especially in the work of Nerval and Baudelaire, but when it reemerges in the literature of the inter-war years, it does so in a complex form, retaining its positive aesthetic properties, but now endowed with a destructive psychological apparatus.[29]

It is this 'destructive psychological apparatus'—separated from any aesthetic preoccupations—which emerges as the central thematic concern of *Le Pion sur l'échiquier, La Proie,* and *Deux.* In many novels of the inter-war period, the aesthetically productive melancholy of the nineteenth century is transformed into a psychologically paralysing malaise. The theme of malaise surfaced in various guises in the inter-war period.[30] In 1919, in his essay 'La Crise de l'esprit', Paul Valéry articulated the anxiety of the post-First World War generation who had come face to face with the truth of the fragility of European civilisation. In their essays in the *Nouvelle Revue française* in 1923–1925, Benjamin Crémieux and Marcel Arland termed the anxiety of the younger generation of post-war writers a *nouveau mal du siècle*. In *Inquiétude et reconstruction* (1931), Crémieux identified the aesthetic forms via which this anxiety had manifested itself in the immediate post-war years: the Dada movement; the literature of travel and escapism; the Proustian dissection of personality.[31] But Arland had also offered a more socio-historical treatment of the theme of the *nouveau mal du siècle* in his 1925 essay, where he identified his generation as disoriented, prepared for a war they were too young to fight, and searching for moral values in a post-war world offering few such certainties. As Hewitt suggests, this aspect of Arland's analysis opened the door to a psycho-social notion of malaise which departs from its original aesthetic definition. Hewitt concedes that, given the importance in the inter-war texts of the theme of sexuality, this slippage from literature to life is justifiable: 'clearly the "nouveau mal du siècle" cannot be seen as a purely intellectual problem, but must be viewed as the expression of a psychological instability, allied to neurosis and suicide, with an essentially sexual cause'.[32] Thus, in French inter-war fiction, we find a more generalised representation of malaise, which is related to, but by no means synonymous with, the *nouveau mal du siècle*, which is a question of theme rather than of form, and which arises from novelists' desire to portray the situation of the individual obliged to negotiate the moral, political and economic uncertainties of the age. Writing in 1931, Crémieux suggested that 1930 constituted a turning point in French literary production: the decade of 'anxiety' was opening out onto a period of 'reconstruction' during which writers were abandoning the search for absolute originality of form and turning instead towards the depiction of collective, social concerns.[33] Writers were moving away from the experimental and destructive conception of writing exemplified by the Dada movement, and were instead turning to works such as Martin du Gard's *Les Thibault* as a model for a literature which would abandon Proustian introspective analyses of highly individual, non-generalisable psychological states in favour of the creation of psychological types, such as the young man of the post-war era.[34] It is in this context that Némirovsky's portraits of the malaise of the post-war French male should be understood.

Le Pion sur l'échiquier establishes the cross-generational nature of inter-war male malaise. Malaise is certainly not limited to the *nouveau mal du siècle* generation, represented here by Philippe. Némirovsky interrogates father–son relationships across three generations: a narrative strategy typical of the *roman-cycle*. Philippe's rebellion expresses itself through his indifference to his grandfather's death, but Christophe suggests a commonality of experience shared by all three men: 'Laisse-le mourir en paix . . . Il a souffert du même mal que nous; il n'avait pas plus que nous de contentement, de paix intérieure' (*Let him die in peace. He has suffered from the same ills as us; he didn't have any more contentment or peace of mind*).[35] The 'mal' afflicting all three generations of the Bohun family is, in origin, financial: it began with the collapse of the family banking business in 1925. The generation of David Golder and James Bohun benefited financially from the boom years but cannot sustain their success; the generation of Christophe Bohun and the Carmontel brothers in *Deux* are exhausted by their experience of the war and unable to overcome their apathy in order to take advantage of the opportunities open to them in the 1920s; the generation of Philippe Bohun and Jean-Luc Daguerre in *La Proie*, sons of war veterans, are in a state of angry revolt against their fathers and against the lack of opportunities for social and financial advancement in the 1930s. Money creates malaise differently for each generation: the first generation is characterised by energy, the second by apathy, and the third by revolt.

Némirovsky was certainly not the only novelist of the inter-war period to link money and malaise: as Hewitt points out, Pierre Mac Orlan identified the economic aspect of the *nouveau mal du siècle* in the 1920s.[36] However, she was careful to distinguish between mere posturing and real financial hardship. Interviewed by Jeanine Delpech in June 1938, shortly after the publication of *La Proie*, she remarked: 'Il y a je crois une grande part de snobisme dans le pessimisme aggressif de certains jeunes gens—c'est une nouvelle forme du mal du siècle. Chez ceux qui sont directement atteints par le chômage, la misère, il y a une souffrance indéniable' (*I think there is a lot of snobbery in the aggressive pessimism of some young people—it's a new form of the* mal du siècle. *Amongst those who are directly affected by unemployment and poverty, there is undeniable suffering*). Némirovsky's portrait of post-war malaise is a social critique as well as a documentary account of contemporary reality and, as usual, Némirovsky is not afraid to underline the unacceptable nature of her characters' behaviour and motivations. *Le Pion sur l'échiquier* demonstrates the highly ambivalent attractions of money in the modern economy. Christophe's passion for motoring illustrates the material benefits of modernity.[37] But ultimately, modernity's superficial pleasures offer no consolation. As he drives, he wonders why he is so unhappy.[38] War had given Christophe a reason to live, but in the post-war era, money cannot fulfil this function: 'J'étais moins malheureux à la guerre. La vie, du moins, paraissait avoir du prix' (*I was less unhappy in the war. At least life seemed to have some value*).[39] Christophe was brought up with the values of the new capitalism, which he despises, rather than with those of the pre-war French bourgeoisie, to which he aspires. By contrast, Geneviève's family represents old-style French provincial wealth:

> Quelle blague, quelle vaste blague! . . . Je voudrais le loisir, la paresse, la tranquilité, ni végéter, ni me battre, mais vivre! . . . Est-ce donc impossible? . . . Pourquoi ne suis-je pas née dans la famille de ma femme? Un petit rentier de province, mais il n'y a plus de petits rentiers. . . . [40]

> *What a joke, what a huge joke! I want leisure, idleness, peace: I don't want to vegetate and I don't want to fight, I just want to live! Is that impossible? Why wasn't I born into my wife's family? A little provincial property owner. But no-one lives off their property any more. . . .*

The war has destroyed apparently invulnerable provincial prosperity, making a certain type of French bourgeois existence a thing of the past and provoking a crisis of identity in those who seek to define their lives according to its values. Christophe's self-righteous, complacent bourgeois wife Geneviève is the target of the narrator's irony because she lacks the self-awareness or the financial insight to recognise that the values of Courtenay, her family's provincial home, are hopelessly outdated:

> C'est par la prévoyance et l'économie que sont fondées les fortunes de notre province, ajouta-t-elle, répétant les paroles entendues dans son enfance, et qui s'échappaient de ses lèvres, dictées sans doute par une lignée de mortes, de sages bourgeoises de Courtenay, endormies dans la paix du Seigneur.[41]

'The wealth of our region is based on prudence and economy', she added,
repeating the words she had heard in her childhood, and which escaped
from her lips, as if dictated to her by a whole line of deceased women,
the wise bourgeoises of Courtenay, sleeping in the peace of Christ.

This theme recurs in *La Proie*, where Jean-Luc's family are eking out a miserable existence in one wing of the formerly prosperous le Vésinet, which
becomes for Jean-Luc the symbol of his family's failure to provide him with
the material means to succeed. Such evocations of the *domaine familial*
recall other contemporary novels on a similar theme, such as Lacretelle's
Les Hauts-Ponts and Chardonne's *Les Varais*. Jean-Luc links his malaise
explicitly to the psycho-social anxieties of the *nouveau mal du siècle* generation through a reference to Stendhal:

> Julien Sorel pouvait encore compter sur une partie de la société. Mais
> nous? . . . Sur quoi s'appuyer aujourd'hui? . . . Tout chancelle. L'argent
> lui-même n'est pas sûr. Et autour de soi, rien. Pas un appui.[42]

> *At least Julien Sorel could still rely on one section of society. But what*
> *about us? What can we cling on to? Everything is unstable. Even money*
> *is not safe. And around you, there is nothing. Nothing to hold on to.*

All that society can offer Jean-Luc is meaningless *arrivisme*, '[l]a cru-
elle et froide passion de parvenir, déguisée sous toutes sortes de noms et
d'étiquettes partisanes' (*the cruel cold desire for social advancement, disguised beneath all sorts of names and political labels*).[43] Like Julien Sorel,
Jean-Luc lives in a world which offers no outlets for his ambition and his
desire for action.[44] Aspects of Jean-Luc's trajectory recall that of Julien: his
love for a woman above his social station; her pregnancy; his frustration
at his inability to transcend his socially and economically modest origins.
But his suicide is a gesture of despair and acquiescence which distinguishes
him from his romatic predecessor, whose death, sometimes interpreted as a
quasi-suicide, might be read as an affirmation of Julien's freedom to choose
the outcome of his *Bildung*.[45] But these young men no longer have the financial luxury of turning against a wealthy family, even if they seek to reject
their outmoded values:

> As-tu songé, dit Jean-Luc, que la parole de Gide n'aura bientôt plus
> de sens? Une famille qui vous assomme, mais qui est là, qui peut vous
> aider, vous faire monter, c'est d'un prix . . . je ne sais pas, moi, d'un prix
> formidable. . . . [46]

> *'Have you ever thought', said Jean-Luc, 'that what Gide said soon*
> *won't mean anything at all? A family which bores you, but which is*
> *there, which can help you, help you progress, that's worth something*
> *. . . I don't know, that's really worth a lot'.*

This passing reference to Gide's 'Familles, je vous hais!' (*Families, I hate you!*) in *Les Nourritures terrestres* (1897) is not an example of the type of complex intertextuality Roger Martin du Gard undertook in *La Belle saison*, the second volume of *Les Thibaut*, where extended quotations from *Les Nourritures terrestres* are woven into the text.[47] Like the reference to Stendhal, it should rather be read as part of Némirovsky's attempt to locate her own writing in relation to well-known French literary models. The erosion of bourgeois family wealth is also a defining factor in Antoine Carmontel's malaise in *Deux*. Antoine's studies were interrupted by the draft; returning from the war, he has no motivation to build a career.[48] The death of his father reveals the extent of his financial difficulties: now married to Marianne and with a family to support, he involves himself in a mediocre business venture. However, in this text, the accent is placed much more firmly on the sexual aspect of malaise. Indeed, the novel was marketed as a book about relationships: it was billed as Némirovsky's first love story.[49]

In all three texts, malaise is explicitly and repeatedly linked to the First World War. René Pomeau remarks in his study of French war fiction of the inter-war period that whilst the 'war novel' exists, the 'peace novel' does not because 'peace' is only meaningful in relation to war.[50] *Le Pion sur l'échiquier*, *La Proie,* and *Deux* might in fact be termed *romans de paix* insofar as the peacetime they depict is only meaningful in relation to the conflict which preceded it. In *La Proie*, the war is primarily present through its economic effects. The war defines the economic identity of the protagonists by undermining their fathers' financial stability. Jean-Luc's father's physical incapacity, which prevents him from working to provide for his family, is a result of his period of wartime captivity in Germany.[51] Jean-Luc's friend Dourdan lost his father in 1917, and although his representatives tried to ensure the survival of the family firm, it was in decline by the late 1920s and did not survive the first months of the crash.[52] In *Le Pion sur l'échiquier*, war is present rather through its psychological effects:

> –La mort m'est familière, dit Christophe. La guerre, malgré tout a eu cela de bon.
> Il tressaillait de surprise en entandant son fils murmurer :
> –Ah ! oui, c'est vrai, tu as été à la guerre, tu as eu de la chance . . .
> –Tu es fou, mon petit.
> Philippe secoua la tête :
> –Si, si, je t'envie. Cela secoue les nerfs, au moins, et puis penser à la mort, ce n'est pas gai, mais à la vie d'à présent, quelle horreur!
> –Tu es donc malheureux, mon chéri? demanda Christophe à mi-voix. A ton âge?
> –Dame, tu crois que c'est gai? Trembler à chaque instant que l'on va rester sans travail, subordonner sa vie à cette malheureuse obligation de gagner le pain quotidien? . . . C'est gai? Tu crois me comprendre? Votre génération était inquiète, ajouta-t-il en ricanant: ah! veinards! . . . Nous ne sommes pas inquiets, nous autres, nous sommes furieux.[53]

> '*Death is familiar to me*', said Christophe. '*Despite everything, that's one good thing about the war.*'
> He trembled with surprise to hear his son whisper:
> '*Ah, yes, that's true, you fought the war, you were lucky . . .* '
> '*You are mad, son!*'
> Philippe shook his head:
> '*No, really, I envy you. At least war sharpens your nerves, and then, thinking about death isn't very cheerful, but thinking about life at the moment, that's appalling!*'
> '*Are you unhappy, then, my dear?*' asked Christophe quietly. '*At your age?*'
> '*Honestly, do you think it's any fun? Terrified all the time that you won't have a job, giving your whole life over to the miserable need to earn your daily bread? Do you think that's fun? You think you understand me? Your generation was anxious*', he added, sniggering. '*Ah, you had it easy! As for us, we aren't anxious, we are furious.*'

Philippe's envy of his father's war experience identifies him as a representative of the *nouveau mal du siècle*. The war defines Christophe's identity both sexually and economically. He married Geneviève, who nursed him in a field hospital, to escape his memories of the war.[54] The war has destroyed the economic stability Christophe craves, and has created the economic instability which he cannot overcome. *Deux*, which begins at Easter 1919 and ends in the early 1930s, has a broader chronological scope than *Le Pion sur l'échiquier*, set in 1934, or *La Proie*, which begins in 1932. This provoked René Lalou to remark that the novel dealt with a time long past, fresh in readers' memories perhaps, but whose preoccupations—particularly financial ones—were very far removed from the present. The culture which surrounds the protagonists is infused with memories of the war: posters in the streets of Paris advertise collections to benefit needy war veterans; the fourteenth of July celebrations of 1919 are an affirmation of patriotism, with music, fireworks, dancing, and a rousing chorus of 'La Madelon de la victoire', a popular song written in 1918 in homage to 'La Madelon' of 1914 to celebrate the victory:

> Madelon, verse-nous à boire!
> Et surtout, n'y mets pas d'eau!
> C'est pour fêter la victoire,
> Joffre, Foch et Clemenceau![55]
> *Madelon, pour us a drink!*
> *And we don't want any water with it!*
> *We're celebrating the victory*
> *Of Joffre, Foch, and Clemenceau!*

As the text progresses, the significance of the war seems to fade. The *dénouement* of this text is the opposite of the two preceding novels. Christophe and Jean-Luc both commit suicide, but Antoine overcomes his malaise and resigns himself to his unadventurous but satisfying marriage with Marianne. In the context of the discourse of patriotism conveyed by the account of the fourteenth of July celebrations and by the inclusion of the text of the 'Madelon', it seems rather more than coincidental that the conclusion of the novel should posit the ultimate triumph of 'Marianne'—France?—over the economic and emotional wreckage which resulted from the First World War. In the final lines of the novel Antoine embraces Marianne lovingly, if resignedly, in the iconic location of the Champs Elysées. When she was drafting the novel, Némirovsky wrote that *Deux* would be the first optimistic book she had written.[56] Did she intend the 'optimism' of this text to be located not only in an assertion of the value and endurance of conjugal love, but also in an affirmation of a mythical 'Frenchness'? Such an interpretation is certainly consistent with the conclusion of her next published work, *Les Biens de ce monde*.

Of course, the optimism of *Deux* also lies in Antoine's choice of life over death. The theme of suicide had been a constant preoccupation in Némirovsky's writing from her very earliest texts, beginning from Ismaël's death by hanging in 'L'Enfant génial'. Gabri throws herself off a balcony in 'L'Ennemie'; Henri's lover dies by her own hand in 'La Comédie bourgeoise'; two more lovers kill themselves in 'Ida'; Marcus shoots himself in *David Golder*; Tatiana drowns herself in the Seine in *Les Mouches d'autonmne*; Christophe slits his throat in *Le Pion sur l'échiquier*; Sarlat takes an overdose and Jean-Luc shoots himself in *La Proie*; Evelyne takes an overdose in *Deux*; Doris Williams kills herself in London in the short story 'Magie'; Florence does likewise in Verona in 'Le Départ pour la fête'.[57] Péraudin hangs himself in 'La Peur', and there is a suggestion of suicide in *Les Feux de l'automne* in relation to the death of Mannheimer. And this is only to list actual deaths: various characters contemplate suicide, but hold back. But it is only in *Le Pion sur l'échiquier*, *La Proie,* and *Deux* that the protagonist's meditations on his despair and desire for death occupy a significant part of the narrative. The theme of suicide is, a Hewitt shows, a crucial aspect of the 1930s novel of malaise. Given the notable rise in suicide rates in the inter-war period, it was 'sufficiently a fact in French society to constitute a real basis for fictional treatments of the theme'.[58] Literary suicide can be either a positive expression of human freedom or a negative expression of despairing acquiescence.[59] Romantic suicide falls into the former category, as a manifestation of a clash between the superior intellect, insight, creativity, and sensibility of an individual and the baseness of the world.[60] Over the course of the nineteenth century, suicide began to be viewed as a sickness rather than as a sin, and, in the last decades of the century, as a manifestation of a social malaise.[61] Durkheim and Freud separate the *nouveau mal du siècle* from the romantic *mal du siècle*. In the inter-war period, suicide was a crucial element of Dada and surrealism, where it was encoded as an escape from reality, as 'the ultimate act of esthetic self-assertion and social and metaphysical transcendence', and as an expression of gratuity.[62] In 1942, in *Le Mythe de Sisyphe*, Albert

Camus rejected suicide in favour of revolt and freedom as the philosophical consequences of absurdity.[63] It is in relation to these literary discourses on suicide that Némirovky's fictional suicides must be understood.[64] Her representations of suicide in the mid- and late-1930s demonstrate the difference between the romantic *mal du siècle* and inter-war malaise. According to J. A. Hiddleston, romanticism proposed that it was

> preferable to be uniquely misguided than to be mediocrely right, so that madness, illness, criminality, and the destructive power of emotion were thought to constitute more alluring values in a literature which increasingly glorified the outcast, the pariah, ancestors of the twentieth-century popular figures of the 'rebel without a cause' and the 'crazy mixed-up kid'.[65]

Némirovsky's suicides are neither rebels nor mixed-up kids: they are mediocrely *wrong*. They do not die positively, for an idea, or to assert their freedom; they die negatively, in a moment of weakness, of acquiescence. Christophe's suicide is pathetically accidental: he slits his throat almost— but not quite—by accident whilst shaving and eventually dies of blood poisoning. Whilst he actively consents to his own death in the closing paragraphs of the novel, he dies of indifference, thinking simply 'Je m'en fous' (*I don't give a toss*).[66] Jean-Luc's suicide is certainly no romantic demonstration of heroic superiority. Jean-Luc is a profoundly antipathetic anti-hero who has been willing to sacrifice his wife, his child, and his best friend in the pursuit of social and financial advancement. In both novels, suicide is the pathetic end of a failed life completely lacking in heroism. Christophe and Jean-Luc are examples of the *raté*, the failed man. If we feel any sympathy for these characters, it is because their suicides are a manifestation of a profoundly social malaise. Evelyne's suicide in *Deux* has a different character. It is rather Gothic: she takes an overdose in a deserted cottage where two other young people committed suicide two years previously.[67] In a suicide note, she presents her death in terms of self-sacrifice: 'Je voulais te quitter. Mais ce n'est pas cela que tu veux, mon amour. Ce que tu veux, c'est d'être délivré du désir de moi, et moi, je veux être délivré de tout désir, et de la vie par surcroît' (*I wanted to leave you. But that isn't what you want, my love. What you want is deliverance from your desire for me, and I want deliverance from all desire, and also from life*).[68] But this is the discourse of romance literature rather than of romanticism. Overall, the 'trilogy' composed of *Le Pion sur l'échiquier*, *La Proie*, and *Deux* opposes the romantic notion according to which, as Paul Morand explained in his 1932 essay on romantic suicide: 'le suicide est une affirmation de vie; être dégoûté de la vie, c'est encore avoir foi en elle' (*suicide is an affirmation of life: to be disgusted with life is to still have faith in life*).[69] In Némirovsky's version of inter-war malaise, suicide is encoded as despair, whilst resignation is an affirmation of the value of life.

How then can we evaluate Némirovsky's engagement with the theme of malaise? Some critics found that, by the late 1930s, the theme was a little dated. Whilst in 1934, Marcel Prévost found Philippe Bohun to be 'tellement "d'à présent"' (*so very contemporary*), André Billy was not convinced that the themes of money and malaise were still relevant in 1938. He described Jean-Luc as a young Rastignac characteristic of 1933, 1935, or 1936, but who was outdated by 1938. Billy thought that readers' interest in the financial scandals in which Jean-Luc becomes enmeshed had been exhausted by the Stavisky crisis of 1934.[70] There is perhaps some justification for such a criticism: the themes Némirovsky was exploring in this period were by no means new ones. However, for Jean-Pierre Maxence, the representative nature of Némirovsky's fiction constituted one of its strengths. *La Proie* was proof that Némirovsky 'a vécu avec son temps' (*has lived with her time*), and that '[e]lle a su, en le comprenant d'une intime comprehension, en le connaissant d'une chaude connaissance, féconder son art, le nourrir' (*has, by understanding it intimately, by knowing it closely, been able to enrich and to nourish her art*).[71] It is a peculiar coincidence of literary history that Maxence should have reviewed *La Proie* in *Gringoire* alongside Sartre's *La Nausée*. Maxence, justifiably, could not imagine a mode of writing more different from Némirovsky's than that of Sartre. His prediction that *La Proie* might come in the future to stand for the experience of a generation has been proved by literary history to be very wide of the mark. Insofar as *La Nausée* is a depiction of melancholia, as Hewitt contends,[72] it could be argued that the theme of the sexual, moral, and intellectual or professional crisis of the mediocre man of the 1930s is at the root of both *La Proie* and *La Nausée*. But here the similarity ends. Jean-Luc is certainly no proto-existentialist, even if at the beginning of the novel he claims 'le droit d'être libre et responsable de ses actes' (*the right to be free and responsible for his actions*).[73] Maxence's purely circumstantial pairing of *La Nausée* and *La Proie* invites the modern reader to reflect on the differences between Némirovsky's writing and the much better known, philosophically sophisticated, and politically engaged fiction of the 1930s. The narrative framework and the structures of characterisation in Némirovsky's texts are simply not designed to support the kind of philosophical or political reflection typical of the inter-war philosophical novel.[74] It is clear from the characterisation of Jean-Luc that *La Proie* was not intended to be an investigation of the absurdity of the human condition in the manner of *La Nausée*, since Jean-Luc's pursuit of freedom is an exercise in shallow and irresponsible self-gratification rather than a quest for authenticity.[75] Rather like the Evelyn Waugh of *Vile Bodies* and *A Handful of Dust*, texts with which she was familiar,[76] Némirovsky's novels of this period are works of acerbic social satire which seek to demonstrate the appalling fates of human beings who allow themselves to be defined by superficial social and economic values. Némirovsky had an uncanny ability to evoke the reader's sympathy for the fate of characters who are fundamentally antipathetic. It is perhaps in this disturbing narrative quality that the value of her texts lies.

The theme of malaise offered Némirovsky a recognisable narrative structure around which she could create representative characters who are products of their socio-historical context. As well as addressing specifically French themes, such as the economic collapse of the traditional French propertied bourgeoisie, Némirovsky attempted to reinforce the national character of her texts through various intertextual references to well-known works of classic and contemporary French literature, including, as well as Gide and Stendhal, the comtesse de Ségur (Christophe likens Geneviève to Madame de Fleurville),[77] Giraudoux,[78] Mauriac,[79] Laclos,[80] and Musset.[81] The function of these references is to establish complicity between author and reader as members of the same national cultural community. This literary strategy was not entirely successful: although Gaston Chéreau could describe Némirovsky as 'Française d'adoption—et bien française!' (*French by adoption—and very French!*),[82] both Noel Sabord and Jeanine Delpech found *La Proie* to be a story of specifically Russian passions.[83] This was no doubt only to be expected, since throughout her career, Némirovsky and her publishers had traded on her 'exoticism' to provoke interest in her books. Clearly, by the late 1930s, the political context was such that Némirovsky had a strong interest in presenting herself through her fiction in terms of Frenchness. She had begun this process as early as 1934. The discourse of patriotism around the First World War in *Deux*, as well as the text's optimistic conclusion, represent her most explicit attempt to date to present a positive and heroic image of French national identity. The fresco of contemporary history which she then attempted in *Les Biens de ce monde*, *Les Feux de l'automne*, and *Suite française* was a much fuller development of this sort of fictional treatment of recent history.

FAMILLE, PATRIE, RELIGION

Les Biens de ce monde, *Les Feux de l'automne*, and *Suite française* tell the story—or rather, a story—of France between the turn of the century and the German declaration of war on the U.S.S.R. in June 1941. *Les Biens de ce monde* and *Les Feux de l'automne* both begin in the *belle époque* and narrate the First World War, the inter-war period and the outbreak of the Second World War. *Les Biens de ce monde* follows the fate of the Hardelot family, owners of a paper factory in the village of Saint-Elme in North East France, which finds itself in the path of the advancing German forces twice over. Destroyed in 1914, the village is rebuilt between the wars only to be destroyed for a second time as the German army breaks through the Maginot line. *Les Feux de l'automne* recounts the effects of two World Wars on a lower middle-class family in Paris. The young Thérèse Brun marries in 1915, is widowed shortly afterwards, and remarries after the

war. The middle section of the novel is reminiscent of the earlier texts insofar as it depicts the malaise of Thérèse's new husband Bernard, a young war
veteran, and the breakdown of their relationship. Both Bernard and their
son Yves are called up in 1939; Yves is killed, but Bernard survives, and
is reconciled with Thérèse at the end of the novel. Broadly speaking, *Les
Biens de ce monde* is an affirmation of the value and permanence of the
conservative ideals of the provincial French bourgeoisie, whilst *Les Feux de
l'automne* is a denunciation of the deficiencies of the inter-war social and
economic values which are blamed for the fall of France in 1940. The second novel also celebrates a certain French conservatism insofar as Thérèse's
petit-bourgeois values triumph over Bernard's rebellion. There is no doubt
that these texts also contain a strong element of satire, often humorous,
which is directed at the social conventions of the French bourgeoisie. Yet
despite Némirovsky's mockery of its habits and certainties, these two novels suggest that its moral values should be cultivated.

Each of these novels resembles a mini *roman-cycle*. Pomeau notes the close
relationship between war and the structure of the French *roman-cycle*:

> Ces chroniques d'une génération, écrites à la génération suivante,
> dépendent étroitement de l'Histoire: les phases alternatives de guerre
> et de paix y sont utilisées avec plus ou moins de chance, selon les dates
> de la composition.[84]

> *These chronicles of a generation, written in the next generation, de-
> pend closely on history: the alternating phases of war and peace are
> used more or less felicitously, according to the date of writing.*

Némirovsky's integration of French history into her fiction, which was
entirely typical of other contemporary writers, became increasingly ambitious through the late 1930s and into the war years. Although *Suite française*
is not an exact sequel to *Les Biens de ce monde* and *Les Feux de l'automne*,
it reads rather like their conclusion. *Suite Francaise* focuses on the here
and now, on the moment of writing, and presents the consequences of the
1900–1939 period. *Les Biens de ce monde* had concluded with the *exode*
and the armistice on 22 June 1940, whilst *Les Feux de l'automne* goes further into the Occupation period, as far as the return of the POWs. The two
volumes of *Suite Française* recount the events of 1940 and1941, beginning
with the fall of France. 'Tempête en juin' begins on 3 June 1940—the end
of the evacuation from Dunkirk—and finishes in the spring of 1941. 'Dolce'
narrates the following three months, finishing with the German declaration
of war on the U.S.S.R. on 22 June 1941 and the resulting departure of the
Germans from the occupied village on 1 July. Thus, *Suite française* differs
structurally from the previous texts, since the chronological period covered
is very much more concentrated and the story is told via a series of separate
but interrelated stories, rather than via a single story. However, to prevent

readers from forgetting the characters as the story progressed, Némirovsky had decided that the final work should be one single text of around 1,000 pages, rather than a series of separate volumes.[85] *Suite française* would then have been formally closer to the *roman-cycle* than her earlier work, but would not have fully embraced its structural conventions. Given the significant literary differences between *Suite française* and the earlier novels, as well as the importance of the novel's publication and reception in 2004, I reserve my discussion of this text for Chapter 6. However, I do not wish thereby to understate the crucial continuities which link *Suite française* to the works which preceded it: indeed, it is my contention that this work can only make sense in relation to Némirovsky's inter-war fiction. Nonetheless, just as the appearance of *Le Pion sur l'échiquier* in 1934 was a literary turning point, so too was the writing of *Suite française*. In 'Tempête en juin', Némirovsky abandoned strict chronological sequence in favour of an interweaving of narratives; the depiction of the situation of Occupation in 'Dolce' required a return to the type of narrative concentration which characterises her short stories, and a departure from the depictions of generational progression she had constructed in the novels of the later 1930s and early 40s.

Les Biens de ce monde and *Les Feux de l'automne* use the French bourgeois family as a vehicle for a generally favourable depiction of the French nation and its values. As we noted in Chapter 2, the fictional interrogation of family, and specifically marital, relations has a specific history in the inter-war French literary field. As Fernande Gonthier points out, the study of the couple—rather than of the individuals which constitute it—was a new literary preoccupation in the period, which derived from a new conception of marriage in the social field:[86]

> A côté de la conception traditionnelle du couple fondé sur des impératifs économiques et sociaux et sur une relation de dominant-dominé, va se substituer au XXe siècle l'idée du couple comme entité fondamentale et constitutive d'un nouvel ordre social fondé sur la liberté de l'individu.[87]

> *Alongside the traditional conception of the couple based on economic and social imperatives and on a relationship between dominant and dominated, in the twentieth century, we also find this model replaced by the idea of the couple as an entity which is fundamental to and constitutive of a new social order based on the freedom of the individual.*

As we have noted, it was in the work of writers such as Jacques Chardonne and André Maurois that this fictional trend was established.[88] Némirovsky told Frédéric Levèvre that she particularly liked Chardonne's *L'Epithalame* (1921), a classic example of the novel of love and marriage in this period.[89] Gonthier identifies three types of representations of women in inter-war

French literature: novels which respect the established, pre-First World War hierarchies of race, sex, age and money and in which a woman is either an adolescent or 'pré-femme', a wife or a mother; novels such as Victor Margueritte's *La Garçonne* which present female freedom and individuality via sexual liberation; and politically militant novels which discuss women's emancipation within a leftist political agenda.[90] Némirovsky's novels fall very clearly into the first category. She certainly did not seek to present herself in terms of a radical gender identity. Interviewed by J. d'Assac as part of a series of articles on the husbands of famous women, Némirovsky explained that at the end of a day's writing, she became just like other wives: 'Mon mari rentre. J'arrête mon travail, à partir de ce moment je suis l'épouse tout court' (*My husband comes home. I stop working, and from that moment I am simply a wife*).[91] Asked whether her work occupied her mind when she was not writing, she replied, 'pas plus que le souvenir d'une robe que l'on vient de choisir en se demandant si elle ira' (*no more than the memory of a dress you have just chosen, wondering whether it will suit you*).[92] Such trivialisation of the act of writing and the affirmation of very conventional gender roles was doubtless a means of seeking popularity through acceptability in a period when the woman writer was certainly not universally welcomed as a legitimate feature of the cultural landscape, as we saw in Chapter 1, and should not necessarily be taken as proof that Némirovsky held retrograde views about female identity. But there is no doubt that the types of female identity she presents in her fiction are traditional ones: the adolescent, the wife, the mother, the lover, the grandmother. All of Némirovsky's female characters exist as a function of heterosexual relationships, past, present, or future. As Stemberger notes, unlike Colette's female characters, the women in Némirovsky's fiction have no independent 'economic competence'.[93] Némirovsky was particularly interested in the coexistence of the two conceptions of marriage Gonthier cites: her fiction demonstrates the ways in which men and women were obliged to negotiate the potentially contradictory exigencies of the marriage of social and economic convenience and the marriage of inclination. In *Les Biens de ce monde* and *Les Feux de l'automne*, the account of male malaise and the consequent breakdown of marital relationships Némirovsky had presented in *Le Pion sur l'échiquier, La Proie,* and *Deux* is inverted almost point for point. Stemberger remarks that 'Némirovsky's texts [. . .] dismantle a whole series of mythified, seemingly "natural" human relationships—the myth of "family" as well as the myth of "motherly love" and the myth of "romantic love"'.[94] But in these later novels, the family, motherly love, and romantic love are all strongly affirmed. In *Les Biens de ce monde*, Pierre chooses a marriage of inclination to Agnès over a marriage of economic convenience to Simone. Their union is an idyll of faithful companionship and service to the family and to the community of Saint-Elme. In *Les Feux de l'automne*, Bernard's malaise and rebellion do not end with his suicide, but with his safe return from the war, redemption from his past misdemeanours, and a touching reunion with the ever-faithful Thérèse. This inversion of the account of marriage in the earlier novels appears particularly clearly through depictions of eroticism. Prior to *Les Biens de ce monde*, Némirovsky's depictions of sex were almost without exception either mechanical or brutal. Bourgeois marriage was equated with an absence of desire, as in the case of Christophe and Geneviève in *Le Pion sur l'échiquier*:

> Machinalement, il la prit dans ses bras, et, les yeux ouverts dans l'obscurité, fixant le point d'or d'une petite lampe de métal que touchait parfois le rai de clarté d'un phare d'auto, dans la rue, il lui donna la ration normale, prévue de caresses. En éprouvait-elle du plaisir? . . . Depuis longtemps, il avait cessé de se le demander . . . Mais il baisa ses cheveux, avec une machinale politesse.[95]

> *Mechanically, he took her in his arms; his eyes open in the darkness, staring at the golden glow from a small metal lamp, which was occasionally caught by the ray of light from a car headlight in the street. He gave her the normal, agreed ration of caresses. Did she feel any pleasure? He had long since stopped asking himself. But he kissed her hair with a mechanical politeness.*

Male malaise resulted in violent sexual encounters, for example, between Christophe and Murielle, or between Antoine and Marianne in *Deux*:

> Christophe s'assit sur le lit, lui prit les seins avec une brutalité soudaine qui l'étonna lui-même. Elle ne dit absolument rien; une sorte de grimace légère de souffrance entr'ouvrit ses lèvres, elle poussa un soupir las et retomba en arrière.[96]

> *Christophe sat down on the bed and seized her breasts with a sudden brutality which surprised even himself. She said absolutely nothing; a sort of slight grimace of suffering parted her lips, she let out a weary sigh and fell back.*

> Il l'avait prise brutalement, presque avec rancune, comme s'il eût voulu la saccager, assouvir une mystérieuse vengeance, lui faire cruellement mal.[97]

> *He took her brutally, almost with resentment, as if he wanted to desecrate her, to satisfy a mysterious desire for revenge, to hurt her cruelly.*

In the case of Pierre and Agnès, sex is mostly discretely elided; when it is narrated, it is tender and loving:

Il était de temperament ardent; il avait eu des aventures. Ce n'était pas le plaisir qu'elle lui avait procuré qui l'attachait si vivement à elle. C'était autre chose, qui prenait naissance dans une région plus subtile que la chair, plus chaude que l'âme. 'Dans notre sang, murmura-t-il. Cela naît dans le sang.' Il sentait le sien courir plus vite. Il n'avait jamais été si heureux.[98]

He was passionate by nature; he'd had affairs. But it wasn't the physical pleasure she gave him that made him feel so strongly attached to her. It was something else, a feeling that arose in a domain more subtle than the flesh, more ardent than the soul. 'It's deep within us', he whispered. 'It's in our blood'. He felt his own rushing faster. Never had he been so happy.[99]

The trajectory of Pierre and Agnès's son Guy reinforces the idea that the French bourgeois family is strong enough to withstand the crises it encounters. This message is quite different to that of the earlier novels, which tend to suggest rather that the social and economic breakdown of the family is beyond the control of individuals. The related themes of adultery and suicide now function as a means to affirm both the superiority and the robustness of traditional values. Although in *Les Biens de ce monde*, an adulterous woman again precipitates male malaise, the narrative now treats malaise with suspicion, insists on the possibility of recovery, and even allows the adulteress to make up for her wrongdoing. Guy's unfaithful mistress Nadine redeems herself when, in a typically Némirovskian narrative coincidence, she meets Guy's wife Rose by chance during the *exode* when both are seeking refuge at a mill. Nadine gives up her comfortable bed to the pregnant Rose, with the result that Guy's baby is safely delivered.[100] Guy had previously attempted suicide when Nadine's unfaithfulness was revealed. The discourse on suicide in this text is quite different from that of the previous novels: suicide is no longer an inevitable and tragic consequence of a socially and economically induced malaise, but a sin, an act of cowardice and a contravention of God's law.[101] The courage and resilience of the entire Hardelot family are rewarded at the end of the novel through a series of positive resolutions: Pierre survives the destruction of Saint-Elme after heroically rescuing many of its inhabitants; Agnès survives the *exode*, having ensured the safety of Rose and her baby, and is eventually reunited with Pierre in Saint-Elme after crossing the demarcation line; Guy has not been killed, as his parents fear, but is a POW in Germany. The novel's optimistic conclusion is summed up in Agnès's final words: 'On rebâtira. On s'arrangera. On vivra' (*We will rebuild. We will get by. We will live*).[102] There is a strong tradition in French cultural representations of war in which woman functions as the personification of the nation.[103] Agnès is the fulfilment this motif, which Némirovsky had already sketched via Marianne in *Deux*. The motif recurs in *Les Feux de l'automne* where Thérèse's faithfulness is also rewarded by the return of her husband. In both *Les Biens de ce monde* and *Les Feux de l'automne*, female faithfulness results in the re-composition of the French family. Given the historical and political context, it is difficult not to read a patriotic message from these stories: traditional French values will prevail and will facilitate the re-composition of the nation. We will return to the difficult question of the ideological significance of these happy endings.

Much has been made of Némirovsky's tendency to present monstrous, Medean mother figures in her fiction. Némirovsky's biographers have interpreted this aspect of Némirovsky's *œuvre* as a more or less direct transcription of personal experience, given that Némirovsky's difficult relationship with her own mother, Anna, or Fanny, is well-documented. According to Philipponnat and Lienhardt, '*Jézabel* solde une fois pour toutes les comptes d'Irène Némirovsky et de Fanny devant le jury des lecteurs' (Jézabel *finally settles the score between d'Irène Némirovsky and Fanny before the jury of her readers*).[104] Martina Stemberger devotes a considerable proportion of her analysis to Némirovsky's representations of bad mothers. The list is certainly long: Gloria Golder in *David Golder*, Rosine Kampf in *Le Bal*, Bella Karol in *Le Vin de solitude*, and Gladys Eysenach in *Jézabel* all inflict humiliation and damage on their daughters; as regards the short stories, one might also cite 'L'Ennemie', 'Film parlé' and 'L'Ogresse'.[105] These characters suffer from a pathological fear of ageing: mothers detest their daughters because they are proof of the passing of the generations, proof that they themselves will not be young and desirable for ever. Since these women acquire their economic and emotional viability from the men who desire them, the loss of their physical power to please means the total collapse of their identity. This theme reached its apotheosis in *Jézabel*, which recounts Gladys Eysenach's trial for the murder of a young man, Bernard Martin. The bulk of the narrative is a retrospective reconstruction of the events leading up to the trial: the death of Gladys' daughter in childbirth, and the fate of the child, who turns out to be Bernard Martin, Gladys's own grandson. When he finds Gladys again in Paris and threatens to reveal how old she really is, she shoots him. Némirovsky presented this macabre novel as a portrait of a female malaise which, like that of Christophe Bohun, Jean-Luc Daguerre, and Antoine Carmontel, is socially and historically specific:

> J'ai voulu peindre une *passion* qui n'ait pas été trop exploitée par la littéraure [. . .] et qui dépend, en quelque manière, du temps où nous vivons. [. . .] Autrefois—un autrefois qui date d'avant la guerre— une femme, même oisive, même riche, ne pouvait pas prétendre à plaire à tous les âges. Avant la guerre, quarante ans, c'était un âge terrible, l'âge-limite. Aujourd'hui, il n'est pas rare qu'une femme de soixante ans soit encore séduisante: cela est dû, pour beaucoup, à la pratique des sports, à l'usage des produits de beauté et à la chirurgie esthétique.[106]

I wanted to depict a passion which has not perhaps been much used in literature [. . .] and which, in a way, is a result of the age we live in [. . .] In the past—before the war—a woman could not hope to be appealing for ever, even if she was leisured and rich. Before the war, forty was a terrible age, a deadline. Now, it is not unusual for a woman of sixty still to be seductive. For many, this is a result of doing sports, using beauty products and having cosmetic surgery.

However, with the exception of Henri de Régnier, who discussed this contemporary female problem at some length in *Le Figaro*,[107] most critics of *Jézabel* were more interested in the technical difficulties posed by the retrospective narration and by the focusing of the story on such a disagreeable character than they were in the novel's thematic content.[108] It may well be plausible to suggest a biographical source for such mother figures in Némirovsky's work, but it is equally important to bear in mind their literary context. The characterisation of Geneviève Bohun via two references to Mme de Fleurville, the perfect mother figure in the Comtesse de Ségur's *Les Malheurs de Sophie*, which Némirovsky read to her own children,[107] alerts the reader to the importance of the discursive context of literary representations of motherhood. In the case of *Jézabel*, Mauriac's *Genitrix* (1928) is a plausible intertext. The situation which leads to Gladys' daughter's death is almost identical to the death of Félicité Cazenave's daughter-in-law in *Genitrix*: Marie-Thérèse Eysenach dies in childbirth and Mathilde Cazenave dies after a miscarriage because the 'bad mother' neglects to go into the daughter's room, and because the relationship has broken down to such an extent that Marie-Thérèse and Mathilde are unwilling to shout for help. As Gonthier shows, the transformation of positive maternal values into a perverted, devouring, destructive maternal identity was well-established in the inter-war French literary field.[110] Brosman shows that the positive image of woman-as-nation in French war imagery could be inverted to produce an image of 'Madame la Patrie' who, instead of protecting her children, metaphorically devours them by sending them off to be killed by the war machine in the name of patriotism.[111] Given her earlier representations of mothers, one might imagine that Némirovsky would use this narrative resource in her representations of war. But she did not do so. On the contrary, even the negative mother–daughter relationship finds resolution in her last novels. Agnès has a difficult relationship with her daughter-in-law Rose, who cannot relate to her own mother, Simone. But harmony is restored because mothers are now capable of behaving honourably: Simone seeks a reconciliation—which is described as a peace treaty and an armistice[112]—and Agnès puts Rose's need to flee to safety with her unborn baby before her own desire to stay in Saint-Elme with her husband. In *Suite française*, the problematic relationship between Lucille and her mother-in-law Madame Angelier is resolved positively when the latter chooses to support Lucille in her act of resistance, by hiding Benoît, who has shot a German soldier, in her house.[113] Némirovky's representations of French mothers in her later novels convey a discourse of patriotic heroism which is diametrically opposed to the Medean grotesques which populate her earlier texts.

Having considered the family as a vehicle for discourses of patriotism in Némirovsky's texts, let us now turn to her presentation of war itself as a means of interrogating national identity. If *La Proie, Le Pion sur l'échiquier,* and *Deux* are *romans de paix, Les Biens de ce monde, Les Feux de l'automne,* and *Suite française,* are *romans de guerre.* Literary historians have noted a resurgence of interest in war fiction in France after 1930. The early 1920s had witnessed the popularity of the war novel written by an ex-combatant: Barbusse's *Le Feu* and Dorgelès' *Les Croix de bois* are the most famous examples. Later war novels focused less on testimony than on an analysis of the meaning of war—the last war and the coming war—for the contemporary French reader.[114] Brosman's analysis of war imagery across three centuries of French history demonstrates that '[t]he past and its quoted images serve as ways of reading the present; but the present, with its images, is also a way of reading the past'.[115] In her account of twentieth-century cultural representations, she underlines 'the importance of the role of previous wars in mediating the Great War, and, subsequently, its function as a historical mediation for the following great European conflict'.[116] It is precisely this notion of historical repetition and discursive reflection which generates the accounts of war in *Les Biens de ce monde* and *Les Feux de l'automne.* This is particularly obvious in *Les Biens de ce monde* where the two *exodes* of 1914 and 1940 and the destruction of Saint-Elme twice over suggest that the population of North Eastern France did not experience the two World Wars a politically discrete events, but as straightforward historical repetition:

> La guerre ne sera pas finie. Elle durera autant que celle de 1914. Beaucoup le croyait comme elle. Les événements du passé projetaient leur sanglante lumière sur les jours qu'ils vivaient. On ne pouvait imaginer autre chose que la répétition de ces quatres années glorieuses et terribles, une immense, une surhumaine patience avant la fin.[117]

> *The war wouldn't be over. It would last as long as the one in 1914. Many people thought the same. The events of the past cast a long shadow and their bloodstained light coloured the times they were living through. They could imagine nothing but a repeat of those four years of glory and horror, the immense, superhuman need for patience until it might end.*[118]

We find the same idea in *Les Feux de l'automne,* in a passage which echoes Georges Bernanos's now famous 'Nous retournons dans la guerre ainsi que dans la maison de notre jeunesse'[119]:

Comme on entre dans une maison où on a vécu autrefois, comme on se dirige à tatons parmi des meubles familiers, ainsi, sans secousses, sans effort apparent, les Françaises retrouvèrent leurs habitudes de l'autre guerre.[120]

Just as one enters a house where one used to live, feeling one's way amongst the familiar furniture, so without any sort of shock, without any obvious effort, French women went back to doing what they had done in the previous war.

But Némirovsky also underlines the dangers of this particular form of national memory. For Pierre, '[l]a mémoire d'un peuple est une chose terrible' (*a population's memory is a terrible thing*):

Mais eux . . . qui savent que tous les sacrifices ont été inutiles, que la victoire n'a vaincu personne, qui ont lu, ont vu, ou entendu tout ce qui s'est passé alors et depuis, comment veux-tu qu'ils supportent ça? Les jeunes ont été bercés avec nos récits. Combien nous leur avons répété la bêtise de tout ça, l'inutilité de tout ça! Alors? Que se passera-t-il? Les uns, ceux qui sont bien, vraiment bien, n'auront même pas les illusions nécessaires pour mourir à peu près proprement. Les autres . . . la majorité . . . Pour peu que la guerre se prolonge, qu'il n'y ait pas d'éclatantes victoires dès le début, ils se sentiront dupes, comme nous l'avons senti. Nous avions tenu, résisté. Nous continuions par habitude. Mais eux. . . . [121]

But they . . . they know all our sacrifices were useless, that victory conquered no one; they've read, or seen, or heard everything that happened then, and since then. How do you think they're supposed to bear it? The young have heard our stories from the cradle. How often have we told them how stupid it all was, how pointless. And now? What will happen? Some of them, the good ones, the really good ones, won't even have the illusions they need to die a more or less decent death. As for the others . . . the majority . . . if the war lasts, there mustn't be any brilliant victories at first, otherwise they'll feel duped, like we did. But for us it happened towards the end. We held on, put up a fight. We carried on out of habit. But they. . . . [122]

The national memory of the First World War threatens to demoralise the soldiers of 1939 and so to prevent France from holding her own militarily. Némirovsky's account of the difference in French attitudes to the mobilisations of 1914 and 1939 accords precisely with modern historians' interpretations. Jean-Jacques Becker concludes that the French responded to the outbreak of war in 1914 with resolution—the French nation was threatened and a patriotic response was required. But in 1939 the prevailing mood was resignation—the war had to be fought because there was no other option. Becker argues that in 1939, those who had known the 1914–1918 war looked back to it, but without the hope they had then of rebuilding a better world.[123] Némirovsky's decision to write about the First World War in 1940–1941 was a response to the great upsurge in national memory of the last war in the context of the present one. Her interpretation of the relationship between the two wars in the minds of the French is highly representative of contemporary public opinion—Némirovsky's contemporary readers would have found in *Les Biens de ce monde* a confirmation of what they were feeling and remembering.

As is characteristic of Némirovsky's *œuvre*, evocations of politics in these novels are vague, limited to a few disjointed words which the characters overhear from the radio or in conversation. Rather than bearing ideological significance, the representation of war was a means by which Némirovsky sought to achieve identification, and therefore assent, on the part of her 1941 readership. But of course, Némirovsky, who had arrived in France in 1919, did not really share these memories with her French readers. As Denise Epstein says, she herself did not have a French grandfather to tell her stories of the Great War.[124] Némirovsky's notes suggest that the account of the First World War in *Les Biens de ce monde* and *Les Feux de l'automne* was constructed from a variety of sources, including contemporary mémoires, works of history, and literary texts.[125] As well as a bibliography of reference works on the Great War, Némirovsky copied out an extended quotation from Pierre Loti's 'Il pleut sur l'enfer de la Somme' of 1916, and noted John Galsworthy's *The Apple Tree* as a useful point of comparison. There is no very obvious textual connection between Galsworthy's text and Némirovsky's, unless Frank Ashurst's enforced stay at the Devonshire farm was a model for Jean-Marie's stay at the Sabarie's farm in *Suite française*. But this source should alert us to the fact that Némirovsky's fiction is based less on her own experience than many modern readers would like to believe. Némirovsky's skill as a novelist resided in her ability to weave together discourses derived from an impressively wide range of sources to create extremely plausible narratives. In a stimulating discussion of 'collective memory' and 'cultural history', Alon Confino stresses the need to distinguish between 'the memory of people who actually experienced a given event' and memory as 'the representations of the past and the making of it into a shared cultural knowledge'.[126] Research around 'collective memory' in relation to war demonstrates the importance of the fact that Némirovsky was not part of the same 'survivor networks' as her readers.[127] Jay Winter describes the ways in which 'the transmission of "scripts" about the war is based on "autobiographical memory".[128] Because Némirovsky was placed differently in relation to the 'processes of remembrance'[129] compared with her French readers, she could only harvest the results of those processes in order to write plausibly about the French experience of the war. Her account of the First World War is based not on actual memory but on the type of 'shared cultural knowledge' to which Confino refers. That which appears as memory in her novels is actually fiction; the disguising of fiction as memory—like the frequent references to works of French fiction which we have already noted—is a means of creating reader–writer complicity, of persuading the French reader that they are reading a thoroughly *French* novel. Through her accounts of the First World War, Némirovsky was positioning herself as *someone who remembers what the French remember*— that is, *as French*. Memory is, as Benedict Anderson reminds us, and as public memorials of all kinds demonstrate, a crucial ingredient of national identity.[130] Once again, it is because Némirovsky's fiction is recognisable that it is successful. Her evocation of the scandal of the 'embusqués'— those who obtained comfortable positions away from the front line thanks to nepotism—via the character of Détang in *Les Feux de l'automne*, and of visits to the battlefields in *Deux*, are references to sedimented forms of French memory and memorialisation of the Great War in the inter-war period.[131] These motifs are examples of 'collective memory' as Susan Suleiman describes it: 'a set of individual memories' which coalesce as 'the stipulation of what is important to a group at a given time'.[132] Némirovsky had understood which 'sets' of memories were important to her contemporary readers. Her account of the First World War also draws on well-established literary forms, using a repertoire of 'set-piece' scenes which would have been familiar to a contemporary readership with a knowledge of the inter-war French war novel: the soldier's departure for the front; his return on leave; his individual experience of the fighting war; the victory celebrations when the war is over; the soldier's return to civilian life. Némirovsky interpellates the French reader with a discourse on war in which it is ultimately impossible to separate out fiction from history. The scene in *Les Biens de ce monde* in which Charles Hardelot is killed when the Eglise Saint-Gervais is shelled by long-range German artillery during a service on Good Friday of 1918 is likely to have awakened Némirovsky's readers' memories of this real historical event.[133] But equally, they might have read Romain Rolland's fictional account of the same episode which concludes his 1920 novel *Pierre et Luce*.[134]

Les Feux de l'automne offers a much more ambivalent—at times openly critical—account of France and war than is to be found in *Les Biens de ce monde*, and which stands in tension with the discourse of individual patriotism conveyed by the female characters. This progression towards a problematisation of patriotism is further developed in *Suite française*. The accounts of the fourteenth of July celebrations of 1919 in *Deux*, *Les Biens de ce monde*, and *Les Feux de l'automne* highlight this shift in perspective. In *Deux*, as we have seen, Bastille Day 1919 functions, in Brosman's words, as 'a restaging of war as a nationalist spectacle with a positive cultural value'.[135] Némirovsky does not really criticise the state's attempt to foster a certain type of collective memory in this text. In *Les Biens de ce monde* however, although the 'Madelon de la victoire' is quoted again, the attempt to restage war as a nationalist spectacle now appears to be failing: the crowd acclaims the parade of soldiers, but they are 'sad' and 'nervous', suspicious that the survivors paraded before their eyes actually have never seen action, and no longer moved by the spectacle of the war wounded.[136] In *Les Feux de l'automne*, Bernard's cynicism about the victory parade beneath the Arc de Triomphe is part of a much more developed account of the mismatch between the reality of war and the discourses propagated about it: 'Pensez-vous, ceux qui défileront seront les embusqués genre Détang, tandis que moi, j'engraisserai les rats. Bah, on s'en fout!' (*Just think, the ones in the parade will be the ones who escaped the fighting, like Détang, whilst I'll just be food for rats. Who gives a toss!*).[137] The account of the First World War in *Les Feux de l'automne* suggests that official discourses of war do not correspond to its reality. Thérèse's first husband Martial is a doctor in a field hospital. He soon discovers the difference between discourse and reality:

> Martial n'était pas demeuré longtemps dans son beau train sanitaire de l'arrière qui pouvait, assuraient les journaux avec orgueil, contenir jusqu'à huit lits par wagon, au total cent vingt-huit blessés par train. Ils servaient pour la parade, pour la consolation des civils et pour l'édification des neutres; les blessés voyagaient dans les trains de marchandises et les wagons à bestiaux, saignant, agonisant, mourant le long des petites lignes départementales.[138]

> *Martial didn't stay long in his lovely hospital train behind the lines which, the newspapers proudly declared, could hold up to eight beds per carriage, a total of one hundred and twenty eight casualties per train. They were just for show, to reassure civilians and to teach the non-combatants a lesson. The injured travelled in goods trains and cattle trucks, bleeding, expiring, dying all along the local railway lines.*

Martial dies as a result of a spontaneous act of heroism: when his medical station is bombed, he returns to rescue a wounded soldier who was left behind, and is killed by a grenade.[139] The representation of Martial is similar to Albert Camus' later account of the doctor Rieux in *La Peste*: his heroism is of the kind which resists mythologisation. The photograph of Martial in uniform, decorated with a tricolore rosette and a black crêpe ribbon, which has pride of place on the mantelpiece, does not correspond to the reality of Martial: he looks taller and more imposing than he did in life.[140] Public memorialisation—the public display of the photograph with the rosette and the ribbon—conflicts with Thérèse's private memory. Martial's name underlines the opposition between his own real heroism, based on devotion to duty and the personal sacrifice of one human being for another, and Bernard's naïve and exulted notions of heroism. Bernard's Napoleonic fantasies are punctured when he discovers that the Great War is not another Waterloo or another Austerlitz but simply 'une entreprise de massacre en série' (*a process of serial massacre*).[141]

The theme of responsibility in relation to the Second World War in *Les Feux de l'automne* is conveyed via Bernard, who becomes involved in a scheme to import aeroplane parts from the United States, despite doubts about their compatibility with the French planes. When his son Yves later dies in an air crash, it seems that he has been killed in one of the faulty planes. The question of individual responsibility opens out onto a suggestion of national responsibility insofar as Bernard believes that the deficiencies of the French war materials are a result of inappropriate relationships between politics and business in 1930s France, of the sacrifice of national interest on the altar of individual financial gain:

> Il savait mieux que tout autre pourquoi certains appareils étaient perdus dans des accidents qui paraissaient inexplicables, pourquoi il n'y avait pas assez de tanks, pas assez de chars, pourquoi les armes étaient insuffisantes, pour quelle raison le désordre régnait, pourquoi, pourquoi . . . Il savait. Il jeta autour de lui des regards affolés. Il lui semblait que tous devinaient, tous pensaient: "Il a assassiné son fils".[142]

> *He knew better than anyone why some machines were lost in apparently inexplicable accidents, why there weren't enough tanks and vehicles, why the weapons were insufficient, why chaos reigned, why, why . . . he knew. He looked around him, terrified. He had the impression that everyone had guessed, that they were all thinking: 'He killed his son'.*

The fact that this section of the novel was based directly on the Riom trial, proceedings for which began in October 1941, raises the question of the ideological significance of Némirovsky's portrait of generational conflict on a national scale.[143] The Riom trial was an attempt on the part of the Vichy government to bring the political leaders of the Third Republic to justice on the basis that arms deals with foreign powers, specifically the United States, had sacrificed France's national interest to that of other nations. Was *Les Feux de l'automne* intended to be a validation of Vichy's attitude to the Third Republic, and therefore of its ideology more generally? The answer to this question is by no means clear. Jonathan Weiss concludes that the account of France's responsibility for her own defeat is 'pas loin d'une idéologie vichyssoise' (*not far from a Vichylte ideology*),[144] whilst for Philipponnat and Lienhardt, '[o]n aurait [. . .] tort de présenter *Les Feux de l'automne* comme le grand roman de la resignation idéologique qu'il paraît être' (*it would be wrong to present* Les Feux de l'automne *as the great novel of ideological resignation which it seems to be*).[145] They exculpate Némirovsky on the basis that the novel condemns the type of opportunists who in 1941 were to be found within the Vichy government, and that the collapse of the Riom trial was the first serious threat to Pétain's supposed infallibility.[146] It is certainly true that Némirovsky is fiercely critical of the financial improprieties of 1930s France—as she had been in many of her earlier novels. However, an awareness of the contextual aspects of the novel must be combined with an understanding of its *literary* logic. If *Les Feux de l'automne* puts inter-war France on trail via the character of Bernard, he is not condemned in the final pages of the text, but acquitted. In the last line of the novel, Thérèse realises that the Bernard who has returned from the war is 'changé, mûri, meilleur, et, enfin, à elle, à elle seule' (*changed, matured, better, and finally hers, hers alone*).[147] He has learned from his mistakes and has expiated his sin. I use the word 'sin' advisedly, since there is a notable strand of religious discourse in both *Les Biens de ce monde* and *Les Feux de l'automne*. It would be misleading to link this too closely with Némirovsky's conversion to Catholicism in 1939, for as we have seen, this is also the moment she chose to publish her most detailed account of Jewish identity in *Les Chiens et les loups*. In the absence of any clear biographical evidence as to the nature of her conversion, it is more appropriate to focus on the potential impact of her treatment of Christianity on her readers.[148] The evocations of Catholicism in these novels are quite specific. Whilst on active service during the First World War, Pierre attends Mass in a village church. He sees that the altar is covered with personal souvenirs—portraits, wedding garlands, candelabras, clocks—which the villagers had left there for safe keeping as they fled the advancing German army.[149] In the Saint-Gervais episode, the statues in the church are veiled with purple cloth because it is Lent, as is still the practice in Catholic churches today. Perhaps most striking are the Christian resonances of the endings of the two texts. Agnès has been a faithful and patient servant of her family and her community:

> Elle se sentait fatiguée, calme, détachée du monde. Elle avait accompli sa tâche jusqu'au bout. Elle s'état arrachée à Pierre pour suivre jusqu'ici cette fille, cette Rose qu'elle n'aimait pas. Elle l'avait assistée de son mieux. Elle avait aidé à naître l'enfant de Guy. On ne lui demandait maintenant que la soumission, l'espoir, l'attente.[150]

> *She felt tired, calm, detached from the rest of the world. She had seen her task through to the end. She had torn herself away from Pierre to find this young woman, this Rose, whom she did not like. She had helped her as best she could. She had helped bring Guy's child into the world. All she had to do now was to accept, hope, wait.*[151]

The sense of being detached from the world, of a task fulfilled, of resignation to one's fate, and also the importance of the birth of the child, are reminiscent of the Nunc Dimittis, spoken by Simeon in St Luke's Gospel when the child Jesus is presented to him in the Temple: 'Lord, now lettest thou thy servant depart in peace, according to thy word'.[152] Bernard's return is nothing short of a miraculous answer to prayer—an explicitly Christian *deus ex machina*. Moments before his arrival, Thérèse prays: 'Si vous ne m'avez pas abandonnée, faites-le-moi savoir, Jésus, d'un signe, d'un seul! Ne me tentez plus' (*If you haven't abandoned me, let me know, Jesus, give me a sign, just one sign! Do not temp me any more*).[153] The theme of responsibility in these novels points to the possibility of redemption and forgiveness. The somewhat ambiguous optimism of *Deux* has mutated into a full-blown assertion of the possibility of personal and national rebirth.

Whilst the discourses of the family, the nation, and Catholicism in Némirovky's late fiction are traditionalist, and appear to converge towards an image of Frenchness close to that propagated by the Vichy regime, it is important not to draw hasty ideological conclusions. Némirovsky had always sought to write fiction which was directed very precisely at the situation of her readers, fiction which would be recognisable to them in terms of both their literary experience and their socio-historical position. Just as a *literary* logic explains Némirovsky's decision to continue to publish with *Gringoire*, as we saw in Chapter 1, so a certain type of *literary* choice explains the apparent compliance of the thematic content of Némirovsky's 1940s' fiction with the ideology of the Vichy regime. In 1940–1942, Némirovsky's strategy of writing into the readers' situation was inevitably becoming highly problematic from a political point of view. As modern readers approaching Némirovsky with the benefit of hindsight, we must address this issue.

There can be no doubt, as Némirovsky's biographers have shown that financial constraints were a significant determining factor in Némirovsky's choice to publish in *Gringoire* under the Occupation.[154] The correspondence detailing Némirovsky's attempt to persuade Fayard to honour their contract for the publication of *Les Feux de l'automne* in *Candide* is revelatory in this respect.[155] Exiled from her home in Paris, with no means of accessing her money, her range of options was severely limited. A sudden change in publisher would have been culturally improbable, as we saw in Chapter 1, and practically almost impossible. There is of course a causal relationship between the decision to publish in *Gringoire* and *Candide* and the messages conveyed in the texts themselves: 1941 was clearly not the moment to choose to attempt to publish something non-consensual if one's main goal in writing was financial. From a literary point of view, it is not surprising that Némirovsky's sudden shift towards the creation of positive fictional heroes and heroines had a negative effect on the artistic quality of her work. In so doing, she abandoned the strategy that had worked very well for her since 1929—arousing the sympathy of the reader for profoundly antipathetic characters. In *Suite française*, Némirovsky went back to portraying ambivalent characters, which resulted in a more sophisticated text. Because of the lessening of psychological ambiguity in *Les Biens de ce monde* and *Les Feux de l'automne*, Némirovsky's reliance on the *roman-cycle* model produces more formulaic fiction than is the case in the rest of her *œuvre*.

Despite Némirovsky's choice in favour of *Gringoire*, and despite the apparently acquiescent tone of *Les Biens de ce monde* and *Les Feux de l'automne*, it would be abusive to represent Némirovsky's Occupation novels as political literature designed to support the Vichy regime. This would in any case be anachronistic, since the literary roots of both novels predate Pétain's assumption of power: Némirovsky began writing *Les Biens de ce monde* in April of 1940,[156] before the fall of France, and according to her notes, the idea for *Les Feux de l'automne*, which was based on a short story written in 1939,[157] went back to 1937.[158] Although both texts celebrate traditionalist values such as service and self-sacrifice, and both might be read as indicative of the need for some form of national renewal, they do not anticipate the discourses of Pétain's National Revolution except in the most general terms. *Les Biens de ce monde* might be seen as provincialist, but it is certainly not ruralist. There is no affirmation of rural values here, and no return to the land: the protagonists are factory owners who work the capitalist economy, not the French soil. Neither is there any positive affirmation of the authority figure: Julien Hardelot's refusal to leave Saint-Elme in 1914 might be reminiscent of Pétain's refusal to leave France in 1940, but Julien's vice-like grip on the family's wealth and the control he exercises over their lives produces suffering and conflict, not unity. But much more important, Némirovsky had never written politically militant literature, and these two novels are no exception. The literary apparatus of her novels has little in common with inter-war *littérature engagée* and was not intended to act as a vehicle for specific political or philosophical messages. Némirovsky's talent was for storytelling; it was not for proselytising. As we saw in Chapter 1, her Occupation texts fall into the category of legally published Occupation fiction which is ideologically non-specific, expressing neither discourses of collaboration nor discourses of resistance. It has little in common with the work of politico-literary collaborators such as Robert Brasillach or Lucien Rebatet. Robert Pickering warns against both a hasty dismissal of writers who continued to publish legally, and an overly simplistic approach to the relationship between the texts of such writers and the reality they purport to describe.[159] The complex relationships between fiction, history, and memory which we have identified in Némirovsky's fiction demonstrate that her texts do not aim to reflect the reality which surrounded them in any straightforward way. The logic of Némirovsky's positions in the literary and social fields points to the construction of fictional discourses which are socially and culturally conservative, but not ideologically militant. There is a crucial difference. The analyses offered by Bourdieu and Sapiro suggest that Némirovsky had already refused the type of avant-garde positions in the literary field out of which the literary resistance would be born, and that the literary positions she adopted were those out of which collaboration emerged. However, we must avoid syllogistic reasoning here: the fact that Némirovsky's conservative literary choices placed her within the literary milieux of collaboration does not necessarily mean that she was actively pro-Vichy in any ideological sense. The same argument holds in relation to the political significance of Némirovsky's decision to publish in *Gringoire* as in relation to the interpretation of the content of those texts: under the Occupation, non-political choices could be politically encoded by the nature of historical events. As Sapiro argues, '[l]a signification politique que peuvent revêtir objectivement les attitudes les plus apolitiques est directement liée aux transformations des conditions de production' (*the political meaning which, objectively, could be ascribed to the most apolitical attitudes is directly linked to the transformation of the conditions of production*).[160] Contemporary readers will continue to disagree as to the potential political effects of texts such as *Les Biens de ce monde* and *Les Feux de l'automne*, and therefore as to the advisability or otherwise of Némirovsky's decision to publish them. But as I argued in relation to Némirovsky's portraits of Jewish identity, modern readers have a responsibility to avoid what Bernstein terms backshadowing. There can be no doubt that, at the moment of publication, the thematic content of *Les Biens de ce monde* and *Les Feux de l'automne* was the result of an apolitical attitude.

In a modern cultural context in which readers are inevitably more familiar with the post-war condemnation of collaboration and the celebration of resistance than they are with the literary landscape of the inter-war period, it is particularly important that a study such as this one should insist on the avoidance of anachronism. Post-war literary criticism, enmeshed in its own processes of memorialisation, tended, at least until relatively recently, to view resistance literature as representative of the French Occupation period.[161] Attempts to redress the critical balance have resulted in the appearance of studies which also take account of collaboration, but less attention is paid to non-political cultural production, which is perhaps less voluminous, but is in some ways much more problematic. Nonetheless, as John Flower and Ray Davison pointed out in an essay published in 1984, there is a body of French prose fiction published between 1940 and 1942 which needs to be analysed in relation to its own context of production rather than in relation to the *later* appearance of structures of cultural resistance. This literature predates such resistance: Vercors' *Le Silence de la mer*, the first text published by the clandestine Editions de Minuit, appeared in February 1942, whilst *Les Lettres françaises* did not begin to appear until September 1942. William Kidd's suggestive essay 'From Bernanos to Vercors' insists on the fluidity of images and ideas circulating in 1940–1941, demonstrating that the subsequent production of discourses of resistance and collaboration lent specific ideological meanings to particular motifs; yet in 1940, calls for national regeneration were not the exclusive preserve of future collaborators.[162] Narratively, Némirovsky's novels of this period are atypical: unlike the majority of prose fiction published at this time, they are not 'thinly disguised reminiscences or journalistic accounts of personal experience'.[163] However, as regards their thematic content, *Les Biens de ce monde* and *Les Feux de l'autonme* are typical of other contemporary fictionalisations of the defeat. Flower and Davison find that French prose works of 1940–1942 tend to follow a similar pattern, and, notably, that they contain 'a recognition that the nation has deserved its fate usually tempered in the closing pages by a statement of belief in the ultimate re-emergence of a new, spiritually purer and victorious France'.[164] This is a strikingly accurate description of both *Les Biens de ce monde* and *Les Feux de l'automne.* In their corpus,[165] the authors find 'little that can have given the German authorities very much concern'. They go further:

> Indeed, it is fair to say that during the first two years of the invasion and occupation there is no evidence that either the German presence or the Vichy government was directly challenged by anything in imaginative literature.[166]

Whilst the atypicality of some of Némirovsky's narrative choices—particularly her rare ability to fictionalise contemporary events without the benefit of historical distance—accounts in part for the literary value of her novels, such an interpretation should not be too hastily extended to their thematic content. It is only through a contextual reading which respects Némirovsky's typicality that modern readers can avoid bringing inappropriately anachronistic ethical judgements to bear on her work.

Némirovsky wrote Suite *française* without any hope of immediate publication. Deprived of the ability to publish, Némirovsky's discourse on Frenchness changed: it is not simply more critical, as one would expect, but also more complex. By this stage, Némirovsky was tragically aware that there was no longer any point in trying to project herself through her fiction as a French novelist. And yet it is for her last novel that Némirovsky will be remembered in our own time as an archetypal French novelist: a writer who was able to seize the ambiguities of the situation of Occupation in fiction.

6 Conclusions
Second Flowering

Insofar as the aim of this book has been, in Bourdieu's words, the presentation and analysis of '[les] conditions sociales de la production et de la réception de l'œuvre d'art' (*'the social conditions of the production and reception of a work of art'*),[1] it is already at an end. Whilst the initial impetus for its writing—and no doubt for most readers' decision to buy it or borrow it from a library—was the popularity of *Suite française* in 2004, its project has been to situate Némirovsky's *œuvre* in relation to the inter-war French literary field which shaped it and which it helped to shape. Though inevitably received in our own time as an Occupation writer, and as a Holocaust writer, Némirovsky was first and foremost a French novelist of the inter-war period, and it is only through an appreciation of the literary positions available to her in the 1920s and 1930s that we can fully understand her texts. Via the analyses I have presented in this book of the creation of Némirovsky's literary reputation, of her literary beginnings, and of the Russian, Jewish, and French themes in her writing I have sought to investigate the relationships between the literary field of inter-war France, Némirovsky's trajectory though it, and the novels which resulted from her particular navigation of the literary environment. For Bourdieu, the *space of possibilities* constitutes 'ce par quoi tout producteur culturel est irrémédiablement situé et daté en tant qu'il participe de la *même problématique* que l'ensemble de ses contemporains (au sens sociologique)' [emphasis in original] (*'this is undoubtedly how any cultural producer is irremediably placed and dated in so far as he or she participates in the same problematic as the ensemble of his or her contemporaries (in the sociological sense)'*).[2] This does not mean of course that no writer can be read out of their time, nor indeed that we should not seek to establish relationships between writers across temporal divisions. As Bourdieu goes on to say, whilst Diderot evidently did not know anything about the *nouveau roman*, *Jacques le fataliste* might nonetheless be said to prefigure Robbe-Grillet. Conversely, Némirovsky's *irreparable* connection to the literary field of the 1930s does not mean that she cannot be read in our own time. Of course it is both important and valuable to recognise Némirovsky's identity as an Occupation writer, as a Holocaust writer, and as a literary success of the twenty-first century. But we must not thereby seek to *repair*, perhaps to put a patch over, her inter-war identity. We must understand that such readings are retrospective, and whilst this does not invalidate them per se, if we are to avoid misinterpretation, we must respect two crucial facts of chronology: firstly, that Némirovsky's literary identity was defined to a significant extent by the cultural environment of the 1920s and 1930s, and secondly, that her literary identity as an Occupation writer is limited to the period 1940–1942. Our discussion of Némirovsky would of course be incomplete without some consideration of her current reputation. Yet to read *Suite française* now is to read it out of its own time, or rather, it is to read it in a new time. This is a time when popular French literary fiction of the 1930s is little known, when our understanding of the French experience of the Occupation is coloured by our knowledge of various forms of resistance largely dating from 1942–1944, and when the memorialisation of the Holocaust obeys its own logic in relation to current cultural and social imperatives.

SUITE FRANÇAISE IN ITS TIME

One of the main reasons why *Suite française* attracted such attention and success on its appearance in 2004 was its purported exceptionality as a war narrative. As Olivier Le Naire pointed out in *L'Express*, '[o]n peut en effet compter sur les doigts d'une main les témoignages *d'une telle force* écrits non a posteriori, mais bien durant la guerre' [emphasis added] (*you can count on the fingers of one hand testimonies* of such force *written not after the events, but actually during the war*). What struck Le Naire was the rare combination of literary quality with a narrative based on events occurring literally at the time of writing. Commentators reproduced the view dominant amongst historians and literary critics, according to which artistic quality is generally lower when the moment of writing coincides with the events narrated. This, incidentally, is one of the reasons for the denigration of the literary quality of the inter-war political *roman à thèse*. As Ian Ousby writes,

> Inevitably, the written record of people's immediate impressions is scanty by comparison to the flood of reminiscence, and even the diaries and other contemporary accounts which do survive can seem oddly un-informative. The pressure of historic events might make people feel the need to put down their reactions, but, by its nature, does not usually prompt more than jotting. Sustained description, deliberate meditation and the literary topoi constructed from them come only in safety or in leisure after the event. There was little place for them during the Occupation [. . .].[3]

In one sense, the critics were right, and *Suite française* proves Ousby wrong. However, an understanding of the genesis of the novel in relation to Némirovsky's previous writing goes a long way towards explaining how she managed to achieve the apparently impossible task of writing well about the Occupation as it was happening.

Although *Suite française* of course is profoundly linked to its moment of production, it is also a rewriting of themes which Némirovsky had been working on throughout her literary career. There are very clear connections between this novel and her works on both Russia and inter-war France. *Suite française* is inevitably a novel about exile. It was written by a Russian exile who, because of the Occupation and the increasingly obvious dangers it posed for foreign Jews in France, had been exiled for a second time, from Paris to the village of Issy-L'Evêque, just inside the demarcation line. The 'Tempête en juin' section of *Suite française* recounts the internal exile of the populations of northern France caught up in the *exode* in May and June of 1940. Exile had been the subject of what was probably Némirosky's very earliest story, 'La Niania'. As we have seen, this account of the flight of Russian landowners from the advancing Bolsheviks would be amplified in *Les Mouches d'automne* and again in *Le Vin de solitude*. The account of the *exode* in *Suite française* is part of a more general literary reworking of the theme of exile in Némirovsky's fiction in the late 1930s and early 1940s, nourished not only by the present but also by the past. In a brief text entitled 'Souvenirs de Finlande', which was never published, Némirovsky evokes the Finnish landscapes and way of life she had experienced twenty years previously during her first exile:

> Certains pays, connus et aimés autrefois, sont comme des amis perdus de vue: leur visage s'est effacé dans votre souvenir. Mais on apprend tout à coup qu'ils sont inquiets, menacés; on pense à eux avec tendresse et on voudrait retrouver leurs traits et les montrer à ceux pour qui ils ne sont que des noms étranges sur une carte. C'est pourquoi je voudrais vous parler de la Finlande et de ses habitants.[4]

> *Some countries, which you have known and loved in the past, are like friends you have lost touch with: their face has faded from your memory. Then you suddenly learn that they are anxious, threatened; you think of them tenderly and you want to be able to recall what they looked like and to show them to people for whom they are just strange names on a map. That's why I would like to tell you about Finland and its people.*

Finland during the Russian revolution also provided the narrative framework for a short story entitled 'Aïno', published in the *Revue des deux mondes* in January 1940.[5] In 'Et je l'aime encore', published in *Marie-Claire* in February 1940, the narrator tells the story of her friend Olga, another Russian émigré, separated from her lover in Russia in September 1917.[6] These stories are in a continuum with the various evocations of Finland

and Russia which occur in Némirovsky's short stories even after she had largely abandoned the Russian theme in her novels—'Les Fumées du vin' (1934); 'Espoirs' (1938); 'La Confidence' (1938); 'Magie' (1938); 'Destinées' (1940); 'Le Sortilège' (1940).[7] These texts suggest that exile provided an already familiar narrative context via which Némirovsky could approach the representation of the *exode* in *Suite française*.

In notes dating from 1942, Némirovsky wrote,

> Les Français étaient las de la République comme d'une vieille épouse. La dictature était pour eux une passade, un adultère. Mais ils voulaient bien tromper leur femme, ils n'entendaient pas l'assassiner. Ils la voient maintenant morte, leur République, leur liberté. Ils la pleurent.[8]

> *The French grew tired of the Republic, as if she were an old wife. For them, dictatorship was a brief affair, adultery. But they intended to cheat on their wife, not to kill her. Now they realise she's dead, their Republic, their freedom: dead. They're mourning her.*[9]

This quotation is richly suggestive from various perspectives. It is immediately striking that Némirovsky now positions herself as an outsider in relation to the French Republic and its discourses of freedom, whereas in her novels of the second half of the 1930s, these very discourses had permitted her to position herself as an insider, as a French novelist offering a French perspective on contemporary France. But there is also continuity here. If Némirovsky was able so effectively to portray the French as a murderer weeping over the corpse of his victim in *Suite française*, this is because she had already worked and reworked the theme of the disintegration of his marriage in *Le Pion sur l'échiquier*, *La Proie,* and *Deux*. The malaise of the sons of the French bourgeoisie in a post-war society which had failed, economically and socially, to win the peace remains pertinent in *Suite française*, as Hubert's echoing in 'Tempête en juin' of Jean-Luc Daguerre's reference to Gide's 'Familles, je vous haïs' in *La Proie* suggests.[10] *Suite française* is a literary meditation on defeat: the failure of 1940, certainly, but also the failures of the entire inter-war period which resulted in the various suicides Némirovsky had narrated in the texts of the late 1930s. In a draft of *Le Pion sur l'échiquier*, Némirovsky wrote: 'Défaite? Mais il y a toujours une défaite, et c'est pour cela que C. B. [Christophe Bohun] misait sur les deux tableax' (*Defeat? But there is always a defeat, which is why C. B. was hedging his bets*).[11] She had populated these novels with characters who constantly try to play the game both ways, in love and in business, with disastrous consequences. The type of collaboration Némirovsky portrays in the 'Dolce' section of *Suite française* is a continuation of this type of behaviour. The vicomtesse de Montmort also knows there will be losers, and she does not wish to be among them, whichever side they turn out to be on. She hedges her bets, trying to maintain a relationship both with the Occupier and with her French neighbours. She is a character inspired not only by the specific situation of Occupation, but also by her fictional antecedents.

We saw in Chapter 5 the various ways in which *Les Biens de ce monde* might be read as an inversion of the themes of the earlier 'trilogy': the negative themes of the earlier texts find positive resolution in this novel. When Agnès, Rose, and Simone are stranded, they meet only with kindness: a child indicates where they might find shelter; when they reach the mill, they find a warm welcome despite the difficult conditions; the imminent arrival of Rose's baby provokes overwhelming female solidarity. The women present act with simple and spontaneous kindness, doing everything that is necessary—heating water, fetching towels, calling for the doctor, watching over Rose. There is plenty of hot coffee and fresh bread. Even petrol—a scarce and precious resource—is available: Nadine gives Agnès what she has left to enable her to get back to Saint-Elme.[12] In *Suite française*, the positive account of the *exode* in *Les Biens de ce monde* is inverted in its turn: the *exode* is used throughout 'Tempête en juin' to demonstrate the ways in which a situation of dire emergency brings out the base selfishness of human beings, which is concealed under the normal social conditions of peaceful civilisation. The town of Gien links the two texts: this is where Rose and Simone stop on their flight from Saint Elme, and where the Péricand family make an enforced stop on their way to Nice.[13] Where *Les Biens de ce monde* demonstrated generous charity, in 'Tempête en juin', the same narrative situation functions to illustrate the limits of Mme Pericand's benevolence and her hypocrisy as she refuses to share her ample provisions with the other victims of the *exode*:

> La charité chrétienne, la mansuétude des siècles de civilisation tombaient d'elle comme de vains ornements révélant son âme aride et nue. Ils étaient seuls dans un monde hostile, ses enfants et elle. Il lui fallait nourrir et abriter ses petits. Le reste ne comptait plus.[14]

> *Christian charity, the compassion of centuries of civilisation, fell from her like useless ornaments, revealing her bare, arid soul. She needed to feed and protect her own children. Nothing else mattered any more.*[15]

Various key motifs are common to both accounts of the *exode*, but they signify in opposite ways. Petrol is given freely by Nadine. But in 'Tempête en juin', the wealthy Charles Langelet, again near Gien, cunningly contrives to take a working class couple into his confidence in order to steal their petrol.[16] In *Les Biens de ce monde*, as we have seen, the mistress becomes a positive influence when Nadine, who caused Guy (Rose's husband and Agnès's son) to attempt suicide, turns out to be Rose's saviour. By contrast, Arlette Corail in 'Tempête en juin' remains mired in her own ultimately criminal self-centredness. Having taken the place in the car reserved for the Michauds, thereby preventing them from leaving Paris,[17] she goes on to seduce the young Hubert Péricand[18] and, at the end of the text, callously runs over Charles Langelet and kills him. Unconcerned, she is confident that 'elle connaissait quelqu'un d'influent qui arrangerait tout pour elle' (*she knew someone influential who would fix everything for her*).[19] The Michauds, on the other hand, are a reincarnation of Agnès and Pierre Hardelot. But their heroism is more convincing because it is more sparingly evoked, and because it is put into relief by the reprehensible actions of many of the other protagonists. Compared with *Les Biens de ce monde* and *Les Feux de l'automne*, *Suite française* is characterised by an impressive narrative concision. Nothing here is superfluous. The economy of expression achieved in *Suite française* must surely be ascribed to the close relationship between this novel and the texts which preceded it. *Suite française* is the tip of the iceberg: its concision and sophistication derive from the fact that the themes it addresses and the narrative modes it employs had been worked out in detail by Némirovsky over the course of her ten-year writing career.

The opposing representations of the *exode* in terms of goodness, heroism and generosity in *Les Biens de ce monde* and cynicism, cunning, and self-centredness in 'Tempête en juin' are obviously linked to issues of textual acceptability related to the possibility or impossibility of immediate publication. Having failed to secure a publishing contract for *Les Feux de l'automne* because of the restrictive legislation against Jews, Némirovsky was fully aware that *Suite française* would not be published until after the war, if at all. On 11 July 1942, two days before her arrest, Némirovsky wrote to her publisher, Albin Michel: 'Cher Ami . . . pensez à moi. J'ai beaucoup écrit. Je suppose que ce seront des œuvres posthumes, mais ça fait passer le temps' (*My dear friend . . . think of me sometimes. I have done a lot of writing. I suppose they will be posthumous works, but it helps pass the time*).[20] Much research on the testimonies of Holocaust victims and survivors has stressed the impulse to write as a means of affirming both historical truth and personal identity in the face of the potential annihilation of an entire group and of the individual. In Annette Wieviorka's words, '[w]riting [. . .] becomes a vital way to preserve a record of events that defied the imagination and to assure immortality'.[21] These 'writings from beyond the grave' come to us 'always via strange paths': Wieviorka discusses writings saved from the Warsaw ghetto and documents buried at Auschwitz and later discovered.[22] The story of the survival of the manuscript of *Suite française* is one of these 'strange paths'. In Chapter 5, discussing Némirovsky's representation of the First World War, we distinguished between actual autobiographical memory and 'collective memory' understood as a bank of cultural representations to which a particular group gives assent. It is tempting to read the account of war in *Suite française* as an example of spontaneous testimony, as evidence of Némirovsky's desire to bear witness to her personal experience of the Occupation, and therefore to set it against her transcription of established French cultural memory in her accounts of the First World War. However, this would only be partially accurate. It is true that, in her notes, Némirovsky herself sets her fictional project in the context of personal testimony when she exclaims: 'Mon Dieu! que me fait ce pays? Puisqu'il me rejette, considérons-le froidement, regardons-le perdre son honneur et sa vie' (*My God! What is this country doing to me? Since it is rejecting me, let us consider it coldly, let us watch as it loses its honour and its life*').[23] Nonetheless, in terms of narrative technique, Némirovsky continued quite deliberately to represent war in *Suite française* via the tropes of cultural memory which would emerge as recognisable aspects of the conflict in the future. As the structure of the text began to take shape, she wrote: 'Quels sont les tableaux qui méritent de passer à la postérité?' (*Which scenes deserve to be passed on for posterity?*').[24] She goes on to list the early morning queues, the arrival of the Germans, people's indifference (which she thought was more important than the raids and the shootings of hostages), the contrast between frivolous prosperity and the human tragedies of the war, and food shortages. There is no doubt that her foresight is impressive, and this is one reason why the text has become so popular. This focus on set-piece scenes which were to become recognisable to future French readers in terms of their cultural memory of the Occupation is in fact exactly the same narrative technique Némirovsky had used in *Les Biens de ce monde* and *Les Feux de l'automne* to describe the First World War. Even in 1942, Némirovsky was writing with her future readers in mind: 'Tâchez de faire le plus possible de choses, de débats . . . qui peuvent intéresser les gens en 1952 ou 2052' (*Try to create as much as possible: things, debates . . . that will interest people in 1952 or 2052*'); 'Ne jamais oublier que le public aime qu'on lui décrive la vie des "riches"' (*Never forget that the public likes having the life of the 'wealthy' described to them*').[25] Throughout the novel, Némirovsky imagines the making history of the war in the future:

> L'occupation finira. Ce sera la paix, la paix bénie. La guerre et le désastre de 1940 ne seront plus qu'un souvenir, une page d'histoire, des noms de bataille et de traités que les écoliers ânonneront dans les lycées.

> *The Occupation would end. There would be peace, blessed peace. The war and the tragedy of 1940 would be no more than a memory, a page in history, the names of battles and treaties children would recite in school.*[26]

In some cases, Némirovsky's analysis is almost disturbingly prescient. She anticipates Henry Rousso's thesis of the post-war myth of *résistancialisme* when she has a young peasant remark that 'nous oublierons après 1940 que nous avons été battus, ce qui peut-être nous sauvera!' (*we'll forget after 1940 that we were defeated, which will perhaps be our salvation*'),[27] and when Hubert imagines that 'il y aura autour de ça une telle conspiration de mensonges que l'on en fera encore une page glorieuse de l'Histoire de France. On se battra les flancs pour trouver des actes de dévouement, d'héroïsme' (*'there will be such a conspiracy of lies that all this will be transformed into yet another glorious page in the history of France. We'll do everything we can to find acts of devotion and heroism for the official records'*).[28] In other cases, the narrative is less prescient: the narrator suggests that no one will remember that French women slept with German soldiers: 'Ce serait une de ces choses que la postérité ignorerait, ou dont elle se détournerait par pudeur' (*'It would be one of those things that posterity would never find out, or would refuse to see out of a sense of shame'*).[29]

In his discussion of *Suite française* with Susan Suleiman, Richard J. Golsan asks what might account for the 'ambitiousness' and 'richness' of this novel in relation to Némirovsky's earlier fiction.[30] Part of the explanation lies precisely in its close relationship to the works which preceded it. It was not an impulsive or unprecedented response to the very particular situation of the Occupation, but rather a development and a refinement of a long-term literary project dating back to the mid-1920s. The sophistication of characterisation and thematic content must also be attributed at some level to the newly critical distance between author and subject matter provoked by Némirovsky's tragic discovery that the French nation into which she had attempted to assimilate and whose cultural environment she had made her own was now rejecting her as a foreigner and a Jew. *Les Biens de ce monde* and *Les Feux de l'automne* are ultimately fairly formulaic novels written for largely commercial reasons with the explicit purpose of securing publication in *Gringoire* and *Candide* respectively; it is unsurprising under the circumstances that considerations of readership should have constrained the thematic content of these works. Némirovsky recognised that because *Suite française* would not be published immediately, she could allow herself more freedom: 'ce n'est pas pour maintenant. Alors il ne faut pas se retenir, il faut taper à tour de bras où on veut' (*'this is not for now. So mustn't hold back, must strike with a vengeance wherever I want'*).[31] And for this reason, despite and even because of her own appalling circumstances, she felt she must allow herself to be ambitious: 'Il faut faire quelque chose de grand et cesser de se demander à quoi bon' (*'I must create something great and stop wondering if there's any point'*).[32] The more varied and complex structure of *Suite française* was made possible by a new freedom from the constraints posed by serialisation which partly account for the formally unambitious nature of the earlier texts. Némirovsky's notes suggest that the construction of *Suite française* resulted from serious meditation on narrative technique inspired by her reading of E.M. Forster's *Aspects of the Novel* (1927) and Percy Lubbock's *The Craft of Fiction* (1921). She drew on Lubbock's discussion of 'ironic contrast' and his analysis of Flaubert's 'impersonality', and on Forster's account of the presence of history in *War and Peace*.[33] In 1940, Némirovsky was also working on *La Vie de Tchekhov*, which contains insightful reflections on Chekhov's narrative technique as well as on the contributions of Maupassant and Mérimée to the short story genre, as we saw in Chapter 2.

Golsan also raises the question of the ideological significance of *Suite française*. He notes that some critics have suggested that the absence of Jews from *Suite française* implies that Némirovsky was indifferent to their fate under Vichy and that the novel is more generally indifferent to politics.[34] Such arguments are rejected by Suleiman and Golsan. As time went on, and readers became more familiar with Némirovsky's life story, particularly after the publication of Weiss's biography in 2005, the apparently apolitical nature of *Suite française* began to be read rather simplistically in the light of Némirovsky's associations with *Gringoire* and *Candide* and the stereotyped portrayals of Jews in *David Golder* and elsewhere. However, as I suggested in Chapter 1, this was primarily a feature of English and American reviews of *Suite française*. One searches in vain for any hint of these arguments in the French press. The French reception was overwhelmingly positive and celebratory; one of its dominant themes was the idea of reparation, both for the post-war critical neglect of Némirovsky and, more problematically, for her death.[35] Michaëlle Petit summed up the mood when, discussing the 2004 award of the Renaudot prize, she remarked that 'il ne sera jamais assez dit que ce n'est que justice rendue à un auteur majeur' (*it cannot be said often enough that this is simply doing justice to a major writer*). In Britain by contrast, the byline to Stuart Jeffries' *Guardian* article 'Truth, Lies and Anti-Semitism' suggested that 'the charge that she might have been anti-Semitic—even though she was Jewish—threatens to stain her reputation', whilst the cover of the supplement in which the article appeared carried the title 'The Troubling Truth about Literary Sensation Irène Némirovsky'. In the *Telegraph*'s review of *David Golder*, entitled 'George Walden Is Disturbed by a Nazi Victim's First Novel', the author wondered, 'But what was Némirovsky doing writing it at all?'. In America, criticism has been even more pointed. In the *Washington Post*, Ruth Kluger noted the absence of Jews from *Suite française*, and suggested that 'when one thinks of the threat the Jewish population endured even at this early stage of persecution, one feels the significant gap here'. In *The Nation*, Alice Kaplan noted that the absence of Jewish characters was '[t]he most surprising aspect of *Suite française*', and found this to be indicative of 'how little her particular situation seems to have influenced her story'. The most critical article was Ruth Franklin's 'Scandale française: The Nasty Truth about a New Literary Heroine', published in *The New Republic* on 30 January 2008, where the author dismissed *Suite française* as an 'accomplished but unexceptional novel' which 'capped the career of a writer who made her name by trafficking the most sordid anti-Semitic stereotypes'. The only hint of criticism of Némirovsky in the French press has been more recent, provoked by the question of the possible transfer to France of the exhibition on Némirovsky hosted by the New York Museum of Jewish Heritage, entitled 'Woman of Letters: Irène Némirovsky and *Suite française*'.[36] In an article significantly

entitled 'L'offense faite à Irène' (*Irène slighted*), François Dufay noted that
no French museum was so far willing to host the exhibition because of the
polemic around the question of anti-Semitism; the Musée d'art et d'histoire
du judaïsme in Paris had refused it because of Némirovsky's supposed Jewish self-hatred and because the museum is devoted to Jewish culture and
not to the Shoah. Although Dufay's article rehearses the arguments—that
Némirovsky sinned by omission, that she converted to Catholicism, that
she betrayed her community by creating negative and stereotyped Jewish characters—its title is representative of the continuing refusal of most
French readers to condemn Némirovsky on these grounds. Delphine Peras
rightly characterised the debate as an American one when she noted that
the topic had caused much ink to flow in the United States.[37] The *New York
Times* review of the exhibition focuses almost entirely on the question of
the absence of Jews from *Suite française*:

> But why does no foreshadowing emerge in the novel? Given that
> Némirovsky and Epstein fled Paris for the small town of Issy L'Evêque,
> in Burgundy, where they were the only citizens required to wear the yel-
> low star, why is there not the slightest hint of that reality in this book,
> which features no Jews and no mention of that Nazi obsession?[38]

For the author, this is sufficient to justify the opinion that 'there is no
sense of history' in *Suite française*. It is interesting that the author should
have chosen the term 'foreshadowing', for this type of criticism is a clear
example of Michael André Bernstien's notion of 'backshadowing'. It is
profoundly anachronistic, insofar as it does not seek to read the novel
either in relation to the literary trajectory which preceded and produced it,
or in the context of the literary environment of 1940s France. The resurgence of Jewish memory of the Holocaust in relation to Vichy France is a
relatively recent phenomenon. Cultural history resists precise chronology,
and interpretations differ: Wieviorka cites the appearance of texts such
as Elie Wiesel's *La Nuit* in 1958, André Schwartz-Bart's *Le Dernier des
justes* in 1959 and Anna Langfus' *Les Bagages de sable* in 1961, whilst
Philippe Burrin suggests that the genocide began to be discussed in the
1970s as part of the more general re-evaluation of Vichy after May 1968
and the death of de Gaulle, and Olivier Lalieu affirms that silence surrounded the issue until the 1980s.[39] What is certain is that the persecution
of the Jews was not central either to public opinion or to official discourses
in the 1940s and 1950s:

> Les honneurs rendus au lendemain de la guerre à la seule déportation
> politique, la confusion opérée entre camps de concentration et camps
> d'extermination, le désintérêt massif de l'opinion et, subsidiairement,
> le silence accablé de beaucoup de survivants avaient fait descendre un
> voile qui mit longtemps à se déchirer.[40]

The fact that immediately after the war, only the victims of political deportations were honoured, the confusion between concentration camps and extermination camps, the overwhelming lack of interest on the part of the public, and, secondarily, the appalled silence of many survivors means that a veil descended, which took a long time to be torn.

Neither was the Jewish experience of Vichy central to public opinion or to political discourse at the time Némirovsky was writing *Suite française*. The major wave of arrests and deportations of Jews from France dates from the summer of 1942. Némirovsky's arrest took place very early in the process, on 13 July 1942, before the infamous round-up of Jews at the Vélodrome d'hiver—the *rafle du Vél d'hiv*—on 16–17 July 1942. Jean-Marie Flonneau and Pierre Laborie have described in precise detail the shifts in French public opinion between 1940 and 1944. After the meeting between Pétain and Hitler at Montoire in the autumn of 1940, the general consensus in favour of Pétain developed into a rejection of the politics of collaboration, which manifested itself as hostility to the Vichy regime but did not exclude continuing attachment to Pétain himself. In 1941, the problem of food shortages dominated French public opinion, and the prevailing mood was one of political apathy. Vichy's anti-Semitic policies did not induce hostility towards the regime until July–August 1942, and this type of hostility was not overtly expressed until the end of 1942 and the beginning of 1943. As I have sought to demonstrate throughout this book, Némirovsky always sought to write into, not against, the situation of her readers. Her notes clearly demonstrate that *Suite française* was no exception in this respect. Her personal situation under the Vichy regime certainly motivated her to write a novel which was profoundly critical of Vichy's politics of collaboration, but she sought to do this first and foremost in the terms her readers would remember, and not via a straightforward transcription of her own situation. *Suite française* thereby demonstrates a strikingly clear sighted and accurate sense of history. The absence of any account of the persecution of the Jews is explicable by the literary logic of the novel's genesis and by its historical context. A simplistic and anachronistic biographical reading can only deform Némirovsky's text. These inappropriate ethically based criticisms have more to do with our own twenty-first century cultural environment than with Némirovsky's situation in 1940–1942.

There is a hint in Némirovsky's notes that the Jewish situation would have been treated in later parts of the text.[41] In the light of Flonneau's analysis, this would have been perfectly in line with the text's historical logic. However, we can only discuss the extant text, and it is more productive to focus on what it actually contains than on what it does not. 'Tempête en juin' is both an impressive portrait of the confusion and disarray of the *exode*, and a biting and effective satire on French bourgeois *mœurs*. As we have noted, one of the reasons why its portrait of the *exode* has resonated with contemporary readers is that it is very recognisable. Although it has been widely presented in the press as an account of Némirovsky's own experience, this is not in fact the case. Némirovsky had left Paris definitively for the village of Issy l'Eveque in May 1940, before the *exode* had begun in earnest. In Issy, which fell inside the occupied zone, she first lived in the Hotel des Voyageurs, and then in a rented house where she stayed with her family until her deportation. Her departure was well planned and well prepared—Némirovsky had been visting Issy since 1938, and her two daughters had been there since the outbreak of the war.[42] Thus, although the family saw the *exode* pass by the village, they were not themselves part of it.[43] Because Némirovsky conveys the *exode* via the scenes which have in fact been passed on for posterity—the spectacle of vehicles piled high with mattresses and all sorts of personal belongings, the fear of the fleeing civilians caught up in bombing raids, the shortages of food and petrol—the reading public have recognised her account and therefore received it positively.[44] The conditions for a positive reception were ideal: *Suite française* simultaneously fulfilled the criteria of familiarity and of authenticity. However, we must recognise that this is a result of a deliberate narrative strategy on Némirovsky's part. If the text really had been a direct transcription of a personal and therefore very particular experience, it is likely that it would have been less familiar to readers, and therefore potentially less popular.

One of the key themes of *Suite française* is class division. Just as in *Les Chiens et les loups* Némirovsky had demonstrated the ways in which economic identity complicates ethnic identity and defines the experience of persecution, so in *Suite française* she illustrates the relationship between class stratification and the experience of—and response to—the invasion. As Jeanne Michaud cries out in a moment of frustration, it is the lower middle classes who suffer most: 'Les ouvriers se défendent, les riches sont forts. Nous, nous sommes les moutons bons à tendre' (*'The workers fight back, the rich are powerful. We're just sheep to the slaughter'*).[45] Collaboration in this novel is always a result of habits of opinion and behaviour formed under the Third Republic and which, before Vichy, were certainly reactionary, but not fascist. Collaboration is not a positively chosen or politically conscious act in *Suite française*. It derives from the type of anti-republicanism the Péricands illustrate, people happy to describe the republic as a rotten regime whilst taking all the social and financial benefits it has to offer people of their class; it also derives from the unthinking complacency of the *grande monde*, who, like the writer Gabriel Corte, bury previous political disagrecments under a veneer of luxury and plenty, which turns out to be what they value most.[46] The force of the novel might perhaps be ascribed to its illustration of the ease with which both bourgeois self-centredness and working-class frustration can, under a situation of extreme national crisis, turn into shocking brutality. Fleeing from the burning village, concerned only with the task of maintaining her position at the top of the pecking order, which in this case means being the first to get out, Madame Péricand bribes a passing farmer to transport her and her children to safety. But she completely forgets about her father-in-law, who is left behind.[47] The violence festering amongst the deprived children in the care of the priest Philippe Péricand erupts uncontrollably when they camp in the grounds of a wealthy country house; their rage becomes senselessly focused on Philippe, and they murder him by throwing him into the lake and stoning him until he drowns.[48] These narrative climaxes are set against the day-to-day absurdity of the situation of Occupation. For most people, it is simply that 'la routine était plus forte que la peur' (*'their need to follow a routine was stronger than their terror'*).[49] This is why remembering to collect the ironing board and the embroidered sheets is a crucial, though ludicrous, aspect of the departure from Paris.[50]

'Dolce' is an effective and engaging account of the moral and personal ambiguities created by the Occupation. Its focus on the strange relationship between the occupying Nazi forces and the rural French population is foregrounded in 'Tempête en juin' when the villagers, expecting the arrival of some vision of the Apocalypse, some terrifying monster, are brought face to face with the disturbing normality of the German soldiers:

> Et la résonance humaine de cette parole, ce geste, tout ce qui prouvait jusqu'à l'évidence que l'on avait affaire non à quelque monstre altéré de sang mais à un soldat comme les autres, cela brisa tout à coup la glace entre le village et l'ennemi, entre le paysan et l'envahisseur.[51]

> *And the humanity of his words, his gesture, everything proved they were not dealing with some bloodthirsty monster but with a simple soldier like any other, and suddenly the ice was broken between the town and the enemy, between the country folk and the invader.*[52]

Structurally, 'Dolce' is clearly modelled on Némirovsky's earlier fiction. It is a chronologically continuous story in which the conflicts which drive the narrative are derived from interactions between complex personal relationships and the socio-political environment in which they are played out. The Vicomtesse de Montmort's patriotism and her anti-communism soon shade into overt collaborationism, anti-Semitism and a devotion to Pétain, none of which are impeded by her instinctive Germanophobia:[53]

> Bon gré, mal gré, il fallait suivre la politique du gouvernement. Et puis enfin, ces officiers allemands, c'étaient des gens bien élevés après tout! Ce qui sépare ou unit les êtres, ce n'est pas le langage, les lois, les mœurs, les principes, mais une manière identique de tenir son couteau et sa fourchette![54]

> *Whether they liked it or not, they had to follow the government's orders. And besides, these German officers were cultured men after all! What separates or unites people is not their language, their laws, their customs, their principles, but the way they hold their knife and fork.*[55]

Némirovsky constantly underlines the idea that it is the fracturing of French society along class lines which makes collaboration a reality. In common with her earlier novels, there is little ideological specificity here: whilst *Suite française* is a denunciation of day-to-day collaboration, it is by no means a political attack on fascism as an ideology. Némirovsky's account of France losing her honour is a social satire but it is not a political novel. The dilemmas posed by the text are personal, social and ethical, but never explicitly ideological. The seamstress who is sleeping with a German soldier is attracted not by his politics but by the fact that he is more refined than the 'gars du pays' she is used to.[56] Lucille's relationship with the German officer is ambiguous not because it indicates any sympathy on her part for the politics of the Occupier, but because it illustrates the capacity of affective human relationships to transcend political oppositions. Her loyalty to France is never in doubt, as is made clear by her willingness to use her friendship with the German to retrieve items of personal value from the Perrin's requisitioned house and to get hold of petrol and a travel permit to facilitate Benoît's escape after he has shot a German soldier. Benoît's crime is also ambiguous: although his action results in his becoming involved with the resistance, it is by no means clear that it was politically motivated. It is a crime of passion and of class hatred against the man who has attempted to seduce Madeleine; it is not a protest against Nazism. In the final pages of the novel, as the occupying Germans depart for the Eastern front, the message is much more one of the universal waste of human life which war causes than it is of ideological conflict:

> Il était tard, mais personne ne songeait à dormir. Tous voulaient voir le départ des Allemands. En ces dernières heures, une sorte de mélancolie, de douceur humaine liait les uns aux autres, les vaincus et les vainqueurs.[57]

> *It was late, but no-one even considered going to bed. Everyone wanted to see the Germans leave. In these final hours, a kind of melancholy and human warmth bound them all together: the conquered and the conquerors.*[58]

The German soldiers are leaving the safety of the village to be exposed to Russian bullets: 'Combien resteraient ensevelis dans les plaines russes?' (*'How many of them would be buried on the Russian steppes?'*), the narrator wonders. There is then no strong ideological conclusion to *Suite française*. As was the case with *David Golder*, a fundamentally apolitical text has been politicised by its context of reception, though this time to its advantage rather than to its detriment. It is easy to represent *Suite française* as an indictment of Vichy France, and in a sense this is accurate, however it is not a novel of political protest; it is in a clear continuum with the novels which preceded it and, as such, it is certainly no *roman à these*.

SUITE FRANÇAISE IN OUR TIME

The Final Solution permanently altered the moral, intellectual and aesthetic climate in which French and German literary artists tried to write about World War II and its aftermath [. . .] in the aftermath of the Final Solution, the production of literary artefacts could not continue as in the past, as if nothing radically different had happened.[59]

Est-il possible, pour paraphraser le mot prêté à Theodor Adorno, de prétendre écrire encore l'histoire après Auschwitz, et d'écrire précisément cette page-là? Sommes-nous en possession des outils, des concepts, de l'éthique nécessaire qui permettraient à l'historien d'appréhender la rupture profonde induite par un tel événement?[60]

Is it possible, to paraphrase the words attributed to Theodor Adorno, to imagine that one can still write history after Auschwitz, that one can write about exactly that period? Do we have the necessary tools, concepts, ethics which would allow the historian to understand the profound rupture caused by such an event?

Literary critics and historians have discussed at length the problem of writing after Auschwitz. Némirovsky poses the problem of reading after Auschwitz. In her case, post-war France seemed to have given a definitive answer: reading Némirovsky after Auschwitz was not possible. Hardly anyone did. In the light of Henry Rousso's analysis of the 'Vichy syndrome' in his 1987 book of that title, the critical neglect of Némirovsky's writing in the post-war period is not surprising. Although some critics have objected to his use of psychoanalytic metaphors, the chronology of Rousso's account of the development of representations of the Vichy period is still broadly accepted. Rousso characterised the immediate post-war period (1944–1954) as one of 'unfinished mourning' when the French nation was incapable of processing the trauma of the Occupation. The period from 1954–1971 was a period of 'repression', when the Gaullist myth of *résistancialisme* dominated the political and cultural landscape. According to this myth, de Gaulle, the resistance, and France constituted an organic unity, Vichy and collaboration were taboo, and national reconstruction proceeded according to the fiction that France's *grandeur* was firmly rooted in its unwavering identity as a nation of Resistants. The post-Gaullist period (1971–1974) saw the beginnings of a reassessment of the Vichy period which permitted the articulation of different discourses. After 1974, France entered a period of 'obsession' characterised by the proliferation of memorialisations of Vichy and the Holocaust. Annette Wieviorka's succinct account of the 'era of the witness' in which organisations such as the Yale Video Archive and the Spielberg Foundation have collected millions of hours of testimony from Holocaust survivors suggests that the period of 'obsession' is ongoing and extends far beyond the Hexagon. *Les Biens de ce monde* was published as a book in 1947 and *Les Feux de l'automne* in 1957. Neither of these moments was auspicious for a positive reception of novels about the fall of France written by a Holocaust victim. *Les Feux de l'automne* could not be further from a work of Jewish testimony: there could have been no possibility of integrating this novel into the literary context provided by the publication of Wiesel's *La Nuit* and the award of the Goncourt prizes to Schwartz-Bart and Langfus in 1959 and 1961, respectively, which for Wieviorka indicate the beginnings of an interest in France in the Jewish experience of the genocide. But it was not only a question of *la mémoire juive*. As Catharine Savage Brosman points out:

> The challenge for authors dealing with the second great world conflict of the century would be to find forms appropriate to its peculiar features and especially to the sense of historical repetition, whether by renewing old techniques, carrying farther the techniques of modernism, or developing new ones, which would convey the growing twentieth-century angst in the face of history.[61]

Post-war French literature was enthralled first by Sartrean engagement and later by the narrative experiments of the *nouveau roman*. In the 'era of suspicion', according to Nathalie Sarraute, 'les personnages tels que les concevait le vieux roman (et tout le vieil appareil qui servait à les mettre en valeur), ne parviennent plus à contenir la réalité psychologique actuelle' (*characters as the old novel conceived them (and the entirety of the old structure which gave them prominence) can no longer contain contemporary psychological reality*).[62] Némirovsky's fiction, so heavily dependant on character that she began each novel by writing a biography of all the protagonists, and so devoid of any obvious political message, was out of tune with the literary preoccupations of post-war France. Further, the traditionalist representations of gender roles and the lack of any obvious narrative experimentation or self-reflexivity in her fiction meant that, like most other female-authored realist fiction of the inter-war period, her novels were not interesting to feminist critics of the 'second wave' as they developed the idea of *écriture féminine*. How could a novel by a Jewish woman writer, a victim of the Holocaust, which did not deal with Jewish identity, which relied on outmoded notions of plot and character, and which celebrated traditional gender roles possibly find an audience in 1957?

Yet, thanks to the literary career of her younger daughter, Elisabeth Gille, Némirovsky was not completely forgotten. Gille's *Le Mirador* won the Cazes prize in 1992. Gille's novel about Vichy, *Un Paysage de cendres*, won *Elle* magazine's *Grand prix des lectrices* in 1997, after the author's death from cancer in 1996. A second edition of *Le Mirador* appeared in 2000 along with the first of two collections of Némirovsky's short stories, under the title *Dimanche et autres nouvelles*. A second collection, *Déstinées et autres nouvelles*, would follow in 2004, before the appearance of *Suite française*.

The period of 'obsession' provided propitious territory for the reception of these works, though they did not attract anywhere near the same volume or variety of attention as *Suite française*. In the light of the post-2004 discussion of Némirovsky, the paratextual material included in the new edition of *Le Mirador* is extremely interesting. The book contains a substantial preface entitled 'Mère et fille' by René de Ceccatty, and an interview de Ceccatty had conducted with Gille, which was first published in Italy in 1992. De Ceccatty was quite pointed in his description of the social milieux in which Némirovsky moved and which provided the material for her novels:

> Une bourgeoisie éclairée mais naïve, rapidement irresponsable à force de ne pas lire les signes annonciateurs mais aussi un milieu intellectuel d'une grande veulerie. Assurément Irène Némirovsky tarda à en prendre conscience, puisque, comme Elisabeth le rappelle, elle ne sut pas se montrer assez attentive aux dérapages d'un Paul Morand, d'un Jean Cocteau et plus grave, dans un certain sens, aux incohérences ingénues ou aveugles d'un Daniel Halévy et d'un Emmanuel Berl.[63]

> *An enlightened but naïve bourgeoisie, which quickly became irresponsible because it did not read the warning signs, but also an extremely spineless intellectual milieu. Certainly, Némirovsky took a long time to realise this since, as Elisabeth reminds us, she was not able to be sufficiently attentive to the excesses of a Paul Morand or a Jean Cocteau, nor to the ingenuous or blind incoherencies of a Daniel Halévy or an Emmanuel Berl which, in a way, was more serious still.*

In the 1992 interview, Gille was willing to express overt criticism of her mother's decisions during the Occupation, and was very honest about the effect she felt these decisions had had on her own life. She said that 'je lui en voulais de son inconscience politique' (*I was annoyed with her for her lack of political awareness*) and that she found it difficult to accept the fact of her association with *Gringoire*: 'C'est un reproche intérieur que je lui ai toujours fait' (*that's something I have always privately reproached her for*).[64] She also said that she felt her mother's choice not to try to leave France had placed her daughters in danger—something Denise Epstein also mentions in her recent book[65]—and that Némirovsky had not been able, or willing, to see the truth of France's treatment of immigrant Jews:

> Son aveuglement était criminel. Pendant les années trente, jusque dans son œuvre, elle n'était nullement émue par ce qui arrivait aux petits Juifs des quartiers populaires de Paris.[66]

> *Her blindness was criminal. During the 1930s, even in her novels, she was not in the least bit moved by the fate of poor Jews in the working-class areas of Paris.*

It would be inappropriate to pass judgement on such opinions and emotions; it is rather the fact of the inclusion of this material in the text which interests me. In her analysis of the contemporary British literary marketplace, Claire Squires stresses the crucial importance of paratexts in defining the way readers respond to texts. Drawing on the work of Gérard Genette, she writes,

> Genette turns the physical borders of the book—its cover, its pages— into a more fluidly metaphorical site. He presents the paratext as an invitation, which may be accepted or rejected, and at which the potential reader either 'step[s] inside or turn[s] back'. This invitation is one of marketing's methods of appeal, by which texts are represented to the potential reader.[67]

For Squires, marketing is both representation and interpretation; marketing includes book design, format, and the text included on the book's cover and in the preliminary pages, as well as more obvious sales presenters and point of sales materials. The paratextual material around *Le Mirador* invites the reader into a critical—though by no means hostile—relationship with the text; the reader is encouraged to explore the ambiguities of Némirovsky's position in France of the 1930s, as well as the inevitably difficult, but ultimately positive, relationship between Gille and her mother which produced the complex and fascinating homage to Némirovsky that is *Le Mirador*. The paratextual material around *Suite française* did not shy away from addressing difficult issues in relation to Némirovsky: Myriam Anissiomv's preface used the concept of Jewish self-hatred and presented a litany of the stereotypes which occur throughout her fiction, and the correspondence presented after the main text includes Michael Epstein's letter to Otto Abetz in which he cites the testimonial written in the Epstein family's favour by one of the occupying Nazi soldiers, and seeks to prove that his wife had no sympathy for either Bolshevism or Judaism.[68] But the crucial difference is that the paratextual material also presented *Suite française* in starkly ethical terms, by defining it as *testimony* and as an *assault on intolerance*. Denise Epstein presented the novel very overtly as her mother's testimony and as a bridge between the dead and the living in a brief epigraph, which reads: 'Sur les traces de ma mère et de mon père, pour ma sœur Elisabeth Gille, pour mes enfants et petits-enfants, cette Mémoire à transmettre, et pour tous ceux qui ont connu et connaissent encore aujourd'hui le drame de l'intolérance' ('*I dedicate this novel to the memory of my mother and father, to my sister Elisabeth Gille, to my children and grandchildren, and to everyone who has felt and continues to feel the tragedy of intolerance*').[69] The fact that Myriam Anissimov, herself a Jewish writer and the child of Holocaust survivors, wrote the preface defines the text in terms of Jewish memory. Anissimov's introduction begins with a detailed account of Némirovsky's Jewish, specifically Yiddish, origins, detailing her birth in

Kiev, in 'Yiddishland', underlining her knowledge of Yiddish, mentioning her father's Hebrew name, and giving details of the pogroms which caused the Némirovskys to flee.[70] The editorial choice to begin the selection of extracts from Némirovsky's notebooks with her anguished cry 'Mon Dieu! que me fait ce pays?' sets the text very clearly—and very personally—in the context of Vichy's persecution of the Jews. The inclusion of Michael Epstein's incredibly moving correspondence documenting his attempts to locate and rescue his wife lend an almost overpowering emotional force to the text as a whole. This paratextual material is at the origin of the French press's response to *Suite française*, which quickly defined the publication and celebration of book as a long overdue, though obviously insufficient, reparation for the appalling injustice the nation had inflicted on Némirovsky. According to Clémence Boulouque: 'Autant qu'une consécration, c'est une justice faite, enfin faite la reconnaissance d'une romancière qui a donné aux lettres françaises d'admirables pages et qui a été sacrifiée par Vichy' (*As much as a consecration, it is a matter of justice, of finally giving recognition to a novelist who gave French literature some admirable pages and who was sacrificed by Vichy*). The French novelist J.M. Le Clézio defended the award of the Renaudot prize on the same basis.[71] De Ceccatty presented Némirovsky's fate as an indictment of France, as an opportunity for a nation still in its period of 'obsession' to continue to scratch its wounds: 'Le cas tragique d'Irène Némirovsky occupera longtemps la mauvaise conscience française' (*The case of Irène Némirovsky will be on France's conscience for a long time*). Of course, the date of publication was also crucial. That year, the 'Mur des noms', a sculpture bearing the names of 76,000 Jews deported from France under Vichy, was inaugurated at the Mémorial de la Shoah in Paris to commemorate the sixtieth anniversary of the liberation of the concentration camps.[72] This type of 'packaging' of the Némirovsky phenomenon, via which the text is presented to the reader as *already having been interpreted*, has been a major factor in its phenomenal success both in France and abroad.

Claire Squires argues convincingly that in the contemporary literary marketplace, genre has become a function of marketing.[73] Although, as we have seen, *Suite française* is a carefully constructed work of fiction which owes as much to Némirovsky's career as a novelist as it does to her personal experience of the Occupation, it has been presented and received as if it were a piece of pure testimony. The cover text tells the reader that the work was 'écrit dans le feu de l'histoire' (*written in the heat of the moment*) and that it describes the events of the Occupation 'presque en direct' (*almost live*). Discussing *Suite française* in *L'Express*, Olivier Le Naire quoted Denise Epstein, who said that although *Suite française* is a novel, 'c'est surtout le journal de bord de ma mère, écrit au fil des années noires' (*it is first and foremost my mother's day to day diary, written during the dark years*). This notion was picked up in the reviews: Olivier Le Naire's qualification of the text as 'un livre testament' (*a work of testimony*) and 'un roman vérité' (*a novel of truth*) in the same article are typical. Reviewers presented the novel as though it were a direct transcription of reality. For *Le Point*, 'une mouche chargée d'encre semble composer en temps réel la partition du désastre' (*a fly covered in ink seems to be composing the score of the disaster as it happens*).[74] Boulouque pointed out that the novel was written 'presque au jour le jour' (*almost day by day*) and Annie Coppermann suggested that the scenes in the novel were so effective because 'elles ont la force du vécu' (*they have the force of lived experience*). *Le Temps* called *Suite française* a '[r]adiographie de la débâcle française' (*a radiograph of the fall of France*), and specified that '[e]ntre 1941 et 1942, Irène Némirovsky écrit à chaud les deux premiers chapitres de *Suite française*' (*between 1941 and 1942, Irène Némirovsky wrote the two first chapters of* Suite française *in the heat of the moment*).[75] The reception of *Suite française* is an excellent illustration of Pierre Nora's idea that history is our new collective imagination.[76] Because contemporary culture looks to history rather than to fiction for imaginative stimulation, there is a danger that historical fiction will be read as if it were history. And fiction written by an author personally implicated in the events can easily be recast as testimony. Furthermore, as war crimes trials have increasingly been used to teach Europe a history lesson,[77] there has been a tendency to treat testimony as if it were history.[78] The marketing of *Suite française* as testimony was so effective because it derived from, and responded to, the desire for witnessing, which Wieviorka has identified as a dominant element in current discourses on the Holocaust. Wieviorka dates the surge in interest in witnessing to the 1961 trial of Adolph Eichmann, one of the most infamous Nazi war criminals deemed primarily responsible for the organisation and execution of the Final Solution:

> The Eichmann trial freed the victims to speak. It created a social demand for testimonies, just as other trials would later do in France—the trials of Klaus Barbie, of Paul Touvier, and of Maurice Papon—and just as two fictional films would do, the U.S. television miniseries *Holocaust*, and Steven Spielberg's *Schindler's List*.[79]

The demand for testimony has become *le devoir de mémoire*, the *duty* to remember.[80] The witness is now called upon to function as the carrier of authenticity, identity, truth, and history.[81] Michael André Bernstein argues that 'one of the most pervasive myths of our era, a myth perhaps even partially arising out of our collective response to the horrors of the concentration camps, is the absolute authority given to first-person testimony'.[82] Because the novel was written as events were happening by an author who was so tragically implicated in them, Némirovsky's novel has been accorded the authority of a first-person testimony. Némirovsky has been transformed into a witness. In contemporary culture, remembering is seen as an arm in the fight against the rise of the far right, and as a means of promoting human rights and world peace.[83] Remembering Vichy in France is part of 'l'impossible espoir d'inscrire dans les consciences une mémoire-rédemption qui vaincrait définitivement et solennellement l'oubli' (*the impossible hope of inscribing a redemptive memory into consciousnesses which will definitively and solemnly overcome forgetting*).[84] *Suite française* is such a *mémoire-rédemption*, as the reviews demonstrate: its publication was both a means of pricking France's conscience, and of offering reparation. For Denise Epstein, though not for Némirovsky, the publication of the text is an act of commemoration with a political subtext, as her epigraph to the novel makes clear. In *Survivre et vivre*, Epstein says that her life has been dedicated to Memory (the capitalisation is her own), and that *Suite française* is the culmination of that trajectory.[85] Némirovsky's 'Que me fait ce pays?', which many reviewers quoted, taps into the 'discourse of resentment toward France' which Wieviorka identifies as an important feature of recent French testimonies.[86] The constant re-telling of Némirovsky's life story by critics and the excessively biographical reading of her fiction is a manifestation of what Wieviorka calls the culture of intimacy, the need 'to return a name, a face, a history to each of the victims of mass murder', which dominates not only our memorialisations of the Holocaust, but all our current cultural representations.[87] In one sense, the desire to remember Némirovsky in terms of the Holocaust is justified and appropriate: *Suite française* provides contemporary readers with another way of approaching the unapproachable. But in another sense, it is problematic. It risks enclosing Némirovsky within the single identity of the deportee, which some survivors have strongly resisted.[88] In this context, it is easy to see how and why the transformation of *Suite française* into a work of Holocaust testimony has caused contemporary commentators to vilify Némirovsky on the basis that her novel does not talk about Jews. It is of course both fitting and important to honour Némirovsky's memory; it is not appropriate to disparage her for failing to live up to our twenty-first century expectations.

Some reviewers were critical of the marketing of Némirovsky in terms of the Holocaust, particularly in relation to the controversial award of the Renaudot prize. Josyane Savigneau argued that Némirovsky's reputation had no need of 'cette opération de marketing déguisée en "devoir de mémoire"' (*this marketing campaign disguised as the 'duty to remember'*). She continued,

> Tout cela relève d'une cuisine assez piteuse, dans laquelle la mémoire d'Irène Némirovsky est instrumentalisée, et sa mort tragique mise en avant pour empêcher toute contestation d'un choix ayant moins à voir avec la défense d'une œuvre qu'avec un coup publicitaire—pour le Renaudot.

> *All this derives from pathetic intriguing which instrumentalises Irène Némirovsky's memory and highlights her tragic death to prevent any criticism of a choice which has less to do with the defence of a book than with a publicity stunt: for the Renaudot.*

Savigneau's article was a denunciation not of the value of Némirovsky's novel—quite the contrary—but of the Renaudot prize itself. The issue was all the more controversial since André Brincourt, the secretary of the Renaudot prize committee, had objected to the award on the basis that the point of the prize was to support living authors.[89] There is no doubt that the award of the prize, and the controversy surrounding it, played a significant part not only in the construction of Némirovsky as a literary success, but also in the affirmation of the literary and historical value of her text. James F. English's work on the cultural significance of literary prizes argues convincingly that the opposition between the type of commercialism our contemporary prize culture represents, and the notion that cultural value is above such venal concerns, no longer obtains. English is of the view that Bourdieu's opposition between the *champ de production restreinte* and the *champ de grande production* has been a useful model for analysing twentieth-century cultural production, even into the 1960s: he suggests that Sartre's refusal of the Nobel prize can still be read as an affirmation of his belief in the former and rejection of the latter.[90] But in our postmodern culture, the relationships between cultural and financial consecration have become more complicated. No writer can stand outside the economic circulation of cultural products, and readers simultaneously do and do not believe in the *illusio* as Bourdieu conceives it, that is, as disinterested literary value:

> We are, rather, dealing with a kind of suspension between belief and disbelief, between the impulse to see art as a kind of ponzi scheme and the impulse to preserve it as a place for our most trusting investments. Under these circumstances, cultural prizes can be, at one and the same time, both more dubious—more of a joke—than they used to be, and more symbolically effectual, more powerfully and intimately intertwined with processes of canonization.[91]

English argues that 'journalistic capital', which he defines as visibility, celebrity, and scandal, now mediates between pure cultural consecration and commercial success, such that each type of capital is constantly being converted into its opposite.[92] The literary prize is one means via which this *capital intraconversion* occurs. Visibility, celebrity, and scandal have certainly been present in the discussions around *Suite française*. The Renaudot was a classic example of a 'scandalous' literary prize. The story of the manuscript's survival and that of Némirovsky's exceptional life and tragic death provided ample material for the creation of a new literary celebrity. The traditional notion of the *illusio* was also affirmed—as had been the case with *David Golder*—when the commissioning editor, Olivier Rubinstein, professed to have been overwhelmingly impressed by the sheer quality of the manuscript.[93] What Juliet Gardiner has called the 'author function' has operated very effectively in relation to *Suite française*, as it did in 1929 in relation to

David Golder. Gardiner argues that in the contemporary cultural marketplace, the author is central to marketing strategies: it is via the author that a
book is sold to consumers as a brand, rather than via the publishing house
or the imprint, except in quite rare cases of specialist imprints, such as, in
Britain, Virago for women's literature, or Faber for poetry:

> [. . .] the Romantic definition of the author as stand-alone source
> of meaning and authority, becomes conflated with a more overlooked
> root of the word author, the Latin, 'agere' to act or perform. The au-
> thor not only writes the text, increasingly in various ways she or he
> speaks it, circulating its meaning through media interviews, reviews,
> business reports and so-called news items, in 'personal appearances', at
> readings and literary events.[94]

Although Némirovsky could no longer 'speak' her text in this way, as she had
'spoken' *David Golder*, Denise Epstein's participation in the presentation
and discussion of *Suite française* has fulfilled this function. As Clémence
Boulouque remarks in the preface to *Survivre et vivre*, Denise received the
honours in Némirovsky's place.[95] Because Epstein herself is a Holocaust
survivor, her own testimony has been of great interest to Némirovsky's
readers, as is indicated by the recent publication of her own work of testimony, *Survivre et vivre*, the cover of which carries a banner which reads:
'La fille d'Irène Némirovsky témoigne' (*Irène Némirovsky's daughter bears
witness*). Pursuing a similar line of argument to English, Gardiner suggests
that even a 'literary' author can no longer reject this sort of participation
in the marketplace:

> [. . .] in the case of the non-mass market author, it had been possible for
> him or her to shelter under an ideological cover of the 'transcendent' au-
> thor who happens to sell but whose value is represented as being largely
> due to the fact that he or she is unbeholden to the fickle vagaries of the
> marketplace. With the competitive economic demands of the post 1980s
> expansion and aggregation of publishers and book selling outlets, the
> so-perceived literary author has been required to achieve a high profile
> in the marketplace in ways that do not compromise his or her 'value' by
> being associated with an 'unknowing' mass market.[96]

In Némirovsky's case, the demands of marketing have been easily satisfied
without any danger of compromising the author's reputation because the
'author function' has been split between two individuals: Epstein's presence ensures visibility, whilst Némirovsky's radical absence as a posthumous success allows her 'transcendence' to remain intact. Thus, the two
potentially opposing aspects of the 'author function'—aesthetic autonomy
and cultural value, and media celebrity—have reinforced, rather than con-
tradicting, each other. There is no doubt that Némirovsky is now a media

phenomenon. But neither the award of the Renaudot prize, nor her celebrity, has called the legitimacy of her work into question: quite the opposite. Any criticism of Némirovsky has been politically rather than aesthetically motivated. British and American critics of Némirovsky's attitude to Jewishness have, in common with much ideologically based criticism, used political criteria to make aesthetic judgements: Ruth Franklin's article, which condemns *David Golder* as 'an appalling book by any standard', is a case in point. Savigneau is right to problematise the definition of the Némirovsky phenomenon as *un devoir de mémoire*.

Némirovsky's life and work are in many ways exceptional, and it is right that her achievements should be celebrated and her tragic fate remembered. But in this book I have sought to show that, if her *œuvre* is understood within its own context of production, it is highly typical. Stressing Némirovsky's exceptionality is important insofar as it allows contemporary readers to respect her accomplishments and to condemn those who persecuted her. It is also hazardous because it tends to draw too much attention to the ethical or moral issues posed by her work. Because we read Némirovsky in our own time with the benefit of hindsight, it is all too easy to accuse her of a lack of foresight. Nonetheless, Michael André Bernstein's rejection of 'backshadowing' in favour of 'sideshadowing' is not a rejection of the possibility of retrospective readings. These are inevitable:

> Sideshadowing, then, can also be thought of as the entire set of alternative interpretations, subsidiary plots, and interrogations that history encourages us to add to a work by uncovering new connections, ramifications, or contradictions between it and the world of lived actuality.[97]

The challenge posed by Némirovsky's work in the twenty-first century is to uncover new connections without attempting simplistically to resolve contradictions.

Notes

NOTES TO THE INTRODUCTION

1. See Epstein 140, 164; Le Naire.
2. *Ida* also includes 'La Comédie bourgeoise'.
3. *Suite Française*; *David Golder*; *Le Bal*, which also includes *Snow in Autumn*; *Fire in the Blood*; *The Courilof Affair*; *All Our Worldly Goods*.
4. Weiss's *Irène Némirovsky* appeared in English translation as *Irène Némirovsky: Her Life and Works*. Philipponnat and Lienhardt's book is to appear shortly in English translation.
5. Stemberger's *Irène Némirovsky: Phantasmagorien der Fremdheit* is the only book-length study to date. Cegarra; Kershaw, 'Finding Irène Némirovsky'; Lloyd; Kedward; Tritt; Stemberger, 'Selling Gender; Golsan and Suleiman.
6. The lecture, entitled 'Language, Foreignness and the Canon: Beckett/Némirovsky', took place on 15 May 2008.
7. See Kershaw, *Forgotten Engagements*.
8. Relevant articles by Bourdieu include 'La Production de la croyance'; 'The Field of Cultural Production'; 'Le Champ littéraire'; 'Une Révolution conservatrice dans l'édition'.
9. English, *The Economy of Prestige* 8.
10. Ibid. 10.
11. See also English, 'Winning the Culture Game' 119–120; Gardiner.
12. Sapiro, *La Guerre des écrivains*; 'Forms of Politicization'.
13. Meizoz, *L'Œil sociologique* 15. All translations are my own unless otherwise indicated.
14. Iser 9.
15. Eagleton 87–88.
16. English, *Economy* 12.
17. Bourdieu, *Les Règles de l'art* 314–15.
18. Confino 1395.
19. Epstein 25.

NOTES TO CHAPTER 1

1. Bourdieu, *Les Règles de l'art* 280.
2. Bourdieu, *The Rules of Art* 167.
3. Hutcheon and Valdés xi, x.
4. Bourdieu, *Les Règles de l'art* 469; *The Rules of Art* 287–88.
5. Bourdieu, *Les Règles de l'art* 495–96; *The Rules of Art* 304.
6. On the relationship between meaning, field, and ideology, see Sapiro, 'Pour une approche sociologique'.

7. *L'Ennemie* and *Le Bal* were published under the pseudonym Pierre Nerey.
8. Chartier and Martin 220.
9. Hewitt 8. See also Cornick, 'Marcel Arland'. See Crémieux, 'Bilan d'un enquête' and Arland, 'Sur un nouveau mal du siècle'.
10. These stories were originally published as follows: 'Ida', *Marianne*, 16 May 1934; 'Film parlé', *Les Œuvres libres* Vol 121, July 1931; 'La Comédie bourgeoise', *Les Œuvres libres* Vol 132, June 1932; 'Les fumées du vin', *Le Figaro*, 12 and 19 June 1934.
11. See also Weiss, *Irène Némirovsky* 54; Philipponnat and Lienhardt 168–174.
12. Weiss, *Irène Némirovsky* 54.
13. Bellenger 589; Chartier and Martin 220.
14. Chartier and Martin 220.
15. Ibid. 207.
16. Pierrey, review of *David Golder*, 8 March 1930 in IMEC FSQ315 *David Golder*. Part of Pierry's text is reprinted in Philipponnat and Lienhardt 429–30.
17. Chartier and Martin 207, 209.
18. On the *Revue des deux mondes*, see Cornick, *The* Nouvelle Revue Française 39; Sapiro, *La Guerre des écrivains* 261.
19. Todd 42.
20. *Le Matin*, 18 January 1930, p. 2. The text, which includes quotations from positive reviews, is accompanied by a photograph of Némirovsky. See also Philipponnat and Lienhardt 178.
21. IMEC NMR11.1 Dossier critique. See also Weiss, *Irène Némirovsky* 55.
22. Charle, *Le Siècle de la presse* 329–30.
23. Bellanger 595.
24. Bourdieu, *Les Règles de l'art* 375.
25. Bourdieu, *The Rules of Art* 229.
26. Bourdieu, *Sur la télévision* 25.
27. Ibid. 88.
28. Bourdieu, 'La production de la croyance' 28.
29. Bourdieu, 'The Production of Belief' 284.
30. See Weiss, *Irène Némirovsky* 79–85; Philipponnat and Lienhardt 261–62
31. Charle, *Le Siècle de la presse* 329–30.
32. See Bourdieu, *Les Règles de l'art* 353–65; *The Rules of Art* 215–23.
33. Discussions of this type relevant to the present study include Gardiner; Squires, 'Fiction in the Marketplace'; Squires, *Marketing Literature*. See also Mounier 242–50, for an account of critical engagements with Bourdieu's remarks on journalism and culture.
34. Bourdieu, 'Une révolution conservatrice dans l'édition' 16.
35. Bourdieu, 'A Conservative Revolution in Publishing' 138.
36. See also Bourdieu, 'The Field of Cultural Production'.
37. Bourdieu, *Les Règles de l'art* 357.
38. These are part of the Fonds d'éditeurs held at IMEC. FSQ315 Fonds Grasset et Fasquelle has dossiers on *David Golder*, *Le Bal*, *Les Mouches d'autômne*, and *L'Affaire Courilof*. The archive also includes a typewritten dossier which contains transcriptions of a selection of reviews: NMR11.1 Dossier Critique.
39. See Weiss, *Irène Némirovsky* 55–56; Philipponnat and Lienhardt 177–78.
40. See for example *Comœdia*, February 1930 in IMEC NMR11.1 Dossier critique; Raymond Millet in *Paris Presse*, 30 January 1930 in IMEC FSQ315 *David Golder*.
41. *Comœdia*, 1 October 1931 in IMEC NMR11.1 Dossier critique.
42. Pierrey, review of *David Golder*, 8 March 1930 in IMEC FSQ315 *David Golder*; Philipponnat and Lienhardt, *La Vie d'Irène Némirovsky* 429–30.
43. Raimond 109.

44. Ernest-Charles, 'Une romancière', *L'Opinion*, 3 June 1933 in IMEC FSQ315 *L'Affaire Courilof*.
45. Raimond 106–07.
46. Ibid. 112.
47. Ibid. 11.
48. Ibid. 11–12.
49. Ibid. 117, 130.
50. Ibid. 139.
51. Ibid. 14.
52. Ibid. 15.
53. Reviews of *Le Bal* in *Le Petit provenençal*, 1930 and *Chantecler*, 20 September 1930 in IMEC NMR11.1 Dossier critique.
54. Raimond 160–61.
55. *Comoedia*, 21 January 1930 in IMEC FSQ315 *David Golder*.
56. Raimond 30–33.
57. *Paris-Presse*, 30 January 1930 in IMEC FSQ315 *David Golder*.
58. For an account of the classicism/romanticism debate, see Sapiro, *La Guerre des écrivains* 120–27; Renard 82–89. On the position of naturalism in the literary field, see Raimond 171–72.
59. On the Goncourt academy, see Sapiro, *La Guerre des écrivains* 317–75, particularly 323–24 on the question of naturalism.
60. De Pawlowski.
61. Augagneur.
62. Sapiro, *La Guerre des écrivains* 321.
63. Pierrey, review of *David Golder*, *Chantecler* 8 March 1930 in IMEC FSQ315 *David Golder*. Ernest-Charles, 'Une romancière', *L'Opinion* 3 June 1933 in IMEC FSQ315 *L'Affaire Courilof*.
64. Bourdieu, *Les Règles de l'art* 373–78.
65. Ibid. 281–83.
66. Larnac 223.
67. Ibid. 248.
68. Pierrey, review of *David Golder*, 8 March 1930 in IMEC FSQ315 *David Golder*. On women and inter-war French literature, see Milligan; Kershaw, *Forgotten Engagements*.
69. André Billy, source illegible in IMEC FSQ315 *David Golder*.
70. *Monde*, 11 January 1930 in IMEC FSQ315 *David Golder*.
71. *L'Intransigeant*, 29 October 1932 in IMEC FSQ315 *L'Affaire Courilof* ; *L'Intransigeant*, 1 June 1933 in IMEC FSQ315 *L'Affaire Courilof* ; Franc-Nohain, *Echo de Paris*, 4 March 1933 in IMEC FSQ315 *L'Affaire Courilof*.
72. André Billy, source illegible in IMEC FSQ315 *David Golder*.
73. J. Ernest-Charles, *Le Quotidien*, 4 February 1930 in IMEC FSQ315 *David Golder*.
74. *L'Intransigeant*, 29 October 1932 in IMEC FSQ315 *L'Affaire Courilof*.
75. *L'Intransigeant*, 1 June 1933 in IMEC FSQ315 *L'Affaire Courilof*.
76. *Toulouse Spectacles*, 26 December 1931 in IMEC FSQ315 *Les Mouches d'automne*.
77. Larnac 5.
78. Ibid. 224–25, 242.
79. Ibid. 231–32.
80. Ibid. 254, 256.
81. On lesbianism in literature in the inter-war period in France, see Benstock; Lesslier.
82. *Toulouse Spectacles*, 26 December 1931 in IMEC FSQ315 *Les Mouches d'automne*.
83. *Journal des débats*, 13 February 1930 in IMEC NMR11.1 Dossier critique.

84. Pierre Loewel, *L'Ordre*, 29 January 1930 in IMEC FSQ315 *David Golder*.
85. Renard 119.
86. Ibid. 123.
87. 'Ecrivains francisés', *Le Figaro*, November 1933 in IMEC FSQ315 *L'Affaire Courilof*.
88. *Le Quotidien*, 4 February 1930 in IMEC FSQ315 *David Golder*.
89. *Les Annales*, 1 February 1930 in IMEC FSQ315 *David Golder*.
90. Sapiro, *La Guerre des écrivains* 122; Renard 24–25, 35ff.
91. For an account of this debate, see Cornick, 'In Search of the Absolute' 15–32.
92. Raimond 12, 166–70.
93. For example, in Lefèvre's interview 'Une révélation: une heure avec Irène Némirovsky', Némirovsky cites a comment by Noel Sabord in *Paris-Midi*, and in Delpech's interview, 'Chez Irène Némirovsky ou La Russie Boulevard des Invalides', *Les Nouvelles littéraires*, 4 June 1938, Némirovsky objects to the opinion of certain critics that she is guided by her characters.
94. Raimond 19.
95. Sapiro, *La Guerre des écrivains* 78–79.
96. Bourdieu, *Les Règles de l'art* 411.
97. Bourdieu, *The Rules of Art* 249–50.
98. Bourdieu, 'The Production of Belief' 278.
99. Lefèvre; Delpech.
100. Pierrey, review of *David Golder*, 8 March 1930 in IMEC FSQ315 *David Golder*; Philipponnat and Lienhardt 429–30.
101. Cornick, *The* Nouvelle Revue Française; Sapiro, 'Forms of politicization' 644; Sapiro, *La Guerre des écrivains* 377–466.
102. Sapiro, *La Guerre des écrivains* 381–88.
103. Decourdemanche; Saurat
104. Sapiro, *La Guerre des écrivains* 90.
105. For an account of the relationship between politics and literature in the period, see Sapiro, 'Forms of politicization', where Sapiro draws on Bourdieu's framework.
106. Kershaw, *Forgotten Engagements* 48–63.
107. Sapiro, *La Guerre des écrivains* 69–82.
108. Defez.
109. *Monde*, 3 June 1933 in IMEC FSQ315 *L'Affaire Courilof*.
110. J.-B. Severac, 'Russie d'hier et Russie d'aujourd'hui', 24 June 1932 in IMEC FSQ315 *L'Affaire Courilof*; *Le Populaire*, June 1933 in Dossier biographique—Irène Némirovsky, Bibliothèque Marguerite Durand.
111. See for example reviews of *Suite française* by Finas, *Libération*, 20 November 2004; Boulouque, *Le Figaro*, 9 November 2004.
112. See for example 'Le Dilemme identitaire d'Irène Némirovsky', *Le Temps*, 12 March 2005, and the much less balanced review by Valérie Marin la Meslée, 'Les années Némirovsky', *Le Point*, 7 July 2005.
113. Weiss, *Irène Némirovsky* 67–71 (67), 85–92, 120–32, 144–58, 209–14.
114. Ibid. 158.
115. Ibid. 212.
116. Philipponnat and Lienhardt 224, 285.
117. Ibid. 224.
118. Ibid. 243–45.
119. Ibid. 284–85.
120. Ibid. 284
121. Ibid. 353–56.
122. See Weiss, *Irène Némirovsky* 164; *Irène Némirovsky, Her Life and Works* 132–33.
123. Némirovsky, *Suite française* (French) 11.

124. Némirovsky, *Suite Française* (English) 395.
125. See in particular Sapiro, *La Guerre des écrivains*, Chapter 1; 'La Raison littéraire'.
126. Sapiro, *La Guerre des écrivains* 21.
127. Ibid. 30.
128. Ibid.
129. Ibid. 93.
130. Charle, *Le Siècle de la presse* 262.
131. Juliard and Winock 666.
132. Sapiro, *La Guerre des écrivains* 36.
133. Bellenger 72, 76.
134. Juliard and Winock 668.
135. On the *épuration* of French intellectuals, see Assouline esp. 42–45 on Bérard. See also Rubenstein; Sapiro, 'Ecrivains en procès'.
136. Philipponnat and Lienhardt 224, 244–45.
137. On the right-wing political affiliations of some assimilated French Jews in the inter-war period, see Schor, *L'Antisémitisme* 210.
138. Grépon; Rousseaux; Defez.
139. Juliard and Winock 527–32.
140. Le Diable, 'Causerie littéraire'; Brasillach, 'Causerie littéraire', *L'Action française* 7 Jan. 1932; Rocher, 'A la petite semaine'; Brasillach, 'Causerie littéraire', *L'Action française* 31 May 1934.
141. Renard 18–19.
142. Brasillach, 'Causerie littéraire', *L'Action française* 7 Jan. 1932.
143. See Renard 138–44, for a discussion of anti-Semitism in *L'Action française's* literary pages.
144. de Pawlowski; Loewel
145. Sapiro, *La Guerre des écrivains* 121–24.
146. Ibid. 161.
147. Prévost, 'Romans imagines et vécus'.
148. The *NRF* published Sartre's short story 'Le Mur', and Sartre was also contributing literary reviews to the journal. See Sapiro, *La Guerre des écrivains* 389.
149. Maxence, 'Les Livres de la semaine', *Gringoire* 10 June 1938.
150. Prévost, 'Romans'; 'Deux nouveaux romans'.
151. Maxence, *Histoire de dix ans* 225.
152. *Comœdia*, 1 October 1931 in IMEC NMR11.1 Dossier critique.
153. Nettlebeck 258.
154. Sapiro, *La Guerre des écrivains*, 402–22.
155. Ibid. 470, 492, 498.
156. Ibid. 539–44.
157. Ibid. 478.
158. Pickering, 'The Implications of Legalised Publication' 165–66; Sapiro, 'Ecrivains en procès' 228; Golsan 44.
159. Pickering, 'The Implications of Legalised Publication' 187.

NOTES TO CHAPTER 2

1. IMEC NMR13.1 'La Niania'. See Philipponnat and Lienhardt, 126, 184.
2. Bourdieu, *Les Règles de l'art* 352.
3. Bourdieu, *The Rules of Art* 215.
4. Meizoz, *L'Age du roman parlant* 39. See also *L'Oeil sociologique et la littérature* where the author raises the same issue.
5. See Philipponnat and Lienhardt's discussion of Némirovsky's university education, 107, 122–23, 132, 143. The following account of Némirovsky's

educational trajectory is based on evidence in the Archives nationales AJ16 series (Académie de Paris), specifically AJ/16/4817–1826 Licence-es-lettres—certificats d'études supérieures—liste des candidats inscrits par séances; AJ/16/5006 Fiches individuelles des étudiants; AJ/16/8329 Affiches des enseignements supérieures: Faculté des Lettres de Paris; AJ/16/8332 Affiches des enseignements supérieures: Instituts d'université.

6. Archives nationales, AJ/16/4820.
7. Philipponnat and Lienhardt 107.
8. Archives nationales, AJ/16/4824.
9. Weisstein 4. On Baldensperger, see Harvitt; Bataillon; Charle, *Les professeurs de la faculté des lettres de Paris* 19–21. The first volume of the *Yearbook of Comparative and General Literature* includes articles on Baldensperger and van Tieghem 39–41.
10. Weisstein 176–80.
11. Baldensperger was seconded to the new University of Strasbourg between 1919 and 1923. See Harvitt. During this period, Baldensperger was replaced at the Sorbonne by Paul Hazard. See 'Chronique'.
12. Archives nationales AJ/16/8329/p95; AJ/16/8329/p96; AJ/16/8329/p97.
13. Weisstein 172, 176.
14. On this point, see also Philipponnat and Lienhardt 132.
15. Archives nationales AJ/16/4825.
16. On the *roman d'analyse* (and its opposition to the *roman de moeurs* and the *roman idéaliste*), see Braunschvig 125–26.
17. Raimond 380–82.
18. Gonthier 47–48, 53.
19. Némirovsky, 'Le Malentendu', 297–98.
20. Némirovsky told Lefèvre that 'Le Malentendu' was written in 1925.
21. Némirovsky, 'Le Malentendu', 227–233.
22. Philipponnat and Lienhardt 112, 129, 142.
23. Némirovsky, 'Le Malentendu' 244–48.
24. Ibid. 253–55.
25. Ibid. 294–300, 318–27, 329–32.
26. Philipponnat and Lienhardt 121–22.
27. Némirovsky, 'Le Malentendu' 280–83, 336, 340; 267–68.
28. Ibid. 222–23, 259.
29. IMEC NMR 15.2 Nouvelles 1940, projets.
30. Némirovsky, 'Le Malentendu' 280. See Daudet 486: 'Seulement la force d'écrire sur la muraille ce proverbe tarasconais que j'ai entendu si souvent dire à Bravida, qui les savait tous: Rester au lit sans dormir/Attendre sans voir venir/Aimer sans avoir plaisir/Sont trois choses qui font mourir.'
31. Némirovsky, 'Le Malentendu' 271.
32. Ibid. 272.
33. Ibid. See Baudelaire 62: Ils me disent, tes yeux, clairs comme le cristal: / Pour toi, bizarre amant, quel est donc mon mérite? /—Sois charmante et tais-toi! Mon cœur, que tout irrite, / Excepté la candeur de l'antique animal, / Ne veut pas te montrer son secret infernal, / Berceuse dont la main aux longs sommeils m'invite, / Ni sa noire légende avec la flamme écrite. / Je hais la passion et l'esprit me fait mal!
34. Némirovsky, 'Le Malentendu' 305.
35. 'Destinées' in Némirovsky, *Destinées et autres nouvelles* 251; 'Le Sortilège' in Némirovsky, *Dimanche et autres nouvelles* 302.
36. IMEC NMR14.19 'En raison des circonstances': brouillon.
37. Ramon Fernandez, review of *Jézabel*, *Marianne*, 24 June 1936 in Dossier biographique—Irène Némirovsky, Bibliothèque Marguerite Durand.

38. Raimond 416–20.
39. Holmes 20.
40. Ibid. 22–23, 26.
41. Guillén 251.
42. Sapiro, *La Guerre des écrivains* 258. The reference to Daudet in 'Le Malentendu' might however represent a counter example, since his 1888 novel *L'Immortel* is a satire on the Académie, to which he was never elected.
43. Raimond 100–01.
44. 'En marge de *L'Affaire Courilof*', radio interview with Frédéric Lefèvre, published in *Sud de Montpellier*, 7 June 1933 in FSQ315 *L'Affaire Courilof* and reprinted in Philipponnat and Lienhardt 432–35.
45. Lefevre.
46. 'En marge de *L'Affaire Courilof*', radio interview with Lefèvre, published in *Sud de Montpellier*, 7 June 1933 in FSQ315 *L'Affaire Courilof* and Philipponnat and Lienhardt 432–35.
47. In Auscher. Reprinted in Philipponnat and Lienhardt 435–36.
48. On the potential pitfalls of the study of literary influence, see Guillén 54–59, and on literary relations more generally, see 240–87.
49. Lefèvre.
50. Némirovsky, *Un enfant prodige* 9–10.
51. Philipponnat and Lienhardt 140.
52. IMEC NMR13.3 Notes pour *Le Pion sur l'échiquier*. Némirovsky wrote: 'V. Barrès [= voir Barrès]: Toujours rattacher, par quelque côté, ce qu'on écrit à sa propre vie'.
53. Némirovsky, 'L'Enfant génial' 337.
54. Ibid. 339–40.
55. Ibid. 346.
56. Ibid. 349–50.
57. Ibid. 360–61.
58. Ibid. 371–75.
59. Ibid. 362–63.
60. Higgins.
61. Némirovsky, *Suite française* 398, 399, 405; see Chapter 6.
62. Némirovsky, *La Vie de Tchekhov* 131.
63. Weisz; Ringer 237–47. See also Sapiro, *La Guerre des écrivains* 108–20.
64. On the theme of the 'mauvais maître' in the inter-war and Occupation periods, see Sapiro, *La Guerre des écrivains* 161–207.
65. Némirovsky, 'L'Enfant génial' 369.
66. Ibid. 369.
67. See the discussion of Gennep in Nora 641–75. Gennep's *Manuel de folklore français contemporain* was published between 1937 and 1988.
68. See for example Thompson's foundational categorisation of folktale motifs: *Motif-Index of Folk Literature*.
69. Thompson labels this motif as S210 'Children sold or promised'. Thompson also indicates a source for the motif of selling of children in Jewish folk tales (H491.1).
70. Owens 223.
71. Némirovsky, 'L'Enfant genial', 337. Stemberger links the bird motif in this story to the Jewish theme. Stemberger, *Irène Némirovsky* 144.
72. Zipes 45, 56.
73. Lefèvre; Deyroyer, reprinted in Philipponnat and Lienhardt 431.
74. IMEC NMR4.38 Entretien d'Irène Némirovsky par Marie-Jean Viel. See also Bourget-Pailleron, 'La nouvelle équipe'.
75. Higgins.

76. 'En marge de l'affaire Courilof', radio interview with Frédéric Lefèvre, published in *Sud de Montpellier*, 7 June 1933 in FSQ315 *L'Affaire Courilof* and Philipponnat and Lienhardt 432–35; Higgins; Delpech; Lefevre.
77. IMEC NMR14.19 'En raison des circonstances': brouillon.
78. IMEC NMR14.13 'Fraternité': brouillon et journal d'écriture. This text is dated 8 October 1936.
79. IMEC NMR14.19 'En raison des circonstances': brouillon.
80. For a concise presentation of the conception of comparative literature promoted at the Sorbonne in the early 1920s, see Baldensperger; van Tieghem.
81. Némirovsky, *La Vie de Tchekhov* Chapter 24, 131–36.
82. Raimond 147–55.
83. Ibid. 154–55.
84. Ibid. 149.
85. Bourget, *Nouvelles pages*, I, 12–13.
86. IMEC NMR14.19 'En raison des circonstances': brouillon.
87. Némirovsky, *La Vie de Tchekhov* 131–32.
88. Némirovsky, *A Life of Chekhov* 117.
89. Némirovsky, *La Vie de Tchekhov* 94–95, 95.
90. Némirovsky, *A Life of Chekhov* 86.
91. IMEC NMR14.19 'En raison des circonstances': brouillon; Bourget, *Nouvelles pages*, I, 19, 20–21.
92. IMEC NMR13.8 *Le Vin de solitude*: projets et brouillons.
93. Raimond discusses this in detail in Part IV, 257–410.
94. Ibid., pp.243–254.
95. Némirovsky, 'Le Malentendu' 250.
96. Raimond 148.
97. Godenne, *Etude sur la nouvelle française* 7–8; *La Nouvelle* 54–61.
98. See Gratton and Le Juez 14–15.
99. Ibid. 13–14; Godenne, *Etude sur la nouvelle française* 7–8.
100. Némirovsky, 'L'Enfant génial' 331.
101. Ibid. 375.
102. IMEC NMR13.1 'La Niania'.
103. Figes 125–30.
104. Thompson, *The Folktale* 4.
105. IMEC NMR14.19 'En Raison des circonstances', brouillon. 'Le Sortilège' is reprinted in Némirovsky, *Dimanche et autres nouvelles* 293–311.
106. Némirovsky did return to the theme of artistic creation in some of her later short stories. See for example 'Le Spectateur'; 'M. Rose'; 'La Confidente'; 'L'Ogresse', all reprinted in Némirovsky, *Dimanche et autres nouvelles*.
107. Maxence, 'Les Livres de la semaine', *Gringoire* 22 March 1935.
108. IMEC NMR4.38 Entretien d'Irène Némirovsky par Marie-Jean Viel.
109. Némirovsky, *Dimanche et autres nouvelles* 331–49; 351–70.
110. Raimond 12, 246, 264–69.
111. Chaumeix, 'Revue littéraire: Trois aspects du roman (I)'.
112. Review of *Films parlés* in *Le Figaro*, 9 February 1935 in Dossier biographique—Irène Némirovsky, Bibliothèque Marguerite Durand.
113. Godenne, *La Nouvelle* 95–102; *Etudes sur la nouvelle française* 195–98, 202–05, 220–21.
114. Qtd. in Godenne, *Etudes sur la nouvelle française* 224; Poe 7.
115. IMEC NMR14.13 'Fraternité': brouillon et journal d'écriture.
116. Godenne demonstrates that many critics dismissed the short story in these terms. *Etudes sur la nouvelle*, 204, 195.
117. Ibid. 199.
118. Sapiro, *La Guerre des écrivains* 261, 271, 382.

119. Cornick, *The* Nouvelle Revue Française 14, 39–40.
120. Philipponnat and Lienhardt 264–65.
121. Chaumeix, 'Revue littéraire: Romans d'automne (I); Chaumeix, 'Revue littéraire: Littérature féminine'; Bourget-Pailleron, 'Revue littéraire: Romans et critique (I).
122. Bourget-Pailleron, 'La Nouvelle équipie'.
123. 'Jour d'été' and 'La Confidence' reprinted in Némirovsky, *Destinées et autres nouvelles* 11–34; 36–62; 'Aïno' and 'Liens du sang' reprinted in Némirovsky, *Dimanche et autres nouvelles* 57–71; 127–79.
124. Sapiro, *La Guerre des écrivains* 89.
125. Chartier and Martin 260–61.
126. Philipponnat and Lienhardt 241.
127. Ibid. 281–87.
128. Renard 200–01.

NOTES TO CHAPTER 3

1. Qtd. in Bhabha 63. See Fanon 11: 'souvent ce qu'on appelle l'âme noire est une construction du Blanc'.
2. Bourdieu, *Les Règles de l'art* 341.
3. Bourdieu's theory of the literary field does not address in detail the question of international cultural exchange. Recent work in the domain of the sociology of literature has sought to rectify this omission through a focus on literary translation. See Heilbron and Sapiro. See also the review essay on their volume by Meylaerts and Boyden. For an overview of research in the sociology of translation, see Wolf and Fukari; Inghilleri.
4. Baldensperger and van Tieghem wrote programmatic accounts of their particular understanding of the nature and purpose of comparative literature. See Baldensperger; van Tieghem.
5. Guillén 27.
6. Ibid. 35–36.
7. See Renard 118.
8. Baldensperger 29.
9. Eagleton 62.
10. Bhabha 7.
11. Ibid. 41.
12. de Vogüé vii–lv, vii.
13. Ibid. xlvii.
14. Ibid. liii.
15. This has been done elsewhere, by Stemberger in *Irène Némirovsky*; in Thau, on which Stemberger draws heavily, and, to a lesser extent, in the biographies by Weiss and Philipponnat and Lienhardt.
16. Schor, *L'Opinion française*. See also Schor, 'Le Paris des libertés'.
17. Schor, 'Le Paris des libertés' 14.
18. Ibid. 13.
19. Ibid. 14.
20. Schor, *L'Opinion française* 152.
21. See Schor's discussion of Russian emigration *L'Opinion française* 152–61.
22. Ibid. 347–68, esp. 367.
23. Ibid. 366–67; Weisz 255. See Weisz's discussion of the influx of foreign students, 252–69.
24. Weisz 257, 260.
25. Archives nationales, AJ/16/4820 and AJ/16/4825.

26. IMEC NMR5.2 Lettres d'Irène Némirovsky à Madeleine Avot.
27. Archives nationales AJ/16/8332 Affiches des enseignements supérieurs—Instituts d'université. (AJ/16/8332p21 and AJ/16/8332p24). The collection of posters in the archive is incomplete.
28. Sapiro, *La Guerre des écrivains* 127. See Sapiro's tracing of the detail of the debate 127–42.
29. Bourget, *Nouvelles pages*, I, 121–30, esp. 127.
30. Ibid. 128.
31. Ibid. 128–29.
32. Ibid. 129.
33. Gide 8.
34. Ibid. 162–63.
35. See Cornick, *The* Nouvelle revue française 127.
36. Peyre 42. On Gide and Dostoevsky, see also Rayfield.
37. Livak studied the 'studio franco-russe' in detail in *How It Was Done in Paris* and in various articles: 'Nina Berberova et la mythologie culturelle de l'émigration russe en France'; 'Le studio franco-russe, 1929–1931'; 'La dimension littéraire du studio franco-russe'; 'L'émigration russe et les élites culturelles françaises, 1920–1925. Les débuts d'une collaboration'. See also Bérard-Zarzycka.
38. Livak, 'Le studio franco-russe', 110; *How It Was Done in Paris* 34.
39. Livak, *How It Was Done in Paris* 14–15.
40. See Ibid. 14–44, for a detailed account of the use of the terms *French* and *Russian* in this context.
41. The meetings of the 'studio franco-russe' were transcribed and the reports published in the *Cahiers de la Quinzaine* between 1929 and 1931 (Livak gives full bibliographical details in 'Le studio franco-russe, 1929–1931'). Némirovsky's name does not figure in any of the transcripts, and she did not mention the 'studio franco-russe' in interviews.
42. Livak, *How It Was Done in Paris* 10–11.
43. Ibid. 19.
44. Stemberger, *Irène Némirovsky* 351–52; see also 157.
45. 'En marge de *L'Affaire Courilof*', radio interview with Frédéric Lefèvre, published in *Sud de Montpellier*, 7 June 1933. FSQ 315 *L'Affaire Courilof*; Philipponnat and Lienhardt 432–35; see also 210.
46. Livak, 'La Dimension littéraire du studio franco-russe' 487.
47. Schor, *L'Opinion française* 153–54.
48. Max du Veuzit was the pseudonym of Madame Simonet. Todd 68.
49. Ibid. 157–61.
50. On the ethnographic concept of the 'Russian soul', see Cœuré 19–21.
51. Ibid. 19; Peyre 23.
52. Peyre 24.
53. Livak, *How It Was Done in Paris* 17.
54. Higgins.
55. See Poulson's identification of this source, 171, note 34. The article appeared in *Chisla* No 5, 248–50.
56. IMEC NMR7.3 Notes pour 'La Vie amoureuse de Poushkine' et notes de travail.
57. Némirovsky, *La Vie de Tchekhov* 11.
58. Stemberger, *Irène Némirovsky* 289.
59. Némirovsky *La Vie de Tchekhov*, p.80.
60. Ibid. 22.
61. Ibid. 51.
62. Ibid. 182.
63. Ibid. 85.

64. Némirovsky, *A Life of Chekov* 76.
65. Némirovsky, *La Vie de Tchekhov* 30–33.
66. Ibid. 48.
67. Todd 65.
68. IMEC NMR7.3 Notes pour 'La Vie amoureuse de Poushkine' et notes de travail.
69. IMEC NMR13.5 'Le Pion sur l'échiquier': brouillon et journal d'écriture, première version.
70. IMEC NMR15.2 Nouvelles 1940, projets.
71. Némirovsky, *Les Mouches d'automne* 24, 67, 114; Némirovsky, 'Snow in autumn' in *Le Bal* 59, 75, 93.
72. Némirovsky, *Les Mouches d'automne* 25, 40.
73. Ibid. 62, 74, 78; *Le Vin de solitude* 191.
74. Némirovsky, *Les Mouches d'automne* 102.
75. Ibid. 117–18, 124.
76. Ibid. 119.
77. Némirovsky, *Le Vin de solitude* 9.
78. Némirovsky, *La Vie de Tchekhov* 17; *A Life of Chekhov* 13.
79. Némirovsky, *Le Vin de solitude* 57.
80. Ibid. 29–31.
81. Ibid. 35.
82. Ibid. 83.
83. 'Et je l'aime encore . . . ' in Némirovsky, *Déstinées et autres nouvelles* 179–86, esp. 185.
84. 'Le Sortilège' in Némirovsky, *Dimanche et autres nouvelles* 293–311; 'Magie', *L'Intransigeant*, 4 August 1938.
85. 'La Confidence' in Némirovsky, *Déstinées et autres nouvelles* 35–62.
86. 'Destinées' in Némirovsky, *Déstinées et autres nouvelles* 254.
87. Némirovsky, *Les Chiens et les loups* 42.
88. Bourdieu, *Les Règles de l'art* 447–48.
89. Ibid. 411.
90. Bourdieu, *The Rules of Art* 249.
91. Maurice Bazy, *Les Nouvelles littéraires*, 27 February 1932 in IMEC NMR11.1 Dossier critique.
92. *L'Européen*, 9 June 1933 in IMEC FSQ315 *L'Affaire Couirilof*.
93. *L'Intransigeant*, 1 June 1933 in IMEC FSQ315 *L'Affaire Couirilof*.
94. *Marianne*, 14 June 1933 in IMEC FSQ315 *L'Affaire Couirilof*
95. *Le Populaire*, 14 February 1932 in IMEC FSQ315 *Les Mouches d'automne*.
96. *Echo de Paris*, 31 December 1931 in IMEC FSQ315 *Les Mouches d'automne*.
97. *Excelsior*, 28 January 1932 in IMEC FSQ315 *Les Mouches d'automne*.
98. Brasillach, 'Causerie littéraire', *L'Action française* 7 Jan. 1932.
99. Anonymous review of *La Proie* in Dossier biographique—Irène Némirovsky, Bibliothèque Marguerite Durand.
100. *L'Intransigeant*, 18 January 1932 in IMEC FSQ315 *Les Mouches d'automne*.
101. For example, the anonymous reviewers of *L'Affaire Courilof* in *Le Journal de l'ouest* of 16 July 1932 and *La Revue française*, June 1933 in IMEC FSQ315 *L'Affaire Courilof*.
102. IMEC NMR13.8 *Le Vin de solitude*: projets et brouillons.
103. IMEC NMR13.9 *Le Vin de solitude*: brouillon et journal d'écriture (1/2).
104. Némirovsky, *Les Mouches d'automne* 80.
105. Némirovsky, 'Snow in autumn' 80.
106. Némirovsky, *Le Vin de solitude* 239.
107. Némirovsky, *Les Chiens et les loups* 115.

108. Ibid. 150.
109. Némirovsky, *Destinées et autres nouvelles* 137–66.
110. Ibid. 140–41.
111. Ibid. 141.
112. Bourdieu, *Les Règles de l'art*, p.170–178 (p.173, p.178).
113. IMEC NMR14.14 'Espoirs': brouillon et journal.
114. Philipponnat and Lienhardt 211.
115. IMEC NMR13.1 'La Niania'.
116. Ibid.
117. In 'La Niania' the nanny also dies after a confused peregrination around Paris, but in this earlier story she is accidentally hit by a taxi.
118. See for example 'Liens du sang', reprinted in Némirovsky, *Dimanche et autres nouvelles* 127–79.
119. Milligan esp. 128–32.
120. The third section of Stemberger's *Irène Némirovsky* entitled 'Imaginationen des "Weiblichen"' is devoted to Némirovsky's depiction of female identity.
121. Stemberger, 'Selling Gender'.
122. *Toute l'édition*, 12 October 1935 in Dossier biographique—Irène Némirovsky, Bibliothèque Marguerite Durand.
123. See Fuderer; Fraiman; Abel, Hirsch, and Langland; Marrone whose works identifies coincidences between autobiography and the *Bildungsroman* in women's writing. On male-authored *Bildungsroman*, see Buckley.
124. On the use of the *Bildungsroman* structure in female-authored political fiction of the inter-war period, see Kershaw, *Forgotten Engagements* 70–88.
125. As Stemberger also states in *Irène Némirovsky* 296.
126. See Marrone 21.
127. Qtd. in Greene 13.
128. Némirovsky, *Le Vin de solitude* 311.
129. Stemberger, *Irène Némirovsky* 197–98.
130. Carco 45; Kessel, *Nuits de princes* 141.
131. Carco 244.
132. Kessel, *Nuits de princes* 173.
133. Némirovsky, *Le Vin de solitude* 241.
134. Ibid. 300.
135. émirovsky, *Le Vin de solitude* 23–33.
136. Anonymous review of *Les Mouches d'automne*, *Excelsior*, 28 January 1932 in IMEC FSQ315 *Les Mouches d'automne*.
137. Anonymous review of *Les Mouches d'automne*, *La Métropole*, 27 December 1931 in IMEC FSQ315 *Les Mouches d'automne*.
138. Némirovsky, *Le Vin de solitude* 44.
139. Ibid. 24, 210.
140. Ibid. 62.
141. J. Ernest-Charles, 'Une romancière', *L'Opinion*, 3 June 1933 in IMEC FSQ315 *L'Affaire Courilof*.

NOTES TO CHAPTER 4

1. de Beauvoir, *La Force de l'âge* 191.
2. de Beauvoir, *The Prime of Life* 165–66.
3. Part of this essay appeared in *Les Temps modernes* in 1945, and it was first published in its entirety in 1946.
4. Sartre, *Réflexions sur la question juive* x–xi.

5. Levi and Rothberg 1–2.
6. Sartre, *Réflexions sur la question juive* 61; *Anti-Semite and Jew* 57.
7. Levi and Rothberg 10.
8. Ibid. 10.
9. Weiss, *Irène Némirovsky* 231.
10. Bernstein 16. Extracts from Bernstein were reprinted as 'Against Foreshadowing' in Levi and Rothberg 346–53.
11. Wieviorka and Rosset 137, 139. They refer to Jacques Darville and Simon Wiché né, *Drancy la juive ou La Deuxième inquisition*.
12. Cheyette 272–73. Cheyette defines *semitism* in Chapter 1.
13. Sartre, *Réflexions sur la question juive* 156.
14. Sartre, *Anti-Semite and Jew* 147.
15. Bernstein 69.
16. Bourdieu, *Les Règles de l'art* 351; *The Rules of Art* 214.
17. On the history of Jewish immigration into Paris, see Weinberg 1–10.
18. Ibid. 5.
19. Ibid. 11.
20. Philipponnat and Lienhardt 149. Denise Epstein notes that her paternal grandparents were the only religiously observant Jews in her family. Epstein 45.
21. Weinberg viii–ix.
22. See ibid. 45–63.
23. Malinovich, *French and Jewish* 5, 10.
24. Gousseff 14.
25. Némirovsky, *Le Vin de solitude* 174.
26. Lefèvre; Claude Pierrey, review of *David Golder*, 8 March 1930 in IMEC FSQ315 *David Golder*; Philipponnat and Lienhardt 429–30.
27. On the Jewish theme in the work of the Tharaud brothers, see Leymarie. See also Malinovich, *French and Jewish* 196–200; Lehrmann 106–08.
28. See Czerny n.3; Becker and Wieviorka 140–42; Weinberg 25.
29. Nina Gourfinkel, 'L'Expérience juive d'Irène Némirovsky', *L'Univers israélite*, 28 February 1930 in IMEC FSQ315 *David Golder*.
30. Janine Auscher, 'Nos interviews: Irène Némirovsky', *L'Univers israélite*, 5 July 1935 in IMEC FSQ315 *David Golder*.
31. Philipponnat and Lienhardt 268.
32. The most accessible recent works on the 'réveil juif' of the 1920s are *Archives juives* 39.1 (2006) and Malinovich's *French and Jewish*. Malinovich's book includes a useful bibliography of 'fiction on Jewish themes' published in the period. See also Trebitsch; Lehrmann 103–58.
33. On Fleg, Spire, Cohen, and other Jewish writers of the period, see Malinovich, *French and Jewish* 38–56; 162–200.
34. On Elissa Rhaïss, see ibid. 188–90; Milligan 93. The 'Siona' series comprised *La Petite fille de Jérusalem* (1914), *Siona chez les barbares* (1918), *Siona à Paris* (1919), *Le Tendre cantique de Siona* (1922), and *Siona à Berlin* (1927).
35. On Myriam Harry, see Malinkovich, *French and Jewish* 165–66.
36. On Sarah Lévy, see ibid. 182–83, 193; Astro.
37. For a detailed account of the representation of Jews in inter-war French works by non-Jewish authors, see Wardi; also Lehrmann, which deals with Jewish and non-Jewish writers.
38. Chartier and Martin 223–24, 228–29. See also Malinovich, *French and Jewish* 162–63, for a list of titles in the Rieder series.
39. Fhima 36–38, esp. 39.
40. Chartier and Martin 227.

41. Franc-Nohain, review of *David Golder*, *Echo de Paris*, 16 January 1930 in IMEC FSQ315 *David Golder*.
42. Lunel 102–03.
43. Lehrmann 129.
44. Feigelson 41.
45. Malinovich, 'Littérature populaire' 51. See also Malinkovich, *French and Jewish* 184–85.
46. Poliakov 328–31.
47. Astro 242–44, 246.
48. Thau 216, n.11.
49. Némirovsky, *Suite française* 14.
50. Weiss, *Irène Némirovsky* 211, n. 4, n. 5.
51. Ibid. 211–12.
52. The French text here reads: 'Here we are in the presence of an example of 'Jewish self-hatred'.
53. Weiss, *Irène Némirovsky: Her Life and Works* 171.
54. Némirovsky, *Le Maître des âmes* 23.
55. Ibid. 24. 'Haine de soi? Haine du reflet de soi'.
56. Philipponnat and Lienhardt 138, 153
57. Ibid. 139, 184
58. Stemberger, *Irène Némirovsky* 109.
59. Ibid. 12.
60. Ibid. 17.
61. Ibid. 15–16.
62. Ibid. 69–70.
63. Ibid. 80–83.
64. Thau 434.
65. Némirovsky, 'L'Enfant génial' 334.
66. Ibid. 330.
67. Ibid. 334.
68. Malinovich, 'Littérature populaire' 47–48; *French and Jewish* 170–73.
69. Malinovich, 'Littérature populaire' 53.
70. Malinovich, 'Le "Réveil juif"' 4, 6.
71. Ibid. 6.
72. Némirovsky, *David Golder* (French) 32, 61; *David Golder* (English) 14, 33. For an account of the Jewish stereotypes which occur in *David Golder*, see Tritt.
73. Némirovsky, *David Golder* (French) 158, 235; *David Golder* (English) 94, 142.
74. Némirovsky, *David Golder* (French) 55, 66, 74.
75. Marks 7.
76. Stemberger, *Irène Némirovsky* 115–16.
77. Bhabha 95.
78. Cheyette and Marcus 2.
79. Golsan and Suleiman 323–24.
80. Bhabha 97.
81. Ibid. 107.
82. Ziv and Zajdman 41.
83. See Bhabha's preface to Cheyette and Marcus.
84. Bhabha 117.
85. Némirovsky made reference to this text in her notes for *Le Vin de solitude*. IMEC NMR13.10 *Le Vin de solitude*: brouillon et journal d'écriture (2/2).
86. Morand, *France la doulce* 209–11.

87. Philipponnat and Lienhardt link *Le Maître des âmes* and *David Golder* to Morand's *France la doulce* and his *Lewis et Irène* in their preface to *Le Maître des âmes*.
88. Malinovich, 'Littérature populaire' 50–53, 58–59; *French and Jewish* 180–85.
89. Nina Gourfinkel, 'L'Expérience juive d'Irène Némirovsky', *L'Univers israélite*, 28 February 1930 in IMEC FSQ315 *David Golder*.
90. Bernstein 70.
91. Janine Auscher, 'Nos interviews: Irène Némirovsky', *L'Univers israélite*, 5 July 1935 in IMEC FSQ315 *David Golder*.
92. Némirovsky, *Le Bal* (French) 16; Némirovsky, *Le Bal* (English) 6.
93. Némirovsky, *Le Pion sur l'échiquier* 9–11.
94. Stemberger, *Irène Némirovsky* 31.
95. Drieu la Rochelle 83.
96. Malinovich, *French and Jewish* 235–37.
97. Weinberg 72, 105.
98. Stemberger, *Irène Némirovsky* 58–59.
99. See Prazan 17.
100. Weinberg 93.
101. 'Fraternité' in Némirovsky, *Dimanche et autres nouvelles* 87, 86.
102. IMEC NMR14.13 Fraternité: brouillon et journal d'écriture.
103. This doubtless stemmed in part from financial necessity: at the beginning of the manuscript, dated 8 October 1936, Némirovsky had written: 'Aucune envie de travailler, mais bientôt deux enfants à nourrir . . . besoin d'une nouvelle et d'un roman'.
104. IMEC NMR14.14 'Espoirs': brouillon et journal d'écriture.
105. Qtd. in Philipponnat and Lienhardt 338.
106. Ibid. 318. On Némirovsky's conversion, see 310–18.
107. Stemberger, *Irène Némirovsky* 180–86.
108. Némirovsky, *Les Chiens et les loups* 9–10.
109. Stemberger, *Irène Némirovsky* 176.
110. Némirovsky, *Les Chiens et les loups* 182.
111. Ibid. 197, 198.
112. Malinovich, *French and Jewish* 9, 202–03.
113. Thau esp. 128 on *David Golder* and 131 on *Les Chiens et les loups*; Stemberger, *Irène Némirovsky* 12, 79–80, 199–200.
114. Némirovsky, *Les Chiens et les loups* 241–42.
115. See for example Thau 214; Stemberger, *Irène Némirovsky* 99–104.
116. Némirovsky, *Les Chiens et les loups* 124–28, 160.
117. Ibid. 21–22.
118. Qtd. in Philipponnat and Lienhardt 341.
119. Thau 317–18.
120. Stemberger, *Irène Némirovsky* 80–99.
121. Malinovich, *French and Jewish* 238.
122. Marks 83.
123. Némirovsky, *Le Maître des âmes* 21.
124. Némirovsky, *Le Maître des âmes* 44–45.
125. The only explicit reference to a Jewish character is Clara's father, who was a Jewish clockmaker. Ibid. 109.
126. See the annexe to Némirovsky, *Suite française* where Epstein's correspondence with André Sabatier and others is reprinted 422.
127. Ibid. 214.
128. Anonymous review of *David Golder* in *D'Artagnan*, 20 February 1930 in IMEC FSQ315 *David Golder*.

129. Robert de Saint-Jean, review of *David Golder* in *Revue hébdomadaire*, 1 February 1930 in IMEC FSQ315 *David Golder*.
130. André Bellesort, review of *David Golder* in *Le Journal des Débats*, 13 February 1930 in IMEC FSQ315 *David Golder*.
131. François Porché, review of *Le Pion sur l'échiquer*, *Le Jour*, 28 June 1934 in Dossier biographique—Irène Némirovsky, Bibliothèque Marguerite Durand.
132. Jean Blaise, review of *David Golder* in *La Dépêche*, 23 January 1930 in IMEC FSQ315 *David Golder*.
133. Ida R. See, review of *David Golder* in *Le Reveil juif*, 31 January 1930 in IMEC FSQ315 *David Golder*.
134. Nina Gourfinkel, 'L'Expérience juive d'Irène Némirovsky', *L'Univers israélite*, 28 February 1930 in IMEC FSQ315 *David Golder*.
135. Nina Gourfinkel, 'De Silbermann à David Golder', *Nouvelle revue juive*, March 1930 in IMEC FSQ315 *David Golder*.
136. Robert Bourget-Pailleron, review of *David Golder* in *L'Opinion*, 18 January 1930 in IMEC FSQ315 *David Golder*.
137. Jean de Pierrefeu, 'Un roman juif', *La Dépêche*, 30 January 1930 in IMEC FSQ315 *David Golder*.
138. Benjamin Crémieux, review of *David Golder* in *Les Annales*, 1 February 1930 in IMEC FSQ315 *David Golder*.
139. Emile Bouvier, 'Le roman juif', *La Lumière*, 9 October 1931 in IMEC FSQ315 *Les Mouches d'autonme*.
140. Philipponnat and Lienhardt 339.
141. Nina Gourfinkel, 'L'Expérience juive d'Irène Némirovsky', *L'Univers israélite*, 28 February 1930 in IMEC FSQ315 *David Golder*. Quoted in Philipponat and Lienhardt 189.
142. Lacretelle, *Silbermann* 44.
143. Ibid. 109.
144. Némirovsky, *David Golder* (French) 20; *David Golder* (English) 6.
145. Lacretelle, *Le Retour de Silbermann* 69–70.
146. A version of the text appeared in *Candide* between May and August 1929, and the definitive version appeared in a luxury edition in late 1929, before its publication with Gallimard. See Alden 137, 156.
147. Ibid. 157.
148. Griffiths 302.
149. Ibid. 306.
150. Ibid. 306–07.
151. It is worth pointing out however that Cohen's play *Ezéchiel* (1930) encountered a hostile response when it was performed in 1933, with anti-Semitic critics finding in it a justification for their arguments, and Jewish audiences berating Cohen for betraying his people. See Coward 224–25.
152. Nina Gourfinkel, review of *Le Bal*, *Nouvelle revue juive*, September/October 1930 in IMEC FSQ315 *Le Bal*.
153. Coward 223.
154. Ibid. 224.
155. Bernstein 1.
156. Ibid. 93.

NOTES TO CHAPTER 5

1. Philipponnat and Lienhardt 224.
2. Prévost, 'Romans imaginés et vécus': '[. . .] l'auteur de David Golder a tenu, par goût, par caprice, ou par effort de mieux faire, à changer quelque peu sa manière dans le roman récent'.

3. Bourdieu, *Les Règles de l'art* 150.
4. Bourdieu, *The Rules of Art* 88.
5. Thibaudet 556.
6. Philipponnat and Lienhardt 235.
7. Némirovsky, *La Proie* 27.
8. Ibid. 120, 173, 212.
9. For an accessible overview of this type of literature, see for example Bruézière.
10. Brée 183–84.
11. Review of *David Golder*, *Le Temps*, 10 January 1930 in IMEC NMR11.1 Dossier Critique.
12. Todd 67.
13. Brée 184.
14. Prévost, 'Romans imaginés et vécus'.
15. IMEC NMR13.8 *Le Vin de solitude*: projets et brouillons; IMEC NMR14.19 'En raison des circonstances: brouillon. See Philipponnat and Lienhardt 394.
16. Lefèvre; Claude Pierrey, review of *David Golder*, 8 March 1930. IMEC FSQ315 *David Golder*; Philipponnat and Lienhardt 429–30; 'En marge de *L'Affaire Courilof*', radio interview with Frédéric Lefèvre, published in *Sud de Montpellier*, 7 June 1933 in FSQ315 *L'Affaire Courilof*; Philipponnat and Lienhardt 432–35.
17. Bourget-Pailleron, 'La Nouvelle équipe'.
18. IMEC NMR13.5 *Le Pion sur l'échiquier*: brouillon et journal d'écriture, première version.
19. Ibid.
20. Ibid.
21. Ibid.
22. See Morand, *Chroniques* 215–18, where Morand's preface is reproduced in full.
23. West, 'Babbitt' 24. The essay first appeared in *The New Statesman*, 21 October 1922.
24. Schorer, 'Sinclair Lewis: *Babbitt*', 364.
25. IMEC NMR13.5 *Le Pion sur l'échiquier*: brouillon et journal d'écriture, première version.
26. Némirovsky, *Le Pion sur l'échiquier* 134, 154, 155, 202.
27. The song was written by Herman Hupfeld; see Mattfeld 474; on Rudy Vallée, see Larkin 2571–72. In the early 1930s, Vallée hosted a weekly variety show on the NBC radio network entitled 'The Fleischmann Hour'.
28. Némirovsky, *Le Pion sur l'échiquier* 196.
29. Hewitt, '*Les Maladies du siècle*' 23–24; see pp.22–40 for a discussion of the various manifestations of 'melancholia' in the period, in texts by, for example, Léon Daudet, Jean-Paul Sartre, and Louis Guilloux.
30. See Livak, 'La Dimension littéraire du studio franco-russe', 475–476, for a concise overview.
31. Crémieux, *Inquiétude et reconstruction* 53–94.
32. Hewitt, '*Les Maladies du siècle*' 17.
33. Crémieux, *Inquiétude et reconstruction* 25–34.
34. Ibid. 176–78.
35. Némirovsky, *Le Pion sur l'échiquier* 146.
36. Hewitt, '*Les Maladies du siècle*' 62.
37. Némirovsky, *Le Pion sur l'échiquier* 87.
38. Ibid. 89.
39. Ibid.
40. Ibid. 163.
41. Ibid. 199.

42. Némirovsky, *La Proie* 30–31.
43. Ibid 30.
44. Ibid.
45. Hiddleston 218.
46. Némirovsky, *La Proie* 34.
47. See Brosman, 'Roger Martin du Gard'.
48. Némirovsky, *Deux* 78.
49. Advertisement for *Deux*, *Les Nouvelles littéraires*, 25 March 1939.
50. Pomeau 77.
51. Némirovsky, *La Proie* 12, 14–15.
52. Ibid. 33.
53. Némirovsky, *Le Pion sur l'échiquier* 144–45.
54. Ibid. 105.
55. Ibid. 47.
56. IMEC NMR13.8 *Le Vin de solitude*: projets et brouillons.
57. 'La Comédie bourgoise' reprinted in Némirovsky, *Ida* 69–119; 'Le Départ pour la fête' reprinted in Némirovsky, *Destinées et autres nouvelles* 187–206.
58. Hewitt, 'Les Maladies du siècle' 39.
59. The two most substantial works on suicide in French literature are Minois 11; Cahn.
60. Hiddleston 210; Minois 308–21.
61. Cahn 303, 4.
62. Livak, 'The Place of Suicide' 247, 252.
63. Minois 375; Cahn 363–94.
64. See Philiponnat and Lienhardt 71, 131, where the authors seek to draw a (rather speculative) biographical conclusion from the profusion of suicides in Némirovsky's fiction.
65. Hiddleston 216.
66. Némirovsky, *Le Pion sur l'échiquier* 240.
67. Némirovsky, *Deux* 185.
68. Ibid. 177.
69. Morand, 'A propos du centenaire du Romantisme' 553.
70. André Billy, unattributed review of *La Proie* in Dossier biographique—Irène Némirovsky, Bibliothèque Marguerite Durand.
71. Maxence, 'Les livres de la semaine', *Gringoire* 10 June 1938.
72. Hewitt 32–37.
73. Némirovsky, *La Proie* 26.
74. For a discussion of this term, see Hewitt 1–4.
75. Némirovsky, *La Proie* 26.
76. IMEC NMR7.3 Notes pour 'La vie amoureuse de Poushkine' et Notes de travail. This source includes extensive notes on Waugh and other contemporary British and American writers.
77. Némirovsky, *Le Pion sur l'échiquier* 24, 171.
78. Némirovsky, *La Proie* 21, 44.
79. Ibid. 74.
80. Némirovsky, *Deux* 25.
81. Ibid. 224.
82. Gaston Chéreau, article on Némirovsky in *L'Intransigeant*, 25 October 1933 in Dossier biographique—Irène Némirovsky, Bibliothèque Marguerite Durand.
83. Noel Sabord, unattributed review of *La Proie* in Dossier biographique—Irène Némirovsky, Bibliothèque Marguerite Durand; Delpech.
84. Pomeau 88.
85. Némirovsky, *Suite française*, 403–04.
86. Gonthier 47–48.

87. Ibid. 53.
88. See Bruézière 147–54, on André Maurois; esp. 219–22, on Jacques Chardonne.
89. Lefèvre.
90. Gonthier 26–27, 31.
91. J. d'Assac, 'Maris de femmes célèbres: Monsieur Irène Némirovsky', unattributed article in Dossier biographique—Irène Némirovsky, Bibliothèque Marguerite Durand.
92. Ibid.
93. Stemberger, 'Selling Gender' 610.
94. Ibid. 612.
95. Némirovsky, *Le Pion sur l'échiquier* 83.
96. Ibid. 128–29.
97. Némirovsky, *Deux* 45–46.
98. Némirovsky, *Les Biens de ce monde* 58.
99. Némirovsky, *All Our Worldly Goods* 34.
100. Némirovsky, *Les Biens de ce monde* 308–11.
101. Ibid. 188, 190.
102. Ibid. 318.
103. See for example Brosman's discussion of women as the incarnation of the nation in French war imagery in *Visions of War in France* 44–54.
104. Philipponnat and Lienhardt 270. See also 69–71.
105. 'L'Ogresse' reprinted in Némirovsky, *Dimanche et autres nouvelles* 313–29.
106. Qtd. in Langhers.
107. Henri de Régnier, review of *Jézabel* in *Le Figaro*, 23 May 1936 in Dossier biographique—Irène Némirovsky, Bibliothèque Marguerite Durand.
108. See for example Maxence, 'Le Livre de la semaine'; Bourget-Pailleron 'La Nouvelle équipe'; Chaumeix, 'Revue littéraire: Littérature féminine'.
109. Epstein 31.
110. Gonthier 71–73.
111. Brosman, *Visions of War in France* 48.
112. Némirovsky, *Les Biens de ce monde* 270.
113. Némirovsky, *Suite française* (French) 360–63.
114. On literary representations of war in the inter-war period in France, see Pomeau; Brosman, *Visions of War in France;* Hurcombe; Rieuneau; Garguilo and Ablamowicz; Klein, *The First World War in Fiction.* Sherman focused primarily on an analysis of war memorials, but also addresses the question of memorialisation in narrative (see esp. 13–35).
115. Brosman, *Visions of War in France* 28.
116. Ibid. 145.
117. Némirovsky, *Les Biens de ce monde* 274.
118. Némirovsky, *All Our Worldly Goods* 174–75.
119. This well-known quotation was the first line of a text Bernanos published in *La Nouvelle Revue française* on 1 May 1940. See Kidd 49.
120. Némirovsky, *Les Feux de l'automne* 283.
121. Némirovsky, *Les Biens de ce monde* 258.
122. Némirovsky, *All Our Worldly Goods* 164.
123. Becker 38.
124. Epstein 51.
125. IMEC NMR15.2 Nouvelles 1940, projets.
126. Confino 1386.
127. Winter; Winter and Sivan.
128. Winter and Sivan 18.
129. Ibid. 32–39.
130. Anderson 197–206.

131. Becker 42; Winter and Sivan 37.
132. Suleiman 4.
133. *The Times Diary and Index of the War* 140; Némirovsky, *Les Biens de ce monde* 109–17.
134. Rolland 173–77. Némirovsky's notebooks do not tell us whether Rolland was a direct source for her account of this episode, although she was certainly familiar with Rolland's fiction.
135. Brosman, *Visions of War in France* 168.
136. Némirovsky, *Les Biens de ce monde* 127–28.
137. Némirovsky, *Les Feux de l'automne* 130.
138. Ibid. 52.
139. Ibid. 79–80.
140. Ibid. 91.
141. Ibid. 39–45, 93.
142. Ibid. 294.
143. Némirovsky's transcription of the initial proceedings of the trial is conserved in the IMEC archives (IMEC NMR 7.2). See Weiss, *Irène Némirovsky* 161–62; Philipponnat and Lienhardt 398–99.
144. Weiss, *Irène Némirovsky* 162.
145. Philipponnat and Lienhardt 399.
146. Ibid. 398–99.
147. Némirovsky, *Les Feux de l'automne* 356.
148. See Philipponnat and Lienhardt 310–14; Weiss, *Irène Némirovsky* 113–20. Denise Epstein said that she believes Némirovsky's conversion to have been an attempt to protect herself and her family, but she finds this difficult to understand. Epstein 52.
149. Némirovsky, *Les Biens de ce monde* 107–08.
150. Ibid. 313.
151. Némirovsky, *All Our Worldly Goods* 199.
152. *King James Bible* Luke 2:29.
153. Némirovsky, *Les Feux de l'automne* 354.
154. Philipponnat and Lienhardt 353–56.
155. Weiss, *Irène Némirovsky* 148–54.
156. Philipponnat and Lienhardt 337.
157. Ibid. 394.
158. Weiss, *Irène Némirovsky* 154, note 64.
159. Pickering 'Writing under Vichy'.
160. Sapiro, 'La Raison littéraire' 4.
161. See Flower and Davison's objection to this view (59).
162. Kidd, esp. 51–52.
163. Flower and Davison 52.
164. Ibid. 52.
165. The authors cite Léo Dartey (a pseudonym of Henriette Fechy), *Après la nuit* (1940); André Chamson, *Quatre mois* (1940); René Roques, *Le Sang de nos fautes* (1941); Christian Mégret, *Jacques* (1941); Jean de Baroncelli, *Vingt-six hommes* (1941); René Balbaud, *Cette drôle de guerre* (1941); Claude-Armand Masson, *Ligne Maginot, bastion inutile* (1942).
166. Flower and Davison 58.

NOTES TO CHAPTER 6

1. Bourdieu, *Les Règles de l'art* 15; *The Rules of Art* xvii.
2. Bourdieu, *Les Règles de l'art* 387; *The Rules of Art* 236.
3. Ousby 163.

4. IMEC NMR4.30 'Souvenirs de Finlande'.
5. Reprinted in Némirovsky, *Dimanche et autres nouvelles* 57–71. The names of the characters and the setting in this story are the same as 'Les Fumées du vin', also reprinted in *Dimanche et autres nouvelles* 89–126, but the story is different.
6. Reprinted in Némirovsky, *Destinées et autres nouvelles* 179–86.
7. 'Les fumes du vin' and 'Le Sortilège' reprinted in Némirovsky, *Dimanche et autres nouvelles* 89–126; 293–311; 'Espoirs', 'La Confidence' and 'Destinées' reprinted in Némirovsky, *Destinées et autres nouvelles* 137–66; 36–62; 245–62.
8. Némirovsky, *Suite française* (French) 396.
9. Némirovsky, *Suite Française* (English), 350.
10. Némirovsky, *Suite française* (French) 34.
11. IMEC NMR13.3 Notes pour *Le Pion sur l'échiquier*.
12. Némirovsky, *Les Biens de ce monde* 302–13.
13. Ibid. 289–90; *Suite française* (French) 73–77.
14. Némirovsky, *Suite française* (French) 77.
15. Némirovsky, *Suite Française* (English) 49.
16. Némirovsky, *Suite française* (French) 140–47.
17. Némirovsky, *Suite française* (French), 64–67.
18. Némirovsky, *Suite française* (French) 123–30.
19. Némirovsky, *Suite française* (French) 215; *Suite francaise* (English) 177.
20. Némirovsky, *Suite française* (French) 22; *Suite française* (English) 400.
21. Wieviorka 15. First published as *L'Ere du témoin* (Paris: Plon, 1998).
22. Ibid. 21, 14.
23. Némirovsky, *Suite française* (French) 395; *Suite française* (English) 347.
24. Némirovsky, *Suite française* (French) 398; *Suite française* (English) 348.
25. Némirovsky, *Suite française* (French) 402, 406; *Suite française* (English) 356, 362.
26. Némirovsky, *Suite française* (French) 250–51; *Suite française* (English) 211.
27. Némirovsky, *Suite française* (French) 364; *Suite française* (English) 320.
28. Némirovsky, *Suite française* (French) 180; *Suite française* (English) 146.
29. Némirovsky, *Suite française* (French) 292; *Suite française* (English) 250.
30. Golsan and Suleiman 325.
31. Némirovsky, *Suite française* (French) 400; *Suite française* (English) 353.
32. Némirovsky, *Suite française* (French) 400; *Suite française* (English) 353.
33. Némirovsky, *Suite française* (French) 398, 399, 405. Other manuscript sources show that her familiarity with Forster dated back at least to the mid-1930s: IMEC NMR 7.3 Notes pour 'La vie amoureuse de Pushkin' et notes de travail also contains a reference to Forster's *Aspects of the Novel*.
34. Golsan and Suleiman 323, 325.
35. On this question, see Garnett, in which she discusses the award of the Renaudot prize to *Suite française*.
36. The exhibition ran from 24 September 2008 to 30 August 2009. See <http://www.mjhnyc.org/irene/index.html>.
37. Peras's article is a review of Philipponnat and Lienhardt's biography.
38. Rothstein. Némirovsky was not of course a 'citizen' of France: since her demand for naturalisation was ignored, she remained a stateless person.
39. Wieviorka 60; Burrin 340; Lalieu 89.
40. Burrin 340.
41. Némirovsky, *Suite française* (French) 401.
42. Philipponnat and Lienhardt 329–30.
43. Epstein 63.
44. On the *exode*, see Diamond.
45. Némirovsky, *Suite française* (French) 204; *Suite Française* (English) 167.

46. Némirovsky, *Suite française* (French) 191–92.
47. Némirovsky, *Suite française* (French) 135–39.
48. Némirovsky, *Suite française* (French) 162–71.
49. Némirovsky, *Suite française* (French) 56; *Suite Française* (English) 30.
50. Némirovsky, *Suite française* (French) 55–56.
51. Némirovsky, *Suite française* (French) 126.
52. Némirovsky, *Suite Française* (English) 94.
53. Némirovsky, *Suite française* (French) 288, 337–40.
54. Némirovsky, *Suite française* (French) 340.
55. Némirovsky, *Suite Française* (English) 297.
56. Némirovsky, *Suite française* (French) 302.
57. Némirovsky, *Suite française* (French) 389.
58. Némirovsky, *Suite Française* (English) 343.
59. Cloonan 1–2.
60. Rousso 680.
61. Brosman, *Visions of War in France* 174.
62. Sarraute 73.
63. Gille 17.
64. Ibid. 419.
65. Epstein 147.
66. Gille 417–18.
67. Squires, *Marketing Literature* 75. Squires refers to Genette's *Paratexts: Thresholds of Interpretation.*
68. Némirovsky, *Suite française* (French) 14–15; 421–22.
69. Némirovsky, *Suite française* (French) 9; *Suite française* (English).
70. Némirovsky, *Suite française* (French) 12; *Suite française* (English) 395.
71. 'J. M. G. Le Clézio défend le choix du Renaudot, attribué à un auteur décédé', *Agence France Presse*, 9 November 2004.
72. See <http://www.memorialdelashoah.org>.
73. Squires, *Marketing Literature* 70–101.
74. Arnaud.
75. 'Radiographie de la débâcle française'.
76. Nora xlii: 'l'histoire est notre imaginaire de remplacement'.
77. Wieviorka 66.
78. Rousso 678–710.
79. Wieviorka 87.
80. Ibid. ix.
81. Rioux 164.
82. Bernstein 47.
83. Lalieu 85.
84. Rioux 160.
85. Epstein 109, 110, 115, 122.
86. Wieviorka 138.
87. Ibid. 140–43.
88. Ibid. 128.
89. de Larminat.
90. English, 'Winning the Culture Game' 119–20.
91. Ibid. 118.
92. Ibid. 123, 126.
93. Qtd. in Nivelle.
94. Gardiner 65. See also Squires 85–94.
95. Epstein 11.
96. Gardiner 70.
97. Bernstein 81.

Bibliography

ARCHIVE SOURCES

Archives nationales:

AJ/16/5006 Fiches individuelles des étudiants.
Licence-ès-lettres—certificats d'études supérieures—liste des candidats inscrits par séance:
AJ/16/4820 Session de juillet 1922.
AJ/16/4824 Session de juin-juillet 1924.
AJ/16/4825 Session des mars 1925.
AJ/16/8329 Affiches des enseignements supérieures—Faculté de lettres de Paris.
AJ/16/8332 Affiches des enseignements supérieures—Instituts d'université.

Bibliothèque Marguerite Durand:

Dossier biographique—Irène Némirovsky.

IMEC (Institut Mémoire de l'édition contemporaine):

Fonds Némirovsky – IMEC NMR
Fonds Grasset et Fasquelle – IMEC FSQ315 *David Golder*; IMEC FSQ315 *Le Bal*; IMEC FSQ315 *Les Mouches d'automne*; IMEC FSQ315 *L'Affaire Courilof*.

FICTION BY IRÈNE NÉMIROVSKY

'Le Malentendu', *Les Œuvres libres* Feb.1926: 221–344.
'L'Enfant génial' *Les Œuvres libres* April 1927: 331–75.
'L'Ennemie', *Les Œuvres libres* July 1928: 279–379.
David Golder. Paris: Grasset, 1929.
Le Bal. Paris: Grasset, 1930.
Les Mouches d'automne. Paris: Grasset, 1931.
L'Affaire Courilof. Paris: Grasset, 1933.
Films parlés. Paris: Gallimard, 1934.
Le Pion sur l'échiquier. Paris: Albin Michel, 1934.
Le Vin de solitude. Paris: Albin Michel, 1935.
Jézabel. Paris: Albin Michel, 1936.

'Magie'. *L'Intransigeant*, 4 Aug.1938.
La Proie. Paris: Albin Michel, 1938.
Deux. Paris: Albin Michel, 1939.
Les Chiens et les loups. Paris: Albin Michel, 1940.
'La Peur'. 1940. IMEC NMR4.28.
'Les Revenants'. *Gringoire*, 5 Sept. 1941.
La Vie de Tchekhov. Paris: Albin Michel, 1946.
Les Biens de ce monde. Paris: Albin Michel, 1947.
Les Feux de l'automne. Paris: Albin Michel, 1957.
Un enfant prodige. Paris: Editions Gallimard Jeunesse, 1992.
Dimanche et autres nouvelles. Paris: Stock, 2000.
Destinées et autres nouvelles. Pin-Balma: Sables, 2004.
Suite française. Paris: Denoël, 2004.
Le Maître des âmes. Paris: Denoël, 2005.
Ida. Paris: Denoël, 2006.
Chaleur du sang. Paris: Denoël, 2007.
Les Vierges et autres nouvelles. Paris: Denoël, 2009.

WORKS BY IRÈNE NÉMIROVSKY IN ENGLISH TRANSLATION

A Life of Chekhov. Trans. Erik de Mauny. London: Grey Walls Press, 1950.
Suite française. Trans. Sandra Smith. London: Chatto and Windus, 2006.
Le Bal. Trans. Sandra Smith. London: Vintage, 2007.
The Courilof Affair. Trans. Sandra Smith. London: Chatto and Windus, 2007.
David Golder. Trans. Sandra Smith. London: Vintage, 2007.
Fire in the Blood. Trans. Sandra Smith. London: Chatto and Windus, 2007.
All Our Worldly Goods. Trans. Sandra Smith. London: Chatto and Windus, 2008.

SECONDARY TEXTS

Abel, Elizabeth, Marianne Hirsch, and Elizabeth Langland, ed. *The Voyage In. Fictions of Female Development*. Hanover: University Press of New England, 1983.
Alden, Douglas. *Jacques de Lacretelle. An Intellectual Itinerary*. New Brunswick: Rutgers University Press, 1958.
Anderson, Benedict. *Imagined Communities*. 1983. London: Verso, 2006.
Archives juives 34.2 (2002), special issue on 'Juifs russes à Paris'.
Archives juives 39.1 (2006), special issue on 'Le Réveil juif des années vingt'.
Arland, Marcel. 'Sur un nouveau mal du siècle', *Nouvelle Revue française* 22 (1924): 149–58.
Arnaud, Claude. 'Irène Némirovsky—le manuscrit retrouvé'. *Le Point* 30 Sept. 2004.
Assouline, Pierre. *L'Epuration des intellectuels*. Bruxelles: Editions Complexe, 1985.
Astro, Alan. 'Two Best-selling French Jewish Women's Novels from 1929' *Symposium* 52.4 (1999): 241–54.
Auganeur, Marcel. 'Une tranche de vie'. *Gringoire* 24 Oct. 1930.
Auscher, Jeanine. 'Sous la lampe. Irène Némirovsky', *Marianne* 13 Feb. 1935.

Azéma, Jean-Pierre, and François Bédaria, ed. *Vichy et les Français*. Paris: Fayard, 1992.

Baldensperger, Fernand. 'Littérature comparée: le mot et la chose'. *Revue de littérature comparée* 1 (1921): 5–29.

Barrès, Maurice. *Les Déracinés*. 1897. Paris: Plon, 1972.

Bataillon, Marcel. 'L'Héritage de Fernand Baldensperger, 1971–1958'. *Revue de littérature comparée* 32 (1958): 159–67.

Baudelaire, Charles. *Œuvres complètes*, Vol. 1. Paris: Bibliothèque de la Pleïade, 1961.

Becker, Jean-Jacques. 'Les Entrées en guerre', *Les Sociétés en guerre 1911–1946*. Ed. Bruno Cabanes and Edouard Husson. Paris: Armand Colin, 2003. 29–46.

Becker, Jean-Jacques, and Annette Wieviorka, ed. *Les Juifs de France. De la Révolution française à nos jours*. Lonrai: Liana Lévi, 1998.

Bellenger, Claude, ed. *Histoire générale de la presse française, III, De 1871 à 1940*. Paris: Presses Universitaires de France, 1972.

Benstock, Shari. *Women of the Left Bank: Paris 1900–1940*. London: Virago, 1987.

Bernanos, Georges. 'Nous retournons dans la guerre'. *Nouvelle Revue française* 54 (1940): 577–98.

Bérard-Zarzycka, Ewa. 'Les écrivains russes—Blancs et Rouges—à Paris dans les années 20'. *Le Paris des étrangers*. Ed. Kaspi and Marès. 351–69.

Bernstein, Michael André. *Foregone Conclusions: Against Apocalyptic History*. Berkeley: University of California Press, 1994.

Bhabha, Homi K. *The Location of Culture*. London: Routledge, 2004.

Bidou, Henry. 'Le mouvement littéraire'. *La Revue de Paris*, 1 January 1934.

Bocker, John T., and Allan Pascoe, ed. *The Play of Terror in Nineteenth-Century France*. Newark: University of Delaware Press, 1997.

Bouissounouse, Janine. 'Femmes écrivains: leurs débuts'. *Les Nouvelles littéraires*, 2 Nov. 1935.

Boulouque, Clémence. 'Echec à l'oubli'. *Le Figaro* 4 Nov. 2004.

Bourdieu, Pierre. 'Le Champ littéraire'. *Actes de la Recherche en Sciences Sociales* 89 (1991): 4–46.

———. 'La Production de la croyance'. *Actes de la recherche en sciences sociales* 13 (1977): 3–43.

———. 'A Conservative Revolution in Publishing'. Trans. Ryan Fraser. *Translation Studies* 1.2 (2008): 123–53.

———. 'The Field of Cultural Production, or: the Economic World Reversed'. Trans. Richard Nice. *Poetics* 12 (1983): 311–56.

———. 'The Production of Belief: Contribution to an Economy of Symbolic Goods'. Trans. Richard Nice. *Media, Culture and Society* 2 (1980): 261–93.

———. *Les Règles de l'art*. 1992. Paris: Seuil, 1998.

———. 'Une Révolution conservatrice dans l'édition'. *Actes de la Recherche en Sciences Sociales* 126–127 (1999): 3–27.

———. *The Rules of Art*. Trans. Susan Emanuel. Cambridge: Polity Press, 1996.

———. *Sur la télévision*. Paris: Liber, 1996.

Bourget, Paul. *Le Disciple*. 1889. Paris: Plon, 1901.

———, *Nouvelles pages de critique et de doctrine*. 2 vols. Paris: Plon, 1922.

Bourget-Pailleron, Robert. 'La Nouvelle équipe', *Revue des deux mondes* 1 Nov. 1936: 94–103.

———. 'Revue littéraire: Romans et critique (I)'. *Revue des deux mondes* 1 July 1938: 220–231.

Brasillach, Robert. 'Causerie littéraire'. *L'Action française* 7 Jan. 1932.

———. 'Causerie littéraire'. *L'Action française* 31 May 1934.

Braunschvig, Marcel. *La Littérature française étudiée dans les textes (de 1850 à nos jours)*. 1926. Paris: Armand Colin, 1947.

Brée, Germaine. *Twentieth-Century French Literature*. Trans. Louise Guiney. Chicago: University of Chicago Press, 1983.

Brosman, Catherine Savage. 'Roger Martin du Gard, *Les Thibaut* et *Les Nourritures terrestres*'. *Retour aux Nourritures terrestres*. Ed. David H. Walker and Catherine Savage Brosman. Amsterdam: Rodopi, 1998. 87–106.

———. *Visions of War in France: Fiction, Art, Ideology*. Baton Rouge: Louisiana State University Press, 1999.

Bruézière, Maurice. *Histoire descriptive de la littérature contemporaine*, 2 Vols. Paris: Berger-Levrault, 1975, 1976.

Buckley, Jerome. *Season of Youth: The Bildungsroman from Dickens to Golding*. Cambridge, Mass: Harvard University Press, 1974.

Burnet, Etienne. *Loin des icônes, roman des émigrés russes*. Paris: Flammarion, 1923.

Burrin, Philippe. 'Vichy'. *Les Lieux de mémoire*, III, *Les France*. Ed. Pierre Nora. Paris: Gallimard, 1992. Vol 1. 320–45.

Cabanes, Bruno, and Edouard Husson., ed. *Les Sociétés en guerre 1911–1946*. Paris: Armand Colin, 2003.

Cahn, Zilla Gabrielle. *Suicide in French Thought from Montesquieu to Cioran*. New York: Peter Lang, 1998.

Cain, James. *Le Facteur sonne toujours deux fois*. Trans. Sabine Berritz. Paris: Gallimard, 1936.

Callil, Carmen. 'May God Help Us All'. *The Guardian* 3 Feb. 2007.

Camus, Albert. *Les Justes*. 1950. Paris: Gallimard, 1977.

Capitano, Sarah, Lisa Downing, Paul Rowe, and Nicholas Whire, ed. *Currencies: Fiscal Fortunes and Cultural Capital in Nineteenth-Century France*. Bern: Peter Lang, 2005.

Carco, Francis. *Verotchka L'étrangère ou le gout du malheur*. Paris: Albin Michel, 1923.

Cegarra, Marie. 'Secrets et silence: comment ne pas voir? Pourquoi ne pas dire? A propos d'Irène Némirovsky'. *Ethnologie française* 35.3 (2005).

Charle, Christophe. *Le Siècle de la presse (1930–1930)*. Paris: Seuil, 2004).

———. *Les professeurs de la faculté des lettres de Paris, dictionnaire biographique 1909–1939*. Paris: Institut national de recherches pédagogiques/CNRS, 1986.

Chartier, Roger, and Henri-Jean Martin, ed. *Histoire de l'édition française, IV: Le livre concurrencé 1900–1950*. Paris: Fayard/Cercle de la Librairie, 1991.

Chaumeix, André. 'Revue littéraire: Trois aspects du roman (I)'. *Revue des deux mondes* 15 March 1935: 457–66.

———. 'Revue littéraire: Romans d'automne (I)'. *Revue des deux mondes* 1 Dec. 1935 : 688–97.

———. 'Revue littéraire: littérature féminine'. *Revue des deux mondes*, 15 Nov. 1936. 454–63

Cheyette, Bryan. *Constructions of 'the Jew' in English Literature and Society. Racial Representations, 1875–1945*. Cambridge, England: Cambridge University Press, 1993.

Cheyette, Bryan, and Laura Marcus, ed. *Modernity, Culture and 'the Jew'*. Cambridge, England: Polity Press, 1998.

'Chronique'. *Revue de littérature comparée* 3 (1923): 473.

Cloonan, William. *The Writing of War. French and German Fiction and World War II*. Gainesville, Florida: University Press of Florida, 1999.

Cœuré, Sophie. *La Grande lueur à l'est: les Français et l'Union soviétique, 1917–1939*. Paris: Seuil, 1999.

Cohen, Hennig, ed. *Landmarks of American Writing*. Washington, D.C.: Voice of America Forum Lectures, 1970.

Confino, Alon. 'Collective Memory and Cultural History: Problems of Method'. *American Historical Review* 102.5 (1997): 1386–1403.

Coppermann, Anne. 'Une résurrection bouleversante'. *Les Echos*, 19 Oct. 2004.

Cornick, Martyn. 'Marcel Arland, le "Nouveau mal du siècle" et la politique éditoriale de la *Nouvelle Revue Française* de Jean Paulhan'. *Australian Journal of French Studies* 41.1 (2004): 85–101.

————. *The* Nouvelle Revue Française *under Jean Paulhan, 1925–1940.* Amsterdam: Rodopi, 1995.

————. 'In Search of the Absolute: the *Nouvelle Revue française* and Uses and Meanings of the Orient (1920–1930)'. *Modern and Contemporary France* 14.1 (2006): 15–32.

Corpet, Olivier and White, Garret, ed. *Woman of Letters. Irène Némirovsky and Suite française.* New York: Five Ties Publishing, 2008.

Coward, David. '*Les Valeurex* d'Albert Cohen: cousins et frères humains'. *Uncertain Relations. Some Configurations of the 'Third Space' in Francophone Writings of the Americas and of Europe.* Ed. Rachel Killick. Oxford: Peter Lang, 2005. 221–34.

Crémieux, Benjamin. 'Bilan d'un enquête'. *Nouvelle Revue française* 21 (1923): 287–94.

————. *Inquiétude et reconstruction.* Paris: Corrêa, 1931.

Czerny, Boris. 'Paroles et silences. L'affaire Schwartzbad et la presse juive parisienne (1926–1927)'. *Archives juives* 34.2 (2002): 57–71.

Daudet, Alphonse. *Tartarin de Tarascon, collection le roman populaire du XIXe siècle.* Malesherbes: Alterdit, 2007.

de Beauvoir, Simone. *La force de l'âge.* Paris: Gallimard, 1960.

————. *The Prime of Life.* Trans. Peter Green. London: Penguin, 1965.

de Ceccatty, René. 'Le "Guerre et paix" d'Irène Némirovsky'. *Le Monde* 1 Oct. 2004.

Decourdemanche, D. Review of *David Golder. Nouvelle Revue française* 34 (1930): 278–80.

Defez, René. 'La menace de troubles politiques influe-t-elle sur vos projets littéraires?'. *Candide* 26 Sept. 1935.

de Lacretelle, Jacques. *Le Retour de Silbermann.* Paris: Gallimard, 1931.

————. *Silbermann.* Paris: Gallimard, 1922.

de Larminat, Astrid. 'Assaut à la mousquetaire contre l'institution'. *Le Figaro* 9 Nov. 2004.

Delpech, Jeanine. 'Chez Irène Némirovsky ou La Russie Boulevard des Invalides'. *Les Nouvelles littéraires* 4 June 1938.

de Musset, Alfred. *La Confession d'un enfant du siècle.* Paris: Gallimard, 1973.

de Pawlowski, G. 'David Golder, de I. Nemirovsky'. *Gringoire* 31 Jan. 1931.

de Vogüé, Eugène Melchior. *Le Roman russe.* Paris: Plon, 1892.

Diamond, Hanna. *Fleeing Hitler. France, 1940.* Oxford: Oxford University Press, 2007.

Deyroyer, Michelle. 'Irène Némirovsky et le cinéma' *Pour vous* June 1931.

Drieu la Rochelle, Pierre. *Le Feu follet.* 1931. Paris: Gallimard, 1959.

Drumont, Edouard. *La France juive devant l'opinion.* Paris: Marpon & Flammarion, 1886.

Dufay, François. 'L'offense faite à Irène'. *L'Express* 18 Sept. 2008.

Du Veuzit, Max. *John, chauffeur russe.* Paris: Tallandier, 1931.

Eagleton, Terry. *After Theory.* London: Penguin, 2004.

English, James F. *The Economy of Prestige: Prizes, Awards and the Circulation of Cultural Value.* Cambridge, MA: Harvard University Press, 2005.

————. 'Winning the Culture Game: Prizes, Awards and the Rules of Art'. *New Literary History* 33 (2002): 109–35.

Epstein, Denise. *Survivre et vivre. Entretiens avec Clémence Boulouque.* Paris: Denoël, 2008.

Fanon, Frantz. *Peau noire, masques blancs.* Paris: Seuil, 1952.

Feigelson, Raph. *Ecrivains juifs de langue française.* Paris: Jean Grassin, 1960.

Fhima, Catherine. 'Au cœur de la "renaissance juive": littérature et judéité'. *Archives juives* 39.1 (2006): 29–45.

Figes, Orlando. *Natasha's Dance. A Cultural History of Russia.* London: Allen Lane, 2002.

Finas, Lucette. 'Mes semblables, mon tourment, mon journal'. *Libération* 20 Nov. 2004.

Flonneau, Jean-Marie. 'L'évolution de l'opinion publique de 1940 à 1944'. *Vichy et les Français.* Ed. Jean-Pierre Azéma and François Bédaria. Paris: Fayard, 1992. 506–22.

Flower, John, and Ray Davison. 'France'. *The Second World War in Literature.* Ed. Holger Klein with John Flower and Eric Homberger. Basingstoke: MacMillan, 1984. 47–87.

Fraiman, Susan. *Unbecoming Women. British Women Writers and the Novel of Development.* New York: Columbia University Press, 1993.

Forster, E. M. *Aspects of the Novel.* London: Edward Arnold, 1927.

Franklin, Ruth. 'Scandale française: The Nasty Truth about a New Literary Heroine'. *The New Republic* 30 Jan. 2008.

Fuderer, Laura Sue. *The Female Bildungsroman in English. An Annotated Bibliography of Criticism.* New York: Modern Languages Association of America, 1990.

Galsworthy, John. *The Apple Tree and Other Stories.* London: Penguin, 1988.

Gardiner, Juliet. '"What is an Author?" Contemporary Publishing Discourse and the Author Figure'. *Publishing Research Quarterly* 16.1 (2000): 63–76.

Garguilo, René, and Aleksander Ablamowicz. *Irruption de l'histoire dans la littérature française de l'entre-deux-guerres.* Katowice: Université de Silésie, 1986.

Garnett, Mary Anne. 'Official stories? Representing the Occupation and Shoah in Recent Prize-winning French Novels'. *Contemporary French and Francophone Studies* 12.3 (2008): 349–56.

Gide, André. *Dostoevsky.* London: Secker and Warburg, 1949.

Gille, Elisabeth, *Le Mirador.* 1992. Paris: Stock, 2000.

Godenne, René. *Etude sur la nouvelle française.* Geneva: Slatkine, 1985.

Godenne, René. *La Nouvelle.* Paris: Honoré Champion, 1995.

Golsan, Richard J. 'Ideology, cultural politics and literary collaboration at *La Gerbe'. Journal of European Studies* 23 (1993): 27–47.

Golsan, Richard J., and Susan Rubin Suleiman, '*Suite française* and *Les Bienveillantes,* Two Literary "Exceptions": A Conversation'. *Contemporary French and Francophone Studies* 12.3 (2008): 321–30.

Gonthier, Fernande. *La femme et le couple dans le roman, 1919–1939.* Paris: Klincksieck, 1976.

Gousseff, Catherine. 'Les Juifs russes en France. Profil et evolution d'une collectivité', *Archives juives* 34.2 (2002): 4–16.

Gratton, Jonnie, and Brigitte Le Juez. *Modern French Short Fiction.* Manchester: Manchester University Press, 1994.

Greene, Gayle. *Changing the Story: Feminist Fictions and the Tradition.* Bloomington: Indiana University Press, 1991.

Grépon, Marguerite. 'Une femme de lettres peut-elle réussir sans accepter certains hommages de ses juges?'. *Candide* 4 June 1931.

Griffiths, Richard. 'Anti-Semitism, Ambiguity and Audience Reception: The Problem of *Silbermann'. French Cultural Studies* 2 (1991): 291–308.

Guillén, Claudio. *The Challenge of Comparative Literature*. Trans. Cola Frazen. Cambridge, MA: Harvard University Press, 1993.

'Haine de soi'. *Libération* 1 Mar. 2007.

Harvitt, Hélène. 'Fernand Baldensperger (1871–1958)'. *Comparative Literature* 10.2 (1958): 188–89.

Heilbron, Johan, and Gisèle Sapiro, ed. *Traduction: les échanges littéraires internationaux. Actes de la recherche en sciences sociales* 144.1 (2002).

Hewitt, Nicholas. *'Les Maladies du siècle': The Image of Malaise in French Fiction and Thought in the Inter-war Years*. Hull: Hull University Press, 1988.

Hiddleston, J. A. 'Literature and Suicide'. *The Play of Terror in Nineteenth-Century France*. Ed. John T. Bocker and Allan Pascoe. Newark: University of Delaware Press, 1997. 209–25.

Higgins, George. 'Les Conrad français'. *Les Nouvelles littéraires* 6 April 1940.

Hirschfeld, Gerhard, and Patrick Marsh, ed. *Collaboration in France. Politics and Culture during the Nazi Occpation, 1940–1944*. Oxford: Berg, 1989.

Holmes, Diana. 'Novels of Adultery: Paul Bourget, Daniel Lesueur and What Women Read in the 1880s and 1890s'. *Currencies: Fiscal Fortunes and Cultural Capital in Nineteenth-Century France*. Ed. Sarah Capitano, Lisa Downing, Paul Rowe, and Nicholas Whire. Bern: Peter Lang, 2005. 15–30.

Hubert, Etienne-Alain, and Michel Murat, ed. *L'Année 1945. Actes du colloque Paris IV—Sorbonne (janvier 2002)*. Paris: Honoré Champion, 2004.

Hurcombe, Martin. *Novelists in Conflict, Ideology and the Absurd in the French Combat Novel of the Great War*. Amsterdam: Rodopi, 2004.

Hutcheon, Linda, and Mario Valdés. *Rethinking Literary History. A Dialogue on Theory*. Oxford: Oxford University Press, 2002.

Inghilleri, Moira, ed. 'Bourdieu and the Sociology of Translation and Interpreting'. *The Translator* 11.2 (2005).

Iser, Wolfgang. *How to do Theory*. Oxford: Blackwell, 2006.

Jeffries, Stuart. 'Truth, Lies and Anti-Semitism'. *The Guardian* 22 Feb. 2007: G2.

'J.M.G. Le Clézio défend le choix du Renaudot, attribué à un auteur décédé'. *Agence France Presse* 9 Nov. 2004.

Juliard, Jacques, and Michel Winock, ed. *Dictionnaire des intellectuels français. Les Personnes, les lieux, les moments*. 1996. Paris: Seuil, 2002.

Kaplan, Alice. 'Love in the Ruins'. *The Nation*, 29 May 2006.

Kaspi, André, and Antoine Marès, ed. *Le Paris des étrangers*. Paris: Imprimerie nationale, 1989.

Kedward, Rod. 'The Pursuit of Reality: The Némirovsky Effect'. University of Reading: The Stenton Lecture, 2008.

Kershaw, Angela. 'Finding Irène Némirovsky'. *French Cultural Studies* 18.1 (2007): 59–81.

———. *Forgotten Engagements: Women, Literature and the Left in 1930s France*. Amsterdam: Rodopi, 2007.

Kessel, Joseph. 'La Nouvelle littérature russe'. *La Revue de Paris* 15 Sept. 1925: 309–29.

———. *Nuits de princes*. Les Editions de France, 1927.

Kidd, William. 'From Bernanos to Vercors'. *France 1940: Literary and Historical Reactions to Defeat*. Ed. Anthony Cheal Pugh. Durham: University of Durham, 1991. 47–56.

Killick, Rachel, ed. *Uncertain Relations. Some Configurations of the 'Third Space' in Francophone Writings of the Americas and of Europe*. Oxford: Peter Lang, 2005.

Klein, Holger, ed. *The First World War in Fiction*. Basingstoke: MacMillan, 1976.

Klein, Holger with John Flower and Eric Homberger, ed. *The Second World War in Literature*. Basingstoke: MacMillan, 1984.

Kluger, Ruth. 'Bearing Witness. A Gripping Novel about the German Occupation of France, Written as the Nazis Closed in on the Author'. *The Washington Post*, 14 May 2006.

Laborie, Pierre. *L'Opinion française sous Vichy*. 1990. Paris: Editions du Seuil, 2001.

Lalieu, Olivier. 'L'Invention du "devoir de mémoire"'. *Vingtième siècle. Revue d'histoire* 69 (2001).

Lalou, René. 'Les livres de la semaine: *Deux*'. *Les Nouvelles littéraires* 8 April 1939.

Langhers, Pierre. 'Mme Irène Némirovsky, peintre de mœurs'. *Toute l'édition* 4 July 1936.

Larkin, Colin, ed. *The Guinness Encyclopedia of Popular Music*, Vol. 4. London: Guinness Publishing, 1992.

Larnac, Jean. *Histoire de la littérature féminine en France*. Paris: Kra, 1929.

le Diable, Robert. 'Causerie littéraire'. *L'Action française* 9 Jan. 1930.

'Le Dilemme identitaire d'Irène Némirovsky'. *Le Temps* 12 March 2005.

Lefèvre, Frédéric. 'Une révélation: une heure avec Irène Némirovsky'. *Les Nouvelles littéraires* 11 Jan. 1930.

Lehrmann, Chanan. *L'élment juif dans la littérature française*. Paris: Albin Michel, 1961.

Le Naire, Olivier. 'La Passion d'Irène'. *L'Express* 27 Sept. 2004.

Lesslier, Claudie. 'Silenced Resistances and Confidential Anxieties: Lesbians in France, 1930–1968'. *Journal of Homosexuality* 25 (1993): 105–25.

Levi, Neil, and Michael Rothberg, ed. *The Holocaust: Theoretical Readings*. Edinburgh: Edinburgh University Press, 2003.

Lewis, Sinclair. *Babbitt*. 1922. London: Vintage, 2006.

Leymarie, Michel. 'Les frères Tharaud. De l'ambiguïté du "filon juif" dans la littérature des années vingt'. *Archives juives* 39.1 (2006): 89–109.

Livak, Leonid. *How It Was Done in Paris. Russian Emigré Literature and French Modernism*. Madison: University of Wisconsin Press, 2003.

———. 'La dimension littéraire du studio franco-russe'. *Revue des études slaves* 75.3–4 (2004): 473–91.

———. 'L'émigration russe et les élites culturelles françaises, 1920–1925. Les débuts d'une collaboration'. *Cahiers du monde russe* 48.1 (2007): 23–43.

———. 'Le studio franco-russe, 1929–1931'. *Revue des études slaves* 75.1 (2004): 109–23.

———. 'Nina Berberova et la mythologie culturelle de l'émigration russe en France'. *Cahiers du monde russe* 43.2–3 (2002): 463–78.

———. 'The Place of Suicide in the French Avant-Garde of the Inter-war Period'. *The Romanic Review* 91.3 (2000): 245–62.

Lloyd, Christopher. 'Irène Némirovsky's *Suite française* and the Crisis of Rights and Identity'. *Contemporary French Civilization* 31 (2007): 161–82.

Loewel, Pierre. 'Vient de paraître'. *Gringoire* 25 April 1940.

Lubbock, Percy. *The Craft of Fiction*. London: Cape, 1921.

Lunel, Armand. *Les Chemins de mon judaïsme et divers inédits*. Ed. Georges Jessula. Paris: L'Harmattan, 1993.

Malinovich, Nadia. *French and Jewish. Culture and the Politics of Identity in Early Twentieth-Century France*. Oxford: The Littman Library of Jewish Civilisation, 2008.

———. 'Le 'Réveil juif' en France et en Allemagne. Eléments de comparaison en manière d'introduction'. *Archives Juives* 39.1 (2006): 4–8

———. 'Littérature populaire et romans juifs dans la France des années 1920'. *Archives juives* 39.1 (2006): 46–62.

Marin la Meslée, Valérie. 'Les années Némirovsky'. *Le Point* 7 July 2005.

Marks, Elaine. *Marrano as Metaphor. The Jewish Presence in French Writing.* New York: Columbia University Press, 1996.

Marrone, Claire. *Female Journeys. Autobiographical Expressions by French and Italian Women.* Westport: Greenwood Press, 2000.

Mattfeld, Julius. *Variety Music Cavalcade, 1620–1961. A Chronology of Vocal and Instrumental Music Popular in the United States.* Englewood Cliffs, NJ: Prentice Hall, 1962.

Maxence, Jean-Pierre. *Histoire de dix ans: chronique des années 30.* 1939. Paris: Editions du Rocher, 2005.

———. 'Les Livres de la semaine'. *Gringoire* 22 March 1935.

———. 'Les Livres de la semaine'. *Gringoire* 10 June 1938.

Meizoz, Jérôme. *L'Age du roman parlant (1919–1939).* Geneva: Droz, 2001.

———. *L'Œil sociologique et la littérature.* Geneva: Slatkine, 2004.

Meylaerts, Reine, and Michael Boyden. *Target* 16.2 (2005): 363–68.

Milligan, Jennifer. *The Forgotten Generation: French Women Writers of the Interwar Period.* Oxford: Berg, 1996.

Minois, Georges. *Histoire du suicide. La société occidentale face à la mort volontaire.* Paris: Fayard, 1995.

Morand, Paul. *Chroniques.* Ed. Jean-François Fogel. Paris: Grasset, 2001.

———. *France-la-doulce.* Paris: Gallimard, 1934.

———. 'A propos du centenaire du Romantisme: Le Suicide en littérature (1830–1930)'. *La Revue de Paris* 1 June 1932: 552–64.

Mounier, Pierre. *Pierre Bourdieu, une introduction.* Paris: Pocket/La Découverte, 2001.

Nettlebeck, Colin. 'Getting the story right: narratives of the Second World War in Post-1968 France'. *Collaboration in France. Politics and Culture during the Nazi Occpation, 1940–1944.* Ed. Gerhard Hirschfeld and Patrick Marsh. Oxford: Berg, 1989. 252–93.

Nivelle, Pascale. 'Le livre de ma mère'. *Libération* 29 Oct. 2004.

Nizan, Paul. 'Littérature féminine'. *L'Humanité* 20 Mar. 1937.

Nora, Pierre, ed. *Les Lieux de mémoire.* Paris: Gallimard, 1992.

Ousby, Ian. *Occupation: The Ordeal of France 1940–1944.* London: John Murray, 1997.

Owens, Lily, ed. *The Complete Hans Christian Andersen Fairy Tales.* New York: Gramercy Books, 1984.

Peras, Delphine. 'Irène Némirovsky en toutes lettres'. *L'Express* 11 Oct. 2007.

Petit, Michaëlle. 'Coup de cœur. Un destin français: *Le Maître des âmes*, d'Irène Némirovsky'. *La Croix* 27 Oct. 2005.

Peyre, Henri. *French Literary Imagination and Dostoevsky and Other Essays.* Alabama: University of Alabama Press, 1975.

Philipponnat, Olivier, and Patrick Lienhardt. *La Vie d'Irène Némirovsky.* Paris: Grasset/Denoël, 2007.

Pickering, Robert. 'The Implications of Legalised Publication'. *Collaboration in France. Politics and Culture during the Nazi Occupation, 1940–1944.* Ed. Gerhard Hirschfeld and Patrick Marsh. Oxford: Berg, 1989. 162–89.

———. 'Writing under Vichy. Valéry's Mauvaises pensées et autres'. *Modern Language Review* 83.1 (1988): 40–55.

Poe, Edgar Allan. *Le Sphinx et autres contes bizarres.* Trans. Marie Bonaparte, Matila C. Ghyka and Maurice Sachs. Paris: Gallimard, 1934.

Poliakov, Léon. *Histoire de l'antisémitisme. Tome IV: L'Europe suicidaire, 1970–1933.* Paris: Calmann-Lévy, 1977.

Pomeau, René. 'Guerre et roman dans l'entre-deux-guerres'. *Revue des Sciences Humaines* (Jan-March 1963): 77–95.

Poulson, Leslee. *The Influence of French Language and Culture in the Lives of Eight Women Writers of Russian Heritage.* Lewiston: Edwin Mellen Press, 2002.

Prazan, Michaël. *L'Ecriture génocidaire. L'Antisémitisme en style et en discours.* Paris: Calmann-Lévy, 2005.

Prévost, Marcel. 'Deux nouveaux romans'. *Gringoire* 26 May 1933.

———. 'Romans imagines et vécus'. *Gringoire* 15 June 1934.

Pugh, Anthony Cheal, ed. *France 1940: Literary and Historical Reactions to Defeat.* Durham: University of Durham, 1991.

'Radiographie de la débâcle française'. *Le Temps* 6 Nov. 2004.

Raimond, Michel. *La Crise du roman. Des lendemains du naturalisme aux années vingt.* 1966. Paris: Corti, 1985.

Rayfield, Donald. 'A Virgil to his Dante: Gide's Reception of Dostoevsky'. *Forum for Modern Language Studies* 36.4 (2000): 340–56.

Renard, Paul. *L'Action française et la vie littéraire (1931–1944).* Lille: Presses Universitaires du Septentrion, 2003.

Rieuneau, Maurice. *Guerre et revolution dans le roman français de 1919 à 1939.* 1974. Geneva: Slatkine, 2000.

Ringer, Fritz. *Fields of Knowledge. French Academic Culture in Comparative Perspective.* Cambridge, England: Cambridge University Press and Paris: Editions de la maison des sciences de l'homme, 1992.

Rioux, Jean-Pierre. 'Devoir de mémoire, devoir d'intelligence'. *Vingtième siècle. Revue d'histoire* 73 (2002): 157–67.

Rocher, Gabriel. 'A la petite semaine'. *L'Action française* 25 May 1933.

Rolland, Roman. *Pierre et Luce.* Geneva: Editions du Sablier, 1920.

Rothstein, Edward. 'Ambivalence as part of author's legacy'. *The New York Times* 21 Oct. 2008.

Rousseaux, André. 'Un quart d'heure avec Mme Irène Némirovsky'. *Candide* 14 Feb. 1935.

Rousso, Henry. *Vichy. L'événement, la mémoire, l'histoire.* 1992. Paris: Gallimard, 2001.

Rubenstein, Diane. 'Publish or perish: the *épuration* of French intellectuals'. *Journal of European Studies* 23 (1993): 71–99.

Sapiro, Gisèle. 'Ecrivains en procès: la redéfinition de la responsabilité de l'écrivain'. *L'Année 1945. Actes du colloque Paris IV—Sorbonne (janvier 2002).* Ed. Etienne-Alain Hubert and Michel Murat. Paris: Honoré Champion, 2004. 223–39.

———. 'Forms of Politicization in the French Literary Field'. *Theory and Society* 32 (2003): 633–52.

———. *La Guerre des écrivains, 1940–1943.* Paris: Fayard, 1999.

———. 'La Raison littéraire. Le champ littéraire sous l'Occupation (1940–1944)'. *Actes de la recherche en sciences sociales* 111–112 (1996): 3–35.

———. 'Pour une approche sociologique des relations entre littérature et idéologie', COnTEXTES 2, *L'idéologie en sociologie de la littérature* (Feb. 2007): n. pag. Web. 13 Dec. 2007.

Sarraute, Natalie. *L'ère du soupçon.* Paris: Gallimard, 1956.

Sartre, Jean-Paul. *Anti-Semite and Jew.* Trans. George J. Becker. New York: Grove Press, 1962.

———. *Réflexions sur la question juive.* Paris: Gallimard, 1954.

———. 'Le Mur'. *Nouvelle Revue française* 49 (1937): 38–62.

———. *Les Mains sales.* Paris: Gallimard, 1948.

Saurat, Denis. Review of Les Mouches d'automne. *Nouvelle Revue française* 37 (1931): 670.

Savigneau, Josyane. 'Renaudot, Goncourt et marketing littéraire'. *Le Monde* 12 Nov. 2004.

Schor, Ralph. *L'Antisémitisme en France pendant les années trente*. Brussells: Editions Complexe, 1992.

Schor, Ralph. *L'Opinion française et les étrangers en France, 1919–1939*. Paris: Publications de la Sorbonne, 1985.

———. 'Le Paris des libertés'. *Le Paris des étrangers*. Ed. André Kaspi and Antoine Marès. Paris: Imprimerie nationale, 1989. 13–33.

Schorer, Mark. 'Sinclair Lewis: *Babbitt*'. *Landmarks of American Writing*. Ed. Hennig Cohen. Washington, D.C.: Voice of America Forum Lectures, 1970.

———, ed. *Sinclair Lewis: A Collection of Critical Essays*. Englewood Cliffs, NJ, Prentice Hall, 1962.

Sherman, Daniel J. *The Construction of Memory in Interwar France*. Chicago: University of Chicago Press, 1999.

Squires, Claire. 'Fiction in the Marketplace: The Literary Novel and the UK Publishing Industry 1990–2000'. Diss. Wolfson College, University of Oxford, 2002.

———. *Marketing Literature. The Making of Contemporary Writing in Britain*. Basingstoke: Palgrave MacMillan, 2007.

Stemberger, Martina. *Irène Némirovsky: Phantasmagorien der Fremdheit*. Wützbrg: Königshausen and Neuman, 2006.

———. 'Selling Gender: An alternative View of 'Prostitution' in Three French Novels of the *entre-deux-guerres*'. *Neophilologus* 92 (2008): 601–15.

Suleiman, Susan Rubin. *Crises of Memory and the Second World War*. Cambridge, MA: Harvard University Press, 2006.

Tharaud, Jean and Tharaud, Jérôme. *Quand Israël n'est plus roi*. Paris: Plon, 1933.

Thau, Norman David. *Romans de l'impossible identité. Etre juif en Europe occidentale (1918–1940)*. Bern: Peter Lang, 2001.

The Times Diary of the War, 1914-1918. London: The Times Publishing Company Ltd, 1921.

Thibaudet, Albert. *Histoire de la littérature française*. 1936. Paris: CNRS Editions, 2007.

Thompson, Stith. *The Folktale*. Berkeley: University of California Press, 1977.

———. *Motif-Index of Folk Literature*, 6 vols. Bloomington: Indiana University, 1932–1936.

Todd, Christopher. *A Century of French Best-sellers*. Lewiston: Edwin Mellen Press, 1994.

Trebitsch, Michel. 'Les écrivains juifs français de l'affaire Dreyfus à la Seconde Guerre Mondiale'. *Les Juifs de France. De la Révolution française à nos jours*. Ed. Jean-Jacques Becker and Annette Wieviorka. Lonrai: Liana Lévi, 1998. 169–95.

Tritt, Michael. 'Irène Némirovsky's *David Golder* and the Myth of the Jew'. *Symposium* 62.3 (2008): 193–206.

van Tieghem, Paul. *La Littérature comparée*. Paris: Armand Colin, 1931.

Vignaud, Jean. *Niky*. Paris: Plon-Nourrit, 1922.

Walden, George. 'George Walden is Disturbed by a Nazi Victim's First Novel'. *The Telegraph* 11 Feb. 2007.

Walker, David H., and Catherine Savage Brosman, ed. *Retour aux Nourritures terrestres*. Amsterdam: Rodopi, 1998.

Wardi, Charlotte. *Le Juif dans le roman français, 1933–1948*. Paris: Nizet, 1973.

Weinberg, David. *A Community on Trial. The Jews of Paris in the 1930s*. Chicago: University of Chicago Press, 1977.

Weiss, Jonathan. *Irène Némirovsky*. Paris: Editions du Félin, 2005.

———. *Irène Némirovsky: Her Life and Works*. Stanford: Stanford University Press, 2007.

Weisstein, Ulrich. *Comparative Literature and Literary Theory: Survey and Introduction*. Trans. William Riggan. Bloomington: Indiana University Press, 1973.

Weisz, George. *The Emergence of Modern Universities in France, 1863–1914*. Princeton: Princeton University Press, 1983.

West, Rebecca. 'Babbitt'. *Sinclair Lewis : A Collection of Critical Essays*. Ed. Mark Schorer. Englewood Cliffs, NJ: Prentice Hall, 1962: 23–26.

Wieviorka, Annette. *The Era of the Witness*. Trans. Jared Stark. Ithaca: Cornell University Press, 2006.

Wieviorka, Annette, and Françoise Rosset. 'Jewish Identity in the First Accounts by Extermination Camp Survivors from France'. *Yale French Studies* 85 (1994): 135–51.

Wilde, Oscar. *The Complete Works of Oscar Wilde*, Vol. 3: *The Picture of Dorian Gray*. Ed. Joseph Bristow. Oxford: Oxford University Press, 2005.

Wilfert, Blaise. 'Cosmopolis et l'homme invisible. Les importateurs de littérature étrangère en France, 1885–1914'. *Traduction: les échanges littéraires internationaux. Actes de la recherche en sciences sociales* 144.1 (2002). Ed. Johan Heilbron and Gisèle Sapiro: 33–46.

Winter, Jay. *Sites of Memory, Sites of Mourning. The Great War in European Cultural History*. Cambridge, England: Cambridge University Press, 1995.

Winter, Jay, and Emmanuel Sivan, ed. *War and Remembrance in the Twentieth Century*. Cambridge, England: Cambridge University Press, 1999.

Wolf, Michaela, and Alexandra Fukari, ed. *Constructing a Sociology of Translation*. Amsterdam: John Benjamins, 2007.

Yearbook of Comparative and General Literature. 1952. New York: Russell and Russell, 1965.

Zipes, Jack. *Hans Christian Andersen. The Misunderstood Storyteller*. New York: Routledge, 2005.

Ziv, Avner, and Anat Zajdman, ed. *Semites and Stereotypes. Characteristics of Jewish Humour*. Westport, CT: Greenwood Press, 1993.

Index

*For Product Safety Concerns and Information please contact
our EU representative GPSR@taylorandfrancis.com Taylor & Francis
Verlag GmbH, Kaufingerstraße 24, 80331 München, Germany*

T - #0121 - 270225 - C0 - 229/152/13 - PB - 9780415891035 - Gloss Lamination